THE REICHSTAG FIRE TRIAL

VAN DER LUBBE DURING THE TRIAL

THE

REICHSTAG FIRE TRIAL

The Second Brown Book of the Hitler Terror

based on material collected by the World Committee
for the Relief of the Victims of German Fascism, with
an Introductory Chapter specially written for the book by

GEORGI DIMITROV

a Foreword by D. N. PRITT, K.C.,
an Appendix on Murder in Hitler-Germany introduced by
LION FEUCHTWANGER

HOWARD FERTIG

NEW YORK · 1969

First published in English in 1934

HOWARD FERTIG, INC. EDITION 1969
Published by arrangement with The Bodley Head Limited

Library of Congress Catalog Card Number: 68-9605

PRINTED IN THE UNITED STATES OF AMERICA
BY NOBLE OFFSET PRINTERS, INC.

FOREWORD

By D. N. PRITT, K.C.

So many events of importance have occurred in Europe since the Reichstag fire trial concluded, that public sympathy and interest have flagged somewhat, not because of inherent fickleness but rather from a multiplicity of other interests, since the timely rescue of Dimitrov, Popov and Tanev from their relentless enemies, the German Government, by the Soviet Union. Elements interested in accord, compromise, or alliance with the present rulers of Germany have not been slow to perceive a slackening of public interest and have sought to relegate the Reichstag fire trial and the fire itself to the background of political memory.

Although a conviction of any of the four Communist accused would have constituted a major judicial crime, Germany's apologists not unnaturally sought to welcome the verdict of the Leipzig Court as a triumph of German justice. The voice of praise, however, fell silent when it was seen that, notwithstanding the verdict, the Government still held the acquitted prisoners in custody; but after the release of three of the four innocent men the wisdom of Germany's rulers was once again the propagandists' theme, Torgler's fate and the tragic end of van der Lubbe being conveniently forgotten.

This book is timely, and should reawaken public interest; it is apposite in the minuteness with which it surveys the whole proceedings and the thoroughness with which it exposes the conduct of the prosecution by the German Government.

It was difficult for anyone who closely followed the course of the long trial, or studied the reasons given by the Court for its verdict, to be under any illusions about the measure and quality of what was done at Leipzig; but the more superficial observer might well be deceived, and the full analysis contained in the book is calculated to dissipate any illusions that still survive. In this respect its value and importance is twofold. In the first place, it reveals in their full shame the methods pursued by the Government in the endeavour to secure the conviction of the four innocent men. These methods, it is unfortunately too clear, had their effect upon the Supreme Court itself; the treatment of the accused van der Lubbe and his condemnation to death under legislation passed only after the burning of the Reichstag, the demeanour permitted to politicians before the Court itself, the exclusion of Dimitrov from large parts of the trial and the disallowance of the bulk of the questions formulated by him, all produce a very disquieting impression. In the second place, the book reminds us forcibly of the fact that the trial was largely intended to serve an ulterior purpose, and that in the furtherance of that purpose certain sources of evidence were ignored, and on the other hand other lines of investigation were zealously pursued. Far more important for the German Government than that the guilty incendiary should expiate his crime was the securing of a legal pronouncement in favour of the alleged complicity in the fire of their most feared and hated political opponents, the Communist Party of Germany. The main current of the trial was directed to that end and the reasons of the Court for its judgment, however unconvincing they may appear, crowned these efforts with some measure of success. The terror, the persecution and attempted political and economic annihilation of the Jews, the working-class movement, and the progressive thinkers of Germany, thus received some shadow of apparent legal justification.

This attempt to fasten the guilt of the fire on the Communist Party tends to make the foreign observer reflect on the circumstantial evidence tending to implicate the National-Socialists, the one Party which was likely to gain and did in fact gain in strength as a result of the fire. The trial was of course used for the white-washing of the National-Socialists and the blackening of their enemies. But the white-washing process was a very superficial one, since no serious investigation or inquiry was made into many circumstances of suspicion which had become the object of widespread public interest. With these matters the book deals fully, and it is impossible to read it without drawing the conclusion that the case against the National-Socialists has been strengthened and not weakened, and that the concrete indications of National-Socialist complicity in the burning of the Reichstag are far greater than those which tend to show the guilt of any other person or political group in Germany.

If there is interest lost, this book should revive it. The world-wide campaign in the interests of the four innocent men, which has attained so great a measure of success, is an object lesson for all who sympathise with those whom the present rulers of Germany are seeking to crush and destroy. It indicates not merely a sentiment but a power which transcends national boundaries. The exposure of the methods and aims of the present rulers of Germany in connection with political trials, which the book effects, should serve as a reminder that there are still many thousands of victims and potential victims of exactly similar activities; especially perilous is the position of the political opponents of the National-Socialists, in particular Torgler and Thälmann. The menace to their lives has been rendered more grave and imminent by the recent creation of special tribunals for dealing with political offenders. The majority of the Judges in the so-called People's Court are to be laymen, appointed for political reasons. Far-reaching inroads are made into the most elementary rights of those accused before it. Its proceedings are designed to be carried out summarily, and largely in secret. Political expediency, not justice, is the basis of the constitution and the jurisdiction of the Court.

As long as the terror reigns, as long as the present rulers of Germany hold sway, it must not be forgotten that they climbed to despotism through a crime in which, although it has been avenged upon others, their own party appears to be plainly implicated.

D. N. PRITT.

The Temple.

May 1934.

CONTENTS

CONTENTS

APPENDIX: MURDER IN HITLER-GERMANY

LIST OF ILLUSTRATIONS

THE REICHSTAG FIRE TRIAL

INTRODUCTORY CHAPTER BY GEORGI DIMITROV

NATIONAL-SOCIALISM
AND THE REICHSTAG FIRE TRIAL

THE "Brown Book" is inseparably bound up with the history of the Reichstag fire trial. It was more than a mere book; its effects were far greater than those commonly produced by a literary work. It was a factor, a decisive factor, in the struggle which was waged between two different worlds around the Reichstag fire trial.

Although the Brown Book did not come into my hands before I reached Moscow, I had long known of its existence. Even during the course of the preliminary examination I learned from the National-Socialist press, the only newspapers which we were permitted to receive, of the existence of a mysterious 'lying propagandist work' which appeared at least to be a fly in the ointment of National-Socialism in Germany. Later I came to know its title and something of its contents. Even later I caught once or twice a glimpse of our unknown ally.

On the very first day of the proceedings at Leipzig the Brown Book made its entrance into the Court. It was, so to speak, the sixth accused. As the object of bitter antipathy it provided many hours of discussion from the commencement of the trial onwards. Our so-called defending counsel who, had they seriously wished to defend us, could have made effective use of the book hastily retreated from its allegations. I burned to get a copy between my fingers. From its effect I had perceived the immeasurably great services which it could perform in my battle. As is well known, in accordance with the provisions of the Criminal Procedure Code I applied to be furnished with a copy. The Court had no interest in handing me so powerful a weapon and my request for a copy of the 'pamphlet' as the unhappy Public Prosecutor styled it, was flatly declined, albeit quite contrary to law.

I

Nevertheless the Brown Book was of great assistance not only because it obliged the Court and the counsel for the prosecution and the 'defence' to attempt the contradiction of its allegations, but also because it indicated to us the international solidarity with which we felt our case to be supported throughout the proceedings, during the preliminary investigation during the trial and within the very Court-room itself.

Now there appears a second Brown Book, I trust that it will not be the last of its kind for the battle is still raging. At this moment Ernst Thälmann, the clearest and best brain of the German working class which through its efforts during the trial contributed so much towards our acquittal, sits in chains in prison. Thälmann is one of the best of our comrades in the fight. With him are held in prison hundreds and thousands of brave men, warriors in our cause. My foremost and most urgent task at the present time is this; to exhort all those who helped me and my Bulgarian colleagues to liberty to apply themselves just as enthusiastically and as energetically to securing Ernst Thälmann's release. In this campaign the second Brown Book and others, if need be, have a great role to play.

By way of introduction to this work I would like to present a comprehensive view and estimate of the Reichstag fire trial, to indicate what was its purpose and what its significance.

A General Attack upon Marxism

The Reichstag fire was designed to serve and in fact did serve as the point of departure for a campaign of action, for the general attack of the Fascists upon the revolutionary movement of the German working class. The object of this campaign was the extirpation of Marxism, that is, of the whole revolutionary movement. These Fascist blockheads wished to parade themselves before the world as the saviours of all Europe from the terrors of the proletarian revolution.

The Leipzig trial, the greatest political trial of modern history, was staged by the National-Socialist leaders in order to prove that in February 1933 they had saved Europe from Bolshevism. They hoped to win recognition as the champions, the saviours of capitalist society. The text of the indictment, which was kept a carefully guarded secret throughout the trial indicates definitely that the trial was directed not only against Communism in Germany but also against the Communist International and the Soviet Union.

At the commencement of the trial the German Press did not appear to regard it as in the least necessary to conceal the full extent of these intentions. We, my fellow accused and myself, were accused of being emissaries of the Russian Communist Party sent from Moscow in order, by setting fire to the Reichstag, to organise an armed revolt in Germany with the aim of setting up Soviets throughout Europe. Witnesses during the course of the preliminary investigations, carefully schooled by the prosecuting officials, alleged that following the burning of the Reichstag, similar acts of arson were planned to take place in Warsaw, Prague and Vienna so that the whole of Europe should be set ablaze.

Such were the propagandist purposes to be served by the staging of the trial. They did credit to the great brain of the diminutive Dr. Goebbels. Berlin, Germany even, was too small for him!

Their Concrete Tasks

The concrete tasks which National-Socialism set itself in holding the trial in Leipzig were four in number.

Firstly, they desired to rehabilitate the real Fascist incendiaries, upon whose guilt the whole world, within and without Germany was already clear, to shield them by a legally established decision that the Communists were guilty.

Secondly, they desired to provide a justification for the barbarous terror and the monstrous suppression of the revolutionary proletariat. This persecution, this savage destruction of cultural wealth, this rage against progressive science, against free thought, and literature, the mass murders and the 'suicides' had raised so many enemies against them that the National-Socialists sought to provide an excuse which would assuage the abhorrence and revulsion which their activities had produced and which would wash them clean of guilt.

Thirdly, the trial was to furnish the pretext for a new anti-communist campaign and to serve as the basis for a fresh monster trial of the Communist Party in Germany.

Fourthly and lastly, logically ensuing upon these tasks was

the design of National-Socialist foreign policy to use the heads of the accused men as currency in the imminent bargaining with the imperialist powers. In return for his historic services in ridding Europe of the spectre of Bolshevism, Hitler hoped to come by concessions in the question of equality of armaments and other matters. In the eyes of the National-Socialists this task was of wide significance and far-reaching importance.

Preparations for the Trial

To assure the successful carrying through of this fourfold task, large-scale preparations were made to furnish material; the whole police and judicial machinery, not to mention the gigantic propaganda apparatus, was put at the disposal of the National-Socialists. This was not done so much for the purposes of preparing the charges as to find and to rehearse suitable witnesses. For six months the Fascists frantically and desperately searched for witnesses, and even later, up to the last days of the trial suitable evidence was sought and procured.

The Fascists were particularly interested in procuring persons from the ranks of the working class, from amongst Communists or leading officials of the revolutionary movement. The Fascist incendiaries had planned that such witnesses should furnish proofs that the German Communist Party and the Red Front Fighters' League had made preparations for an armed insurrection in February and March 1933, that directions to this effect had been given to them and that the Reichstag fire was to be the signal for the breaking out of this insurrection. They stopped at nothing in the endeavour to obtain such witnesses. Thousands and thousands of Communists and revolutionary workers were subjected to the most frightful mental and physical torture in the prisons and concentration camps in order to render them witnesses pliable to the requirements of the National-Socialists.

But these plans failed miserably. Despite all their efforts the only witnesses they were able to produce in support of the charges in the indictment were National-Socialist deputies, Fascist journalists, criminals, coiners, recidivists, mental defectives and drug addicts. They did not succeed in bending to their will a single worker or official of the revolutionary movement. This was the Achilles' heel of the case for the prosecution. Their miserable failure served at the same time strikingly to demonstrate to the world the magnificent steadfastness and fidelity, the boundless devotion of the German workers to the cause of the proletarian revolution, to Communism and to the Communist International.

The debut upon the European stage which German Fascism made in the role of protector of European culture against Bolshevism ended in an utter fiasco. German Fascism went to Leipzig as proud as a lion and returned like a whipped cur.

A Triumph of Solidarity

The trial was an acid test for the revolutionary working class of Germany. It came through with flying colours. Those warriors of the German revolution who were dragged into the Court displayed such proofs of fidelity and devotion that one can indeed be sure that the future fight of the German workers for freedom will be carried on to victory. The marks of sympathy which reached me wherever I was during the long months, in prison, under guard, or in the very Courtroom itself, the many letters, greetings and expressions of solidarity which came to me, often through inexplicable channels, even into my cell, all furnished irrefutable proof that despite the heavy reverses which the German working class has sustained through the treachery of the Social-Democrats it has neither lost its head, nor let its courage fail but carries on the struggle even under the most difficult conditions.

The trial has shown once again what a force, a living force is constituted by international solidarity. Fascism, and above all classical German Fascism is the most unbridled bellicose nationalism and chauvinism. In the field of ideals, where Fascism is most active, all its efforts are aimed at destroying, at extirpating the spirit of international solidarity from the German working class. International solidarity is a fatal poison to any kind of Fascism as it is the life blood to the working-class movement. This is the most important reason for the antipathy of the National-Socialists to the Communist International.

The trial and the events which have taken place in the world

5

without the Court-room have shown that international solidarity is a living and a mighty force. Through the mobilising of the working classes in Germany and abroad, through the adherence of the best elements of international opinion to our cause, the Court-room at Leipzig became a battlefield. The blow which the Fascists had aimed at International Communism recoiled with fearful force upon their own heads.

After our liberation I have often been asked whether whilst the trial was going on I believed that we should ultimately be set free. I must confess that I never considered the matter in this way at all. I was and am still deeply convinced that the cause for which I have fought all my life and for which I am ever fighting will triumph in the end. It was this conviction, the fruit of deep research into the events of history armed with the weapon of Marxist-Leninist dialectic, which gave me strength and courage in my struggle. My determination and resolution, however and wherever I was situated, to do my utmost to bring forward the historically inevitable triumph of the Socialist revolution thrust any thoughts of the eventual outcome of the trial, as far as I was personally concerned, far into the background.

My belief in the ultimate victory of Socialism has been confirmed by the events which have passed in the world during the last weeks of our imprisonment. The news of the great achievements of the French workers and of the mighty struggles of the Austrian workers reached our ears in prison. Numbers of *Pravda* which despite the strongest possible guards and the strictest censorship of my letters reached me on several occasions told of the Seventeenth Congress of the Communist Party of the Soviet Union and the picture of the successful building up of Socialism which was there displayed. Since apart from this we were permitted only National-Socialist newspapers it was not until after my arrival in Moscow that I was able fully to study the whole course of the events in France and Austria and their true significance. My heart swelled when I read of them; I was moved with joy at the heroic efforts of the French and Austrian workers against Fascism, but with regret at the shameful role played by the leaders of Social-Democracy on these occasions and with disgust and hatred at the conduct of the bourgeois who lash like monsters about them when their end is near. I would

6

that all those who stood by us during our long ordeal shared these sentiments with me.

We, my Bulgarian comrades in adversity and myself, are safely in the land of victorious Socialism, whose Government capped the world campaign for our release with receiving us demonstratively into its citizenship. Those same gentlemen who, trotted out as witnesses against us during the trial, sought to blacken and defile the name of this land have now been forced, like naughty schoolboys, to give way to its might and power. Like the trial itself, their malicious and vile abuse has recoiled on their own heads.

The fight which Fascism fought and lost at Leipzig was a triumph for international Socialism, a victory for the Communist International. This should be understood by all those who have lined up alongside us. From it should be drawn the inspiration for further struggle against Fascism, the worst and lowest enemy of the working class, of true culture, of science and art, of all progressive elements in mankind.

GEORGI DIMITROV.

Moscow, March 18th, 1934.
 Anniversary of the Paris Commune.

THE FIGHT FOR A TRIAL

"My conscience hath a thousand several tongues,
And every tongue brings in a several tale,
And every tale condemns me for a villain.
Perjury, perjury, in the high'st degree;
Murder, stern murder in the direst degree;
All several sins, all used in each degree,
Throng to the bar, crying all, Guilty! guilty!"
(*Richard III.* Shakespeare.)

"Late at night on November 29th, 1933, the condemned men were informed by the Public Prosecutor in the presence of the prison Governor that the carrying out of the death sentence was fixed for the following morning. All the condemned men, but particularly Hammacher and Moritz, strenuously protested against this order and once again affirmed their innocence. They were the victims of the perjury of Nazi witnesses.

"In the prison courtyard stood the scaffold, in the place formerly occupied by the guillotine. On the scaffold was only a bench and the headsman's block. On the same spot where the notorious murderer Kurten was guillotined in 1931, the six political criminals were to be beheaded. Their execution was to be carried out with the short-handled axe.

"Whilst the prison bell tolled for them, the condemned men were bound and were led out one by one by their warders under exceptionally strong police and S.A. guards. A number of people were gathered in the courtyard; the President and the other members of the Court of Assize, the legally prescribed dozen members of the public to act as jury. The executioner and his assistants stood behind the scaffold. As well as a large throng of Storm Troopers, there were present some secret police officials, doctors and priests of both creeds. The route from the prison building to the table at which the officials were seated and to the foot of the scaffold was lined by police and S.A. men. Behind the officials' table, draped in black cloth, sat the Public Prosecutor with officials from the Registrar's office. The prisoners whose heads had been shaven and whose throats were bared were led in their bonds before the Public Prosecutor. To them was read out the sentence of the Court, which done the Public Prosecutor read in loud tones the ministerial decree—'His Excellency, the Prussian Prime Minister has decided not to exercise his standing prerogative of commutting the death sentence in the present case.'

"To these words the condemned men, who had obviously undergone great sufferings during their confinement, aggravated as it was by the burden of their fetters and by the sentence upon them, replied with a cheer for the world revolution. Immediately the executioner's assistants seized the first of the condemned men and dragged him to the scaffold. Scarcely had he kneeled at the block before his head was severed by a blow of the axe. The second and third of the prisoners were decapitated with one blow in the same way.

"But it was apparent that in order to go through with their terrible work the headsman and his assistants had fortified themselves with spirits. This had its effect when the fourth of the condemned men mounted the scaffold. The

9

headsman's first blow missed its mark and his axe stuck in the victim's skull. The second blow was dealt with no different result. Not until he had struck thrice was his fourth victim's head severed. This horror was not without its effect on the bystanders. Those of them who still nourished a spark of human sensitiveness experienced feelings of abhorrence and disgust. Following this the executioner's first blow at the fifth victim missed and a further blow was needed to complete his beheading.

"The last decapitation, that of the window cleaner Josef Engel was accomplished with one mighty sweep of the headsman's axe. Attendance at the execution of these six workmen was the worst experience which I have been fated to undergo during the whole term of my service."

THE event described above took place on November 29th, 1933, in the Klingelpütz prison in Cologne. The six executed men were Communist workmen. The description was furnished by an official of long standing who was present as an eye-witness at the execution.

Had Hitler and Göring had their way the same fate as was suffered by these six workmen in Cologne lay in store for the four Communists, Dimitrov, Torgler, Popov and Tanev, accused by the German Government of complicity in the burning of the Reichstag. From the very night of the fire never once did the rulers of Germany conceal their intention of surrendering these four innocent men into the hands of the executioner. Before an audience of S.A. men in the Berlin Sportpalast on the night of March 4th, 1933, their passions at fever pitch, raged Göring:

"If I had had my way, we should have set up the gallows on the very same night beside the Reichstag and then and there should have hanged the Communist crooks!"

More moderate in tone, Reichschancellor Hitler himself took advantage of the opening of the new Reichstag on March 23rd to say:

"Since certain sections of the foreign press have been seeking in some way to identify this monstrous crime with the re-awakening of the German nation, my own determination to avenge this sin in the shortest possible time by the public execution of the incendiary and his accomplices has been greatly strengthened."

The cry 'to the gallows'—for the innocent accused men was not only raised by the National-Socialists during the maddened days of March. On November 4th, 1933, when thirty-one days of the trial of Dimitrov, Torgler, Popov and Tanev had passed without the shadow of a case being established against them, when the whole world was convinced of their innocence, Göring could not restrain himself. Throwing aside all self-control during his encounter with Dimitrov, he shouted:

"You are a crook; your place is the gallows!"

The police and the Storm Troops were only too ready to respond to these outbursts of their Ministers. The cry—'to the gallows'—fell upon willing ears. It was carried into deadly effect in the S.A. barracks, the police prisons and the concentration camps, on the streets of the cities and on the highways and byways of Germany. Three thousand anti-fascists have been done to death—tortured, beaten, shot, 'committed suicide' or 'shot while trying to escape.' These were no chance happenings. The rulers of the Third Reich deliberately sought to wash out in blood the memory of the crime which brought them to the attainment of power. But in vain, for the burning of the German Reichstag will fade from the memory of man only when it has been avenged. It will not be forgotten whilst the murders, the executions and the tortures of prison, barrack and concentration camp are unexpiated, whilst the campaigns of suppression against the working classes, the persecution of the Jewish people and the obliteration of progressive thought are unavenged. It will be remembered daily until its authors have been hunted from their hiding-places and until the political adventurers whose purpose it served have been laid low.

National-Socialist Revolution—Through the Backdoor!

Hitler's path to power and the history of the events from the time of his accession to the Reichschancellorship until the burning of the Reichstag have been treated exhaustively in the "Brown Book of the Hitler Terror." For the present purposes it is therefore necessary only to summarise briefly those events standing in direct relation with the Reichstag fire trial.

Thirteen years, almost to a day, before the burning of the Reichstag the political programme of the National-Socialist German Workers' Party was published. On February 24th, 1920, in the banqueting hall of the Hofbrau at Munich, Hitler promulgated the celebrated twenty-five points of which it was composed. In his speech on that occasion Hitler characterised the programme as the weapon with which

National-Socialism would cleave its way, even into the hearts of its opponents. During the ensuing thirteen years the National-Socialists learned that the German working classes rejected and bitterly opposed it. But the despondent middle classes, exhausted and ruined by the effects of inflation and the economic crisis, fell prey to the 'idealism' of the National-Socialists. Jobless ex-officers, students without hope of practical outlet for their college learning, the sons of shop-keepers, who saw their inheritance threatened, large sections of officials and clerical workers into whose heads the idea that the destruction of Marxism would bring in its train employment and higher wages had been sedulously driven, all these elements threw themselves, with all their doubts and confusions into the arms of National-Socialism. The progress of the theories of the National-Socialists came to a halt at the gates of the working-class areas and factories. Although Hitler and his satellites devoted themselves fervently to the task of encompassing the minds of the German workers but small fractions of the working classes, demoralised by chronic and incessant unemployment, deserted to the camp of National-Socialism. These gains were transitory, for late in 1932 it became apparent that a movement of disillusioned followers away from the National-Socialist ranks had begun. At the Reichstag elections of November 6th, 1932, Hitler's Party lost no less than two million votes against which the Communists registered an advance of some half-million. A tide was rising in Germany, hostile to Fascism, which was expressed in mighty demonstrations in which Social-Democratic, communist and non-party workers took part, shoulder to shoulder. The policy of the united working-class front against Fascism found support in constantly widening circles. The growth of revolutionary sentiment amongst the working class was expressed in a growing wave of strikes, foremost amongst which was the strike of the Berlin transport workers in November 1932.

These portents, the meetings and demonstrations, the growth of the anti-fascist sentiment in factory and workshop were observed anxiously by the Junker-landowners and the barons of heavy industry and finance. To counter the swelling revolutionary tide, they planned the formation of a reactionary block. The only popular basis upon which this reactionary alliance could be erected was Hitler's Party. It was here that the ruling powers of Germany saw the rock against which the growing wave of revolution would shatter. It was planned, with the aid of the National-Socialist Party, to deprive the working class of the last few rights of which former governments had allowed them to retain possession, to carry through a programme of re-armament and thus bring about a pre-war economic situation, a forced revival of industry on a war basis. In the National-Socialist Party was seen the force essential for the preparation of internal despotism and foreign war. The hand was proffered to Hitler, and he reached greedily for it. Moved by his lust for power Hitler approached the proposed alliance.

The National-Socialists did not attain power through struggle and victory; power was conferred upon them. Incessantly stressed in their Party's propaganda were the 'German' virtues—manliness and honour—and the spirit of the true old Germans who stood up and fought for their ideals, but its achievement of power was altogether lacking in these qualities. The barricades of the 'German revolution' were no more than the backstairs of the Presidential Palace. Hitler came into power as the result of a sordid and worldly bargain struck with von Papen, whom up till that moment the National-Socialists had abused as the representative of a petty clique of antiquated noblemen, in the elegant private office of the Cologne banker, Schröder. The way into the Palace of the Reichschancellor did not lie through struggle in the streets, nor through insurrection; flunkies opened the door of President von Hindenburg's study to Hitler and there the aged Field-Marshal handed to him the decree of nomination.

Thus the National-Socialist 'Workers' Party lined up with Hugenberg's pan-German reactionaries. The National-Socialists joined the fighting front with von Hindenburg's circle and the Herrenclub. On January 30th, 1933, the Hitler-Hugenberg Cabinet was born, with the Junkers and the barons of heavy industry and finance standing beside its cradle.

Even after the formation of the Government the National-Socialist Party shrank from immediate open conflict with the working class. It sought rather to lull the fears of the anti-fascist majority of the people by means of pacific declarations. Hitler's Ministers pledged themselves to uphold that very constitution against which during the last fourteen years they had so relentlessly fought. They lost no opportunity of proclaiming their staunch adherence to constitutional methods. On the day following the formation of the Government, through the mouth of the Minister of the Interior Frick they went even to the length of declaring that they intended neither to ban the Communist Party nor to impose any restrictions on the freedom of the press.

Through von Papen's good offices Hitler and Hugenberg entered into alliance on January 30th, 1933. From the very moment when they sealed their compact with a handshake, these two "German" statesmen had but one thought, how to adhere to the letter of the alliance whilst they violated its spirit.

Behind each of these opponents waited a horde of job-hungry hangers-on. The official positions in the administrative apparatus of the States and Communes up till then occupied with Social-Democrats, Democrats and Centre Party supporters were to be divided up afresh between the followers of Hitler and Hugenberg. Each of them designed to cheat the other in dividing up the spoils. For Hitler it was vital and essential to extricate himself from Hugenberg's clutches, while the latter's aim was to consolidate the power of the Nationalists in the Reich and Prussian Ministries of Economy which were in his hands and thence to draw the noose tighter round the neck of his new bed-fellow. But he either failed to reckon with or else underestimated the importance of two factors, the Prussian Police Ministry and the mass military formations of the National-Socialists. Here the Nazis enjoyed mastery and it was from these quarters that they began their struggle for sole political power. Although united with the National-Socialists in the government Hugenberg was apprehensive of their political voraciousness and saw a useful handicap to Hitler's aspirations in the continued existence of the opposing political Parties. While Hugenberg was clear upon the importance of preserving the political opposition to the Cabinet, even the Communist Party, as a support for himself and a burden for Hitler, the Leader, Göring and Goebbels, on the other hand, realised that the suppression or at least the decisive weakening of the political parties in opposition was the essential step, without which they could not venture into the lists against the Nationalists.

In his statement to the Supreme Court in Leipzig on November 4th, 1933, Göring explained in some detail how, from the formation of the Coalition-Cabinet, he carried out the re-organisation of the police in the interests of his Party. In order to prepare for the great task of extirpating Marxism, not only were the key positions in the Prussian police and administrative services filled with National-Socialists, but thousands of the lower ranks were dismissed and their places filled from members of the Storm Troops. Daluege, S.S. Commander, Göring's closest collaborator, was appointed director of the Prussian Ministry of the Interior, and in that capacity controlled the Prussian police force. Not content with this packing of the police force, on February 22nd, 1933, bodies of auxiliary police composed as to seven-eighths of S.A. men and as to the rest of members of the Stahlhelm, were established all over Prussia. Carrying batons was forbidden— the revolver was the chosen weapon. Orders to shoot at sight were issued to the police. They were instructed to employ their firearms regardless of consequences and any policeman who failed to carry out these orders to the letter was threatened with punishment and dismissal.

When the election campaign began early in February 1933 the internal tension was strained to its utmost. The indignation of the working class with the Government's policy and measures grew daily—anti-fascist demonstrations increased in number. This reversion the National-Socialist leaders sought to counter by introducing oppressive measures, by throttling the working-class press and by instigating attacks, usually taking place at night, by Storm Troopers on isolated workers. Press, cinema, poster-hoarding and even wireless were put almost entirely at the disposal of the National-Socialists' election propaganda. Their battle-cry—'Death to Marxism'—was blazoned from press and hoarding, was incessantly repeated on screen and loud-speaker. In such atmosphere, charged with electricity, the Reichstag suddenly burst into flames.

It is unnecessary and would be out of place here to repeat the tragic tale which is known to the whole world. It is sufficient to recall that the Terror which has not ceased to hold sway over Germany was deliberately let loose on the selfsame night as the Reichstag fire. For the mass arrests, for the cynical violation of the last remaining legal shreds of individual liberty, for the annihilation and destruction of all that was best in Germany the burning of the Reichstag was used as the pretext and justification.

Building the Case

The complete political monopoly which the National-Socialists were quick to achieve after the burning of the Reichstag gave them complete self-confidence. The police and investigating officials were in their hands; wireless and press broadcast the news dictated by the National-Socialist press chiefs of the Reich and the Prussian Government; the opposition was effectively gagged. The National-Socialists ordered whom was to be arrested and what was to be written. Having furnished the immediate solution that the Communists had burnt the Reichstag, the next task of the National-Socialists was to build their case in such a way not only to provide the electorate with material of a sufficiently convincing nature, but also to furnish a basis for the criminal and judicial investigations which might follow. This task they set about forthwith, employing their vast propaganda apparatus in its service.

The first official statement upon the Reichstag fire, contained in the Amtliche Preussische Presse Dienst (A.P.P.D.) bulletin of February 28th, 1933, indicated that no time had been lost by the National-Socialists. It was stated that the arrested incendiary, van der Lubbe, was a Communist and had admitted membership of the Dutch Communist Party. The official wireless announcement made on the night of the fire went further in declaring that a Communist [Party membership card had been found in van der Lubbe's possession. This was followed up on the next day by a bulletin of the A.P.P.D. stating that van der Lubbe had attended meetings of the "Communist Committee of Action" and had been selected there to take part in the burning of the Reichstag. Incidentally and in order to spoil the election prospects of the Social-Democratic Party, it was also officially announced that van der Lubbe had been in contact with Social-Democratic circles.

Some of these points will be further alluded to, for the present suffice it to say that each and every one of the statements was shown at the trial to be demonstrably and even admittedly untrue.

The first official bulletin announced the issue of warrants for the arrest of two important Communist deputies who were strongly suspected of complicity. It was well known that Torgler was accustomed to working late in the Reichstag, it was further known that he and Koenen, another leading Communist deputy, had been amongst the last persons to leave the building on the night of the fire. This sufficed to supply the link connecting van der Lubbe with the German Communist Party. The official bulletin of March 1st, 1933, therefore stated that Torgler and Koenen were the last persons to leave the Reichstag on the night of February 27th, that they had been observed leaving the building as if in flight at about ten o'clock and that they had been seen together with van der Lubbe in the Reichstag that afternoon—"at about eight o'clock"—by three independent witnesses. Again it is enough at this point to remark that all these statements were entirely false. But published in this way, they furnished their quota of mischief. One of the immediate consequences of the statements of the A.P.P.D. was that Torgler went in person to the police headquarters on the morning after the fire to protest against and to answer the allegations which had been spread abroad concerning him. He was there arrested. This voluntary call upon the police by Torgler hardly suited the plans of the National-Socialists who therefore announced on March 1st in the official bulletin that it was incorrect that he had presented himself voluntarily at the police headquarters but that it was true that he asked for a safe conduct when he realised that escape was impossible; thereby implying that he had gone into hiding but had been tracked down.

No less false in their tenor, although somewhat later in point of time, were the statements published concerning the Bulgarian Communists, Dimitrov, Popov and Tanev. These men, be it remembered, were not arrested on account of any clue having been unearthed during the investigations—before their arrests not one statement was made to the authorities which implicated them in any way. Their arrest was in fact purely fortuitous. At a time when arrests of foreigners, especially of South Europeans were an hourly occurrence in Berlin, a National-Socialist waiter in a restaurant on the Potsdamerstrasse, his attentions attracted, as he admitted later, by the twenty thousand marks reward offered for information, denounced the three "suspicious foreigners" to the police, asserting that he had seen van der Lubbe frequently in their company in the restaurant. These statements which gave the National-Socialists the possibility of implicating three more foreigners in the conspiracy which they had already built up around the persons of van der Lubbe and Torgler, were welcomed by the police. When the identity of the three Bulgarians and their political allegiance was established, the authorities were more than content : witnesses implicating them began to come forward and the allegation, made quickly after the fire, that the burning of the Reichstag was a crime of International Communism was powerfully fortified. Thus the Examining Magistrate in a statement to the press issued on March 22nd, 1933, asserted that he held proofs that van der Lubbe had been in direct contact with the three Bulgarians and that they themselves had been involved in the blowing up of Sofia Cathedral in 1925, on account of which they had been sentenced to death or to long terms of penal servitude. These statements again were admitted to have been false.

Side by side with the accusations against van der Lubbe, Torgler and the Bulgarians, the Hitler government announced that it had accumulated absolute and convincing proof of the complicity of the German Communist Party in the burning of the Reichstag. The A.P.P.D. circulated the following statement on February 28th, 1933 :

"This act of incendiarism is the most monstrous act of terror yet carried out by Bolshevism in Germany. Amongst the many hundredweights of subversive documents which the police found in their search of the Karl Liebknecht House were discovered instructions for the carrying through of a Communist terror on the Bolshevist model.

"According to these instructions, government buildings, palaces, museums and essential undertakings were to be set on fire. Further, orders were given that women and children, wherever possible those of police officials, should in case of disorder or clashes with the police be placed in front of the terrorist groups. By the discovery of these documents the systematic carrying through of the Bolshevist revolution has been prevented. Despite this the burning of the Reichstag was to be the signal for bloody rioting and civil war. Looting was to break out in Berlin at 4 o'clock on Tuesday morning (February 28th). It has been established that terrorist acts were to begin to-day throughout Germany against individuals, against private property and against the life and safety of the peaceful population and that civil war was to break out."

The preparation of the ground for the reception of these statements implicating responsibility for the crime to the Communists and detailing their insurrectionary plans, had been undertaken some little time previously. The headquarters of the Communist Party in Berlin, Karl Liebknecht House, were occupied by the police on General Göring's instructions as early as February 17th. Although a thorough search of the building brought nothing to light, the police continued in occupation. A change in the Police Presidency of Berlin was brought about, the Nationalist Dr. Melcher being replaced by the National-Socialist Admiral von Levetzow on February 22nd. The new police chief ordered a further search of the Karl Liebknecht House. On this occasion, in the absence of any official of the Communist Party and without any check on the material removed, the desired result was forthcoming. On the evening of February 24th and during the next four days, until the Reichstag fire, the press was packed with reports of a highly sensational character anent the "astounding discoveries in the catacombs of the Karl Liebknecht House." These reports alluded to and discussed in purely general terms the "criminal character of the documents." No indication was given as to the actual nature or contents of the alleged discoveries.

During the month following the Reichstag fire and during the trial itself the discoveries in the Karl Liebknecht House were relegated to the political lumber-room. Not unnaturally the attention of the world was captured by the human figures around whose fate the drama of the Reichstag fire trial was enacted. But the fact that the cited extract from the official bulletins was the very kernel of the National-Socialist accusations at the trial, just as it had been the pretext for the loosening of the terror, must not be lost sight of. The criminal and treasonable nature of the discoveries was broadcast during March 1933 throughout Germany by every speech and every article emanating from the members of the German Government relating to the Reichstag fire. The word 'Fanal'—a beacon-fire, or signal—was bandied from mouth to mouth. This name given in a moment of inspiration by Göring to the Reichstag fire, on the steps of the Reichstag on February 27th, became the very measure of the guilt of the Communists and of the five accused men at Leipzig. In a speech by Göring broadcast from Berlin on March 1st he declared on his word of honour that when the full character and content of the discovered material was revealed to the German people, they would resolve to extirpate the Communists root and branch.

Dr. Goebbels spoke in the Berlin Sportpalast on the evening of March 2nd. He also upon his honour declared:

> "We have found incontrovertible proof of the guilt of the Communists in the Karl Liebknecht House. The German people do not sufficiently realise the dreadful fate which threatened them. The tongue falters in giving utterance to the kind of crimes which the Communists had prepared. The publication of the material discovered in the Kark Liebknecht nest of murderers will open the eyes of the world."

As early as March 1st Göring saw fit through the channel of the A.P.P.D. to announce that the documents discovered in the Karl Liebknecht House, whose immediate publication was impossible for reasons of state safety, would be given over to the public at the earliest moment possible. Twenty-one days passed by. Then on March 23rd, at the opening ceremony of the newly-elected Reichstag, Reichschancellor Hitler took the opportunity of re-affirming the attitude of the Government to these documents. He said:

> "The burning of the Reichstag, the abortive attempt to bring a deep-laid plot to fruition is an indication of the fate which awaits all Europe should this devilish doctrine triumph. The real extent of the designs which were to have been carried into effect by this gang has never been fully realised by the German people or by the outside world. A development the catastrophic results of which would have shaken Europe to the roots was averted only by a lightning stroke of your Government."

Thus the 'absolute proof' of the guilt of their political opponents was provided by the alleged documents from the Karl Liebknecht House, the central point of the National-Socialist accusations. Based upon this material began the crusades against the working class, against Marxism, against the Jews and the 'un-German' and pacifist members of the intellectual classes. For proofs the National-Socialists proffered merely the official announcements, seeking on the strength of these alone to be appraised as the saviours of Europe from the universal Bolshevist menace.

Not only did the world outside Germany come quickly to realise the truth about this material, but even within that land the doubts expressed as to its authenticity grew in volume and strength. Ex-Chancellor Brüning in the course of a speech made at Paderborn on March 2nd, 1933, urged the publication of the alleged documents:

> "We do hope that the Government will see its way to publish the material discovered at the earliest possible moment. It is 'difficult to imagine that a political party should so lightly surround itself with incriminating documents. But the Government holds proofs and it has promised to publish them."

The official announcement that Göring intended to publish the finds, made in the A.P.P.D. bulletin of March 1st, 1933, was reiterated by the Reichschancellor himself a few days later for the allaying of Brüning's qualms:

> "Herr Brüning may rest assured we shall publish the material."

But the material was not published. The elections and the opening of the new Reichstag passed by. March ended, then April, then May. Even after six months of National-Socialist rule the Government's alleged 'finds' did not see daylight. No wonder that the doubts entertained from the first by the outside world and by large sections of the German people grew to scepticism. Little wonder that the leaders of the Government sought to provide assurances. The most extraordinary of these is to be found embodied in an interview with Hitler published in the *New Yorker Staatzeitung* of August 6th, 1933.

> " As incomprehensible as the rebirth of Germany seems to be to the outside world, is to us the new war obsession and the atrocity propaganda against Germany. America, France and England have rather to be thankful to the members of the S.A., S.S. and Stalhelm that the Bolshevist flood which would have flowed from Germany over the entire world was stemmed on the night of the burning of the Reichstag. Supposing that a comparatively large proportion of the population of America consisted of organised Communists, and supposing that the White House instead of the Reichstag had gone up in flames on the crucial night, what would you in America have done? Would you not have retaliated more harshly than I, with my order to the S.A., S.S. and Stalhelm to carry out the arrest of the Bolshevist leaders so that the threatened destruction of the council chambers, theatres and public buildings all over Germany should be averted, the secret organisations of the conspirators crushed and their plans nipped in the bud ?
>
> "On the very night of the fire, while we were receiving moving appeals by telephone, telegram and letter from all over Germany for protection against the impending Bolshevist conspiracy and insurrection, I determined there and then, irrespective of the forces on my side, forthwith and with all the means at my disposal to take action. The watch-word was 'Break or be broken.' The course I had taken was completely justified by the discoveries which the two succeeding hours revealed. An immediate search of the public buildings in Berlin alone, including the university, library and the district council chambers,

brought to light the preparations which had been made for arson. Fuses, cotton-waste soaked in petrol and explosives were found ready. If during the decisive hours I had not opposed the Bolshevist plans for setting Germany ablaze with all my might, who knows but that all the public buildings throughout the land, and even through the whole western world might have been laid in ashes.

"The coming legal proceedings will open the eyes of the world to the sensational events of that night. These will be proved by means of the material which was discovered and which hitherto on account of the investigations in progress has not been published. This evidence will constitute absolute proof of the existence of a Bolshevist world plot."

This statement is truly an amazing one. The amount of specific detail which it contains is the more extraordinary in that much was quite new and that nothing has been published, before or since, to indicate that a single word of it could be supported in fact. The concluding phrases of the interview might have justified the assumption that the material discovered was really being withheld by the National-Socialist leaders on account of the approaching trial, but the trial was itself held and concluded without one single piece of the alleged material being laid before the Court or given to the world.

As is well known, a special stage of the proceedings was set aside for the proving of the general accusations against the Communists. These accusations were dealt with in a special section of the secret indictment, which in the midst of a series of police reports and hearsay statements, referred in a general way to the subversive documents discovered in the Karl Liebknecht House on February 24th, 1933. The so-called political stage of the trial in which the bulk of the contents of this part of the indictment were reproduced called aloud for the production of at least some part of the alleged 'discoveries.' But despite this and despite the fact that their publication had been promised and their withholding before the trial justified by the forthcoming proceedings, not a page, not a photograph and not a scrap of proof of the discoveries was produced throughout the trial. To-day a year has passed and the promises of the National-Socialist leaders remain and will remain unfulfilled. As far as the alleged 'discoveries' in the Karl Liebknecht House go, the Nazis' statements of the impending insurrection, the wave of Bolshevist terror and the world plot rest on nothing more substantial than the 'official reports.'

But it is by no means to be imagined that there existed no documents "discovered in the Karl Liebknecht House" from which the allegations of the official reports and the minute details given to the world by the leading National-Socialist could have been drawn. There were certainly some 'documents.' Had it not been for the wisdom of the German Nationalists the Hitler Government would probably have been sufficiently foolish to publish their 'finds' shortly after the fire. Bitter and protracted disputes arose within the Cabinet on the subject and Göring's outspoken intention to give the 'finds' over to publication was frustrated only by the threat of the Nationalists to resign from the Cabinet, a threat which at that time would have had very serious consequences for Hitler. The 'finds' were in fact so obviously and clumsily forged that the Nationalists feared that their publication would be disastrous for the prestige, and even for the power of the Government. The course which these disputes took is described in the celebrated Oberfohren Memorandum which played an important part in the Reichstag fire trial.

The truth of the account of the disputes in the Cabinet furnished in the Memorandum compiled under Dr. Oberfohren's direction has been borne out by further information received since his 'suicide' in Kiel, from another prominent member of the Nationalist Party.

Von Papen and Daluege

During February 1933 Göring nominated Daluege, S.S. Commander for Berlin-Brandenburg, one of his closest and most trusted confidants, to the position of director of the Prussian Ministry of the Interior. Daluege before his appointment was little known to the wide public, he was a man in the background. He belongs to the inner circle of National-Socialists who are fully instructed of the truth about the Reichstag fire. He was the highest ranking official present at the first examination of van der Lubbe on the night of the fire; from him the first bulletins of the fire seem to have emanated and it was he who first interviewed the three National-Socialists Karwahne, Frey and Kroyer whose incriminating statements against Torgler and Popov will be later discussed.

While the Nationalists prevented the publication of the discoveries made by the National-Socialists in the Karl Liebknecht House, they nevertheless for obvious political reasons set great store upon getting the material into their own hands. To that end, one day in March 1933 von Papen, then Vice-Chancellor and Reich Commissioner for Prussia, thus Göring's immediate superior, came perhaps by chance to visit the Ministry of the Interior when Göring himself happened to be absent. Daluege had been left in charge. He had taken a leading part in the production of the originals of which his chief's 'finds' were composed. His fate thus, as well as Göring's would be sealed by the exposure of the original documents, the withholding of which had then been decided upon; little wonder that von Papen should find Daluege reluctant to hand over the documents to him.

Von Papen began the interview by discussing the ordinary political events of the day. During the course of the conversation he mentioned incidentally that he would require to see the documents which constituted the 'finds.' Daluege did not counter with a direct refusal, but explained that the documents could be disclosed only upon the specific instructions of his immediate superior, Göring. Von Papen retorted that as Vice-Chancellor and Commissioner of the Reich he was the highest authority in Prussia. Daluege was unmoved and replied, indicating his garb, that there were higher authorities in Prussia who, although not occupying official positions, wore black uniforms. Von Papen now faced with a direct refusal threatened the intervention of von Hindenburg. Daluege was adamant. Von Papen threatened dismissal, public exposure—to no effect. Not until Hitler himself intervened in the dispute did von Papen give up his quest for the documents. Daluege's promotion by the grateful Göring followed almost immediately.

The crudity of the German Government's falsehoods about the accused men—all admittedly baseless—and the clumsy treatment of the 'finds' in the Karl Liebknecht House is to be explained only by the fact that they were assigned primarily as means of serving the political aims of the National-Socialist leaders and only secondarily as furnishing the basis of any legal proceedings. The primary purpose was well served. Since the Nazis through the accomplishment of their immediate political aims had it in their power to drive the "enfuriated soul of the German people" to resort to lynch law, it is doubtful whether their leaders during the first frenzy of power foresaw that a trial would have to be held. The clumsiness of their accusations can be only reasonably explained upon this assumption. But it is quite certain that the Cabinet, confident of its political monopoly and despotic powers, had little fear of being able to control the progress and result of a trial should it eventually become essential.

Having provided the politically suitable solution to the riddle—who fired the Reichstag?—the National-Socialists took little care to ensure the accuracy of the proofs which were to be adduced to support their accusations. They miscalculated that, in their hands, the burning of the Reichstag could be relegated to the realm of forgotten things and that only the legend of themselves as the saviours of the world from Bolshevist incendiarism and terror would remain. They had no reason to fear that any proof of the accusations directed against their political opponents, particularly the Communists, would ever be called for. During their fourteen years' experience of propaganda, they had been accustomed to overwhelm their supporters with promises and to cover their opponents with accusations and slanders without limit. They had never been called upon either to fulfill their promises or to justify their slanders—indeed the occasion for them to do so had never arisen. The National-Socialists were confident that it would go no differently with their master-stroke, the burning of the Reichstag.

The World Fights for the Trial

The Reichstag fire and its bloody consequences—the organised persecution of the German working class, the intellectuals and the Jews, even in the first days of March 1933 produced marked and world-wide repercussions. Whilst Hitler and the other Nazi leaders never tired of asserting that international solidarity was a myth, the world movement brought into being by the Hitler terror demonstrated that international solidarity was more powerful and vigorous a force than ever before. The rulers of Germany were quick to change their tale—they sought to capture the world's support and sympathy with the blood-curdling stories of international conspiracies, they painted themselves as the saviours of the world, with the first claim on the world's gratitude.

But slowly and quietly the full extent of the revulsion of the world's feelings from the present rulers of Germany was revealed. The word was spoken in the factories and labour exchanges, in the universities and colleges, in the learned societies and parliaments of every land. Anti-fascist demonstrators marched to the German Embassies and Legations—sometimes breaking their way through cordons of police. Danish workmen burnt effigies of Göring in the public squares. The swastika emblems flaunting over the German Embassies in Brussels and Madrid were hauled down. The German Consulates in Liverpool and Stockholm, in Antwerp, in Philadelphia, Chicago and New York were painted with slogans against the Hitler terror. One night a squad of anti-fascists painted the German Consulate in Rotterdam blood-red. The resentment of the opponents of Fascism found its expression in hundreds of meetings and demonstrations. For weeks the Embassies in London, Paris and Washington were besieged by deputations and demonstrations. Dockers in Holland, France and Belgium refused to discharge cargo from ships which flew the hated swastika emblem at their mast-heads. The Jewish populations in New York and London summoned monster meetings to honour their persecuted co-religionists. The foremost representatives of culture in every land, the leaders of modern art and literature raised their voices in protest and added themselves to the ranks of the opponents of Fascism. The workers all over the world although reduced to the verge of penury by constant wage and dole cuts gave of their last to aid the victims and the active fighters against Hitler Fascism. The stupendous events of the Hitler terror and the campaign of destruction against the German working classes swept masses of Communist, Social-Democratic, Christian and non-party trade unionists into united activity against Fascism. Samples of the illegal Communist literature, produced and distributed by men and women who had often paid for their activity with their lives, contrived to be smuggled by devious ways out of Germany, were exhibited amidst almost sacred silence to vast audiences who realised that it was written in the blood of their fellow anti-fascists. Meanwhile, the world over, representa-

NEW YORK
A Protest Demonstration to the German Consulate

LONDON
Frau Schütz, wife of the murdered Communist deputy, addressing a protest meeting in
Hyde Park

tives of the working and intellectual classes came together to build up committees for the relief of the victims of Hitler Fascism.

With the aid of the Reichstag fire, Hitler had achieved sole political power. It was the deliberate aim of his Government to obliterate the memory of that crime of provocation as speedily as possible whilst continuing to enjoy none the less the benefit of its consequences. The counter-aim of the opponents of Fascism was, therefore, to make that crime unforgettable and to force the Hitler Government to produce the alleged proofs of the guilt of the accused men and of its political opponents to the world; to compel the examination of these proofs in the critical searchlight of foreign opinion. Whilst it was essential in the interests of the accused men that the holding of a trial should be forced, no opponent of Fascism nourished any illusions as to the course and outcome of any legal proceedings conducted under the sole auspices of the Hitler Government and in the obscurity of the Fascist terror. The forcing of a trial was the first aim, but by itself insufficient; the trial must be expedited and its course must be followed with the closest attention. Four Communists lay in prison, accused of complicity in the burning of the Reichstag. Cut off from all the world outside they would be unable to defend themselves, they would be forced to be dumb. If they could secure the forum of a public trial even Hitler justice could not prevent them from defending themselves and in defending themselves to reveal and to prosecute the real incendiaries before the world.

The Manœuvres of the Hitler Government

Not even its own emissaries were able to conceal from the Hitler Government the mighty wave of indignation which had been produced abroad by the burning of the Reichstag and the terror. Even foreign governments, some of them otherwise anxious to be well disposed towards the 'reborn' Germany, were affected by the irresistible pressure of the anti-fascist movement within their lands. The events in London, Paris, New York and the other capital cities of the world were duly notified to the Wilhelmstrasse by the representatives of the foreign governments in Berlin. The German

Government sought for a way of escape and a means of staving off the universal indignation by announcing that a Reichstag fire trial would be held. Between March 30th and June 1st the Examining Magistrate was responsible for issuing no less than five different statements in each of which the approach of the time for the holding of the Reichstag fire trial was announced. These attempts to mislead were in vain. The world was not to be satisfied with the announcement of the fact that a trial would be held, it demanded to know when the trial was to be commenced.

Again serious differences of opinion were aroused within the German Cabinet, which gave rise to long and bitter argument. While Göring not unnaturally was against the holding of any trial, Neurath and Goebbels were strongly in favour of a trial for reasons of foreign policy which, they insisted, made it indispensable. They were astute enough to realise that Germany's isolation in the realm of foreign politics was partly conditioned by the pressure which was being brought to bear upon their respective governments by the indignant anti-fascist masses abroad, on account of the delay in holding the Reichstag fire trial. By the beginning of June this view appeared to have got the upper hand, for the *Völkischer Beobachter* reported on June 3rd, 1933, in the following terms that the Examining Magistrate had concluded his labours:

"It has been announced by the Press Chief of the National-Socialist Parliamentary Group that the preliminary examination conducted by Judge Vogt, the Examining Magistrate attached to the Supreme Court, into the case against van der Lubbe, Torgler, Dimitrov, Popov and Tanev, all accused of complicity in the burning of the Reichstag and of high treason was completed on June 1st, 1933. All the documents have now been sent to the Public Prosecutor at Leipzig. The results of the investigations will be revealed at the forthcoming trial.

"This announcement will at last silence the slanderers who at the hest of the Jewish-Marxists, have been spreading through the world the rumour that the President of the Reichstag himself, Prime Minister Göring, set the Reichstag on fire. From the outset it was apparent that the incendiary who was captured must have had a number of accomplices, and it was to the discovery and identification of these accomplices that the painstaking and protracted investigation has been devoted. The results at which Judge Vogt has arrived as well as the clues which he has been able to discover will be revealed at the forthcoming trial. In any case the dastardly attempt against the Reichstag, that edifice dedicated to the German people, will be expiated in a fitting manner."

Although the preliminary investigation and the interrogation of the witnesses had been concluded at the end of April 1933, Judge Vogt did not transmit the documents to the Public Prosecutor until June 2nd. Once again General Göring intervened and succeeded in further delaying the date for the holding of the trial. He induced the Public Prosecutor to send the papers back to the Examining Magistrate on the pretext that they required to be completed. It is obvious that the holding of the trial would have been postponed to the Greek Kalends had Göring had his way.

The Fates of Rosenberg and Luther

In June 1933 the Reichschancellor sent Alfred Rosenberg on a mission of foreign politics to England. Besides being editor-in-chief of the *Völkischer Beobachter* Rosenberg was chief of the important National-Socialist Foreign Policy Department. Rosenberg's task was to break through Germany's isolation in the realm of foreign politics. His stay in London was unpleasant enough for him and quite unproductive of results. He was shunned by the politicians and treated almost as a leper by the public. A young woman threw one of the many anti-Hitler pamphlets—*The Brown Plague*— in his face. The London workers demonstrated in long processions before the hotel in which he was staying and went in throngs to speed his departure. Thousands of letters addressed to Rosenberg demanded to know when the trial, the approach of which had so frequently been announced, was actually to take place. Rosenberg left London a disappointed man. A few days after his return to Germany, the first despatch of the newly-appointed Ambassador to the U.S.A., Luther, arrived in Berlin. Its contents showed that Luther was panic-stricken. On his landing he had been received with most patent distrust by the assembled journalists. Out of the eighty questions which were put to him some sixty-eight of them dealt with the Reichstag fire. Coming on the heels of Rosenberg's fruitless journey, Luther's despatch forced the issue. Göring had to give way. The German Government definitely decided that the Reichstag fire trial must take place. Accordingly the *Völkischer Beobachter* announced on July 22nd:

"Reliable information has reached us respecting the position in the Reichstag fire case. The judicial investigation of the cases against some of the accused was completed some time ago. Now the Examining Magistrate attached to the Supreme Court has completed the investigation into the case against the remaining accused. On account of the wide range of the inquiries which had to be undertaken, the investigation has been unusually protracted. In a few days' time the complete documents, together with the indictment against the principal accused, will be laid by the Public Prosecutor before the Fourth Criminal Court of the Supreme Court. It can therefore be estimated that the actual proceedings will be opened during the first half of September."

This announcement throws a glaring light on the unreliability of all the official reports and announcements. It is interesting to compare it with the report made in the same paper on June 3rd, 1933, reproduced above, in which it was announced that Judge Vogt had completed the investigations against the accused on June 1st. The two reports are in fact hopelessly and inexplicably contradictory.

All the original calculations of the National-Socialists were thus upset. Their hopes of avoiding a trial were frustrated; while the conditions had already arisen which ensured that the trial could not be conducted in the secrecy and obscurity of the terror.

The Brown Book

The first round had been won. The hand of the Hitler Government had been forced. A trial was to be held. The next immediate goal of the anti-fascist movement was to develop the conditions which had already arisen, to fight for the holding of the trial in circumstances ensuring the fullest publicity and to determine the direction and content of the proceedings. Conditions had been created in Germany, particularly in relation to the Reichstag fire—amongst them the practical denial of legal assistance to the prisoners—so that it was impossible to anticipate that even the holding of a public trial would be more than a solemn pretence. For this reason it was essential for the opponents of Fascism to set their aims as high as the influencing of the course of the trial itself. Any doubt of the propriety of this course was strikingly removed by the actual events of the trial.

Numerous pamphlets and publications appearing during the first seven months of 1933 had painted partial and incomplete pictures of the events in Hitler-Germany. The first complete account of the terror was published on August 1st, 1933, by the World Committee for the Relief of the Victims of Hitler-Fascism. After a short interval the work appeared in France and England, where it was published before the opening of the Reichstag fire trial. Subsequently it ran through another seventeen editions. The Brown Book as it came to be called, gave the first complete and circumstantial account of the burning of the Reichstag—as far as the details were then known. It furnished the international anti-fascist movement with a picture of the Reichstag fire both as a crime of provocation and as the work of National-Socialist incendiaries. It was not, therefore, surprising that the Brown Book played a prominent part in the new wave of world revulsion which arose towards the end of the summer of 1933. The publication of the book was heralded with notices and extracts from it in the world press. The allegations of the book, marshalling as they did the proofs of National-Socialist complicity in the burning of the Reichstag were a crushing blow for the German Government. Before the Public Prosecutor laid his indictment before the Supreme Court charging the four innocent Communists with the guilt of the Reichstag fire an irrefutable indictment of the Hitler Government itself was before the public. Whilst the Public Prosecutor laboured at his task alone, the Brown Book passed into a million hands. The accusations relating to the fire formulated in the Brown Book against the German Government and the leaders of the National-Socialist Party were repeated in almost every newspaper of importance in the world. A few extracts may be reproduced from the press as typical:

"Perhaps the most serious case ever brought against a responsible government." (*News Chronicle*, September 1st, 1933.)

The *Manchester Guardian* paid tribute to the important role of the Brown Book in the fight against the Hitler Government in several long paragraphs, in which it was described as:

"The most important work that has yet been published on the Hitlerite dictatorship."

The world press warned the Hitler Government against under-estimating the importance of the Brown Book. The *Oesterreichische Abendblatt*, the official organ of the Dolfuss Government formulated this warning in the following terms:

" The sensational revelations, the accusations which are made in this publication are of such gravity and weight that the Prussian Prime Minister Göring cannot easily ignore them."

The *Ceske Slovo*, the organ of the Czechoslovak Foreign Minister, expressed the universal indignation which had been produced through the Brown Book's exposure of the Hitler terror and the Reichstag fire.

"This uncoloured testimony of facts, proofs, quotations, names and dates awakens a sense of shame and burning indignation. If these things are true, then this book must shock the conscience of the world."

The Hitler Government attempted, as far as it was humanly possible to do so, to discredit the Brown Book. It mobilised its entire press and propaganda apparatus. Despite the fact that the book was banned in Germany and that severe penalties were imposed on those found with it in their possession, it attained a large circulation both in its large edition and in a specially produced disguised form. Many persons were arrested and sentenced for being in possession of it, but yet its circulation mounted in Germany before the Reichstag fire trial to some twenty thousand copies.

The Commission of Inquiry

Not only did the anti-fascist movement give rise to this remarkable international movement of solidarity and resistance to Hitler Fascism, but it also gave to the world the first independent public tribunal which, as even the Nazis themselves conceived it, virtually sat in judgment upon Hitler and his colleagues. In April 1933 the World Committee for the Relief of the Victims of Hitler Fascism proposed that a Commission should be set up to inquire into the origins of the Reichstag fire and into the guilt of the accused men. It was thought that such a Commission composed of impartial and eminent jurists would be able to throw important light upon the Reichstag fire and its related events. Prominent lawyers of many nationalities declared themselves ready to take part in the work of such a Commission.

Ultimately a Commission was constituted of the following members: Chairman: Mr. D. N. Pritt, K.C., England; Maître Moro-Giafferi, France; Maître Gaston Bergery, France; Arthur Garfield Hays, U.S.A.; George Branting, Senator, Sweden; Dr. Betsy Bakker-Nort, Deputy, Holland; Vald Huidt, Denmark; Pierre Vermeylen, Belgium. In addition to the above, Francesco Nitti, former Prime Minister of Italy, and Wilhelm Huber, President of the Swiss National

Council, participated in single sessions of the Commission of Inquiry but were prevented the one by ill health and the other by the duties of his office from being present at the full session of the Commission in London.

From April 1933 the Secretariat of the Commission devoted itself to the difficult and arduous task of collecting the materials relating to the Reichstag fire which were to be laid before the Commission of Inquiry. It had neither the machinery nor the unlimited financial resources of the Hitler Government at its disposal; it could not command a host of police and investigating officials, or of eager witnesses. The finances of the Secretariat were raised by collections amongst sympathising supporters. Reliable agents of the Secretariat worked secretly in Germany, many of them at the risk of their lives, collecting material for the Inquiry. Statements from more than a hundred witnesses were taken. Expert opinions were obtained from chemists and criminologists of universal repute. A volume of material was collected which subsequently went to form the nucleus of the newly-founded anti-fascist archives. Just before the opening of the Reichstag fire trial the Secretariat published a brochure in several languages in which the course of its work was outlined. The preliminary session of the Commission of Inquiry was held in Paris on September 2nd, 1933. On that occasion it was decided to send a sub-committee of three of its members to investigate the material relating to van der Lubbe which was available in Holland. The sub-committee held sessions in Holland on September 6th and 7th; it completed its work with a report which was laid before the Commission at its full session.

With the approach of the middle of September interest in the Reichstag fire trial was at its keenest. The chief sections of world opinion were almost unanimous in expressing their conviction that the four Communists whose trial was fast approaching were innocent and even in pointing to the shoulders upon which the guilt of the fire seemed to rest. Accusation and counter-accusation had raised the excitement of the public to a high degree—and scarcely a voice could be heard outside Germany expressing belief in the guilt of the men who were to be tried as the incendiaries.

It was in this atmosphere that the opening session of the Commission of Inquiry took place. Promptly at 10 a.m. on

September 14th, 1933, in the Court-room of the Law Society, the ex-Solicitor-General, Sir Stafford Cripps, K.C., M.P., opened the proceedings with a short speech in which he outlined the reasons for the holding of the Inquiry. He expressed the universal disquiet at the prospects for the forthcoming trial in Germany. After he had declared the proceedings opened, the Chairman, Mr. D. N. Pritt, K.C., rose and indicated the order of procedure.

From then onwards the proceedings of the Commission of Inquiry took their course before the eyes of the world. It was the first time in history that such a tribunal had assembled. Composed of jurists from many lands, it commanded international respect. Its mandate was conferred by the conscience of the world and it was to the ears of the world that its findings were ultimately spoken.

The opening session of the Inquiry showed with what sympathy and expectation the world was following its proceedings. Shoulder to shoulder sat the foremost leaders of English thought, of political life and of the anti-fascist movement. Every important newspaper and press agency in the world had sent its own representative to attend the Commission. As the Chairman rose at the commencement of the hearing the audience felt the solemnity of the occasion. Here were independent men and women gathered together to assist in the search for the truth, to aid the cause of right and justice.

The Commission of Inquiry was no court—for no accused sat in the dock before it. Neither was it a prosecutor for it had no case to prove. It was not the aim or object of the Commission to pronounce any persons, accused or otherwise, guilty or not guilty. It was the task of the Commission to examine all such evidence as might be laid before it, independently of its source and regardless of its tendency. It was upon the results of the examination of all these materials, being duly weighed and tested, that the Commission was to pronounce its findings. Quite without basis are all those attempts to discredit the Commission by challenging its political impartiality or by suggesting that its purpose was merely to perpetuate the statements in the Brown Book. In fact the members of the Commission were drawn from the most diverse of political allegiances; the Brown Book was hardly mentioned and certainly never made use of as evidence throughout the proceedings.

The public session of the Commission lasted for five days. Statements were received from some thirty witnesses all of whom were subjected to exhaustive questioning. Amongst them were famous German politicians such as Professor Bernhard, and Social-Democratic leaders like Dr. Breitscheid and Dr. Hertz. Witnesses, the writer Freek van Leeuwen amongst them, were brought from Holland. Concerning the arrests on the night of the fire there came to testify the dramatist Ernst Toller whose works had been burned by order of Goebbels. The Communist Deputy Wilhelm Koenen on whose head the German Government had set a price came secretly from Germany to describe the movements of Torgler and himself on the night of the fire. Torgler's close colleague Otto Kühne, secretary of the Communist Parliamentary group also appeared. Dimitrova spoke on behalf of her brother while young Kurt Torgler described his father's movements and activities. The Commission examined responsible journalists who furnished first-hand accounts of the actual fire and the events which preceded and followed it. Many of the witnesses who came to testify before the Commission did so at risk of their lives and many of them returned in greater peril to Germany to pursue their hidden campaign against the Hitler terror.

Day by day it became apparent that the world regarded the London session of the Commission of Inquiry as the real Reichstag fire trial. Day by day the world's press fortified its readers' convictions that the four accused Communists were innocent and that the guilt should be lain upon other shoulders. Detailed summaries of the proceedings of the Commission appeared in every newspaper of note—even in Germany. The Commission carried its first full session to completion attuned to a daily growing support of public opinion, the force of which could be neither ignored nor diminished. The effect of the Commission's work was so weighty that the German Government sought but without success, to persuade the British Government to intervene and prevent the Commission from continuing its work.

Of even more importance than the favourable reception of the work of the Commission of Inquiry in the world's press, which qualified it as a task accomplished in the cause of justice, was the attitude of the politically co-ordinated press in Germany. The comments of this press showed how deep a wound the work of the Commission had made in the side of Hitler Fascism and its venial justice. A quotation from the *Frankfurter Zeitung* of September 15th, 1933, may be taken as typical:

"Even though to-day's proceedings of the Commission were not at the commencement conducted in a very orderly fashion, it is nevertheless to be feared that the Commission's work will create a great impression on public opinion in England. Even to-day so strong was the attraction of the Commission that the Court-room, designed to hold eighty, was accommodating about two hundred persons. Amongst the audience were to be seen prominent public figures like H. G. Wells. At the present time English public opinion is predominatingly anti-German. The proceedings of this International Commission of Jurists will, in all probability, heighten the antipathy of the English public towards Germany."

Even more instructive were the comments of the *Danziger Volkstimme*, a newspaper both politically co-ordinated and subject to the censorship of the National-Socialist Danzig Senate, which in its issue of September 15th published a full-page account of the proceedings of the Commission.

"The International Commission of Inquiry into the origins of the Reichstag fire has begun its first session in London. All the important foreign newspapers have devoted leading articles to the proceedings. It is, at the outset, remarkable that the Law Society (the most important legal professional body) should have put its Court-room at the disposal of the Branting Commission. The building lies in the legal quarter of London. It is further announced that a reception was held on the eve of the opening of the Commission's session, at which leading jurists, judges and practising lawyers, as well as other persons prominent in English public life, accepted invitations to be present.

"Seeing the great effect which the Commission of Inquiry had produced in English public opinion and the apparent silent toleration of the English Government, the German representative in London decided to take diplomatic steps. This was announced by the semi-official Wolff Telegraph Bureau in the following report: 'The German Chargé d'Affaires in London charged the British Government with responsibility on the grounds that it had allowed the proceedings of the Commission of Inquiry to take place. The Foreign Office, however, informed the Chargé d'Affaires that the Government had no legal powers to prevent private proceedings of such a character from taking place.'

"The English press agency, Reuters, announced that the Foreign Office had stated that the proceedings of the International Commission of Inquiry bore no official character.

"The comments of the English press are directed against the German Government and are, moreover, couched in the most hostile language and tone. Reich Minister Dr. Goebbels declared some days ago to a meeting of N.S.D.A.P. leaders in Berlin that he did not believe that the world would take these proceedings seriously. Unfortunately the comments and tone of the foreign press do not confirm this view."

The Findings of the Commission

On September 20th, 1933, the Chairman, Mr. D. N. Pritt, K.C., read the Commission's findings to a large audience assembled in the Caxton Hall. Thirty printed pages in length the documents conclude as follows:

"The Commission accordingly concludes on the investigations which it has so far made as follows:

(1)   That van der Lubbe is not a member but an opponent of the Communist Party;

That no connection whatever can be traced between the Communist Party and the burning of the Reichstag;

That the accused Torgler, Dimitrov, Popov and Tanev, ought to be regarded not merely as innocent of the crime charged but also as not having been concerned with or connected in any manner directly or indirectly with the arson of the Reichstag.

(2)   That the documents, the oral evidence and the other material in its possession tend to establish that van der Lubbe cannot have committed the crime alone.

(3)   That the examination of all the possible means of ingress and egress to or from the Reichstag make it highly probable that the incendiaries made use of the subterranean passage leading from the Reichstag to the house of the President of the Reichstag;

That the happening of such a fire at the period in question was of great advantage to the National-Socialist Party.

"That for these reasons and the others pointed out in the third part of this report grave grounds exist for suspecting that the Reichstag was set on fire by or on behalf of leading personalities of the National-Socialist Party.

"The Commission considers that any judicial organism exercising jurisdiction in the matter should properly investigate these suspicions. If during and after the trial at Leipzig there should be any need that this Commission should reassemble to take into consideration the facts elucidated at the Leipzig hearing or any further available facts, and to prepare a further report on the basis thereof, every effort should be made to bring the Commission together again."

The findings of the Commission of Inquiry were thus promulgated one day before the commencement of the trial before the Supreme Court at Leipzig. The outcome of the investigations and deliberations of the independent and impartial jurists, representative of international opinion, were announced by the broadcasting stations of London, Paris and the United States on the same night; on the following morning there was scarcely a newspaper in the world which did not prominently reproduce them. When the Presiding Judge Bünger opened the proceedings at Leipzig on the morning of September 21st, 1933, in the judgment of the world pronounced in the press, on the wireless and in stormy meetings all over Europe the four accused men, then solemnly marched into the dock, had already been acquitted. From September 20th, 1933, the force of world opinion had pronounced the four innocent: one party only, the National-Socialists, were accused of the guilt of the crime.

II

THE PREPARATIONS FOR THE TRIAL

IN the Prussian State Archives, amongst the papers of the year 1850 may be found a letter dated November 11th, which runs:

"My good Mantreffel,

"I have just read the news of little Kinkel's escape. It has put an idea, which I cannot classify as of the purest, in my mind. That is, whether Stieber is not just the right man to unweave the web of the Conspirators for Freedom, and so to present to the Prussian people the long and justly awaited spectacle of a conspiracy uncovered and, what is more to the point, punished. Hasten then to get Stieber to work. Have him make a sample of his work. My opinion is that the idea is well worth following up and I set great store by its immediate execution."

The writer of the letter was King Frederick William IV of Prussia, and the letter was addressed to the Prussian Minister of the Interior. Kinkel, who is named in the letter, was the revolutionary poet Gottfried Kinkel who had escaped from the fortress of Spandau. Stieber was a notorious police agent whose activities as a provocateur had smoothed his way to the highest places. Stieber's activities, proposed in this letter, bore fruit during the following two years, with the arrest and trial of the members of the Communist League at the Cologne assizes. This, the first great Communist trial in Germany, bore all the marks of Stieber's activities. He produced an alleged original draft of the constitution of the Communist League (made in London) and the criminal plot (manufactured in Paris). In addition to these there was a host of police officials, spies, provocateurs, and bought and perjuring witnesses. But in the midst of them, a counter-blast to these fabrications, was the young Karl Marx, whose account of the Cologne trial revealed its nature to the eyes of his contemporaries and to posterity.

In a speech made on the opening of the Prussian State Council, Göring, Prime Minister of Prussia, announced that the prerogatives of the former Prussian Royal House had

39

become directly vested in him. There is little doubt that in the prerogative of instigating acts of provocation and in inspiring their authors, his kingly predecessors have found a worthy, if little modest successor in General Göring.

During the eighty odd years which have passed by since the trial of the Cologne Communists the technique of provocation has. been perfected but its methods remain the same. Inspired from above, infecting the minds of the whole hierarchy of officials, inciting and inviting to perjury and fabrication, making use of the lowest of human beings, provocation bears the same stigmata wherever in the world it raises its ugly head.

Scarcely had the fire in the Reichstag begun when Göring prompted by no more than a sudden intuition, as he alleged, pronounced the fire to be the work of Communists. The Reichschancellor himself arriving on the scene a little later recognised, by special divine revelation, the hand of Communism in the arson. Thus without an investigation of the fire, without any interrogation of the arrested incendiary and solely upon the sudden inspirations of two electioneering politicians, went forth the theory of the guilt of the Communists. It was with this goal before it, that that pursuit of those upon whom the fire was to be avenged was set afoot.

By German law the trial of accused men is preceded by a double investigation, one undertaken by the police the other by a magistrate. The former constitutes the basis for the latter. The police are entrusted with collecting information relating to the crime, the identity, antecedents and associations of its authors. The object of the second investigation, conducted by a magistrate specially selected for each case, is to re-examine and analyse the materials collected by the police, to interrogate the accused and the witnesses and to present the results of his labours in the form of written statements, called protocols, to the Public Prosecutor. Passing over the functions of the Public Prosecutor for the time being, it will be observed that in this way all the evidence and other material passes through a double sieve, that of the police and that of the Examining Magistrate, a fact which should, in the ordinary case, furnish a security against error. The Leipzig trial has, however, revealed the methods which were employed in the police and judicial investigation of the arson in the Reichstag.

The Police Investigation

Under the Criminal Procedure Code the police are bound to follow up every clue or suspicious circumstance which may lead to the discovery of the author of a crime. During the post-war period a practice has grown up for the police or other responsible officials at their instance to issue bulletins on the state of the police inquiries from time to time. Publicity to these bulletins which are based on the materials collected by the police is usually given by the Amtliche Pressedienst (the Å.P.P.D.)

In the Reichstag fire investigations a converse method was pursued. The first event was the publication of the A.P.P.D. bulletin, made by Daluege under Göring's authority, and with his knowledge, none of the contents of which emanated from the police or had, indeed, any more solid basis than Göring and his henchman's imagination. But notwithstanding this, the bulletin provided the police with the clue to their efforts and it became their task to provide the proof necessary to support the A.P.P.D. statements.

It was in the channels decided upon by the leaders of the Government on the night of the fire that the energies of the police were confined. Van der Lubbe's alleged connection with the Communists, the baseless suspicions against Torgler and Koenen, the absolute proofs which the Government declared that it possessed against the Communists, these were the guiding light for the police and judicial inquiries. The progress of the police and judicial investigations never faltered from the path on which the Government had set them.

None of the many subordinate officials who only six months before had faithfully served Severing and Grzesinski dared to protest against this manœuvre. Göring has often described the manner in which he utilised February 1933 in preparing the police for the anticipated day when the National-Socialists should attain power. He outlined his methods to the Supreme Court on November 4th, 1933:

"From the first moment I had to point out clearly to my officials that the sole responsibility for their actions lay on my shoulders. I had to make it perfectly plain to them: 'When you shoot, then I am shooting! When a man lies dead there, then I have shot him!' I had to get the officials at grips with the enemy."

Göring had done well during his month. With the Reichstag fire the police were at last brought to grips with the enemy. Thenceforward they had one clue only to follow—this was indicated to them in the official bulletins.

Dimitrov put the question to Göring in Court as to whether the result of the official statements was not to direct the investigations of the police in one fixed direction to the exclusion of all others. To this Göring in a burst of candour replied:

"If the police and judicial investigations were allowed to be influenced in a particular direction, then in any case they were only influenced in the right direction."

This answer is an open avowal of the purpose and effect of the official statements concerning the fire—it explains the methods used in the police and judicial investigations and indicates why innocent men were accused, while no search was made for the guilty.

The fact that the direction of the police inquiries was predetermined by the Government constitutes a flagrant breach of the German Criminal Procedure Code under which the police and public safety officials, in addition to the Public Prosecutor, are the sole bodies competent to investigate criminal matters.

Van der Lubbe's First Interrogation

The conduct of the police investigation fell at once into the hands of Detective Inspector Heisig—one of the confidants of the National-Socialist Party in the Berlin police headquarters. His function, determined as it was by the tenor of the official bulletins, was to furnish convincing proofs of the guilt of the Communists in general and in particular. In pursuance of the Criminal Procedure Code which entitled the police to act on their own initiative in making inquiries when delay would be dangerous, Heisig conducted the first interrogation of van der Lubbe on the very night of the fire.

As far as could be judged from the few phrases which he uttered in the course of the trial, van der Lubbe's German was poor and halting. His linguistic abilities must have declined vastly from the time of this first interrogation. Van der Lubbe's German on that occasion was so fluent that no interpreter was found necessary. Van der Lubbe used 'flowers

of speech' in giving expression to his views and so voluble
was his oratory that Heisig was unable, as he informed the
Court, to extract the kernel of his ideas until the interrogation
had lasted several hours. Incredible as this may appear, even
more extraordinary were the circumstances in which the
interrogation was conducted. In violence to the provisions
of the law and contrary to all practice Heisig permitted the
presence of some forty or fifty National-Socialists in the room
while the interrogation was taking place. Amongst them were
the three who later obtained notoriety as witnesses, Karwahne,
Frey and Kroyer, hot from Daluege. The presence of this
number of persons was little calculated, even in ordinary
circumstances, to secure privacy for the investigation or to
assist in the elucidation of the true facts, within the room and
elsewhere.

It would be superfluous to stress the importance of the
first interrogation of an accused man—particularly one caught
flagrante delicto—whose statements taken down before he has
had the chance of turning them over in his mind or consulting
with an adviser, at a time when he is still psychologically
under the influence of his act, are of the utmost importance
for the direction of the police inquiries and the elucidation of
the crime. Heisig not only omitted to explain to van der
Lubbe the importance of the statement to which he is alleged
to have put his name on that occasion but he omitted by way
of precaution to summon an interpreter or to translate the
statement to that accused. This does not end the matter, for
from the beginning to the end of the trial the alleged statement was neither read nor shown to any of the other accused.
Its contents were alluded to in Court but the tribunal failed
to require its production. Dimitrov's frequent requests and
the letters and telegrams of the Secretariat of the International
Commission of Inquiry failed to bring it to light. It may be
that the taking of van der Lubbe's statement on the night of
the fire was not strictly in accord with the desires of those in
power. Perhaps its contents were disquieting to them. Some
support for this view can be found in Göring's statement to
the Supreme Court:

"I intended to hang van der Lubbe at once and no one could have stopped
me. I only refrained because I thought 'We have one of them, but there must
have been many. Perhaps we shall need him as a witness.' "

In any case, whatever the truth be, the non-production of this first statement of van der Lubbe's is one of the most remarkable points in the actual trial.

The three National-Socialists, Karwahne, Kroyer and Frey, who had been present when van der Lubbe was first interrogated on the night of the fire, appeared before the Reichstag Fire Investigating Commission at the police headquarters on February 28th. They alleged that they had seen van der Lubbe together with Torgler on the previous afternoon. Before taking a description of the person with whom they alleged having seen Torgler, the police led the three men into another room in the same building in which van der Lubbe was seated and permitted them to study his features and head for some five minutes. With their recollections fortified so recently, as well as by the fruits of their presence at the first interrogation of van der Lubbe by Heisig, it was not surprising that the three National-Socialists were able—on the same day —fairly accurately to describe the head and face of Torgler's companion. But their statements were much less definite, and even inconsistent, on the subject of Torgler's companions' clothing. For the police in their guilty haste to fortify the recollection of these witnesses neglected to carry out the confrontation in the prescribed manner. Instead of confronting him with the witnesses of identification in the condition in which they alleged having seen him, the police allowed van der Lubbe to remain seated, wrapped in a blanket. Although taking such pains to confront these three with van der Lubbe the police neglected to confront them with Torgler, who by then had been taken into custody, an obvious and elementary precaution.

Although the Continental practice of confrontation is alien to English criminal law, identification of criminals by witnesses, by parades or photographs, is common and must always be carried out under strict precautions against error or suggestion. Acquittals on appeal have frequently followed a failure strictly to adhere to these conditions. The complete worthlessness of a confrontation carried out in such a manner as that of the three National-Socialists with van der Lubbe will be obvious to any English lawyer. Indeed, it is illustrated by the total collapse of their testimony at the trial and their obvious discomfiture in the witness-box. The fact that their evidence was ultimately rejected by the Court rather lends point to than weakens the criticism levelled against the police in this connection.

Amongst Göring's confidential men was a certain Dr. Lepsius, who later gave evidence at the trial. Occupying a high position in the Air Ministry though he did, Dr. Lepsius certainly had no official authority or competence, and it may be doubted whether he possessed the qualifications requisite to conduct the interrogation of a political incendiary. But this was a minor consideration to his superiors who apparently thought it dangerous to entrust such delicate tasks to the sole hands of the police. Accordingly on the day following the fire Dr. Lepsius conducted an examination of van der Lubbe, without any of the police officials present professing to see anything unusual in such a course. Dr. Lepsius' interest did not cease at this—he proceeded to conduct more extraordinary. On the fourteenth day of the trial he told the Court how, afterwards, he had retraced with van der Lubbe the route which the latter had taken in firing the Reichstag. Bearing in mind the difficulty openly avowed by Judge Vogt:

"It would never be possible from van der Lubbe's statements to reconstruct his movements in the Reichstag."

—one wonders why the Examining Magistrate did not call on the able assistance of the Air Ministry's expert. What precise interest Dr. Lepsius—not a police or a judicial official —had in interrogating van der Lubbe, much more in retracing his path in the Reichstag, remained unexplained. Perhaps it was that Dr. Lepsius was better acquainted with the geography of the Reichstag than van der Lubbe and so was able to assist him in the choice of route.

Heisig in Holland

On the scene of the fire Reichschancellor Hitler declared simply to the world that van der Lubbe was a Communist. It was to the unhappy Heisig that the harder task of proving this statement fell. It could not, of course, have been proved better than by the admission of the arrested man himself. But this admission was recorded only in the first inspired official bulletin—or perhaps also in the record of van der Lubbe's first interrogation. Since the accused strenuously denied the suggestion that he was a Communist—for even Heisig and his colleagues could rely on nothing more substantial than their 'impressions' to the contrary—the Detective Inspector had to set about proving it another way. He journeyed to Holland, to van der Lubbe's native city Leyden. There he sought out and took statements from van der Lubbe's relatives, every one of whom confided in him that van der Lubbe had left the Dutch Communist Party in 1931 and since that time had been a vigorous opponent of the Communists. The Chief of the Leyden police confirmed the accuracy of these statements. Heisig achieved no more success with van der Lubbe's acquaintances. Bitterly disappointed with the first results of his investigations in Holland, Heisig looked around for a way out of the impasse. It was at this point that, on his own initiative, he arrived at the theory that van der Lubbe had set fire to the Reichstag alone. He declared in an interview which he gave to the Dutch press on March 14th 1933:

"As for the important question whether Lubbe had assistants or accomplices, it is probable that he alone started the fire but that the preparations for it had been carried out by his accomplices."

This statement, so contradictory to the official bulletins, had an immediate result. Judge Vogt hastened to issue a statement contradicting Heisig's interview in the following terms:

"A report has been published in a number of papers that van der Lubbe started the fire in the Reichstag by himself. This is not correct. The judicial investigation has given good reason to believe that van der Lubbe did not commit the crime on his own initiative. Details cannot at present be given in the interests of the pending investigation."

Heisig's thoughts were thus abruptly recalled to what he was expected to discover. He turned from his ill-fated theory and set himself to composing a report containing exactly the opposite from what had been communicated to him by van der Lubbe's friends and relations in Leyden. This remarkable composition was revealed on the second day of the proceedings. The Court was informed:

"Van Albada (a student) had become convinced that van der Lubbe was an individual selected by the Dutch Communist Party for the purpose of carrying out important activities in which the Party desired to remain in the background.

Van der Lubbe was thrust forward and was always agreeable to take the blame on himself.

"Vink informed me that on February 28th, 1933, the Dutch Communist Party had sent a representative to collect some of van der Lubbe's important notes, particularly a diary, since it feared otherwise to be compromised."*

No sooner was Heisig's evidence given than van Albada and Vink publicly protested. It appeared that not only had Heisig completely changed their statements but that he had included in them parts entirely of his own invention. Both these former acquaintances of van der Lubbe requested that they should be summoned to Leipzig to testify and to contradict Heisig's report. Their requests, likewise those of the Secretariat of the Commission of Inquiry, the Supreme Court ignored and Heisig left the Court a free man, with an unsmirched reputation.

The Police Witnesses

The curious might be forgiven for wondering how and where the police discovered their witnesses against Torgler and his Bulgarian colleagues. They certainly collected ruffians with the most unenviable criminal records. Putting on one side men like Heines, condemned for a brutal and cold-blooded murder, there were four particularly worthy of mention: Weinberger, with many convictions for fraud, who tried to worm information out of Popov in prison; Kunzack, with a long list of convictions for crimes of violence and sexual offences, to whom was allotted the role of testifying as to Torgler's experiments with explosives and as to secret Communist gatherings in which van der Lubbe had taken part; Lebermann, another old lag, "specially selected" by Torgler in 1931 for the job of blowing up the Reichstag, who when asked by the Presiding Judge how much he had got for his most recent theft replied: "Twenty-five marks!": Grothe, a mason, formerly insane, now a police spy—whose evidence alone supported the story of the Committee of Action of which the first official bulletins had spoken. In addition to these four, a whole host of police spies, former mental patients and

* Some of van der Lubbe's papers including the diary were taken away by an anarchist friend of his, Harteveld. The diary was later published in the so-called "Red Book" on van der Lubbe, issued by a Dutch anarchist group of which Harteveld was a member.

petty criminals were included in the selection of witnesses made by the police.

In tragic contrast with the type of witnesses last mentioned were those selected by the police from amongst the helpless victims of the prisons and concentration camps. From some of these statements incriminating the accused men or the Communist Party had been wrung by means of threats and worse. Typical was the way in which the world learned of the treatment accorded to three workmen, Jaschke, Nickel and Hieske from the little village of Zinzendorf near Frankfurt-on-Oder. These men had been compelled to confess that the Communist Party had prepared an insurrection to take place in Zinzendorf on February 27th. In giving evidence on December 4th these three workmen withdrew their former confessions which they indicated had been got by means of threats, and Jaschke said:

"I was so badly treated and my head was hurting me so much that I did not know what I was doing any longer. So I just answered 'yes' to all the questions which they put me."

To their honour it must be said that many of these men brought from the concentration camps to the Court, safe from their gaolers for a few brief hours, without thought for the fate which awaited them on their return, spoke the truth in their evidence.

The police who had so grievously ill-treated these witnesses did not stop at the accused. On March 2nd, 1933, in a speech made at the Berlin Sportpalast, Dr. Goebbels related with apparent amusement how Torgler had been led by the police through a dark corridor and had cried for help because he thought he was going to be shot. Goebbels related this story not only publicly to mock the helpless Torgler, but also with a view to discounting the prevalent rumours that Torgler had been subjected to actual ill-treatment. This little comedy which the police played with Torgler in order to extort a confession from him is, however, no isolated incident. Other cases exactly similar are on record. There are, too, many cases in which methods even more brutal have been resorted to by the police and the Gestapo (Secret Police) in order to induce statements. To quote two cases of many: John Scheer, the Communist Deputy, who is said to have been "shot whilst trying to escape" on February 1st, 1934, was put in a heated

48

oven until his flesh hung in ribbons from his body; again Thälmann, the leader of the German Communist Party now in the hands of the police for more than a year is known to have been beaten several times since the end of January 1934.

One of the important points in the case was the means with which the incendiary material had been brought into the Reichstag. Torgler, three days before the fire, had taken a small parcel into the building which according to his account contained cakes for his lunch. The Public Prosecutor alleged that the parcel contained not cakes but incendiary material. A clerk employed by the Reichstag, Schmal, informed the police that he had seen Torgler waiting at a tram stop carrying a small brown parcel at about 2 p.m. on February 27th (or February 25th). Schmal's statement as recorded by the police put the size of this parcel as about twenty by thirty centimetres. Asked how he had been able so accurately to gauge the size of this parcel Schmal replied:

"That is what I was told by the police, so I accepted it."

Dimitrov's Papers

The police were not less unscrupulous in their collection of the documentary materials than in their treatment of the witnesses. The legally prescribed duty, the execution of which Dimitrov specially requested, that his papers should be numbered and sealed was not fulfilled by the police. As a result a pamphlet and a map of Berlin appeared amongst them at the trial. When the pamphlet *The Burning of the Reichstag* was produced in Court on October 6th and it was stated that it had been found amongst Dimitrov's papers, he declared:

"I have never seen, possessed nor read such a document."

This pamphlet was again referred to on the thirty-sixth day of the proceedings. A police official testified that the pamphlet was alluded to in a written summary which had been read through and signed by Dimitrov. Faced by this statement he stood firm:

"I have never read such a document. No mention of this pamphlet was made in the summary which was put before me, nor was it referred to at any time during the police investigation."

It was subsequently established in fact that the statement referred to had neither been shown to nor signed by Dimitrov.

49

On the same day as this pamphlet, a "Pharus" map of Berlin was produced and described as having also been found amongst Dimitrov's papers. This Dimitrov also denied having had in his possession. This map appeared to have undergone extraordinary transformations in the course of the preliminary proceedings. Steinbach one of the detectives who actually searched Dimitrov's rooms stated in Court on November 11th that he had found the "Pharus" map in a closed brief-case of that accused's. He added:

"The 'Pharus' map which I found was found in a different envelope to that containing the map which is produced in Court."

This did not conclude the matter. Another detective, Kynast, swore that he had found crosses indicating the palace, the Reichstag, and the Dutch Embassy on the map discovered in Dimitrov's rooms. He said:

"They were not easy to discover because they were made with a pencil and very lightly. I could only make them out with the aid of a magnifying glass."

The "Pharus" map produced in Court was actually marked with thick pencil crosses, easily visible to the naked eye. The transformation of the map was just as much the work of the police as the planting of the pamphlet and map in Dimitrov's rooms. But the whole thing was carried out so clumsily and stupidly that whatever hopes the police had entertained were destroyed for ever by a short incisive examination.

The failure of the police to make a check of Dimitrov's property had a further consequence. They had found some eight postcards of Berlin in his pockets. But only two of these came to be produced before the Court—one showed the Reichstag, the other the palace—thus, two of the four buildings upon which van der Lubbe carried out his incendiary attempts. The other cards which would once and for all have demonstrated the complete harmlessness of the whole set had been spirited away, where, only the police knew.

The Treatment of the Debris

Amongst the first duties imposed on the police and public safety officials by the Criminal Procedure Code is the preservation of possible clues on the scene of the crime. Under this head in the case of the Reichstag fire fell obviously the duty of preserving untouched the debris of the burnt building. This was not done. Further, despite the invariable practice in all arson trials to-day, of making a chemical analysis of the debris and ashes partly in order accurately to identify the inflammable substances which have been employed, this course was not followed. One of the experts summoned, Dr. Brüning, told the Court that the debris was treated to a superficial examination with spoons: another expert, Wagner, explained to the Court on the same day that he was forced to bare hypotheses for want of a proper chemical examination of the debris. It is obvious that a proper chemical analysis and tests would have established the exact character of the inflammable material employed in the fire, which in its turn would have probably furnished a valuable clue to the identity of the incendiaries. The infractions of the law committed in this connection had only one result, a result which must have been within the contemplation of the responsible officials, to minimise the possibility of elucidating the truth.

Throughout their investigation the police followed in the footsteps of Göring, their leader. They followed the route which he had laid out for them. Some clues they effaced, others they fabricated. They threatened and cajoled witnesses. They manufactured some proofs and suppressed others. From start to finish the police investigation is, to say the least of it, a mass of irregularities and grave infractions of the law. Happily in face of the watchfulness of the world the use of these methods in the Reichstag fire case was a failure. But it can be justly asked in how many cases in Germany have the same means been successfully employed? Who can tell how many witnesses prompted by the police have perjured themselves in the obscurity of the special criminal courts? From how many witnesses have statements been forced by threats and ill-treatment? How often have proofs been effaced and spirited away? How many convictions have been procured by the police and their masters through perjured and fabricated evidence? Little enough is known of the majority of cases in which the enemies of the present regime in Germany are condemned to death or to life-long imprisonment on materials no different from those which were sought without success to be used against the four innocent accused men in the Reichstag fire trial.

Vogt, the Examining Magistrate

The judicial investigation conducted by the sartorially exact Judge of benign countenance revealed the same methods and the same lack of regard for prescribed formalities as had marked the inquiries of the police. Judge Vogt, an Examining Magistrate attached to the Supreme Court was a tried expert in political causes. He had played the same role in the first great framed-up case against the German Communist Party in 1923 the so-called Tscheka trial. Here Vogt had used all his armoury. There were the stories of 'mass poisonings,' to be carried out in that case by means of germ cultures. There were the same 'terror squads' whom Göring made use of in his first official bulletin about the Reichstag fire. There was also the police spy to testify against the Communists, one Felix Neumann, who since Hitler's accession to power has joined the ranks of the National-Socialists.

Beside the difficulties presented by the Reichstag fire trial, the Tscheka case of 1923 had been mere child's play to Vogt. As he went about his work in 1933 a photograph of Göring adorned Vogt's desk. But the Examining Magistrate needed no reminder of Göring's existence more constant and forcible than the daily difficulties with which the Prussian Prime Minister's activities had strewn Vogt's path. He knew that the allegations made in the official bulletins against the accused men and the Communist Party were false and that the material provided by them was absolutely unsusceptible of proof. He was in a quandary. He knew that the falsehoods of the official reports were regarded by the world as seriously incriminating Göring. He knew that to save Göring he must jettison the official bulletins; but that the fact that he had thrown the official statements overboard would of itself immeasurably strengthen the suspicions already entertained against Göring. Finally Vogt decided to bury them without ceremony or mourning. In passing over these reports in silence Vogt had to abandon van der Lubbe's 'confession' that he was a Communist, his 'connections' with the Social-Democrats and his part in the sittings of that mysterious body, the 'Communist Committee of Action.' Vogt did not rely upon the underground passage through which according to Göring's constant and reiterated assertions, the incendiaries had made their escape. He put to one side the many hundred-weights of damning documents found by Göring and his underlings in the Karl Liebknecht House. In fact Vogt suppressed all Göring's materials and set about bringing forward proofs of his own.

The Examining Magistrate seems to have made it his business to assist the witnesses in making their statements. Before they were confronted with the accused men Vogt would show their photographs to the witnesses to assist in the process of identification. Again he got one witness, Frau Meyer, to the point of stating that she had seen Dimitrov with van der Lubbe in a café in the Düsseldorferstrasse in Berlin on February 26th, the day before the fire. But when it was found that Dimitrov's alibi for February 26th and 27th was unchallengeable, the Examining Magistrate allowed the witness silently to disappear. Most painstaking was Vogt's treatment of the engineer Boghun who asserted having seen a strange man stealing out of the Reichstag at about 9 p.m. on the night of the fire. The Examining Magistrate examined this witness at such length and so frequently that he was finally, after several confrontations with Popov, able to describe him with some degree of accuracy and to identify him with the mysterious stranger. Boghun had originally stated to the police that the stranger was wearing light coloured trousers, during his examination by Vogt they darkened perceptibly until they became the identical blue trousers which Popov was wearing. Boghun had told the Police Officer Lateit, on the night of the fire, that he could not say whether the stranger was wearing a hat or a cap; but Vogt so charmed his faculty of memory that in the end Boghun was able, even emphatically, to assert that the stranger had worn a soft hat. The Examining Magistrate displayed the same solicitude as is illustrated by these two examples in attending to all his witnesses.

Hampering the Defence

The Criminal Procedure Code prescribes that the accused must, during the course of the preliminary investigations, be afforded opportunities of making statements in contradiction or explanation of matters appearing to incriminate them and of elucidating facts in favour of their innocence. Vogt, however, declined to accede to the requests of Dimitrov, Popov and Tanev to be confronted with van der Lubbe. Popov and Tanev had stated, quite independently of one another, that at about 9 p.m. on the evening of February 27th they were in the Ufa Pavilion in the Nollendorfer Platz seeing a film. Popov stated that he had left his gloves behind, had gone back later to look for them and had searched with the help of an attendant. His request to be confronted with the attendant Vogt refused. Popov and Tanev gave detailed accounts of the whole of their movements on February 27th. They asked to be confronted with the waiters at the Aschinger Restaurant in the Bülowstrasse where they had had dinner that evening. Vogt declined to do this. He failed to confront Torgler with Karwahne, the most serious of the witnesses against him. Had this been done Torgler would have been able at an early stage to demonstrate the falsity of Karwahne's statements. By refusing to hold any of these confrontations Vogt deliberately deprived the accused men of the benefit of their legal rights.

The same provision of the law requires the attention of the accused to be drawn to all the facts incriminating him. Judge Vogt rooted out a printed engagement card on which the betrothal of a certain Frau Kruger with a Dr. Schaafsma-Schmidt—a name which Dimitrov used during his stay in Berlin—was announced. This card Vogt hid from Dimitrov but concealed amongst the papers of the case in order that it should be possible at the trial to demonstrate the immorality of Dimitrov, who was a married man. When the card first came to light, Dimitrov denied all knowledge of it and sharply criticised Vogt's methods, saying:

"I am learning of this matter to-day for the first time. That is characteristic of the whole course of the preliminary investigation."

On November 12th Frau Kruger herself courageously shattered Vogt's designs and revealed the mystery of the card to the Court. The truth was that she had had the card printed in order to protect herself against the railleries of her women friends; Dimitrov had known nothing of it.

The obligation of strictest accuracy is, not unnaturally, imposed upon the magistrate making the records of the interrogations of witnesses. Two points will illustrate the manner in which Vogt carried out this duty. Schmal, a clerk employed in the Reichstag, when giving evidence on the eighteenth day of the trial swore that he had seen van der Lubbe near the Reichstag on the afternoon of February 27th. He further swore that, possibly on the same day, possibly two days earlier, he had seen Torgler at a tram stop near the Reichstag. The record of his examination by the Examining Magistrate was put to him. It ran as follows:

"I am certain that the meeting of Torgler and van der Lubbe took place on the day of the fire. I myself saw them together in the Reichstag."

Schmal denied that he had ever given such an answer. He declared that he had never mentioned any meeting of Torgler and van der Lubbe either inside or in front of the Reichstag.

Another instance was the absence of any entry in any shape or form of a statement made by van der Lubbe during his interrogation: "The others must have done that." These two examples are typical of a whole series which illustrate that Vogt took his duty of strict accuracy very lightly.

In the office of the Communist Party Parliamentary Group there had hung a list of Torgler's appointments, recording the places and dates after February 27th at which Torgler was due to speak at meetings. This was an important piece of evidence for Torgler's innocence, for a man intending to burn the Reichstag to bring about a political upheaval would hardly go to the trouble of working out a complete list of ordinary engagements to follow his deed. In reply to several requests of Torgler's, Vogt explained that the list of appointments had disappeared. Ultimately a search through the Examining Magistrate's dossier revealed the missing list—an occurrence which can be explained only by assuming that Vogt desired to deprive Torgler of the assistance of this document.

The link connecting the accused Bulgarians with van der Lubbe was forged by the National-Socialist waiter, Helmer, and depended almost entirely upon the accuracy of his testimony. Vogt could easily and indeed should have tested Helmer's statements with scrupulous care. But he accepted them without further inquiry and without taking the least precaution. One visit to the "Bayernhof" restaurant where the meetings were said to have taken place would have shown Vogt the improbability of Helmer's story. A simple inquiry posed in Holland would have elucidated the fact that van der Lubbe did not leave that country from May 1932 until early the next year—for he was in prison in the Hague between June and October and after his release drew and signed for his incapacitation allowance each week in person. It was during this time that Helmer placed the meetings.

Vogt's methods may be finally typified by two examples of particular, and one would have thought, relevant questions which he refrained from pursuing. The statement made in the first official bulletins as to the time at which Torgler had left the Reichstag had this much foundation in fact, that a deputy had left the building at about 10 p.m. in a state of excitement and in great haste. But this man was not Torgler, nor indeed a Communist. It was a National-Socialist deputy, Albrecht. As the last person to leave the Reichstag, in circumstances exactly similar to those which were alleged against Torgler, it might have been presumed that Albrecht's movements would be regarded with suspicion. Vogt, however, refrained from summoning Albrecht before him until nearly a month after the fire and after a brief examination allowed him to depart without having then or at any time taken steps to investigate the truth of his explanations.

From the first it was treated as important to elucidate with the utmost possible detail the course of van der Lubbe's movements on the days preceding the Reichstag fire. It became known at an early stage that van der Lubbe had turned up at the police station in Henningsdorf, near Berlin, on the evening of February 26th and had asked for a night's lodging. Ignoring the fact that van der Lubbe must have somehow got to Henningsdorf and must have been seen by and spoken to persons there, Vogt did not take the first step to investigate van der Lubbe's movements on the day and night before the fire, he did not even take statements from the police at the station which van der Lubbe visited. The seriousness of this omission became all the more striking when van der Lubbe, during the trial, gave his reply to the question as to where he was on February 26th:

"With the Nazis!"

Vogt's Treatment of the Accused

The Criminal Procedure Code prescribes circumstances in which accused persons may be put in fetters. This course should be taken only when they are specially dangerous to other persons or when they have attempted or prepared to attempt suicide or escape.

Neither Dimitrov, Torgler, Popovnor Tanev could be described as specially dangerous to other persons; none of them attempted or prepared to escape; and none of them, before they were put in fetters, attempted suicide. Nevertheless Vogt kept these four innocent men in fetters for five out of the seven months during which they awaited their trial. Released from the German gaol by the force of world indignation, on the anniversary of the Reichstag fire Dimitrov gave his first interview with the press in Moscow. He described the agony of their fetters; the unbearable pain caused by the gashes on their ankles and wrists where the chains cut into them; the sleepness nights which they passed. What Vogt's intentions were in this respect passes almost beyond conjecture. He ignored their requests to be released. Until forced into an ashamed admission he sought at the trial to deny the fact that he had received many written applications in the proper form from Dimitrov for the removal of the fetters. While the German Government, through Göring himself, officially denied that the accused men were being kept in chains, the men lay in prison fettered night and day, undergoing such suffering that at length Tanev was driven to attempting suicide. Tanev who once underwent torture at the hands of the Bulgarian police for three days and nights without breaking down, was driven to the extremity of self-destruction by Vogt's inhumanity. When he was visited in prison by the Bulgarian lawyer Detcheff for the first time in August 1933, Tanev replied to Detcheff's question as to why he had done it, with the answer:

" That thing forced me into it."

The conduct of the German Government and of its subordinate, Vogt, in this connection is not easily susceptible of another explanation than their hope through ill-treatment to destroy the accused men before their trial, to render them physically and mentally unable to defend themselves.

Less cruel but not less unscrupulous was the manner in which Vogt set about poisoning the air for the three Bulgarians. The celebrated announcement of March 22nd was issued by him. It ran:

"The result of the investigations so far has established that the Dutch Communist incendiary arrested in the Reichstag at the time of the fire was, during the time immediately before the fire, in touch not only with German Communists but also with foreign Communists including some who have been condemned to death or to long terms of penal servitude in connection with the blowing up in 1925 of Sofia cathedral."

When this statement was issued the Bulgarians had been in custody for thirteen days. At Vogt's disposal was the information supplied by Helmer and by Boghun and nothing further. Yet Vogt saw fit on the basis of this scanty material to issue his official statement. So obvious was the wantonness with which Vogt conducted himself that on the thirty-third day of the trial the lawyer Teichert was forced to abandon his passive role and to exclaim:

"I regret that the Examining Magistrate should have been led by this witness (Helmer) who, I am convinced is absolutely mistaken, on to a path which has been disastrous for the German people."

Not until the trial was proceeding did it become clear what basis Vogt had for his statement connecting the Bulgarians with the Sofia cathedral outrage. A National-Socialist official, Dr. Dröscher, happened some weeks after the fire to be passing through a part of the Reichstag in which the Examining Magistrate was conducting his investigations with the accused men. He immediately went to Vogt and informed him that he recognised one of them from his pictures as Dimitrov from Sofia, who was one of those who blew up the cathedral. This was enough for Vogt. He did not deem it necessary to lodge an inquiry on this point with the Bulgarian authorities, which would have elucidated the fact that Dimitrov was far away from Sofia at the time of the outrage in question and that he had never in any way been implicated in it. He could have discovered that there was a Stefan Dimitrov Todorov who was implicated in the explosion but that he had no connection with nor any resemblance to Dimitrov. Dröscher and Vogt, on this point, were thus demonstrably mistaken, but instead of acknowledging his error the Examining Magistrate sought firstly to excuse, secondly to blame Dimitrov himself and thirdly to deny that he was mistaken.

On September 28th, 1933, Vogt declared to the Court:

> "It is correct that a statement was issued to the press which inferred that the three arrested Bulgarians had taken part in the setting on fire or blowing up of Sofia cathedral. At a later date I stated to Dimitrov that it appeared that this information was incorrect. He himself, however, is responsible for the error since he failed to correct me when I connected the commencement of the Bulgarian insurrection in 1923 with the outrage in Sofia cathedral which latter did not in fact take place until 1925."

Three minutes after attributing the responsibility for the mistake to Dimitrov himself, Vogt retracted his admission and declared in a loud voice:

> "The accused Dimitrov was involved in the blowing-up of Sofia cathedral. Yes! Mr. Dimitrov, we are a little confused. But you wait awhile for there will be a witness who will swear that you had a part in that affair."

The witness, who was the National-Socialist Dröscher, came and stuck to his identification of Dimitrov with the face on the post card which he had seen many years before. Error was impossible. All this was at a time when the publication of the actual sentences against Dimitrov had made it plain that he had never been accused much less convicted on account of the Sofia outrage.

Despite the provisions of the law which strictly forbid the practice, Vogt did not hesitate to induce the accused men to confess by interviewing them singly and pretending that their colleagues had made a clean breast of it. Thus Vogt told Tanev that Popov had made a confession. He also tried to trap Torgler into incriminating himself, and van der Lubbe into alleging that Torgler had acted as his accomplice, by leading each of them to believe that the other had made a full confession. When examined upon his use of such methods on September 28th, Vogt replied:

> "Firstly, I am a German judge: secondly, my name is Vogt."

This is perhaps unique amongst Vogt's statements in that it cannot be contradicted. It furnishes the explanation of the methods which he adopted in the execution of his judicial functions, it explains his treatment of the evidence and his inhumanity towards the prisoners.

Had the preliminary examination been conducted with the least care and regard for legal requirements, let alone impartiality, it would have been obvious that there was not the shred of a case against any of the four Communists. The exposure of Vogt's methods day by day as the trial progressed furnished convincing proof that he had been guilty of flagrant and deliberate misconduct. Even a newspaper so partial to the regime that its representative alone was permitted to interview van der Lubbe, the Amsterdam *Telegraaf*, recorded its doubts upon Vogt's activity.

"The first stage of the trial has been concluded. The results show that the indictment has by no means been put on its feet. Indeed the competence, not to say the impartiality with which the preliminary investigations have been conducted come seriously into question."

A thorough examination of Vogt's methods and of the results of his investigations leaves no doubt remaining. There are hardly terms strong enough to paint his conduct. But his case is by no means isolated or unique; it is typical of the justice meted out to its victims by the Hitler regime.

The Secret Indictment

The work of Heisig, Vogt and their associates was brought to its conclusion in the indictment. The German press with one voice extolled the size of the indictment which was laid before the Supreme Court by the Public Prosecutor in August. It was two hundred and thirty-five pages long and concluded with a supplement of the names of one hundred and ten witnesses. Its length was the only praiseworthy thing about it.

Protected by legal provisions the Court and the Prosecution veiled the indictment in secrecy. The requests of the Secretariat of the Commission of Inquiry for a copy were totally disregarded. The public was made aware of the nature of the case against the accused men only by closely following the proceedings through the whole fifty and more days of their length. Dimitrov's requests that the indictment should be published were ignored.

But the indictment did not remain quite secret. Opponents of the Hitler regime in Germany managed, at the risk of their lives, to photograph the two hundred and thirty-five pages one by one and to send it secretly and perilously out of Germany. The first attempt to bring the photographs across the frontiers failed—the messenger with the documents was arrested and thrown into prison. The second attempt succeeded and the indictment came into the hands of the Secretariat of the Commission of Inquiry and ultimately before the Commission itself at its final session.

Although shattered piece by piece during the course of the proceedings, the indictment, one of the many hundreds of similar documents composed by the officials of the Hitler regime for the destruction of their political opponents has great importance. Its length obviously debars publication in this work, which must be content with a brief indication of its most salient features.

Similarly in this respect to English law, German law requires that an indictment shall set forth the legal provision contrary to which a crime has been committed, the legal conditions within which the act is punishable and the specific acts carried out by the accused by which he is alleged to have violated the law in question. Whilst charging Dimitrov, Torgler, Popov and Tanev with arson, the indictment in the present case failed at any point to indicate by exactly what acts it was asserted that these four men had made themselves guilty. There is nothing whatever in the indictment indicating if or how any of the accused men, other than van der Lubbe, took part in any stage of the arson, whether obtaining the inflammable material, bringing it into the Reichstag, preparing the ground for the fire or actually setting the building alight. The Public Prosecutor in fact furnished himself with a roving commission, which enabled him to change his grounds against any one of the accused as often as he wished during the trial and to set his sail according to whatever wind was prevalent at any moment. Important to the Public Prosecutor and to his masters, the German Government, was only the fact that the accused men deserved punishment, not that they should be proved to be guilty. The Indictment itself conferred a free hand on the Public Prosecutor by stating:

"It has not been possible to establish in what manner the accused individually participated in the commission of the crime charged."

The Witnesses

No less characteristic of the indictment were the names and particulars contained, or omitted, in the concluding list of witnesses. The criminal convictions of Lebermann, for larceny, Bannert, for fraud, Wehle, for coining, and many others are not mentioned. Nearly a sixth of the list had been sentenced for common law crimes—their sentences totalled more than seventy years altogether.

A half of the witnesses listed were members or supporters of the National-Socialist Party; another fifth of them, members of the other political parties of the Right. Ten of the witnesses listed were police officials, a class whose number rose to twenty-five during the course of the trial. Of the remainder some seven or eight, to whose numbers there was also added during the trial, were brought by the Public Prosecutor from concentration camps—a period in which had in many cases brought them, in the prosecution's view, to a suitable frame of mind. How many of these men heroically shattered the illusions of the prosecution on this point during the trial is well known.

Not even this array of witnesses with which the Public Prosecutor sailed into a trial on which the world's eyes were resting, could extricate him from the quandary in which he, like Vogt, was placed by the official statements for which Göring was responsible. The ten incendiaries who had made their escape through the underground passage, of whom Göring had said so much, so frequently, presented a very awkward proposition. He could not accuse van der Lubbe as being the sole culprit without throwing overboard these statements. But to charge and prosecute the four Communists on account of complicity would be disastrous if it were not attended by success, for in such case the world would rightly inquire where the other ten incendiaries really were. Under strong pressure from the Government the Public Prosecutor had to choose the course, so distasteful to him, of indicting all the accused of responsibility for the fire though the proofs which Heisig and Vogt had provided him with were so pitifully weak that it was impossible even to hope for a conviction in a trial held under independent scrutiny. Somewhat ingeniously the Public Prosecutor framed the indictment so as to give him a line of retreat, upon van der Lubbe's sole responsibility for the fire. In this manner, however, there arose a serious flaw in the indictment built up as it was partly on van der Lubbe's assertion that he was the sole incendiary, and partly on the 'proofs' furnished by Heisig and Vogt implicating the other accused. This contradiction the Public Prosecutor considerably lessened by suppressing van der Lubbe's statement to Vogt: "The others must have done that." And Heisig's account of the first interrogation: "He (van der Lubbe) at first stuck to it that he had started the fire by himself."

Van der Lubbe's Story of the Fire

The route supposed to have been taken by van der Lubbe in setting fire to the Reichstag is described in detail in the indictment. The indictment states (at page 97) that the account given by that accused of his own movements is substantially accurate and the description given in the indictment is alleged to be based on van der Lubbe's own account. According to the statements as to time which are accepted in the indictment the period available for van der Lubbe to carry out the arson, from the time when he succeeded in climbing up the façade of the building on to a first floor balcony until the moment of his arrest was from eleven to, at the most, fourteen minutes. Following through the description of van der Lubbe's movements given by the indictment if his statements be correct he must in this time have executed the following separate actions and movements:

	1	Taken a matchbox out of his pocket;
	2	taken out a match;
	3	lit the match which the wind blew out;
	4	taken out a second match;
	5	lit it, but the wind blew it out;
	6	taken out a third match;
	7	lit, but the wind blew it out;
	8	taken out a fourth match;
	9	lit it, but the wind blew it out;
Indictment.	10	taken out a fifth match;
	11	lit it, but the wind blew it out;
Page 76.	12	taken out a sixth match;
	13	lit it;
	14	put the matchbox back into his pocket;
	15	lit a firelighter with the match;
Pages 55, 56, 76.	16	kicked several times against the window pane, holding the burning firelighter in his hand;
Page 76.	17	impeded by his coat, van der Lubbe jumped into the building;
	18	disturbed by sensation of pain, he felt his fingers burning;

63

Page 76.	19	ran several yards further into the restaurant and behind the tables;
Page 77.	20	threw the firelighter on to the table behind the bar;
	21	took the second packet of firelighters from his pocket;
	22	tore off their wrapper and let them fall on the floor;
	23	lit a second firelighter from the remains of the first packet;
	24	walked through the room to the door leading to the lobby opposite the window through which he had climbed;
	25	set the curtain on the left of the door alight;
	26	waited until the flames caught well;
	27	set fire to the foot of the curtain on the right side of the door;
	28	ran back through the room to the next window, giving on to the balustrade;
Page 78.	29	laid the firelighter on the table standing before the window;
	30	pulled up the heavy curtain and laid its lower end on the table;
	31	set light to the lower part of the curtain;
	32	took out the third packet of firelighters from his pocket;
	34	broke off a piece from this firelighter;
	35	ran back through the room to the opposite wall to a point between the first and second doors;
Page 79.	36	let the piece of the third firelighter fall to the floor;
	37	ran first to the door leading to the lobby;
	38	ignited the remaining piece of the third firelighter by the flames of the curtain of this door;
	39	opened the door behind the burning curtain;
	40	ran through the curtain and the door into the lobby;
	41	ran along to the Kaiser Wilhelm monument;
	42	ran back through the lobby to the large entrance door and back again to the staircase S.22;
Page 80.	43	felt the fire burning his fingers and became frightened;
	44	threw the rest of the third firelighter on to the carpet of the lobby, making a burn there;
	45	took off his coat;
	46	laid it on the floor;
	47	undid his tie;
	48	laid his tie on the floor;
	49	took off his collar;
	50	laid it on the floor;
	51	took off his jacket;
	52	laid it on the floor;
	53	took off his waistcoat;
	54	laid it on the floor;
	55	undid his braces;
	56	let them fall on to the floor;
	57	took off his shirt;
	58	laid it on the floor;
	59	drew up his braces again;
	60	fastened them;
	61	picked up his jacket;
	62	put it on again;

Pages 85-6.   63 took a piece of soap out of his pocket;
                64 placed the soap on the floor;
Page 80.   65 picked up his shirt;
                66 set fire to his shirt with the still burning piece of the third firelighter;
                67 dragging his burning shirt after him, ran back to the restaurant through the burning curtain, several yards inside;
                68 ran backwards and forwards in the restaurant;
                69 went past the bar into the waiters' room;
                70 ran to the old refrigerator in the corner of the room;
Page 81.   71 took a skeleton key from his pocket;
                72 unlocked or broke open the refrigerator; (according to the witnesses Jurgen, Marten, Weinhold, marks could be seen on the lock)
                73 apparently tried to set fire to the pile of cloths lying in the refrigerator;
                74 took one of the cloths out;
                75 unfolded it;
                76 set light to the cloth with the burning remnants of his shirt;
Page 82.   77 ran down the staircase which leads from the waiters' room to the ground floor dragging the burning cloth after him;
                78 came upon a locked door at the foot of the stairs, and observed that the door was locked and that the glass panes were reinforced with wire;
                79 broke one of the panes with his foot;
                80 climbed with the burning cloth through the broken pane;
Page 83.   81 ran into the ante-room to the kitchen;
                82 ran through the ante-room into the kitchen;
                83 the cloth threatened to burn his hand and he became frightened;
                84 laid the burning cloth on the chopping-block;
                85 took his jacket off in the kitchen;
                86 laid it down;
                87 loosened his braces;
                88 took off his vest;
                89 fastened his braces;
                90 picked up his jacket;
                91 put it on again;
                92 lit his vest from the tablecloth;
                93 ran to the way out of the kitchen, found the door locked;
                94 seized hold of a plate;
                95 shattered the 8mm. thick panes of the service hatch with the plate;
                96 climbed through the broken panes of the service hatch, trailing his burning vest after him; he then found himself in Room 24;*

* Here later the bullet fired by P.C. Buwert about two to four minutes after seeing van der Lubbe enter the building was discovered. Van der Lubbe heard the shot when he was here and was disturbed in his activities by it.
Up to this point, following the account of the indictment, van der Lubbe had altogether carried out some ninety-six separate actions in 2—4 minutes. This is absolutely impossible.   [*Continued at foot of next page.*]

Page 84.   97   ran through Room K in the direction of the members' cloakroom;
            98   passed through the revolving door;
            99   ran through into the cloakroom where the burning pieces threatened his wrists;
           100   carrying the burning remains of his vest, ran through the length of the cloakroom into the lavatory;
           101   took a small towel from the rack;
           102   unfolded it;
           103   set it on fire with the still burning relics of his vest;
           104   threw the burning remains of his shirt on the stone floor;
           105   threw the burning towel to the stone floor;
           106   threw an empty paper basket over it, which caught fire;
Page 85.   107   took a large towel from the washstand;
Pages 85-6. 108   with the burning hand-towel he set the large towel alight.
Pages 128, 129, 132.   According to the Indictment, but not to van der Lubbe's statement, there then ensued a sequence of actions of some long duration. The time being now at least 9.16 or 9.18 p.m. As early as 9.10 p.m. probably even five minutes earlier, the witness Boghun states that he saw a strange man (Popov?) emerging from Entrance No. II which had been locked earlier by a porter and which Scranowitz also found locked after the fire. Now according to the indictment, van der Lubbe was the only person in the Reichstag building at that time and must, thus, have let out the strange man. The indictment supports this by saying that van der Lubbe must have
Page 131.   been near Entrance No. II since he spoke of having seen "knights' figures" in the Reichstag.
Page 130. 109   As no traces of fire or skeleton keys were to be found in the door of No. II Entrance, van der Lubbe must have ran to the House Inspector's office by Entrance No. III in order to fetch the key;
           110   opened the door of the House Inspector's office;
           111   took the (right) key from the bracket;
           112   ran some distance with the keys to No. II Entrance;
Page 130. 113   opened two heavy doors (the inner and outer) with many locks and bolts;

Van der Lubbe's declaration before the examining magistrate is quite inexplicable. According to that he was first in the Plenary Chamber and set fire to it afterwards coming, for the first time, into the restaurant and thence running down to the ground floor. During these 2—4 minutes he must, if this be correct, have performed numberless more actions which make more transparently impossible his story that he accomplished the deed alone. Moreover against this account are:

Pages 56-7.   (a)   The first fire was in the restaurant (7 witnesses).
Page 58.   (b)   Ultimately van der Lubbe reached Room 57 near the Plenary Chamber where he was arrested.
Pages 131, 132. (c)   Van der Lubbe must have been by Entrance No. II near the Deputies' cloakroom at 9.10 p.m. in order to let Popov out of the building. A point to be later dealt with.

Page 130. 114 after the man seen by Boghun had crept out, van der Lubbe shut, bolted and locked both doors;

115 ran back to the House Inspector's office;

116 hung up the key on its bracket again where it was later found;

117 shut the doors of the House Inspector's office after him;

118 ran back to the members' cloakroom;

Page 85. 119 ran up the staircase into the lobby, carrying the towel which was still burning;

120 ran through the lobby to the Kaiser Wilhelm Memorial where he came across his abandoned clothes;

Page 86. 121 ran towards the great door which gives on to the western window and then back to his clothes;

Page 85. 122 picked up his coat;

123 picked up his waistcoat;

Page 86. 124 threw the now almost completely burned towel to the floor;

125 with the burning remains of the towel ignited his waistcoat which burned slowly;

126 set his jacket on fire;

127 ran through the lobby into the west corridor;

Page 87. 128 saw a wooden panel on the wall opposite and thinking it was a door tried to wrench it open;

129 van der Lubbe "who had already tried to wrench it off" tore the panel away from the wall;

130 tried to set the panel and the other wall panelling alight by thrusting something between them;

131 set light to two heavy curtains in the door between the ante-room H.68 and the west corridor (H.69);

132 set light to a curtain behind a telephone box on the left hand side;

133 ran several yards along the north corridor and out of it into the Plenary Chamber;

Page 88. 134 in front of the "yes" Exit took the last fragments of the broken firelighter from his pocket;

135 threw the broken fragments of the firelighter on to his burning coat;

136 seized hold of two piles of printed paper on a desk and threw them on to his burning coat;

Pages 88-9. 137 also threw down his overcoat which failed properly to catch fire and was later found in the west corridor;

138 ran along the north corridor towards the east corridor and half way along the latter with some burning material in his hands;

139 opened the door leading into the Plenary Chamber;

140 set light to the curtains at the Speaker's tribune;

141 went up to the stenographers' room;

142 tore down the curtain hanging in the entrance to the stenographers' room;

143 laid this curtain on the burning curtain of the Speaker's tribune;

144 ran through the Plenary Session Chamber with the burning curtain in his hand to the door giving on to the west corridor;

145 opened the door and again went along the west corridor;

Page 90.

146 threw down the burning curtain in Room H.69;
147 ran back to the Plenary Chamber and crossed its whole breadth to the Speaker's tribune;
148 took from the Speaker's tribune some more blazing material;
149 ran out into the east corridor and some yards down it to the south corridor;
150 pushed back a heavy leather sofa in the south corridor;
151 set light to a window curtain;
152 tore down the heavy window curtain;
153 threw a part of this curtain down on the sofa;
154 set light to a window blind;
155 set light to a second blind in the window;
156 set light to another blind in another window;
157 ran back to the east corridor and a small distance along it;
158 ran from the east corridor to the Bismarck Hall to the second door which was locked;
159 ran to the opposite door;
160 opened this door;
161 ran into the south corridor;
162 let a burning brand fall there;

Page 91.

163 ran back to the Bismarck Hall;
164 made burns in the carpet;

Page 65.

165 ran into Room 57;
166 stood in a corner of this room;

Pages 65, 92.

167 tumbled in an exhausted condition from the corner of this room against the witness Scranowitz and was arrested.

The above analysis of the actions set out in the indictment, which are said to be 'substantially accurate' considered from the point of time, demonstrate how impossible it was for van der Lubbe alone to have set fire to the Reichstag in the interval which the indictment accepts as accurate.

Every one of the single actions set out needs at least several seconds for its performance, some of them indeed require minutes. If one takes as an average half a minute for each action, van der Lubbe would have taken 83 minutes, i.e., nearly one hour and a half.

This criminal expert Werner makes believe, however, that van der Lubbe succeeded in performing these 167 separate actions in eleven to fourteen minutes. Even if one takes as an average a bare quarter of a minute for each act some forty-one and a half minutes would be required for their performance, nearly three-quarters of an hour. Van der Lubbe is said to have accomplished them in eleven to fourteen minutes.

Van der Lubbe Passes Through the Fire Unscathed

According to the account in the indictment, van der Lubbe set fire to twenty-three separate places. He used as incendiary material, fire-lighters, cloths, towels and curtains. If his account be accepted as true he must have taken a zig-zag course which led him back frequently to burning places and passing through flames. Nevertheless, he was unscathed, untouched. His hair was not singed; his shoes and trousers were unscorched. If van der Lubbe's statement is accurate then he must have smashed with his hands or feet several windows of thick glass and have passed through the broken panes. When van der Lubbe was arrested neither his hands nor his feet—and his toes were showing through the old shoes which he wore—nor his clothing nor footwear bore cuts or scratches. All of these things, any one of which is sufficiently remarkable, were passed over in silence by the Public Prosecutor.

No less vital is the question from whence this alleged account of van der Lubbe's emanated. Striking were the contradictions as to van der Lubbe's demeanour and replies on the occasion of his first interrogation made in Heisig's evidence. It is certain that van der Lubbe cannot have given this account taken up by the indictment to Heisig. Again, had not Judge Vogt asserted in the trial the impossibility of ever getting a lucid explanation from van der Lubbe of his movements in the Reichstag. Yet here was a full and clear account of what he was said to have done, which van der Lubbe's mumbled acceptance at the trial by no means confirmed. The patent impossibility of the story given in the indictment makes the whole question even more mysterious.

The Opinions of the Fire Experts

The charges formulated against van der Lubbe's co-accused in the indictment were largely based upon the opinions of the three fire experts, Josse, Brüning and Schatz. The two first named attributed the fire to inflammable solids; the third to liquids. These opinions bore on the question of the way in which the material had been brought into the Reichstag.

The possibility of storing the material in the Reichstag could not be entertained for one moment against the accused, because it was well known that frequent searches were made, quite improperly, of the rooms and cupboards used by the Social-Democrat and Communist members of the Reichstag. It was essential for the prosecution to assert that the materials had been brought in shortly before the fire by the accused men. The theory of inflammable solids was directed against Torgler, seen carrying two brief cases; that of inflammable liquids was directed against Tanev who was said to have been seen in the Reichstag with van der Lubbe carrying a box on the afternoon of the fire. Josse stated his view that the fire in the Sessions Chamber had been caused by film scrap or fuses. This went to implicate Popov who, according to the evidence of the witness Grothe, had received fuses for the purpose of setting fire to the Reichstag from the Communist official Kempner.

The conflicting views of the experts, all of whom were agreed on only one point, that the fire was probably prepared by persons with a knowledge of chemistry, indicates the difficulties in which the Public Prosecutor found himself. It was not surprising that the attempt to run four different theories of the cause of the fire at one and the same time by no means assisted the discovery of the real facts of the case. Indeed the prosecution's case ended by being no further forward than it was at the time when the indictment was framed.

In addition to the three points discussed above, the indictment is characterised by a mass of other inconsistencies and omissions.

One of the facts relied on by the Public Prosecutor as indicating Torgler's guilt was the tranquil manner in which he heard of the Reichstag fire whilst supping at Aschinger's restaurant. Against this the fact that Torgler appeared to be excited and nervous when he was 'seen' in the Reichstag on the afternoon of the fire and later the same night, when he was having coffee in a small restaurant with some colleagues was also regarded as suspicious. One cannot but admire the facility with which the experienced hand of the Public Prosecutor extracted from contradictory situations the same evidence of guilt.

It is said on page 72 of the indictment that:

"Van der Lubbe's stay at Spandau is of special importance,"

and further that:

"The police have received reliable confidential information that the thread connecting van der Lubbe with the affair was woven at Spandau."

Although, as has been seen, Judge Vogt neglected to make an inquiry into van der Lubbe's adventures in Spandau and Henningsdorf, one would have thought that the Public Prosecutor having included two statements of this character in his indictment would not have been satisfied without making some effort to clear up the history of van der Lubbe's stay in those places. Not so the Public Prosecutor—the bare pronouncement concerning Spandau contented him. None of the witnesses in his list hailed from Spandau; the Public Prosecutor summoned none from there, and none, indeed, would have been heard had Dimitrov not frequently, in the most urgent terms, insisted on the necessity of their appearance.

There were many others whose testimony was called for by the contents of the indictment, but who were omitted from the Public Prosecutor's list. There was Albrecht, the National-Socialist and last person to leave the burning building on the night of the fire; there was the Fire Chief Gempp; the Communist Deputy Neubauer, then and now in a concentration camp; the two former Communist functionaries Kempner and Singer, who had been in the hands of Göring's police since early April 1933 and whom the irresponsible statements of the witness Grothe had implicated as the emissaries and agents of the German Communist Party entrusted with the task of maintaining communications with the accused men and with preparing for the fire. The pressure of world opinion indeed caused all these to be summoned during the course of the trial to testify before the Court.

The names of the four Communists, Florin, Koenen, Kühne and Professor Halle, with whom Torgler had been at various times during the afternoon of February 27th, were not included in the Public Prosecutor's list and, despite the fact that they all offered themselves as witnesses, the Court did not see fit either to summons them or to direct the taking of their evidence abroad. The fact that the Court similarly omitted to obtain

71

the true testimony, which was available, of van Albada and de Vink, has already been alluded to in this chapter. In addition to these witnesses of the facts of the case, no witnesses of the political situation in February 1933, an important issue since the charge of high treason was seriously raised, other than National-Socialists—and safe ones at that—were admitted. Had the Court and the Prosecution seriously desired to obtain a true picture of the German political issues at the relevant time, it is incredible that no witnesses other than Goebbels and Göring should have been heard on the point. Dimitrov's requests that the German-Nationalists, von Papen, Sedlte, Hugenberg and Duesterberg, Stahlhelm leader, should be heard as witnesses in the political stage of the trial were quickly declined. Although the two first named had undergone 'political co-ordination' perhaps it was still feared that they might let fall a clumsy word; while in all cases it was to be envisaged that their statements might be in confirmation of the allegations of the Oberfohren Memorandum, a chance which could not be so much as risked. Since the attack of the prosecution, particularly so at the political stage, was made against the German Communist Party, Dimitrov's application for the summoning of Thälmann as a witness was not unreasonable. The all-embracing testimony of Grothe, adopted to the last word even in the closing speech of the Public Prosecutor, implicated Thälmann personally in the preparations for the fire; an additional ground for requiring his attendance. But Dimitrov's request was refused—neither the Court nor the Public Prosecutor dared to face the consequences of producing Thälmann in open Court.

The last noteworthy omissions from the indictment's list of witnesses were those National-Socialists who were widely believed to have instigated or executed the arson, Göring, Goebbels, Heines and Helldorf. At a later stage of the trial these men were summoned. The Court provided them with an opportunity by means of their testimony of shielding themselves against accusation and suspicion. In the case of the two Ministers among the four, the Court departed from all rules and practice concerning the treatment of witnesses and permitted them to harangue the Court and the world concerning their own greatness.

The very inadequacy of the Public Prosecutor's work in this

connection, the many omissions from his list of witnesses contrasted with some of the personalities who were included, is less indicative of incompetence than of a conscious intention to present his case without regard for the interests of justice, but with the desire to secure the conviction of political opponents of his Government whom he was personally convinced were not guilty.

At all costs the Public Prosecutor had to prove that the Communists had prepared an armed insurrection to break out on the night of the fire. The indictment found and furnished this proof. At pages 206 and 207 of the indictment it is solemnly suggested that the Communist Party gave the signal for the armed insurrection to break out in the tiny Silesian country town of Seidenburg. In support of this puzzling pronouncement the evidence of a compositor, Neumann, was tendered. Neumann's testimony was to recount his impression that "the question of the practical carrying out of the armed insurrection in Seidenburg had, under the orders of the Central Committee of the German Communist Party, been discussed." One is almost driven to regard this infantile attempt to prove the insurrectionary plans of the Communists as a gesture directed by the Public Prosecutor at Göring and his colleagues. To bear out the 'proofs' which the latter never neglected opportunity to expatiate upon, the Public Prosecutor could produce only the 'impressions' of a compositor from a sleepy country town.

The legal charges against the prisoners are set out with comparative brevity on the last two pages of the body of the indictment. Two pages out of two hundred and thirty-five. It is not surprising that with such facts and with such evidence at his disposal the Public Prosecutor was unable to set them out at greater length.

The Importance of the Indictment

The indictment forms the basis of the trial. The proceedings in Court are carried through on lines which the indictment lays down. It lays before the Court the charges in support of which the Public Prosecutor summons his witnesses, it formulates in conclusive form the precise accusations which are to be proved against the accused man. German law prescribes that the indictment shall be laid before the prisoners a certain time before the commencement of the trial. That the accused should possess and comprehend the indictment is naturally essential for him not only that he may appreciate the exact effect of the evidence and charges against him, but also that he may consult with his lawyer concerning the defence.

For Torgler and Dimitrov, for the latter had sufficient command of the language to be able to express himself with fluency and idiom, it was possible fully to comprehend the indictment. For Popov, Tanev and van der Lubbe the understanding of the indictment as it was written was an impossibility. In answer to a question of Dimitrov's, van der Lubbe stated in Court that he had only read about one-half of the indictment and that part he had not understood. To Popov and Tanev no written translation of the indictment was given. The indictment was translated aloud to them and upon their recollection of this recital their answers to its charges had to be made. Despite the utter impossibility of retaining much detail in the memory from a two hundred and thirty-five pages long oral translation, the Court did not seem to regard this method of communicating the contents of the indictment to the prisoners as irregular.

It was upon the basis of this lengthy indictment, the effect and charges of which were not put within the comprehension of all the accused, that the trial was opened. For five of the seven preceding months the accused had, contrary to law, been kept in chains; the prisoners had been, as will later be shown, deprived of free and impartial legal assistance; they had been dragged through the confusion of many lengthy interrogations; their legitimate requests had been refused by the police and the Examining Magistrate; they had been obstructed and hindered in the preparation of their defence at every turn; now, faced with a hundred and more witnesses, with a hostile Court and with all the force and enmity of a Fascist regime, they came to their trial.

III

DR. GOEBBELS' MANŒUVRES

"The very magnitude of a falsehood contains an element which will ensure its being believed; for in their inmost hearts the bulk of the people are depraved rather than deliberately and consciously evil, in that they fall more easily prey to large than to small lies. They lie so frequently themselves in matters of small importance that they do not jib too much at great ones." (Hitler. *Mein Kampf.*)

WHEN in July 1933 the German Government came to the conclusion that a trial was to be held, they did so with a full knowledge of the risks which that course might hold in store for them. They knew the value and weight of the evidence against the four accused Communists, they knew the character of the incriminating witnesses, they knew the large gaps which the investigations of the police and of Vogt had left in the chain of proof. But there was no other way in which even the possibility of quelling the suspicions against the National-Socialist leaders within and without Germany could be envisaged.

Although wont in their propaganda to paint Germany as the outlaw of world society, the National-Socialist leaders soon became aware of the existence abroad of powerful reactionary circles disposed to be friendly towards the 'new' Germany. While not in principle disapproving of the Terror, such circles nevertheless, for political reasons, attached import-ance to the observance of the forms of justice. As long as the rulers, big and small, of Germany flaunted the Terror and openly disdained the forms of justice, the forging of any international ties was difficult. The implacable enmity of the anti-fascist movement abroad, which from the first realised that under Hitler all 'justice' was measured in political scales, was a factor which impeded the aims of National-Socialist foreign policy both on account of its inherent force and for the pressure which it effectively exercised upon quarters otherwise not hostile. The German Government was thus faced with an almost complete lack of confidence in German justice and the Courts which administered it. No voice, even amongst its

75

sympathisers, was so bold as to defend the treatment meted out to the opponents of the regime under the mask of legality. It was this factor with which the National-Socialist propagandists had chiefly to reckon.

An Objective Tribunal

The German Government sought to discount the foreign distrust of their Courts and justice by a careful selection of the tribunal to whom the trial was to be entrusted. At the Cabinet meeting at which the decision to hold a trial was taken, Goebbels laid down the conditions under which this was to take place. The composition of the tribunal selected was to be such as to ensure acceptance of the wishes of the Hitler Government while at the same time giving no cause to the outside world to say that the accused men had been condemned by a demonstrably partial National-Socialist Court.

Of the divers Courts constituting the Supreme Court some seven are charged with the conduct of criminal cases. Of these the first three deal commonly with appeals and applications for revision of sentences. The remainder form the four Courts before which charges of political importance are commonly tried. The composition of the bench is determined each year by nomination from the Presiding Committee of the Supreme Court. The division of cases amongst the four competent Courts is decided by the initial letters of the accused persons. The Government had thus the choice between three different tribunals. It was by entitling the defendants "van der Lubbe and others" that the case was brought before the Fourth Court.

To the Hitler Government the President of this Court appeared to fulfill the requirements laid down by the Minister of Propaganda Goebbels. For three years from 1924 to 1927 Dr. Wilhelm Bünger had been Minister of Justice in Saxony. For one year later he had adorned the Ministry of Popular Education, while for six months between 1929 and 1930 he was Saxon Prime Minister. He possessed qualifications fitting him exceptionally for the task for which the Fourth Court was chosen. A member of the German People's Party he had nevertheless during his terms of office pursued the Communists with exceptional severity. In addition he enjoyed a reputation of liberal tendencies especially abroad, on account

76

DR. WERNER
Public Prosecutor

DR. WILHELM BÜNGER
President of the Fourth Criminal Court of
the Supreme Court

DR. ALFONS SACK
Counsel for Torgler

of the part he had played in obtaining a revision of two cases
not concerning Communists, which gained international
attention. Supported by these considerations the German
Government hoped to present Dr. Bünger to the world as
an impartial and independent jurist. A communication from
Dr. Goebbels to his propagandists abroad sent in early
August 1933 is instructive.

"In demonstrating the objectivity of the Supreme Court it is of particular
importance to note that the Reichstag fire trial will be in the hands of the Fourth
Criminal Court. The President of this Court is Dr. Wilhelm Bünger. It is to
be stressed that Dr. Bünger was a member of the German People's Party until
its dissolution and is thus not a National-Socialist. Notes of Dr. Bünger's
career are enclosed. Most important are the facts that he was prominent in
working for the re-opening of the cases of Jakubowski and Bullerjahn. Cuttings
containing the opinions of the foreign press upon these cases are enclosed."

The Propaganda Apparatus

Having selected the impartial tribunal necessary for the
trial, Dr. Goebbels then set about bringing his gigantic
propaganda machinery into service. His aim was the preparation of the world for the approaching trial. The direction
of these preparations within Germany is shown by the contents
of the newspapers, magazines, reviews and books which vied
with one another in presenting lurid pictures of the perils of
Bolshevism on the brink of which Germany was alleged to
have stood in February 1933. The nearer the date of the trial
approached the more intense grew Dr. Goebbels' campaign.
Material was issued to the press by the Ministry of Propaganda.
Incessantly in speeches and writings it was announced that
there were as few doubts about the guilt of the four accused
Communists as there were about that of the Communist Party
in general.

In addition to the apparatus of wireless, press and publishing house which was at Goebbels disposal in Germany, there
were practically unlimited financial resources available for his
purposes. These funds were used both within and without
Germany for the influencing and creation of foreign opinion.
In the official Financial Survey for 1933, of the 9.6 million
marks earmarked for the Ministry of Propaganda nearly eight
millions were destined for use abroad. In addition Dr.
Goebbels' Ministry receives the bulk of the revenue from the
wireless in Germany, amounting, according to the Survey,

to nearly eleven million marks. Beyond these items, which are traceable in the specific figures, there are secret funds emanating from the surplus revenue of the radio stations, put in the *Journal de Nation* of November 24th, 1933, at thirty-five million marks and from the confiscated funds and property of the working-class organisations. To the 9.6 million marks specified in the Financial Survey there come to be added the odd 35 millions accounted for in the *Journal de Nation* and subsequently confirmed from other sources; while to the resultant total must be added an unspecified allotment from the proceeds of the confiscated property. One thus arrives at a total sum which cannot be less than fifty million marks. It is doubtful whether even this suffices accurately to measure the whole finances at the disposal of the Ministry of Propaganda. It is for example not improbable that some of the 250 million marks allocated in the 1934-35 Budget to the Storm Troops and the odd 190 millions set aside for the Voluntary Labour Corps find their way into the all-consuming mouth of the Propaganda Ministry.

While this gigantic apparatus and these enormous funds at the disposal of Dr. Goebbels are normally designed to serve the purposes of militaristic and expansionist propaganda, yet during the summer of 1933 they were utilised unreservedly to pave the way for the Reichstag fire trial. To this end the machinery of the National Socialist Party both within Germany and abroad was put in motion.

The Machine outside Germany

Because of the part which they played in the German Government's campaign of preparation for the Reichstag fire trial it is not irrelevant to furnish a brief picture of the world-wide ramifications of the National-Socialists. The ruling party in Germany is closely linked with a whole series of parties, either openly or secretly National-Socialist, organisations and newspapers outside Germany. By means of these, some more, some less patently subordinate to the orders of the "National-Socialist Foreign Policy Department," Dr. Goebbels spreads his propaganda abroad.

Austria is perhaps the land which has been subjected to the most concentrated and diverse propaganda. Hitler has his own "Inspector-General for Austria," a member of the German Reichstag, Herr Habicht who weekly proclaims the German aims regarding Austria and denunciations of Dollfuss from the official wireless station at Munich. The National-Socialist Party of Germany and the Government vie with one another in supporting the proscribed Austrian Nazis both morally and materially. To the encouragement of Habicht's broadcasts and the reception of Nazi refugees from Austria are added financial subsidies and material aid and the services of the German diplomatic machinery for the purposes of communication. The direct responsibility of the German Government for much of the work of the illegal Nazi Party in Austria and its complicity in the bulk of the dynamite and other outrages for which its members are responsible is proved beyond all doubt by the documents published by the Dollfuss Government.

Less concentrated than its manœuvres in Austria is the activity of the National-Socialist Party in other bordering lands. The anti-French aspirations of the German Government and its military advisers find expression in the creation of subsidiary National-Socialist groups and parties in Switzerland and the Netherlands. In 1933 the first Swiss Storm Troop was embodied in Berlin under the leadership of Erich Maey who apparently fled from an asylum in Zurich where he was formerly confined. This Storm Troop was directly and openly under the ægis of the German Party as was the "League of Comrades of the National-Socialists" founded in Germany by the Swiss architect Fischer. In Holland an inspired "National-Socialist Group" under the engineer Mussert has been created. Although this group according to Mussert has no 'official connection' with Hitler's Party, nevertheless the unofficial connections are intimate and the 'Group' closely follows the activities of its German associates, even to the extent of proclaiming a fire in the Amsterdam Telephone Exchange to be the work of Communists and to be the signal for an imminent Communist rising in Holland. In Belgium the National-Socialists have made use of the Separatist controversy in order to create a terrorist organisation of Flamands whose policy and activities are dictated from Berlin.

Particular attention has been paid by Berlin to the development of favourable movements in Scandinavia. The greatest successes in this connection have been registered in Sweden where Count Rosen, the brother-in-law of General Göring, plays an important unofficial role in the direction of the movement. The official head of the movement is Count Erkström and his party is in constant receipt of arms and money from Germany. In Denmark too the activities of the German National-Socialist Party particularly in the former German regions have been a constant source of anxiety to the Danish Government. The methods used there, terrorisation, dynamite and bomb outrages, organised assaults are the same as those employed in Austria and in the Saar by the respective illegal National-Socialist organisations. Throughout Eastern Europe and the Baltic States Hitler has his organised satellite parties, the Iron Front in Rumania, responsible for the murder of the Prime Minister in December 1933, and organiser of anti-French and anti-Semitic agitation, the illegal National-Socialist Party in Czecho-Slovakia, the newly-formed National-Socialist group in Poland and many others.

While the ties between Hitler's Party and the existing Fascist organisations in England are ideological rather than financial, there exists in London a branch of the National-Socialist Party of Germany prominent in whose activities is one Otto Behne, whose name has occasionally appeared in the London press and whose doings have been the subject of questions in the House of Commons. It was Otto Behne who was responsible for a notice which appeared in the London 'Brown House' at the time of the session of the Commission of Inquiry. This notice bore the photographs of thirty-three refugees from Germany some of whom had appeared as witnesses before the Commission, below the photographs appeared the sentence:

"If you see one of them, lay him low!"

As for France, there are more than suspicions that financial ties exist between the German Party and one or two of the more pro-fascist organisations centred in Paris, whose growing and implemented threats to arm against the police and the working-class organisations demonstrate an actual dependence upon Berlin for some part of their activities and inspirations.

Nazi Propaganda in the U.S.A.

Typical of National-Socialist methods, are their propaganda activities in the U.S.A. A large amount of detailed information is available in this connection owing to the fact that the House of Representatives Immigration Committee thought it necessary to hold an official inquiry into the matter, the minutes of which have been published privately in Washington. Since this Committee reported, the House of Representatives has by resolution in March 1934 set up a further public Inquiry Commission to investigate Nazi propaganda in the U.S.A. which has reached alarming proportions and which has taken increasingly undesirable forms. A brief outline must suffice for the present purpose.

At the head of all the Nazi propaganda in the U.S.A. stands the New York association "The Friends of New Germany." This organisation was formerly avowed Nazi, but changed its name on Hitler's accession to power. All the officers of the "Friends of New Germany" are German National-Socialists. At their head formerly stood Heinz Spannknoebel sent over for the specific purpose from the National-Socialist Foreign Policy Department in Berlin. Under Spannknoebel and only second in importance to him are three other National-Socialists, Mentzing, a high official in the Nord-Deutscher Lloyd Shipping Company, Haag, a former Prussian officer, and Count Sauerma-Douglas, one of the circle by whom the murders of Rosa Luxemburg and Karl Liebknecht were carried out. Under the direction of these four the whole of the German-speaking associations in the U.S.A. have been substantially transformed into pro-Hitlerite, anti-Semitic organisations subservient to the "Friends of New Germany."

Of the methods employed by Spannknoebel and his associates the records of the Dickstein Commission provide abundant proof. Nazi propagandists and spies are smuggled into the U.S.A. in violation of the law and under the nose of the immigration officers. From letters produced to the Commission it appears that the services of the German shipping lines are freely employed for this purpose, with or without their knowledge. The anti-Nazi activities of people of German blood in the U.S.A. are carefully observed and spies are sent into such institutions as the Amtorg, Russian Trade Delegation Office. The Nazis have access to a chain of newspapers, German and American, throughout the U.S.A. whose columns are put at the disposal of the "Friends of New Germany" and whose tone is violently anti-Semitic. In addition to these large quantities of pamphlets printed in Germany for dissemination abroad are brought into the country and distributed through the medium of the now co-ordinated German-speaking associations.

The minions of the "Friends of New Germany" do not hesitate to carry out an anti-Semitic campaign against the department stores and against Jewish shopkeepers. This campaign is implemented by the free use of threats and boycott as many letters produced to the Dickstein Commission proved. The same means are used to subsidise the Nazi propaganda in the U.S.A. as are used by their party in Germany. Systematic levies, according to the evidence before the Commission, are made upon all German-American trading concerns. A refusal is met with threats of boycott and retribution, and by actual pressure being brought to bear upon the recusant's affairs or associates in Germany. Second refusals are not common. So notorious have these activities in the U.S.A. become that the Government has considered means to check them. The success of the monster trial of Hitler staged in New York in the presence of the most prominent civic and national leaders of American politics and thought was in no small degree contributed to by the animadversion produced by the activities of the "Friends of New Germany" in the U.S.A.

Renegade Journalists

Amongst the most important of the agents of Dr. Goebbels used particularly in his propaganda abroad are numbers of one-time 'Left-wing' journalists, many of them former foreign correspondents. Foremost amongst this group are Paul Scheffer, would-be liberal Moscow correspondent of the *Berliner Tageblatt*. In 1930 Scheffer was sent to America where he became at the same time enthusiastically pro-American and a fervent supporter of Hitler. Scheffer's contacts amongst the foreign press have been of special value to Dr. Goebbels and he, the one time 'Marxist' has been awarded with the post of Editor-in-Chief of the *Berliner Tageblatt*. A second example of these propagandist agents is Friedrich Sieburg whose political transformation is even more extraordinary. As Paris correspondent of the *Frankfurter Zeitung* he wrote a book in praise of French culture, *God in France*. Sieburg has indeed worshipped at the feet of many idols. When in 1918-19 the revolutionary working class seemed on the point of victory he was a staunch supporter of Karl Liebknecht. Later on he discovered the good qualities of Ebert. Then he sang Noske's praises in the same terms with which he had formerly lauded Liebknecht. Even later he threw himself into the arms of Streseman. Then he swore by Brüning, by von Papen, by Schleicher. Now he swears by Hitler. Sieburg has, indeed, most constantly and impartially, become the devoted adherent of any politician who happened to be momentarily in the ascendant. Sieburg's position in the propaganda apparatus has some importance in that he forms the link between the pro-Hitler sections of the Paris press and the German Government. In an interview with Sieburg published in the journal *Les Annales* in January 1934 he declared that:

"It is true that my Government took me into its counsels. They asked me whether it would be practicable to assist the dissemination of the true facts in the service of co-operation and peace by material means."

To do him justice Sieburg alleged that he had advised his Government not to dissipate their finances on such a project. It may be that Sieburg imparted this advice as the results of experience. It is certain that he was associated with some of Stavisky's henchmen. One of these, Darius, was formerly publisher of a very minor periodical *Bec et Ongles*. Suddenly in September 1933 he managed to acquire sufficient finance to commence the publication of a daily newspaper *Midi*. It has been since revealed that Darius was financed by Stavisky to the tune of some fifteen thousand francs monthly. In the summer of 1933 Darius made a visit to Germany armed with a packet of the famous Bayonne bonds entrusted to him by Stavisky for the purpose of raising finance. It has been widely alleged and there appears to be grounds for believing that Darius took with him to Germany an introduction from Sieburg. He returned from Germany without the bonds and with sufficient funds to commence the *Midi* which was violently pro-Hitler in tone.

Another Paris newspaper remarkable for its pro-Hitlerite propaganda was the *Volonté* whose proprietor Dubarry was also a member of the Stavisky circle and who is now languishing in gaol alongside Darius. Further the Paris newspaper *Liberté* whose director Aymard is also in prison on account of his complicity in the Stavisky scandal, has conducted Nazi and Fascist propaganda of such character and quality that there appear to be grounds for suspecting that Sieburg's influence was not absent. Whatever be the sources from which the finance for these newspapers was actually obtained it may be said that Sieburg's own words indicate that the German Government contemplated subsidies to French newspapers as late as January 1934, when he "advised them not to dissipate their finances." But the connection between Darius and Dubarry and Sieburg was of earlier standing and Darius had made his mysterious journey into Germany more than six months previously.

The French journalist Louis Thomas, formerly a resident of Alsace-Lorraine, has been active in the interests of Goebbels. He has produced a series of pro-Nazi articles firstly in *Nôtre Temps*, latterly when he was driven from access to its columns in no less a paper than Darius' *Midi*. His articles were eagerly taken by the German National-Socialists and reproduced in pamphlet form for propagandist distribution.

The Complete Machine

In the short space available one cannot do more than give the briefest summary of the activities of Dr. Goebbels' agents abroad. The methods of propaganda are of the most diverse nature. They range from openly National-Socialist Parties like those of Austria and Switzerland organised and operated from Germany to associations like the "Friends of New Germany" masquerading under the guise of non-partisan sympathy. Goebbels' agents go abroad either openly like Rosenberg or Spannknoebel, or like the Hitler Youth emissaries who recently visited London, or secretly and illegally, like those who are smuggled into the U.S.A. or Austria. Foreign newspapers are founded or subsidised for the purpose of creating or influencing opinion abroad. Pamphlets and books are published and distributed to stimulate anti-Semitic feeling as well as in praise of the Hitler Government. German and foreign press correspondents are made use of and their associations employed for the dissemination of news items favourable to the National-Socialists and against their opponents.

It is not surprising that from the early summer to the opening of the Reichstag fire trial all this machinery was set in motion and was fully employed with the manufacture of the atmosphere desired for the holding of the trial and the production of the result desired by the German Government. The Hitler partisans abroad by word and writing ceaselessly declared that the four accused Communists and the German Communist Party were guilty of the Reichstag fire, that the National-Socialists as they themselves asserted had saved the world from chaos and Bolshevism, that the Reichstag fire had been lit as the signal for an insurrection which was to overthrow the existing governments throughout the world. No less insistent than the repetition of the stale political hypotheses and fulminations of the National-Socialist leaders was the propaganda designed to evoke the confidence of foreign opinion in the impartiality and objectivity of the tribunal before which the Reichstag fire trial was to be held. Goebbels' instructions to his agents, referred to previously, were faithfully followed; the members of the Court were praised individually and collectively for their impartiality and their independence. The methods of the Ministry of Propaganda went even further. Falsehoods concerning van der Lubbe and the Reichstag fire, the alleged forgery of van der Lubbe's passport and the story of the murder of Gempp were invented and disseminated through secret channels in order that the Ministry could produce striking contradictions of the 'lying propaganda' of the so-called 'Jewish-Marxist refugees.' Although these particular false statements were not accepted by any responsible persons and certainly never used in the propaganda against the National-Socialists, they nevertheless issued the planned contradictions and so endeavoured to reduce the effect of the true facts which had been published. The Court in its judgment stigmatised as false the allegation that van der Lubbe had a forged passport, without indicating that this allegation did not originate either in the Brown Book or in the findings of the Commission of Inquiry. The unfortunate Gempp was produced as a witness in Court, Dr. Sack supplying the necessary comment:

"So you are not dead then!"

In truth no one except the German Government's own Propaganda Ministry had ever caused it to be announced that Gempp was dead.

False Incendiaries

As the Ministry of Propaganda had not hesitated to issue false statements in order effectively to contradict them, it was just as little reluctant to send abroad spies for the purpose of keeping observation on the working of the Commission of Inquiry and of the anti-fascist emigrés. While some of these emissaries confined themselves to keeping watch on the hotels and houses in which the refugees and members of the Commission of Inquiry were staying, others tried to work their way into the heart of the anti-fascist organisations. Amongst these was the sailor Kronburg from Hamburg, a former confidant of the Statthalter Karl Kaufmann, who had entered the ranks of the German Communist Party as a spy and after his exposure went abroad to conduct his activities. Kronburg was exposed and returned in disgrace to Germany.

Yet another group of Nazi agents were entrusted with becoming 'witnesses of the Reichstag fire.' A half-dozen young Germans approached the offices of the Secretariat of the Commission of Inquiry as the time for its session approached and proffered 'first-hand' accounts of the burning of the Reichstag, allegedly carried out by a gang of incendiaries containing various prominent members of the National-Socialist Party. The most notorious of this batch of alleged incendiaries was the Pole, Leizor Kaphan, who supplied to two Swiss lawyers a most circumstantial account of the manner in which he and van der Lubbe had been instructed by Count Helldorf to fire the Reichstag and had been led through the underground passage by him into the building. Strenuous efforts were made in various quarters to get Kaphan's allegations accepted by the Commission of Inquiry. These failed and ultimately Kaphan under strenuous examination broke down and confessed that his whole statement was false and that he had been put up to making it and to getting it accepted by the Commission. These attempts to interfere with or influence the work of the Commission of Inquiry were thus frustrated and, like the bulk of Goebbels' propaganda for the trial, fell on barren soil.

The Public Prosecutor Attacks

Almost simultaneously with the publication of the Brown Book on the Hitler terror on August 1st, 1933, the Secretariat of the International Commission of Inquiry announced the approximate date for the commencement of that body's sessions. This announcement, together with the terrific effect of the indictment against the National-Socialist Party and its leaders, contained in the Brown Book, provided Goebbels with the occasion for a renewed and more vigorous campaign in defence of his Government and in preparation for the Reichstag fire trial.

On August 10th, 1933, the new campaign was opened by two letters addressed by Dr. Werner, the Public Prosecutor, one to the Senator Georg Branting, the Swedish lawyer, the other to Rolland Romain. The object of these letters was to induce the addressees to place the material and evidence to be utilised by the forthcoming Commission of Inquiry in the hands of the Public Prosecutor and the German Government.

While Werner's letter was greeted at home in the politically co-ordinated press as a master-stoke of the German Government against the foreign false and tendentious rumours, its success abroad was much more dubious. In fact Branting's reply was much more favourably received and its contents were re-echoed through the editorial columns of the leading foreign newspapers. This reply submitted to the Public Prosecutor the following ten requests the acceptance of which would have quelled the distrust of the world in the impartiality and objectivity of the Supreme Court and the suspicions entertained against the German Government in the matter. The ten requests were:

1. Free choice of defending counsel by the accused.
2. Permission for foreign lawyers to be selected if desired.
3. Right of defending counsel to see all the documents relating to the trial.
4. Right of the accused to discuss the case with defending counsel without the presence of third parties.

5. Full and unhindered publicity to the whole proceedings.
6. More humane treatment of the accused pending trial, so that they may be mentally and physically in a condition to conduct their defence.
7. Safe conduct and full security for witnesses nominated by the defence or the Commission of Inquiry to enable them to testify without fear or favour.
8. Full security for defending counsel and complete liberty to them to conduct the defence as they think fit.
9. Full right for defending counsel to summon all witnesses.
10. Permission to summon witnesses now or formerly employed by the German Government or any State, in such conditions that they may testify freely and fully.

In his covering letter Senator Branting referred to the threats and menaces which had been repeatedly made in the German press against counsel or witnesses who should be active in the defence of the accused men. Most striking of many of these threats was an article in the official National-Socialist *Dortmunder Generalanzeiger* which in commenting upon Werner's letter and upon the trial in general stated:

". . . Every healthy people will take unto itself the same law of necessity which the German people has long carried out in its actions, to extirpate the Red Peril root and branch. Any State which should move a finger, let alone attempt actively, to protect the murderous minions must justify itself in the eyes of the world. When Marxist swine declare their solidarity with their accomplices, or stand up for them, there can only be one conclusion; that is that they should be accorded the same treatment."

Werner's reply to Branting's letter demonstrated that neither he nor the German Government intended to give way on any one of the ten requests addressed to him. For the most part he answered each point either by evasions or even by cynical denials of facts subsequently admitted to be true. For example, to the request that the accused men should be treated more humanely he asserted that it was quite false to suggest that the accused men were being treated in an inhumane manner or in any way differently from other prisoners awaiting trial. At the trial it became apparent that, together with General Göring's similar assertion, this statement of the Public Prosecutor was untrue. The accused men had been for five months in chains, in violence to legal provisions, at the very time when it was made.

Similar was Werner's reply to the seventh and eighth of the requests:

"Fears for the safety or lives of counsel or witnesses for the defence are without foundation. They can only be based upon the untrue, tendentious statements which appear, in certain sections of the foreign press and which are entirely lacking foundation in fact."

In his reply to Werner's second letter Branting pointed out how very real and well-founded these fears appeared to be. He referred again to the menaces contained in the official organs of the National-Socialist Party and then to the circumstances which appeared to make it impossible in the conditions reigning in Germany for the accused to make free use of their right to retain German counsel. He alluded not only to the experiences of the accused men and their families in their quest for lawyers, a matter which will be dealt with in more detail in the next chapter, but also to the fates which had overtaken numbers of German lawyers either because like Hegewisch they had offered to undertake the defence of Communists after Hitler's attainment of power, or because of their past activities as lawyers to anti-fascist and working-class organisations. The number of lawyers murdered, shot, beaten or thrown into prison purely on account of their professional activities is a formidable one ranging from Joachim, the legal adviser to the Republican *Reichsbanner*, to the conservative Dr. Weiner, an ex-officer and one of the oldest and most honoured lawyers of Chemnitz.

The statements in Branting's reply based, as they were, upon official reports in the German press had undeniable force. Together with the rejection of each of his ten requests, so obviously reasonable and well founded, they served at an early stage to defeat the attempts of the Public Prosecutor to provide fuel for the pro-Nazi propaganda concerning the Reichstag fire and the trial of the accused men. Goebbels' new campaign met with a deserved repulse; frustrated in this direction the Public Prosecutor faded from the picture. His place was taken by a new figure.

Dr. Sack

In mid-August 1933 the news was announced that Torgler had selected Dr. Sack to act as his defending counsel. Dr. Sack, long a member of the National-Socialist Party and in close touch with its upper circles, lost little time in getting into communication with the Secretariat of the Commission of Inquiry. It is sufficient at this juncture briefly to mention the fact of Dr. Sack's appearance and his two journeys, the one to Paris with the object of obtaining a postponement of the

Commission of Inquiry and the other to London with the aim of obtaining publicity unfavourable to the Commission of Inquiry at the time of its session there. It is not unreasonable to suppose, especially having regard to the conclusions which may be drawn from Dr. Sack's complete activities examined in detail in the following chapter, that his appearance next after Dr. Werner in the events leading up to the Reichstag fire trial was another move by the Minister of Propaganda. His activity was not an unqualified success either in Paris or in London, but Dr. Goebbels had other strings to his bow, the next of which he played upon shortly before the trial opened.

The Armed Insurrection

In August 1933 the Eckhart Publishing House announced that a work entitled *The Armed Insurrection*, which dealt exhaustively with the Communist preparations for the insurrection planned to break out the night of the Reichstag fire, was shortly to be published. The publication date was fixed for early September. But with the work itself there were distributed printed slips instructing every bookseller and agent that no copies were to be sold or issued to the public until September 14th, that is the date of the first session of the Commission of Inquiry. The politically co-ordinated German press heralded the approach of the book as the impending long-awaited revelation of the Communist insurrection which had been imminent in February 1933. The ground for the favourable reception of the work was prepared by the publication of long extracts from its contents in the press before its issue. While the work appeared in the showcases of the bookshops all over Germany on the appointed day, and its appearance was welcomed in the most fulsome manner by the German press, the Ministry of Propaganda was careful that no copy should be sent to the world outside until the Commission of Inquiry had finished its work. To allow the Commission to get a copy of the *Armed Insurrection* into its hands would have been truly dangerous, as will be shortly indicated.

The version of the work for publication in France and England, printed in Germany, was released on the opening day of the trial, September 21st. Its reception in the press was poor without exception. In truth the work was a crudely prepared collection of extracts from numbers of well-known Communist books and documents mixed with transparent forgeries and fabrications. Despite the cover design, depicting the burning Reichstag with van der Lubbe imposed menacingly upon it only eleven out of one hundred and eighty-six pages breathe so much as a word about the insurrection planned for February 1933, which gave its name to the work. The first one hundred and seventy-five pages deal wholly with matters of past history, most of them notorious in Germany. Not until page one hundred and seventy-six does the great revelation see the light of day. The revelation consists of a reprint of a document alleged to be the "Central fighting instructions of the Secret Insurrectionary Leadership of the German Communist Party to the Terror and Fighting Squads." The alleged instructions are dated *February 28th*, a curious fact if the insurrection was planned to break out on the night of February 27th, as the Government, the Court and indeed the work itself allege. The document is worth quoting in full:

"Dear Friends (*sic*)

"We have discussed the present situation with other friends and we have together arrived at several decisions. We are herewith forwarding to you those decisions with the execution of which you are entrusted.

1. Mass action to be used where necessary in the struggle against the Fascist terror.
2. Disarm the Fascist terror bands.
3. Arm the workers and poor peasants.
4. Hound the Brown Shirts out of the working-class districts and Labour Exchanges.
5. Anti-fascist policemen fraternise with the workers!
6. Protest strikes against Fascist murder and Fascist terror!

"Break through the ban on demonstrations. Fight for the freedom of the press, for freedom to meet and to demonstrate! These slogans must be used in all quarters. The disarming of the S.A. and S.S., for example, must be everywhere stressed and popularised amongst the widest circles. The building-up of the widest possible mass organisations must be undertaken, a regular patrol service must be set up at once for the protection of Trade Union and working-class buildings in association with the Reichsbanner, the Socialist-Workers Party and the Christian-Socialists. Arrangements for the speedy mobilisation by means of sirens, bugles or whistles of the mass formations to meet Fascist assaults must be made."

These constitute the full extent of the secret fighting instructions to the alleged terror and fighting squads! The first six points are slogans which were to be read daily in the formerly legal Communist press. The latter part is rehashed from an article written in a Ruhr factory paper in October 1932. The date, the alleged source and the commencement of the letter constitute the only new matter.

The above document is the sole piece of evidence which has ever been published in support of the constant allegation that the German Communist Party had planned the armed insurrection to commence on February 27th. The work does not contain a shred of the "finds in the Karl Liebknecht House" announced by Göring and his colleagues. The author, Adolf Ehrt's so-called "Revelations on the attempted insurrection of the German Communist Party on the eve of the National Revolution" have resulted in proving only one thing: that the German Communist Party in fact made no plan or attempt at an insurrection in February 1933, that they had nothing to do with the Reichstag fire and that there exists not a single document or piece of evidence indicating anything to the contrary.

Goebbels' trump card failed to make any tricks! The designs of the *Armed Insurrection* proved abortive. Its fabrications and inventions were so clumsy, and its inconclusiveness so apparent that it was not long before the German Government issued an official denial of any connection with the work. This despite the fact that the German Government and the National-Socialist official press had all heralded the work's approach, had published extracts from it and had controlled its sale and distribution, despite moreover the stamp of official sanction and co-operation which is apparent through the work, which is borne out by the statement from the Reichschancellor which appears on the title page.

The Reporting of the Trial

The publication of the *Armed Insurrection* was designed more for the influencing of the foreign public than for the press. For them Goebbels had made special preparations. The special section of the Ministry of Propaganda for relations with foreign press correspondents occupied itself continuously with the question of the Reichstag fire trial. The section relies on the active co-operation of German journalists in its work. Both official receptions and reports, personal contact and association by German journalists are the means by which the

Ministry of Propaganda seeks to attain influence over the foreign press. The methods which have been used to get rid of foreign journalists deemed to be 'undesirable,' such for example as Mowrer of the *Chicago Tribune* and Panter of the *Daily Telegraph* are well known. It is not therefore surprising to find that elaborate precautions were taken in relation to the reporting of the Reichstag fire trial. The press cards of admission were allotted according to the directions of the Ministry of Propaganda, the representatives of the Socialist and Communist press were, of course, excluded, as were the correspondents of Liberal newspapers deemed to be too hostile to the regime. Until the Soviet Union resorted, following the arrest of the correspondents of the *Izvestia* and *Pravda* for going to Leipzig without police permission, to retaliatory measures no representatives of the Soviet press were admitted to the trial.

For those journalists who were admitted to the proceedings the Ministry of Propaganda arranged preliminary press conferences at which the "objects of the Reichstag fire trial" were explained and prepared special informatory reports. Foreign correspondents were recommended to obtain their information from the Ministry of Propaganda, in order to ensure its accuracy. They were watched, their letters and telephone conversations were subjected to censorship. When the trial opened there lay in the place at the press table allotted to each foreign correspondent a neatly-arranged document "Printed and published by official order" containing a tabulated list of alleged Communist outrages entitled "Memorandum on the Communist Revolutionary Movement in Germany."

Despite his special press service, despite the surveillance and control which he tried to maintain over the reporting of the Reichstag fire trial, Goebbels did not have it all his own way. Each morning there reached every foreign correspondent, through the post and by a variety of other channels, the bulletin of the illegal German Communist Party on the previous day's proceedings. This daily bulletin was one of the most striking features of this side of the trial. It created a great impression on most of the foreign press correspondents present, the bulk of whom did not hesitate to make use of it in forming their commentaries on the proceedings. Even

93

Dr. Sack is forced in his work *The Reichstag Fire Trial* to testify to the importance and the significance of the Communist daily bulletin.

In one way and another the greater part of Goebbels' attempt to influence the foreign press and to sway public opinion abroad to the side of the German Government and against the innocent accused men came to naught. The world did not permit itself to be deceived or misled. Many of Goebbels' efforts were so crude and ingenuous that their acceptance did not for one moment come into question, others of his attempts, more subtle, were wrecked through the foresight of the leaders of the anti-fascist movement or by the exhaustive and sincere work of the Commission of Inquiry and its Secretariat.

On the eve of the Reichstag fire trial the world was convinced that the fate of four innocent men was in the balance and that arrayed against them was the guilty might of the German Government and some of its most prominent members.

IV

COUNSEL FOR THE DEFENCE

GERMAN law while insisting that every accused man shall be legally represented provides that he shall be free to select counsel for his defence from amongst those qualified to plead before German Courts. In accordance with the law, the four Communists accused of complicity in the Reichstag fire arranged for their defences to be conducted by German lawyers. Their relations and friends succeeded in securing lawyers agreeable to act. With the extension of the terror and the application of the law against 'Marxist' professional men the accused found themselves deprived of the services of the lawyers already retained either because they had fled abroad, or because on the grounds of their non-Aryan blood or their political activities they had been deprived of their professional status.

At first other lawyers still permitted to practise were found to take the places of those originally instructed by the accused men. But one by one these new lawyers abandoned their clients and refused to have more to do with the case. All further attempts to obtain the services of German lawyers were unavailing. The Examining Magistrate had definitely threatened lawyers acting in the defence that unless they abandoned their client's case they would be certainly deprived of their professional status and that arrest and confinement would follow, as it had done in so many other cases. These threats secured the retirement from the case of lawyers already engaged and the withholding of other lawyers who might from humanitarian reasons have been willing to act. Lawyers of more prominence either declined to have anything whatsoever to do with the defence or else, like Dr. Habicht to whom Frau Torgler made application, solemnly demanded from her an initial fee of fifteen thousand marks with an additional thousand marks a day if the trial lasted more than ten days. Well might those lawyers still permitted to practise hesitate before taking up the defence of Communists, however wrongly charged, with the words of Dr. Frank, the Reichscommissioner for Justice in their memories:

> "When Communist prisoners are being defended, the question as to whether their counsel have or do frequently defend Communists will be inquired into; also whether they do so from inner convictions."

All the attempts made from March onwards to secure the services of German lawyers to defend the prisoners, whether from within Germany or abroad, met with failure. No different result could, indeed, be anticipated from the politically-co-ordinated remnants of the legal profession.

It was this fact together with the importance and weight of the charges which led to the application of foreign lawyers to be admitted to act on behalf of the prisoners. By German law foreign counsel have a *locus standi* in German Courts and all that is necessary to condition their appearance is the consent of a German lawyer and the permission of the Court. Numbers of foreign counsel were approached by the lawyers who had been formerly acting for Torgler and his co-accused and by the relatives of the prisoners with requests that they should consent to act. Prominent lawyers from all over the world including Mr. D. N. Pritt, K.C., Maîtres Moro-Giafferi, Torres and Campinchi of Paris, Arthur Garfield Hays and Mr. Leo Gallagher from the U.S.A., and many other English, French, Belgian, Dutch, Swiss and Bulgarian advocates gave their consent to take up the defence of the four accused Communists and made formal application, supported by the requests of their relatives and former legal advisers and, as far as was possible, the authorisation of the prisoners themselves. These applications which were made to the Supreme Court from mid-July onwards were one and all rejected. Various reasons were given. It was alleged in some cases that the applicants had not satisfied the Court as to their knowledge of German law or of the German language, or that they had not the consent of the German lawyer acting or that the Court did not deem the case to be one in which the admission of foreign lawyers was necessary. How inconsistent was the attitude of the Court in this matter appeared from its readiness, when the trial opened, to admit a Dutch lawyer to defend van der Lubbe who at least understood some German while it strenuously rejected any application on behalf of Popov and Tanev who were quite unacquainted with the language.

For months the prisoners were without the slightest legal assistance. In the middle of August it was announced to the press that official counsel had been appointed by the Supreme Court to act on behalf of the prisoners.

"Since the accused have not so far selected counsel the Fourth Criminal Court of the Supreme Court has nominated the following as counsel for the defence. For the accused Torgler, Dr. Huber; for van der Lubbe, Dr. Seuffert; for Dimitrov, Popov and Tanev, Dr. Teichert."

With the exception of Dr. Huber the names will be recognised as those of the lawyers who appeared in the trial.

Dr. Huber in fact disappeared from the picture a few days after his nomination, his place was filled by Dr. Sack, the National-Socialist lawyer, with a formidable reputation in political cases, who appeared as Torgler's 'unofficial selected counsel.' Dr. Sack's appearance was preceded by an instructive exchange of letters and telegrams passing between England and Germany. At the end of June Sir Stafford Cripps, K.C., M.P., was approached by friends acting on behalf of Torgler, his wife and his legal advisers and on their behalf he communicated with Dr. Ehlers, a prominent National-Socialist lawyer whom he requested to undertake the defence of the accused men. After a lengthy delay and under pressure Dr. Ehlers eventually answered offering provisionally to take up the case of the accused men but, at the same time, explaining that he could not give a definite answer "before I get the final decision from the Reichsjustizministerium as well as from Hitler or the second leader of the Party." Hardly had Dr. Ehlers expressed his willingness to accept the defence than the Supreme Court announced the official appointments.

The negotiations with Dr. Ehlers are instructive because they suggest that his fellow National-Socialists must have gone through the same process of getting permissions from "Hitler or the second leader of the Party." While Dr. Sack has not vouchsafed any information about such permission in his work *The Reichstag Fire Trial*, nevertheless in his speech in Torgler's defence Dr. Sack proudly informed the Supreme Court that he had been engaged as counsel on one occasion in a case together with Dr. Frank, the Reichscommissioner for Justice and with Dr. Friesler, the Prussian Secretary of State for Justice, and gave the impression that they had approved of his present activities. This communication bears out Dr. Sack's statement to Senator Branting in Paris that he had sought permission to defend Torgler from the German Government. One would indeed be surprised if he had not done so.

The experience of Dr. Ehlers throws some light on the reasons which may have prompted the Supreme Court in rejecting the applications of the foreign lawyers for leave to be admitted to undertake a joint defence of the Communist accused. Foreign lawyers, unlike Drs. Sack and Ehlers would not have consulted the convenience of the German Government and the leaders of the National-Socialist Party, they would have been truly independent and uninfluenced by political considerations. It is difficult to see that their presence and participation in the trial could have done other than assist the Court in the strenuous and exacting task, which it so frequently insisted to be its function, of clearing up the Reichstag fire. By the rejection of independent legal assistance the Court deprived itself of the opportunity to demonstrate its impartiality, it also, as will be shortly indicated, effectively prevented any legal assistance being given to the prisoners.

Perhaps the part of Dr. Seuffert in the trial was the most ignominious. Although he might be excused from failing to conduct an active defence on the ground that his client refused to communicate with him, yet this does not justify his omission to carry out the obvious duty of demanding a thorough expert examination into van der Lubbe's physical and mental condition, the more so as the Court steadfastly refused to take any cognisance of the matter. But not so Dr. Seuffert. He did not make a single move to have the question of van der Lubbe's condition cleared up. He contented himself with sitting beside his client armed with paper handkerchiefs, and wiping van der Lubbe's nose, a function which he was too comatose to perform for himself. In his final speech Dr. Seuffert even after the disclosures which the proceedings had produced concerning the methods and conduct of the police and the Examining Magistrate, stated that they and the Prosecutor:

"Could not have acted otherwise than they did!"

Dr. Teichert with three accused men to defend took a more active part than his colleague, Seuffert, in the proceedings. The foreign lawyers who had gone to Germany in the endeavour to assist the imprisoned men called upon Dr. Teichert shortly after the news of his nomination had appeared. He commenced the discussions by requesting them to produce their passports in order to see whether they bore Moscow visas. He did not hurry himself to visit the accused men whose counsel he was. Popov wrote complaining that although the news of Teichert's nomination had been published nearly a week, he had not so far troubled to communicate with him. Perhaps Dr. Teichert accepted his nomination only with reluctance, perhaps he intended to give "those Bulgarian Communists" a lesson. At all events it is clear that the most superficial perusal of the indictment must have sufficed to convince any man of impartiality that the three Bulgarians from the absence of evidence against them were innocent. Instead of going at once to the succour of men who were innocent, men who had been kept in chains for months, men who knew little of the charges against them, Teichert kept them waiting.

Shortly after the announcement of the nomination of an official counsel to defend Torgler, Dr. Sack announced that he had consented to act as 'chosen' counsel on behalf of Torgler and that he was willing to defend him for a fee of three thousand marks for the whole trial. Without denying Dr. Sack's certain ability, for his reputation in political cases, largely those involving reactionary circles, is formidable, or the fact that the acceptance of the fee stated must have involved some financial sacrifice, one may presume to criticise Dr. Sack's presence in the case and his conduct of Torgler's defence. There can be little doubt that before taking up Torgler's case Dr. Sack was in communication with the Government and with the leaders of the National-Socialist Party. No lawyer other than one thoroughly *persona grata* with the regime would have been permitted to act as 'unofficial' counsel for any of the accused men, a reference to the experiences of the lawyers formerly engaged in the case in its early stages and to the Dr. Ehlers incident suffices to bear out the assumption that Dr. Sack appeared with the consent and indeed the blessing of the ruling powers. His friendship

99

with General Göring dating from the time when they were fellow-officers in the Flying Corps, his long-standing connection with the inner circles of the National-Socialist Party and his professional associations with the highest judicial officials, secured that his presence in the trial should be harmless to the prosecution. Dr. Sack was decidedly *persona grata*, his personality and qualifications marked him out as the man to be entrusted with the conduct of Torgler's defence.

Dr. Sack's first action was to get into touch with the Secretariat of the Commission of Inquiry, a step which he followed by making a journey to Paris. The exact object of his mission was twofold. Firstly he attempted to discover all the evidence which was to be submitted to the Commission of Inquiry bearing upon the fire and Torgler's guilt. Had he intended to use this evidence in order to secure Torgler's acquittal this object would have been perfectly justified, but the fact that he omitted to acknowledge the receipt of a document from Senator Branting setting out, in pursuance to Dr. Sack's own request, some two hundred points which were relevant to Torgler's defence, much less to make use of it seems to indicate that the motive for his inquiries was purely propagandist. That his activities were in fact determined by such motives is borne out by an examination of the record of the discussion which took place between Sack and Branting in Paris. The former constantly inquired as to the relations between the Brown Book and the Commission of Inquiry. He was told that the Commission of Inquiry would examine any material submitted to it in the form of admissible evidence whether it appeared in the Brown Book or elsewhere, that the Commission would not accept any allegation in any book or newspaper as accurate unless it were supported by corroborative evidence. In his book *The Reichstag Fire Trial* Dr. Sack gives an account of the Paris discussions which is at variance in many points with the shorthand record and with the sworn statements of those who took part in them on behalf of the Secretariat of the Commission of Inquiry. Amongst these points is Dr. Sack's statement that those negotiating with him were obsessed by the allegations in the Brown Book. The small part played by that work in the Commission of Inquiry's session together with the fact that Dr. Sack did not see fit at the time although in communication by letter with the members of the Commission to refer to this suggestion seem to ind cate that his recollection is leading him astray.

Dr. Sack further states, in writing of the Paris negotiations, that he got the 'impression' that the Commission of Inquiry were not interested in the question of the innocence of Torgler but merely in the principles which were at stake. Here again it is unfortunate that Dr. Sack did not make such a suggestion to the members of the Commission, or the Secretariat, and that he should first record it at a time some four months after the interview took place. Again Dr. Sack's suggestion, although it is by no means a strong one, resting as it does upon his 'impressions,' is contradicted by the shorthand record of the interview and by the sworn statement of Senator Branting and his colleagues.

One of the points which was seriously discussed in the interview, was the question of van der Lubbe's alleged 'Communism.' To the Commission's offer to provide him with ample material and with the names of witnesses which would prove conclusively that van der Lubbe was no Communist and would thus remove one of the gravest points of the accusations against Torgler, Dr. Sack gave a definite refusal. He stated that he personally was convinced that van der Lubbe was a Communist. Further, Dr. Sack denied that it was important to trace the source of the statements contained in the official A.P.P.D. news bulletins and expressed the opinion that they were mere press inventions and quite irrelevant to the issues of the trial. To the suggestion that he should make use of the material incriminating the National-Socialists with which the Commission was ready in that case to supply him, Dr. Sack at first returned evasive answers; not until he had been pressed did he counter with a direct refusal and with the intimation that he regarded all such material as false or non-existent.

Dr. Sack's second purpose in his journey to Paris was to attempt to procure the postponement of the session of the Commission of Inquiry. He constantly expressed to Branting his confidence in the impartiality of the Supreme Court; he declared that the police and the Examining Magistrate had carried out their duties with the strictest regularity and scruple. He suggested that it was quite unnecessary for the Commission of Inquiry to hold any session, at least at an early date. Further he flatly refused to supply Senator Branting or the Commission with any information concerning the indictment or the accusations against Torgler despite their repeated requests.

Dr. Sack's visit to Paris bore little fruit, either in its propagandist effects or in his attempts to obtain the postponement of the session of the Commission of Inquiry. The effect of the discussions with Dr. Sack in fact served to convince the members of the Commission of the necessity of holding their Inquiry at the earliest date possible. Dr. Sack's resolute denial to accept any of their offers to provide him with material to secure Torgler's acquittal indicated to the Commission that he was more interested in securing the political aims of the German Government and the prosecution than in making sure of his own client's acquittal.

Dr. Sack's next move, the objects of his Paris visit having failed, was to visit the London session of the Commission of Inquiry. He made his way by aeroplane to London after the session had opened, he sat for one day in the Court-room of the Law Society, was much photographed and interviewed, and then he returned to Berlin as he had come. Although Dr. Sack subsequently declared that nothing had transpired in London of any use whatever for Torgler's defence and even suggested that he left London so hurriedly for that very reason, he concealed the fact that the evidence relating to Torgler's alibi, the statements of the persons with whom he had passed the afternoon and evening of February 27th, was received by the Commission on the very day on which he left London. A detailed account of the course of that day's proceedings had been given him by Senator Branting who had visited him on the preceding evening. Dr. Sack thus left London knowing that on the very same day evidence highly important in establishing his client's innocence was to be given before the Commission. In the light of this it is difficult to regard his suggestion that he had the impression that the Commission was not interested in Torgler's innocence as the product of genuine belief.

Any doubts as to the role of Dr. Sack in the Reichstag fire trial which may have been left unresolved after his visits to Paris and London were removed by his conduct during the trial and subsequently. It was his intervention on several occasions during the proceedings both in Leipzig and Berlin which preceded the exclusion of Dimitrov from the trial on the Court's orders. Perhaps the most flagrant instance of this was his rising on October 10th to point out that Dimitrov was making remarks which were intended to convey the fact that van der Lubbe was the misused tool of others and to request the action of the Court. Early the next morning Dimitrov was excluded for no apparent reason. The instances of Dr. Sack's intervention in the interests of suspected National-Socialists in the laying of the accusations against them are too numerous to mention. Dr. Sack took the leading part in 'exposing' the alleged falsehoods of the Brown Book —without troubling whether the allegations were made in the Brown Book or not. It was he who suggested to the unhappy Gempp that he had been alleged to have been murdered and affected surprise that Gempp was alive. He endeavoured to pass off the inspection of the underground passage by S.S. man Weber on the night of the fire as an action undertaken on official orders, until it was revealed that the instructions had come from Göring's private aide-de-camp and that Weber had undertaken the main part of the inspection alone and unaided. Dr. Sack took the most prominent part in getting the allegation of van der Lubbe's 'Communism' on its feet, although to his knowledge there was abundant material to the contrary effect.

Whilst one might be permitted to pass over Dr. Sack's neglect to bring the actual statements in the Brown Book to the notice of the Court, which, as will be later shown, used fictitious extracts as the basis for the rebutting evidence, there can be no explanation of Sack's misquoting the findings of the Commission of Inquiry. In the course of one of his many attacks on the Commission and its work he declared that everything contained in the findings was valueless because the Commission had accepted as facts two matters, the premature dismissal of the Reichstag employees and the failure to give the highest stage of alarm, which he alleged to be completely lacking in foundation. In fact the findings of the Commission, a copy of which was then in Dr. Sack's possession, expressly referred to both of these points only to reject them as unsupported by any evidence submitted to the Commission.

Whereas it is possible that Dr. Sack's impressions of matters may be based upon misunderstanding or faulty recollection, it is quite impossible to assign any such excuse for his deliberate misrepresentation of part of the Commission's findings.

From the outset of the trial Dr. Sack made it clear that he did not intend to defend Torgler the politician, but only Torgler the man. Having regard to the fact that the trial, to his own knowledge, was of the highest political importance and that he himself assisted in its political direction in the sense favourable to the Government and the National-Socialist Party, one may justifiably say that from the commencement Dr. Sack only intended to provide Torgler with half a defence. Indeed had he intended to conduct a political defence of Torgler he could have played no part in the trial at all. Dr. Sack, as a German lawyer, was perfectly aware of the dangers of this course. In German criminal law the principle of 'intellectual complicity' is well established and there was more than a danger that Torgler would be adjudged guilty of high treason on the ground that his views and intentions were the same as those of van der Lubbe or the Communist Party. In the face of this danger Dr. Sack not only declined to contradict or question the assertions of the prosecution that van der Lubbe was a Communist and that the German Communist Party had intended the Reichstag fire as a 'signal' for the planned insurrection, but he frankly supported them. His entire disregard for the political issues of the trial as far as they affected his own client was borne out by his constant absence from the Court during the 'political stage.' Dr. Sack thus left Torgler unprotected against some of the most serious allegations incriminating him. His non-political defence consisted in exposing his own client's flank and co-operating with the prosecution on the political issues either by abstaining from questioning at vital moments or by active intervention to support certain of the Prosecutor's manœuvres.

Space does not permit a fuller investigation into Dr. Sack's conduct of Torgler's defence or his activity in relation to the Commission of Inquiry. In conclusion, a brief allusion to his own work *The Reichstag Fire Trial*, may be made. More than a half of the book is occupied by the speeches made by the Public Prosecutor and counsel for the defence, including himself. The remainder of the book is devoted to proving two theses: firstly, that the Reichstag fire trial and its result was a triumph for German justice, a testimonial to the objectivity and impartiality of the Court; and secondly, that the burning of the Reichstag was the 'signal' for the outbreak of a Communist insurrection. These hypotheses are indeed those maintained by the Court itself in its judgment as well as by the German Government, the National-Socialist leaders and their apologists. Two of the following chapters are devoted to dealing with each of these matters, "German Justice" and "Who Burnt the Reichstag?"

All the counsel for the defence united in their final speeches in support of the two hypotheses contained in Sack's book. They vied with one another in depicting the horrors from which the National-Socialists had rescued Germany by their rapid action, in decrying the slanderous allegations and suspicions which had been entertained against their leaders and in denouncing in the strongest terms the work of the Brown Book and the Commission of Inquiry. Never before have defending counsel in a political trial been so far in agreement with the prosecution upon the vital issues. Never before have lawyers treated and regarded their clients as Sack and Teichert. While Teichert declined to intercede for the release of the three Bulgarians after their acquittal, on the grounds that his work was finished, that excuse did not prevent him from giving an interview to the *Lokal Anzeiger* declaring that the acquitted Bulgarians were in exceptionally good health, and outlining the numerous joys and pleasures of their incarceration. If Teichert thus endeavoured to portray the continued imprisonment of his innocent clients as something quite usual and proper, Dr. Sack had gone much further. He actually applied, before Torgler's acquittal, for him to be taken into preventive custody without his client's knowledge and against his will. Dr. Sack thus furnished the German Government with a reason for holding Torgler in custody and with the opportunity to assert, as they did until it was disproved, that he was re-arrested on his own request and with his consent. With the publication of his book Dr. Sack completed the task he had undertaken with the consent and approval of the German Government and the leaders of the National-Socialist Party. He had aided in securing the "triumph of German justice," he had assisted the Court and

105

the prosecution to fulfil the political objects of the trial, and lastly, he had procured the continued incarceration of his innocent client.

It was thus that Dr. Sack, the ardent National-Socialist and confidant of the German Government fulfilled his task and attained his self-confessed ambition: to be the prototype of National-Socialist counsel for the defence; to display to all the world his conception of the tasks and duties of the German advocate in the Third Reich.

V

A POLICE BARRACKS

"We swear by the Almighty God, we swear by the souls of our dead, we swear by the memory of those who have fallen victim to a justice alien to our people, we swear upon the soul of the German people, that we German Jurists shall follow our Leader on his path to the end of our days." (Oath of the Supreme Court Judges formulated by Reichscommissioner for Justice Dr. Frank on October 1st in the Reichsgerichtsplatz in Leipzig. *German Jurists' Day*.)

THE trial of van der Lubbe and his associates began on September 21st, 1933, before the Fourth Criminal Court of the Supreme Court. The trial was to be held in the Supreme Court building which from the early hours of the morning was encircled by cordons of police. The streets leading to the Reichsgerichtsplatz were patrolled by groups of armed policemen, while at the doors of the Court building were guards who challenged and searched all persons attempting to enter. The corridors of the Courts swarmed with police and officials of all ranks in and out of uniform. Before the door of the Court-room in which the trial was to be actually staged was another police guard which searched thoroughly all who sought admittance. The Supreme Court building had indeed the air of a police barracks!

No less thorough, if less apparent, were the precautions which had been taken to secure the political and propagandist homogeneity of the proceedings. Those who took their places at the press tables had been carefully sifted according to the instructions of the Ministry of Propaganda. One searched in vain for the representatives of Communist, Social-Democratic or even advanced Liberal newspapers. The rest of the audience had been selected by the high officials of the National-Socialist Party. Those whom the National-Socialists declare to have saved from the Marxist yoke, artisans, clerks, small peasants and tradesmen, none of them were present. The masters of the propaganda apparatus did not dare to let the eyes and ears of their underlings whom they feed with forced marches, pomp and mystery bear witness at the trial. It was by means of microphones, gramophone records, by filmed and written 'summaries' that the Minister of Propaganda designed to present the German people with a picture of Bolshevism "in its most frightful form." Without the apparatus of Dr. Goebbels the working millions of the German people could not be trusted to appreciate from the trial the perils from which they had been rescued. But despite Goebbels' precautions, despite the rigour with which the audience was selected and the stringency of the control exercised over the reporting of proceedings, the truth could not so easily be hid and through the medium of the foreign press and the illegal news service of the Communist Party of Germany reached large sections of the German public.

The Trial Opens

At about 8.45 a.m. a string of cars headed by a lorry carrying a body of armed police drove to the door of the Court. Behind the lorry came the cars containing the prisoners who were carefully screened from view, each car bearing a number of armed policemen. At the end of the string came another lorry load of police. Thus were the accused men brought to the Supreme Court.

The murmur of the countless tongues in the Court-room was stilled as the accused men were led in. First came a wreck of a man, with bowed head and vacant expression, the Dutch mason, van der Lubbe. At his heels followed the four Communists: Torgler, thin and wasted, glanced round the Chamber. Many of the journalists present had visited him no less than seven months ago when he was still leader of the Communist Party Parliamentary Group to obtain political information from him. Now it was a different man whom they saw, his face lined with the sufferings of his seven months' imprisonment and the five-month-long torture of his fetters. Each day of their incarceration had left its traces upon the prisoners' faces. But they faced the Court with unbroken courage and determination for all to see.

In the expectant silence and the hush of the Court one could descry the faint clanking of van der Lubbe's chains. The other accused were unfettered. The pressure of world

THE COURT ROOM
A row of Police separates the Court from the 'public'

THE RELATIONS OF THE ACCUSED IN THE COURT ROOM
(Left to right: Torgler's mother; Torgler's wife; Dimitrov's mother; Popov's sister; Tanev's wife)

opinion had secured this small freedom for them shortly before the trial opened. Each prisoner was accompanied by two armed guards who took their places beside them. The accused and the audience were separated by a barrier. The first row of seats was occupied by uniformed members of the Security Police.

Nine red robes entered the room; nine red-clad arms were raised in salute to Hitler, in token of the Court's subservience. *Ave Cæsar, te salutant!* The assembled members of the audience answered the judges with the same greeting. Above the heads of the accused men towered a threatening arch of upraised arms. The members of the Court took their places at the judges' table, the President, Dr. Bünger, the Judges Coenders, Froehlich, Lersch and Rusch. For the prosecution were the Public Prosecutor Dr. Werner and his assistant Dr. Parisius. The charges before the Court were against:

"The mason van der Lubbe, the commercial employee and former Deputy to the Reichstag, Ernst Torgler, the writer Georgi Dimitrov, the student Blagoi Popov and the shoemaker Vassili Tanev."

The charges against them in the indictment ran:

"That in Berlin, within the legal period of limitation, namely on February 25th and February 27th, 1933, they have been guilty of the following connected offences, partially committed in common:

1. All the accused
   a. that they attempted to alter the German constitution by the use of of violence, and
   b. that they set fire with malice aforethought to a building which is used for human habitation and within which at the time human beings were actually present, namely the Reichstag building, and that they committed the said arson with the intention of provoking an insurrection the outbreak of which was to be influenced or facilitated thereby.
2. The accused van der Lubbe,
   c. that he carried into effect his intention to set fire to a building being the property of other persons, namely the welfare office in Neukolln, Berlin, by performing acts in which he commenced to carry out his intentions but did not proceed to the completion of his said intention;
   d. further, that he set fire with malice aforethought, to buildings used for human habitation namely the Town Hall and the Palace in Berlin, and that he committed these said arsons with the intention of provoking an insurrection the outbreak of which was to be influenced or facilitated thereby."

There followed the statement of the legal provisions contrary to which these alleged offences had been committed and a reference to the Emergency Decrees and the retroactive law concerning the Death Penalty which would be applicable should the prisoners be found guilty.

Promptly at 9.15 a.m. Dr. Bünger opened the proceedings. He commenced with a short statement in defence of the Court.

"The enormous repercussions of the event which constitutes the background of this trial have had the consequence of elevating the subject-matter of these proceedings to the rank of universal interest. It has formed the object of passionate discussion and speculation in the press of the whole world. Attempts have been made to anticipate the result of these proceedings. It does not, however, follow that this Court is entering upon its task with preconceived views or with its mind already made up. So far that has never been the custom either in Germany or abroad. Nor has prejudgment of the issues of a trial in the press been usual.

"The struggle between these various conflicting theories has not affected the Court before which these issues come to be tried. This Court will pass sentence solely upon the results of the proceedings within its cognisance. For the purpose of this Court's decision only facts which are revealed in the course of the proceedings before it can have weight.

Not only is this trial open to the public of all lands without restriction but the prisoners are represented by counsel without let, hindrance or condition. It has been said that no foreign lawyer has been permitted to appear for the defence. In this connection it must be observed that the law only permits such a course in exceptional circumstances. In the present case the Court in the free exercise of its unfettered discretion has not seen fit to permit the admission of foreign lawyers. Not only has the Court seen no occasion for their admission but it holds the view that such applications as were made for this purpose were not directed to serve exclusively the interests of the prisoners."

The President of the Court may be excused for beginning the proceedings in an unusual manner, perhaps this was warranted by the great political importance of the trial which was about to commence. But he cannot be excused for his unfortunate choice of words or the tendentious nature of the opinions which he expressed. It may have been a slip of the tongue which led him to speak of the sentence with which the Court was going to end the trial, but it could not be a mistake which led him to describe the defence of the prisoners as being absolutely free and unconditional. Having regard to the history of the attempts to secure legal assistance for the accused men, the President's statement is a travesty of the true facts. No less unfortunate was his statement that the proceedings were open to the public of all lands without restriction, the deliberate exclusion of certain sections of the foreign press has already been remarked upon.

True the prisoners were represented by counsel. But the active defence within the Court was conducted by the four accused men only, and that under conditions of the greatest difficulty. To the efforts of the accused were added the daily endeavours of the illegal Communist Party whose daily reports upon the proceedings containing, as they did, commentary and new material succeeded in bringing into prominence those points which were vital in the interests of the accused men. Of the importance of this daily bulletin, produced at the risk of human lives, even Dr. Sack has to write in his work, *The Reichstag Fire Trial.* Outside Germany the defence of the four accused Communists was carried on in the columns of the world press, the giant meetings and demonstrations organised by the anti-fascist movement. The accused Communists were acquitted. But this was no thanks to the counsel for the defence, no thanks to the Court, whose conduct of the whole proceedings is examined in detail in a later chapter. Because of their own efforts, because of the influence which the illegal Communist Party's hidden hand exercised on the direction of the trial, because of the mighty campaign which was carried on to secure their freedom Torgler, Dimitrov, Popov and Tanev secured their acquittal and the three latter, their eventual liberation.

Dr. Bünger saw fit to attack the foreign lawyers who had applied for permission to assist in the defence. He indicated that their requests had been rejected because the Court did not consider that they were designed to serve the interests of the prisoners. Many other reasons, such as knowledge of German language and law not satisfactorily proved, or failure to obtain the consent of a German lawyer, had been given by the Court in its decisions declining the applications. It was nowhere suggested, before the President opened the proceedings that the real reason for the rejection of all the applications was that the Court regarded them as being designed to accomplish some sinister purpose. In truth Dr. Bünger must have been aware of the weakness of the reasons actually given by the Court in the respective cases and thus have felt it essential to utilise the last opportunity of justifying his own and his brother-judges' action to the world. But the justification miscarried. Some of those lawyers whose applications for leave to appear had been declined, journeyed to Leipzig and sat daily in the Court watching the case on behalf of the prisoners and their families until the majority of them were expelled from the Court and eventually from Germany. It is not too much to say that the Court feared their participation in the trial, for good reason; even more than this, it feared their very presence, and so eventually drove them thence.

Dr. Bünger's opening statement completed the picture. The police barracks into which the Supreme Court building and its environs had been turned, the carefully sifted 'public,' the selected wireless and filmed 'summaries,' the apathetic and broken van der Lubbe, the haggard but obviously innocent accused Communists, the Hitler salute, the Court which began with an excuse and defence; these were the impressions of the opening day of the trial. Even these things made clear what was amply confirmed by the subsequent course of the trial, that its purpose was not to elucidate but rather to conceal the truth.

VI

TORGLER

"This declaration fits in very well with the information and rumours which have been reaching us during the last few days, which plainly and significantly indicate that anything may be expected to happen between now and March 5th. We have been told that a few days before the elections, it may be on March 2nd or 3rd, an attempt is going to be staged on the life of Herr Hitler. No harm will come to him, but the objects of the attempt will resemble those of the attempt by Hoedel on the life of Kaiser William I—with its ensuing 'Socialist' laws. The psychological conditions and grounds for a wild agitation against the Communists and the Communist Party, and for the cancellation of their mandates and other measures are to be prepared in this manner.

"And more still! We have learned that one of the leaders of the Stahlhelm, Herr von Morozowicz . . . during a recent discussion with another Stahlhelm leader referred to the fact that all manner of complications might be anticipated to arise before next polling day and that the Communists had still many things up their sleeves. To this the other party replied, doubtingly, 'Well, what will happen if the Communists do not allow themselves to be provoked into any action?' To which Morozowicz retorted, 'In such a case the complications will be made such as to appear from the outside as if they had.' I would draw the attention of the public to these matters, and would utilise—how was it called —'the last parliamentary forum'—in order to give publicity to these matters and to this information." (Ernst Torgler in the Session of the Prussian State Council held February 23rd, 1933.)

FIVE days after uttering these prophetic words Torgler was the prisoner of Göring's police, accused together with a Dutchman, van der Lubbe, whom he had never seen or heard of before, of having set fire to the Reichstag to bring about the overthrow of the German State. The wheel of fate had turned. He who had prophesied provocation, was the first victim of a provocative plot.

No time was lost. Accusations against Torgler and his party were circulated and broadcast from the very night of the fire onwards. Soon after midnight the official news bureaux were informing the world press that Torgler, with Koenen, had left the Reichstag 'as if in flight' at about 10 p.m. and was seriously suspected of complicity in the Reichstag fire. It was officially stated that he had been seen with van der Lubbe in the corridors of the Reichstag at about 8 o'clock, less than two hours before the fire broke out.

At the time when the bulk of these statements were made, or confirmed from official sources, Torgler was already in custody and had given a full account of his movements on the day of the fire, indicating, not least, that he had left the Reichstag at about 8.15 p.m.—nearly two hours before the time mentioned in the official statements. Despite this, and despite the fact that the account which Torgler had furnished of his movements could have been quickly and completely verified, the police and the Government did nothing to stem the tide of accusations. Indeed the accusations were strengthened by the false account which was furnished of Torgler's arrest, and which has already been referred to. The Government was solely interested in making political capital from the fire and in realising the profits inflated by deliberate misstatements which had accrued from it.

Torgler's Political Career

At the time of the Reichstag fire Torgler was Chairman of the Parliamentary Group of the German Communist Party He had been a member of the Reichstag for nine years before he was accused of having set it on fire.

Torgler was a son of the working class. He was born in Berlin on April 15th, 1893. His father was a labourer in the gas works; his mother was a member of the Social-Democratic Party, a friend of August Bebel. It was she to whom Torgler looked for his upbringing and it was she who educated her son towards Socialism. Torgler was twenty-one when the war broke out in 1914. Alongside many millions of his fellow-workers he enlisted in the army. On active service throughout the war, Torgler learned the horror and the uselessness of imperialist war. The war history of the German Social-Democratic Party drove him from its ranks to the independent Social-Democrats. In 1920 he adhered to the majority decision of that party and joined the Communists. From that time onwards he laboured ceaselessly in the interests of the German Communist Party and the Communist International.

A shop-assistant by profession he interested himself chiefly in the position of the employee class and the black-coated workers. He entered the Reichstag as the representative of the Communist Party in 1924 and was continuously a member to the time of his arrest. He represented his Party on many committees—amongst them the Supervisory Committee of the Reichstag and the Council of Senior Statesmen. His duties as Chairman of the Communist Parliamentary Group required him to pass the greater part of his days, in and out of session, in the Reichstag itself. He was to be found daily in the precincts of the building and his duties kept him there regularly until late in the evening.

But his work in the Reichstag by no means turned him into the mere barren parliamentarian—which some sections of the press in their search for paradox chose to label him. Though a formidable debater and a man much feared for his biting sarcasm, Torgler harboured no illusions on the development of German society. Often in his speeches he castigated the fascisation of the Weimar system. He criticised mercilessly the events of January and February 1933. In his last speech, part of which is quoted above, he denounced the illusion that the Hitler Government would play itself out. He declared:

"It is impossible to say—let us wait, they will vanish of their own accord. No! Nothing will vanish of its own accord. The tyranny of Fascism will remain until the workers themselves rise up and put an end to its bloody terrorism."

In the course of their initial findings the International Commission of Inquiry paid tribute to the personality of Torgler as he had been described to them by many witnesses, the bulk of them drawn from amongst his political adversaries. Even the National-Socialists and their Court were compelled to pay Torgler a grudging respect, so apparent was his moral integrity and political intelligence, even after the ordeal through which he had passed. For some inexplicable reason, even the mighty Göring condescended to throw a crumb to Torgler, who in the past had not spared his talent for irony on any of the National-Socialist leaders. It was with some malice that Goebbels sought to destroy the favourable impression which his colleague's testimonial had faintly bestowed. Goebbels' malice, however, led him so far astray as to attribute to Torgler a speech which, as was later proved, he had never made. It can justly be said that, Goebbels' ill-directed effort apart, no one could say ill of Torgler.

The Accusations against Torgler

Against one of Torgler's calibre and personality the accusations formulated in the official press bulletins were pitifully inadequate for a public trial. With some ingenuity the police, Examining Magistrate and Prosecuting officials worked from the time of his arrest onwards, to build up a case against Torgler which would stand superficial examination. The charge that he had in some manner, directly or indirectly, taken part in the burning of the Reichstag, the Public Prosecutor's roving commission, was supported by a variety of witnesses drawn almost without exception either from the National-Socialist Party or from the very dregs of the criminal classes. The case against him was built upon evidence directed to three different issues; firstly, that he took part in setting the Reichstag on fire; secondly that he was connected with van der Lubbe and the Bulgarians; and thirdly that he acted on the instructions of the German Communist Party in the whole matter.

As it was absolutely out of the question to prove by first-hand direct evidence that Torgler actually took part in the arson, the Public Prosecutor offered in support of the first hypothesis nothing but a series of alleged circumstances from which the required inference, that Torgler took part in the fire, was to be drawn. The use of circumstantial evidence is subject to two grave objections, firstly it is less easy to rebut than direct evidence and secondly, it involves the great danger of error and faulty deduction. Each single link in the chain is liable, unless the main end is kept firmly in view, to become falsely decisive. The Public Prosecutor collected a series of circumstances to ground the required inference, every one of which even had it been proved would to an impartial tribunal have been susceptible of a ready innocent explanation, but which before a partial Court would be capable of magnification into almost conclusive evidence of guilt. The perils involved in the use and acceptance of circumstantial evidence in that it depends upon the accuracy of deductions as well as of facts were in this case completely overlooked.

Passing over the contradictory inferences sought to be derived from Torgler's excitement at one moment and his calm at another, both on the night of the fire, the most vital links in the Prosecutor's chain were three; the allegations that he had left his house with two heavy packages under his arm on the day of the fire; that he was not in the Communist Party office in the Reichstag between 7 and 8 p.m. on that evening; and that he had not left the building until very late.

The first of these allegations was rapidly exploded. It rested upon the concocted evidence of two prying neighbours, a mother and son, which broke down completely in Court. The heavy packages were, as Torgler had said, briefcases, they did, as he had explained long ago and as the search of the Communist Party rooms had confirmed, contain newspapers. The second allegation proved more persistent if just as unfounded, Torgler's alleged absence from the Communist Party office in the Reichstag between 7 and 8 o'clock on the night of the fire had been reported to Göring by Kohls, one of the Reichstag attendants, whom the Minister had apparently whisked away in his motor-car the same night for a private conference. The grounds of Kohls' statement were that he had failed to get a reply from the Communist Group's rooms when he had telephoned up there. In Court, Kohls was unable to explain how he knew there was no reply on the telephone, nor was he able to distinguish the noise from the 'engaged' signal. As the trial progressed the Public Prosecutor relied less on Kohls' statement than on the alleged statement of a journalist Birkenhauer that Torgler's woman secretary had informed him on the telephone between 7 and 8 p.m. that Torgler was engaged. Birkenhauer's actual recollection of the reply was that Torgler could not make a definite appointment with him then but requested him to telephone later—which Birkenhauer in fact did, about 8.10 p.m., and spoke with Torgler. Against the inference which the prosecution sought to draw from these somewhat slender grounds —that Torgler was engaged between 7 and 8 p.m. in making the preparations for the fire—were the statements of Anna Rehme, Torgler's secretary made before the Court, the statements of Koenen, Kühne and Dr. Rosenfeld to the Commission as well as the record of the telephone calls, all of which were in accord on the fact that Torgler did not leave the Communist Party rooms between 7 and 8 p.m. but was engaged during that time in a series of telephone conversations and interviews.

The fallacy of the inference which was sought to be deduced

117

is made apparent by other factors. Even if Torgler was not in his office between 7 and 8 p.m., what was it suggested that he was actually doing? Witnesses who went through the Reichstag building after he had left the Reichstag stated that everything was in order; the postman and the fireman, one of whom passed right through the Sessions Chamber just before 9 p.m. saw nothing unusual there. If Torgler was engaged in making preparations for the fire between 7 and 8 p.m., where did the material come from, who brought it into the Reichstag and where was it put? Any one of these considerations is fatal to the inference which the Public Prosecutor ingeniously sought to draw. But in the process whereby the single link was elevated to actual guilt, each of them was overlooked.

The third link in the Prosecutor's chain of proof of Torgler's part in the actual fire, was to establish the lateness of the hour at which he left the Reichstag. Faced with the position in which it had become abundantly clear that Torgler's movements on the day of the fire were as little suspicious as at any time before it, the Prosecution contented itself with endeavouring to fix his departure from the building as late as possible. The importance of this from the prosecution's point of view was not far to seek. Departing from the main trend of the suggestions in the indictment, with the assistance of the Court's chemical expert, the fire was sought to be attributed to the use of a secret self-inflammable liquid. The most vital characteristic of this substance was that the time of its taking fire could be regulated within a certain margin by the manner of its composition. Whereas the expert in his oral evidence gave the substance a very wide margin, the experiments which he conducted *in camera* before the Court showed that actually the maximum point of time to which its bursting into flames could be postponed was some twenty-five to thirty minutes. With the evidence of the commencement of the fire at 9.10 to 9.14 p.m. at the earliest, the Prosecutor devoted himself to the attempt to prove that Torgler did not leave the Reichstag building until 8.40 or 8.45 p.m.

This is a further indication of the fallacy and dangers inherent in the use of circumstantial evidence. Even if the Public Prosecutor had succeeded in proving, as he did not, that Torgler did not leave the Reichstag until 8.45 p.m., it is obvious on a long view, that this could furnish no possible indication of his guilt. It was never suggested where or how Torgler could have procured the secret inflammable substance spoken of, or when or where he laid it. Although pressing for the death sentence upon Torgler in his final speech solely on the grounds of his 'chain of proofs' the Prosecutor did not see fit to deal with these very vital points.

In fact Torgler together with Koenen and his secretary Anna Rehme left the Reichstag at about 8.15 p.m., by no means hastily, but at a slow walking pace, dictated by the complaint from which the secretary was at that time suffering. Torgler and Koenen arrived at the Aschinger Restaurant at the Friedrichstrasse Station at about 8.30 p.m. where they ordered and ate a three-course dinner which they had finished by 9 p.m. At 9 p.m. a new waiter, Hans Persicke, came on duty and from him Torgler and Koenen only ordered drinks. Torgler and Koenen's statements as to the time of their arrival were supported by sworn statement made by their first waiter, Stubling, which was read in the Court, its author having died in the meantime. Both Stubling and the cook were able to recollect exactly what dishes Torgler and Koenen had ordered and the time of their arrival. All these statements were absolutely opposed to the Prosecutor's attempt to prove that Torgler did not leave the Reichstag until 8.40 or 8.45 p.m., at a time when it was proved beyond question that he was in the middle of his dinner at a restaurant some distance away.

Torgler's Connections with the Co-Accused

The direction of the Public Prosecutor's second line of attack against Torgler was to connect him with van der Lubbe and the Bulgarians. This was supported almost exclusively by the evidence of the three National-Socialists, Karwahne, now a Nazi deputy, expelled in 1925 from the German Communist Party for terrorist activities; Frey and Kroyer, an Austrian National-Socialist official. These three men had visited Daluege at the Ministry of the Interior on the night of the fire and from him had gone post haste to the police headquarters where, after having a good look at van der Lubbe, they were later able to identify him as the man whom they had seen about a yard behind Torgler in a corridor of

the Reichstag on the afternoon of the fire. From the information given by these three the official statement that van der
Lubbe had been seen with Torgler and Koenen in the corridors
of the Reichstag at about 8 p.m. would appear to have
originated.

None of them suggested that van der Lubbe was walking
beside or talking to Torgler, none of them put the time any
later than about 3.30 p.m., none of them mentioned Koenen's
name. During the course of the proceedings Frey's evidence
weakened, he was unable to be definite as to his identification
of van der Lubbe. Karwahne and Kroyer, however, maintained their statements vigorously. The man behind Torgler
was van der Lubbe. Torgler himself had appeared uneasy.
While Frey's identification of van der Lubbe became uncertain,
his identification of Popov as the man, garbed in hat and
overcoat, with whom he had observed Torgler seated in
conversation some twenty minutes later, grew more and more
definite. His two companions were unable to express any
certainty about this second encounter. The strength of their
recollection was confined to what had passed some twenty
minutes before. They were quite unaffected by the darkness
of the room and corridor in which they had made their
observations, a darkness which was natural to a February
afternoon in the unlit inner corridors of the Reichstag building
and by Frey's inability to state in what tongue Torgler and
the alleged Popov were conversing. The improbability of
Torgler's having selected a most public part of the very
scene of his contemplated crime for forging the last links with
his mysterious accomplices, less than six hours before the
conspiracy was to bear fruit did not seem to have occurred
to them.

From the evidence given in Court and the statements made
to the International Commission of Inquiry the complete
history of Torgler's movements and interviews on the afternoon of February 27th was established. Kühne, Halle,
Florin and Birkenhauer, all of whom were with Torgler during
the relevant time, furnished detailed accounts of his movements. None of them had seen van der Lubbe, indeed no
Reichstag attendant alleged having seen the vagrant with
Torgler in the building on that afternoon.

Torgler's companion's identity was established beyond a

doubt when Dr. Neubauer, a former Communist deputy, appeared in the Court. Dr. Neubauer, arrested and severely beaten by the police in August, has since that date been confined in the concentration camp of Papenburg from the obscurity of which he was brought to give evidence. Bearing the marks of his sufferings for all to see, he stated that he had been with Torgler, seated on the sofa in question, and had seen the three National-Socialists pass by. His identity was confirmed by the evidence of a woman employee of the Reichstag, Frau Baumgart who had seen him with Torgler at the time and in the place in question. After his testimony Dr. Neubauer was dragged back to the camp where, seriously ill from the effects of being gassed in 1916, he is unlikely to survive.

In the end all that remained of the conspiracy into which the prosecution sought to elevate the events of the afternoon of the fire, was the fact that Torgler had received visitors in the Reichstag, as indeed he did every day of his life.

Light from the Underworld

The Public Prosecutor's third line of incrimination against Torgler was to prove that he had acted on the orders of his Party. To establish this the strangest trio of witnesses were utilised. These were Lebermann, an old criminal with many convictions for theft and fraud; Kunzack, a miner, with an unenviable record of sentences for crimes of violence and sexual offences; and Grothe, who suffered from mental derangement.

Lebermann alleged that he had met Torgler in Hamburg in the autumn of 1931 at which time he had belonged to a secret anarchist group. Torgler had then told him that he, Lebermann, was kept in reserve for a big job. The nature of this big job was revealed in the following January when Torgler came and offered him sixteen thousand marks if he would set the Reichstag on fire. Lebermann, whose last theft realised some twenty-five marks profit, was not to be bought with Torgler's sixteen thousand. Nor did Torgler's threats to thrash him have any other result. Through Lebermann's integrity the Reichstag stood unscathed for another twelve months. But a chance remark which he let slip in Court led to the explanation of his evidence. Finding his term of imprisonment dull, he had invented the story so that he might have a few days' change, with the chance of gaining his freedom.

The improbability of Lebermann's evidence was closely rivalled by that of Kunzack. The effect of his statements was that he had been ordered to Berlin with some other man in 1930 and had been led to a place in the Wuhlheide near Berlin where, under the direction of a 'chief fireworker,' experiments with explosives had been carried out in which Torgler and Kaspar, another former Communist deputy, had taken part. The Public Prosecutor triumphantly stated that Kunzack had been able to point out to the police the places in the Wuhlheide. where the experiments had been made. The examination of the police witnesses revealed the fact that Kunzack was not able to find the places at first, but that the police had led him to places they had found and then he was able to recognise them. Asked where he had got to know Torgler, the witness stated that he had met him in his office at the Karl Liebknecht House, not apparently knowing that Torgler had never worked in that building. Both Torgler and Kaspar, brought up from a concentration camp, denied the fantastic story of the experiments in the Wuhlheide.

The test of Kunzack's veracity appeared later when he alleged that, as a Communist official, he had attended a secret conference in Düsseldorf in 1925, which was presided over by the well-known Communist Heinz Neumann, and attended by no less a person than van der Lubbe. Shown a photograph of Heinz Neumann, Kunzack was quite unable to say who it might represent. He was certain that van der Lubbe, who could have been only sixteen at the time, had spoken in Dutch: in his original statement he alleged that van der Lubbe had spoken good German.

The reason for Kunzack's evidence appeared later. He had written from prison to the Examining Magistrate offering his services in rooting out the terrorists from their hiding-places "through their female associates," in return for a money payment and for remission of his sentence. Judge Vogt apparently accepted the offer, for Kunzack appeared in court a free man.

It is difficult to conceive the motive with which the Public

Prosecutor and the Examining Magistrate were actuated in accepting the evidence of such witnesses as Lebermann and Kunzack, much less in proferring them, gravely, as witnesses of truth to the Supreme Court. The very circumstances in which they had come into touch with the officials must have aroused the utmost suspicion and their statements when communicated must have appeared as fantastic as they sounded in Court.

The last of the trio, Grothe, compensated for his lack of criminal convictions with the fact that he was admittedly and conspicuously suffering from mental derangement, and that he had been used as a police spy for some period. His evidence, first taken by Heisig early in April 1933, bore out the story of van der Lubbe's connections with an alleged "Committee of Action" which was published in the first official bulletin relating to the fire. All his testimony was hearsay, and from the point of view of the English lawyer, inadmissible. The effect of it was that two Communist officials, Singer and Kempner had informed him, the one, that the Reichstag fire was intended by the Central Committee of the Communist Party to be the signal for a Communist insurrection and the other, Kempner, that it had been decided by the Communist Party that the Reichstag should be burned down. Grothe stated that Kempner had told him that the decision was made at meetings held in the Karl Liebknecht House just before the fire (when incidentally the police were in occupation of the building) at which Thälmann and Scheer had spoken. Torgler was entrusted with carrying out the plan and a meeting of Koenen, Torgler, Popov and Kempner had been held on the afternoon of the fire in the Grösser Stern (an open square in the Tiergarten) to decide on the details. Kempner had been given a bag containing inflammable materials and fuses to be taken to the Reichstag and handed over to the 'big dark one.'

Grothe landed himself in some difficulties. He was unfortunate enough to select a place and date for his meeting with Singer which made the first part of his statement incredible. The tenant, a tailor named Barz, and his sub-tenant, Fraulein Macke, both summoned as witnesses proved that, contrary to Grothe's statements, his flat could not have been used for any meeting. One of the rooms was locked and in the other Barz was in bed suffering with consumption.

No more fortunate was his selection of a date for the alleged meetings with Kempner at which according to his story the bulk of Grothe's interesting information had been derived. He told the Court that the meeting had taken place on April 19th. He was then reminded of the fact that Kempner had been arrested on April 8th, eleven days earlier. He then put the date as being eight days or so before the end of March; until he was faced with his original statement, made to the police on April 5th in which he had placed the date at April 3rd. This he in fact accepted as true! He was no more able to clear up this date than he could explain how long a time had intervened between his first and second meetings with Kempner and the meeting with Singer.

The last shred of credibility for Grothe was removed with the production of both Kempner and Singer, who had first been said to have disappeared, but were found in concentration camps. Singer and Kempner both dismissed Grothe as a police spy and a mental deficient, and strenuously denied that his statements had a grain of truth in them.

But nothing in Grothe's evidence or his history shook the Public Prosecutor's reliance upon him. Even in his concluding speech he stressed the importance of Grothe's testimony and declared it to be borne out by the facts. So strange was Grothe's demeanour in fact that the Court took the trouble to obtain the opinion of a medical expert who characterised that witness as "a psychopathic case, subject to hysteria and psychological disturbances" He had several times been under observation and had been confined in a mental home for a period.

"Things are Brewing!"

The word 'Fanal'—beacon—played an important role in the Reichstag fire trial. Applied by the indictment to the fire itself, meant apparently to indicate that the fire was to be the signal for the beginnings of an insurrection, the word had become almost an obsession with the National-Socialists. According to Heisig, van der Lubbe told him on the night of the fire that he intended the fire to be a 'beacon' (Fanal) for the revolution. On the same night, a little earlier, Göring's intuition revealed to him that the fire was a 'Fanal'—a beacon.

The same word was pronounced by the lips of Herr Hitler through divine revelation; and bruited abroad in the official bulletins. The problem as to who of the many competitors was to be credited with the first use of the word 'Fanal' in relation to the fire was not solved until November 1st, 1933, when a very minor journalist, one Zimmermann, came to give evidence. He informed the Court that a few days before the fire he was in a tramcar with Torgler when they passed by a Nazi demonstration. Torgler then remarked to him:

"Things are brewing! When the beacon blazes, these gentry will creep back into their hiding-places."

If Zimmermann's recollection was correct, then the expression was first used by Torgler himself, and passed by some telepathic process to Göring, to Hitler and to the world at large. But there appeared, during his examination, to be good grounds for doubting the accuracy and even the genuineness of Zimmermann's recollection. He had carried his secret round with him for seven months, and never revealed the fact or content of his conversation with Torgler to a soul until October 1933. Again, questioning revealed the fact that Zimmermann had been engaged for seven years in writing a novel, the villain of which was a "Communist politician of the type of Torgler." If and when the great work is published the world will be able to discover how much of the statement which its author attributed to Torgler was actually made by the villain of his story.

Torgler's Defence

At the outset of the proceedings Torgler stated that he would defend his Party with all his strength and might against the charges of arson and insurrection. He rightly saw that the whole structure of the indictment would collapse if it could be proved that van der Lubbe's alleged membership of and connection with the Communist Party existed nowhere outside the official bulletins and Heisig's report. To this end he referred in his opening statement to letters written to van der Lubbe which showed conclusively that he was not a member of the Communist Party but of a small anarchist group in

Holland. Again Torgler frequently intervened in the questioning of witnesses particularly during the political stage of the trial with the aim of establishing that his Party had not planned any insurrectionary action for February 1933, nor had they anything to do with the Reichstag fire.

How different was the line adopted by Dr. Sack whose position and tactics in the case are dealt with at greater length in another chapter. Sack did his utmost to assist the prosecution in maintaining the connections of van der Lubbe with the Communist Party and he adopted the tactics, dangerous to his client, of entirely neglecting to defend him upon the political issue. As counsel defending a man charged with high treason, even to the extent that he shared the aims and ideals of his Party, Sack did not find it necessary to exert himself to resist the allegation that the Communist Party in February 1933 was actuated by insurrectionary and treasonable aims. No thanks to Sack's defence, Torgler was acquitted. The transparent weakness of the case against him, his own courage and the bold defence of Dimitrov furnished the conditions for his acquittal. The moral pressure of world opinion secured it.

Forseeing his acquittal, Sack made the application for Torgler to be detained in protective custody. This application was graciously granted and together with the three acquitted Bulgarians, Torgler was on December 23rd, 1933, decreed the prisoner of the Third Reich. Sack, who lost no opportunity to vilify and abuse Communism, declared that he had applied for the decree in order to protect Torgler against the revenge of the Communists. In truth Torgler is held in captivity because he defended his Party before the Court, because he declared:

"I must categorically state that the fight for Socialism has been the content and meaning of my life. I have fought for the interests of the working class with all the idealism of which man is capable and I declare that I shall not cease to give of my best to the workers of Germany."

Torgler was able to sustain the ordeals of seven months' preliminary investigation, of five months passed fettered night and day, and of a three-month long trial, as he said:

"In the consciousness of my innocence and the innocence of the Party to which I have devoted and consecrated my life."

126

DIMITROV, POPOV AND TANEV IN LEIPZIG PRISON

ERNST TORGLER
"The Fight for Socialism has been the content and meaning of my life"
(Torgler. 4th day of the trial)

He will be able to bear the new ordeals through which he is passing and the new trials which are threatened against him with steadfastness and courage. Strengthened by the shining example of Dimitrov, encouraged by the world movement which saved him from the headsman's axe, Torgler is fortified with the knowledge that his liberation is yet being fought for.

VII

POPOV AND TANEV

THE fate of Popov and Tanev was more tragic than that of their great countryman Dimitrov. Circumstances made their plight far worse than his. Popov spoke but few words of German, Tanev had no knowledge of the language. The two were arrested on March 9th, 1933, and passed almost a year in prison without being able to communicate with their gaolers and without reading a single book or newspaper. The indictment was incomprehensible to them, they had to rely upon the recollection of a hasty oral translation; they understood not a word of what was said in court. Themselves, they were unable to communicate with their lawyer, Dr. Teichert. The sole link connecting them with the proceedings, the sole window through which light could come to them was their interpreter. But they could not know whether he had translated their words and the words of others with accuracy, the Court indeed took no step to rebuke or warn the interpreter when he was known to be mistranslating within the Court-room.

To tolerate this isolation, to endure the sufferings made more severe by the fetters so cruelly and unjustly imposed upon them, Popov and Tanev must have been strong men indeed. The knowledge of their innocence burned deeply in them; it was the consciousness that even in their loneliness they were bound by invisible ties to a world movement which sustained them during their incarceration.

Both Popov and Tanev were well aware of the fate which awaits a Socialist who falls into the hands of his Fascist enemies. They were steeled in the struggle of the Bulgarian working class and both of them had known torture and imprisonment at the hands of the Bulgarian police. Blagoi Simon Popov, student of law, aged 35, became a member of the Bulgarian Communist Party when he was 16. He fought in the ranks of his Party when it led the heroic insurrection of the workers and peasants against the Tsankov Government in 1923. After the collapse of the insurrection he fled abroad but returned to Bulgaria in 1931 and became a member of the Bulgarian Communist Party's Central Committee. He fell into the clutches of the police. After a short time in prison he succeeded in escaping and fleeing the land. For the second time thus he became a refugee and was active in supporting the struggle of the Bulgarian Communists from abroad. He entered Germany for the first time in his life on November 3rd, 1933.

Vassili Tanev, a cobbler, was the son of a Macedonian railwayman who had fallen in 1906 during the struggle against Turkish domination. Tanev, too, joined the Bulgarian Communist Party at an early age and took a leading part in the struggles of the Bulgarian Communists. In 1925 he was arrested and sentenced to twelve and a half years' penal servitude on account of membership of the Communist Party, but he was subsequently amnestied and continued his work in Bulgaria, occupying a high place in the counsels of the Party there. He undertook journeys abroad, secretly passing out of Bulgaria, on behalf of the Party and it was in the course of one of these that he arrived in Berlin for the first time on February 24th, 1932. He was met at the station by Popov and it was not long before they met Dimitrov and together discussed the affairs which had brought Tanev to Germany, the question of the Bulgarian political emigrés and the amnesty which it was hoped to secure from the more favourably-disposed Bulgarian Government.

Witnesses against Popov

Like the witnesses against Torgler and Dimitrov those against Popov and Tanev were recruited for the most part from the ranks of the National-Socialist Party, or amongst criminals. One of the most serious witnesses against Popov was the National-Socialist Frey who alleged having seen Popov with Torgler in the Reichstag on the afternoon of February 27th. The evolution of Frey's statements has been discussed in the chapter dealing with Torgler; suffice it to say here that it was not until after a considerable time that Frey mentioned this second encounter with Torgler and the suspicious individual in hat and overcoat, and that even then he was unable to identify Popov. The value of his evidence was considerably lessened by the effect of Dimitrov's question to him:

> "In what tongue were Torgler, who knows no Bulgarian, and Popov, who knows no German, conversing?"

Ultimately it was conclusively proved that Frey was in error; that his identification was a false one.

Next in the string was the engineer Paul Boghun who alleged that on his way past the Reichstag he heard a rattle at Door Number Two, that he looked and saw Popov stealthily emerging from the Reichstag. This incident took place at about 9.10 p.m., or as Boghun later put it, at 9 p.m. Boghun looked for a policeman, but finding none, although the neighbourhood was thick with them and one, Buwert, could have been only a few yards away, he went home. Later on hearing of the fire he wended his way back, saw the police officer Lateit and told him that he had seen a man coming out of Door Number Two (which Lateit had found locked at 9.17 p.m.). Boghun was then unable to say whether the man was wearing a cap or hat, a fact which Lateit specially noted in the record of his statement, but only that he was clad in light trousers. Boghun was first interrogated in the police headquarters on March 2nd when he was unable to describe either the man's features or clothing. Three weeks later, after several confrontations with Popov, in the able hands of Judge Vogt, Boghun's recollection became better and better until eventually he was able to furnish a description of Popov as being the man whom he had seen. This could not happen without Boghun making important qualifications and changes in his first two statements, a fact which soon became known and prevented the Prosecutor or the Court from attaching any importance to his evidence. Dimitrov characterised Boghun's evidence with a phrase:

> "I thought that the witness was an inventor, now I perceive that he is a romancer."

Amongst the evidence 'highly incriminating' to Popov was the allegation that he had been staying during the summer of 1932 in the house of a Communist, Kämpfer, where he had engaged in secret work and had held secret gatherings. This evidence was supplied in a typical manner. The tenants of the same block of buildings had apparently on instructions been organised into a minor secret service to spy upon their co-tenants. The secret service was headed by one tenant, a National-Socialist named Jung who alternately with his wife kept Kämpfer's flat under observation with field-glasses—a practice not unknown to the more curious among flat dwellers the world over. These two, together with some five other tenants of the flats were summoned to report the results of their observations to the Supreme Court. The President hastened to explain away the field-glasses as being necessary for the performance of the duties entrusted to Jung and not the outcome of pure inquisitiveness. Jung and his associates were emphatic on their identification of Popov, Jung even stating that he had seen parcels delivered at the flat which from their apparent size and weight indicated machine-guns. All these persons were at one in putting the dates of Popov's stay as between May and September 1932. Kämpfer, 'found' in a concentration camp and haled into Court, confirmed these statements, also spoke of meeting Tanev in Berlin in 1932 and confessed, in the end, convictions for burglary. Evidence involving the presence of both Popov and Tanev in Berlin in 1931 and the summer of 1932 was given by the proprietor of a café in the Lindenstrasse, near the Soviet Trade Delegation's offices, and his waiter, one Hyta. But neither Michalski, the owner, nor Hyta could once accurately describe the men whom they identified with the three Bulgarians. The best Hyta could do was to state that they all had black hair and that the smallest of the three was rather like himself. In fact only Popov had black hair while the smallest of the three, Tanev, was lean and slight, unlike Hyta who was amply proportioned.

Popov's passport proved that he had come to Berlin for the first time on November 3rd, 1932. Witnesses were called from Russia who established beyond all doubt that throughout the summer of 1932 Popov was continuously in Russia, either in Moscow or in a sanatorium in the Crimea. There could be no doubt that all the witnesses who spoke of Popov's presence in Berlin during that time were mistaken if not deliberately romancing.

A further witness against Popov was a stout seventy-two-year-old Frau Hartung also who provided evidence against Tanev and Dimitrov. This good lady's evidence concerning

Popov was that she had met him in 1928 at the house of a friend, one Frau Rischkowski. It appeared later that these two ladies were on terms none too friendly. Frau Rischkowski appeared to testify and turned the tables on Frau Hartung by coupling her indignant denial of the latter's statement with the assertion that Popov had once lodged with Frau Hartung and the suggestion that an affectionate relationship had existed between that good stout lady and her lodger.

So scanty was the evidence of any degree of credibility against Popov that the Public Prosecutor was reduced to the resort of sending a spy, in the guise of a student of psychology, into the prison in which the accused men were confined during their trial. It was in this manner that one, Weinberger, a convicted criminal, was led on November 24th from prison to testify against Popov. Weinberger's evidence consisted in reporting two statements alleged to have been made to him by Popov in confidence. The first was that he had said: "I am done for, a witness saw me in the 'Red Aid' office." The second was that Popov had asked Weinberger to get his wife to telephone his, Popov's, landlady in order to get possession of the papers which Popov had left in his rooms and destroy them. Weinberger was a little discomfited by the revelation that in any case Popov's lodgings were not accessible on the telephone. In the face of Popov's denial of these confessions and the revelations concerning the activities of the "student of psychology," Wolff, in this matter, Weinberger went back to prison without fulfilling his allotted task.

Witnesses against Tanev

The chief witness against Tanev was an ex-officer, Major (retired) Weberstedt, now press representative of the National-Socialist Parliamentary Group. Weberstedt alleged that he had seen Tanev and van der Lubbe together in the ante-room before the offices in the Reichstag of the Communist Group, on the afternoon of February 27th. They were carrying a large box. Asked why he had been able to remember the incident, Weberstedt became more expansive; he explained that one of the men was very tall and the other very short and wearing an overcoat right down to his ankles. They reminded him forcibly of two comedians whom he had often seen performing.

Although the contrast which had struck Weberstedt was not so remarkable and no such overcoat was ever brought to light, to the suggestion of Tanev that he might be mistaken, Weberstedt immediately stood on his dignity:

"A retired German officer does not lie, nor does he make mistakes."

But closer questioning revealed that Weberstedt could not qualify for his own test of infallibility. He admitted that the encounter might have taken place three days before, on February 24th, the day Tanev first arrived in Germany. He went on to supply the facts, the broken window pane in the Communist rooms and the ladder, upon which the suggestion that the incendiaries had escaped on to the roof was based. He also spoke of the fumes of petrol which he, and he alone of the many persons who passed through or by them, noticed issuing from the Communist rooms. With this last statement even the Prosecutor appeared to think that Weberstedt had gone too far. No reliance was ultimately placed on his evidence for apart from the inherent improbability of his statements, Dimitrov's attack on Weberstedt had been only too well justified.

Another witness who inculpated Tanev was the same Frau Hartung who after considerable reflection changed her statement that she had never seen Tanev before to allege that he had been employed as a boot-mender for the 'Red Aid' office in 1928. In support of her came the 'merchant' Bannert, whose qualification for that designation were his several convictions for fraudulent practices. Bannert alleged that he had seen Tanev in the "Red Aid" offices in 1927 and 1928. Against the testimony of these two was the evidence of Tanev himself and the statements of seven persons employed in the "Red Aid" office at the dates in question who denied that Tanev had ever been employed in or visited the place.

An unfortunate workman, Sonke, was also produced to incriminate Tanev. Tanev had lodged with him during the few days that he had been in Berlin until his arrest. Sonke, in order to conceal the manner in which Tanev had come to him, to save himself from persecution, invented a story of friendship struck up on the Rumanian front during the European war, and of a chance meeting in Berlin. Whilst he was making his statement Popov called to him in Russian:

"Speak the truth and nothing will happen to you!"

Whereat the unhappy Sonke broke down, confessed that his story was invented and told the truth about Tanev's arrival and stay. Far different was the treatment meted out to this workman who departed from his previous statement from that accorded to the many National-Socialist and other witnesses for the prosecution, some of whom committed demonstrably deliberate perjury. Sonke was immediately, on the application of the Public Prosecutor, placed under arrest for perjury. He was subsequently sentenced to three years' imprisonment for a stupid lie which had harmed no one and which he had invented merely for his own protection.

The Star Witness—Helmer

One of the most important of the Public Prosecutor's witnesses was the waiter Helmer, of many years standing in the National-Socialist Party and employed in the Bayernhof Restaurant in Berlin. Although Helmer had seen van der Lubbe's photograph coupled with the announcement of the twenty thousand marks reward in the evening paper of March 3rd, 1933, and had at once recognised him as the man whom he had often seen at the Bayernhof accompanied by three suspicious-looking 'Russians,' Helmer did not communicate with the police until four days later. As a result, when Dimitrov, Popov and Tanev entered the restaurant for refreshment on March 9th, 1933, they were scarcely seated before they were placed under arrest by the police.

Although during his first interrogation Helmer asserted that he had frequently seen *all three* Bulgarians at the restaurant in the late spring and summer of 1932, when he learned that Tanev had arrived in Germany for the first time only three days before the fire he changed his statement and stated that he had only seen Tanev there once. As regards Dimitrov and Popov, Helmer was insistent that he had seen them there frequently in the summer of 1932 together with van der Lubbe. He would not admit the possibility of error although it was proved beyond a doubt that van der Lubbe had been in prison in Holland from June until October 1932 and had not left for Germany until early the following February, and that Popov had been in Moscow and the Crimea during the previous summer and had not reached Berlin until November 1932.

If made doubtful by these facts, Helmer's veracity was shattered by his allegation, from which he could not be moved, that he had served Dimitrov in the Bayernhof on the very afternoon of February 27th, at a time when it was conclusively proved that Dimitrov was miles away in Munich and making his preparations to return to Berlin that night. Against the sole testimony of Helmer was the improbability that a vagrant like van der Lubbe would have been admitted to the Bayernhof and even more, the evidence of the manager and seven other waiters employed in the restaurant that they had never seen van der Lubbe there on any occasion.

In the face of the facts Helmer's evidence failed to achieve its aim. There can be little doubt that Helmer was moved by the reward offered for information. He himself advanced as the explanation for his four days' delay the fact that he had discussed the matter and the reward with his wife who had been against his intervening in the matter in any circumstances. Frau Helmer must have been a shrewd judge of her man, it was unfortunate for him that Helmer did not accept her advice. Whether or not he got his reward one can but guess, but his allegations served their purpose. They furnished the basis for the arrest of the three Bulgarians and the tendentious statements published concerning them by Judge Vogt. Even Dr. Teichert, to whom the thought of attacking the methods of the prosecution was abhorrent, openly catechised Judge Vogt for accepting Helmer's wild statements as true:

"The fact that the Examining Magistrate undertook the prosecution of the three Bulgarians on the basis of this statement has gravely injured the reputation of the German people in the eyes of the world outside."

Confronted with the methods of the police and officials, incriminated by the statements of witnesses without conscience or regard for the truth, cut off by their lack of knowledge of German from comprehension of the nature and effect of much of the evidence, weakened by the long sufferings which they had undergone, Popov and Tanev yet stood up and faced their judges courageously. They showed their determination and proved themselves to be steadfast to their ideals. They showed themselves not to be unworthy of their colleague Dimitrov.

VIII

GEORGI DIMITROV

VOLUME B of the secret indictment is labelled "the Bulgarians." It was under this designation that the three Bulgarians accused by the National-Socialists of complicity in the Reichstag fire were also described in the world's press at the time when the trial began.

The examination of Georgi Dimitrov commenced on the third day of the proceedings and from that moment his name became separated from the collective expression "the Bulgarians." From that moment his personality stood out head and shoulders above his judges and his prosecutors. He became the shining light of the trial to the world, and to millions the symbol of the battle which was being fought at Leipzig, a hero of the struggle against Fascism. Dimitrov was indeed a voice which could not be ignored, an opponent who, despite the severe restrictions under which he was labouring, was to be feared and a figure to whom even his political adversaries and millions of the adherents of National-Socialism in Germany could not gainsay respect and admiration.

The President commenced Dimitrov's examination by warning him that for his own sake he had better behave in Court in a less disorderly manner than that in which he had conducted himself during the preliminary proceedings. Dimitrov replied:

"Herr President, if you were a man as innocent as myself and you had passed seven months in prison, five of them chained night and day, you would understand that one becomes perhaps a little strained."

Thus began the battle which lasted throughout the proceedings and which was only stayed by the exclusions of Dimitrov from the Court. Nothing, no threat of the President, no silence imposed upon him, no expulsion could move Dimitrov from the direction and course which he regarded as necessary for the defence of himself, his colleagues and his Party. His relentless pursuit of this course, his untiring search for the truth concerning the Reichstag fire, his intransigence in the face of threat and command determined that Dimitrov instead of an accused, became an accuser. Göring chose to abuse and vilify the Communists and their leaders before the Court. He styled them "hangmen's apprentices," "gaolers of the most pronounced sadistic tendencies," and "crooks." One of the leaders of Communism stood before the Court who took openly upon his shoulders responsibility for the actions and decisions of the Communist International, who without blenching faced the terrible General whose threats were unavailing to protect him from the fire of Dimitrov's questions. Dimitrov never lost his self-control, every word he spoke was considered, every comment measured to the service in which it was destined. The representatives of the world press present at Leipzig joined in paying tribute to Dimitrov's courage, ability and intelligence.

So astounding, so inexplicable to some was this phenomenon of an indubitably innocent Communist standing up fearlessly to insult, rebuke and expulsion, that they sought to explain it in the terms of a miracle. Perhaps it was that such a description best set off the contrast between the Bulgarian Communist leader and the apathetic vagrant Dutchman with whom he was said to have conspired, but in truth there was nothing miraculous about Dimitrov's conduct, nothing of inspiration in his words. Dimitrov's intelligence, his courage and his personality were all the fruits of a long experience in the Bulgarian working-class movement, they were the product of his lifelong practical and theoretical study of the working-class movement. This same experience had endowed him with perspicacity and foresight, it taught him to feel his unity with the masses of the world whose force was with him, although he was isolated by chains, bars and unscaleable walls from them, and whose solidarity with him gave him the strength and courage to endure his long confinement. Dimitrov challenged and vanquished the Judges who were to pass judgment upon him, he challenged and vanquished the witnesses, even the redoubtable Göring, who testified against him and he challenged and vanquished the whole force and power of the National-Socialist dictatorship as embodied in the charges against him. He turned the trial, destined to convict the Communists of the Reichstag fire, into a trial of the National-Socialists themselves. He became the accuser and his charges fell with increasing weight and gravity on to the heads of his prosecutors.

Scenting difficulties, on the first day of Dimitrov's examination the President sought to restrain him from doing more than answer questions. Dimitrov would not be gainsaid and with a wave of his hand brought the President to silence:

> "I am a proletarian revolutionary. I am a Socialist revolutionary by conviction. I am not of that type of Socialists amongst whom is numbered the German ex-Crown Prince. I am a member of the Central Committee of the Bulgarian Communist Party and of the Executive Committee of the Communist International. I may therefore call myself one of the leaders of the Communist Movement and in such capacity I undertake here and now responsibility for all decisions, all publications and all activities of the Bulgarian Communist Party and the Communist International.
>
> "This, moreover, is the reason why I am not to be regarded as a mere terrorist adventurer. I am an enthusiastic supporter of the proletarian revolution because I realise that it presents the only way out of the crisis of capitalism."

Communism has been outlawed in Germany, it is visited with the death penalty; thousands of its supporters languish in police prisons and concentration camps. But the German Government was compelled to provide it with a forum, with a pulpit for the propagation of its aims and ideals. From the midst of the bludgeons and bayonets of the police and Storm Troopers, from the Court-room at Leipzig, there was raised the voice which proclaimed to the working class of Germany that Communism was living and was fighting. The voice of Dimitrov found its way, by the medium of thousands of secret pamphlets and leaflets through the walls of the prisons and concentration camps, into the ears of millions of German workers; it gave them hope and courage in their continued fight against Fascism.

The President informed Dimitrov that he had been sentenced to death in Bulgaria. Dimitrov replied:

> "I have heard that was the case. I have not made further inquiries because the matter was one which did not interest me."

To all those who heard it it was plain that this remark came straight from Dimitrov's heart. His fearlessness during the trial, his action after his acquittal in immediately demanding his re-admission and public trial in Bulgaria, all his words and actions combined to show that he was a man to whom thought of self was far distant, a man who submerged personal fear or aspiration to the cause of which he was the outspoken servant.

Dimitrov's Mother

Each day while the incessant struggle between Dimitrov and the Supreme Court was being waged, an old woman sat in the fourth row of the audience. Each day, accompanied by two other women, she appeared punctually a quarter of an hour before the time when the proceedings were due to commence and took her place. She was shrouded in a black shawl from amidst which her furrowed, intelligent face peered out; her bright dark eyes captured the attention as she followed the proceedings closely. The same eyes shone from below Dimitrov's brows. The old woman was Parashkeva Dimitrova, his mother.

Aged seventy-two years, she had never left Bulgaria and never travelled by train before she went to Leipzig. In order to obtain permission to leave the country she had to pay a tax. The Dimitrovs were poor and the tax was a large sum. Within fifteen minutes the whole amount was collected from Bulgarian workmen themselves condemned to labour at starvation wages. Wherever she went Dimitrov's mother encountered a mighty sentiment of affection and solidarity. She was greeted by a crowd of French workers at the railway station in Paris and some ten thousand of them assembled to hear her make a short speech in a language which but few of them could understand. Every day hundreds of letters reached her in Leipzig. She was dauntless and her courage was indomitable. After the acquittals she remained in Germany in the face of discouragement and veiled threats. Sick with anxiety, deprived by the Government's order of expulsion against him of the services of her interpreter, she remained in Berlin until her son was released. Abused by high officials, her requests ignored, turned back disappointed from the gates of her son's prison, she yet remained sustained by hope and courage in the midst of a hostile world.

Parashkeva Dimitrova had brought eight children into the world. Three of her six sons had already fallen in the fight for liberty. Nicholas had died in exile in Siberia whence he was banished from Russia in 1909. Konstantin, the fourth son, fell in the Balkan war. Theodor, the youngest son, died in prison in 1925 at the hands of the Bulgarian police shortly after having been arrested. Another son, Boris, a railwayman, has been frequently imprisoned for his political activities and was released less than twelve months ago from his last spell in prison. Of her daughters, Magdalena was one of the founders of the Bulgarian Tailors' Trade Union, played and still to-day plays a prominent part in the workers' movement in Bulgaria. The younger daughter, Eleanor, also suffered imprisonment on account of her political activities as a member of the Bulgarian Communist Party. It was she who shortly after her brother's arrest journeyed through Europe to raise up the workers for the liberation of the accused men. She too made her way at an early stage in the trial to Leipzig and there testified to her brother's character and political beliefs.

Dimitrov's Career

The eldest child of Parashkeva Dimitrova, Georgi Dimitrov was raised in a hard school. His father was a Macedonian worker forced to flee his native soil at the time of the Turkish massacres. The family settled first in Radomir, later in Sofia. As Macedonian refugees they were at the mercy of the police to whom his father had constantly to report and whose visits to the Dimitrov household were frequent and brutal. Even in his early childhood and later, when he was old enough to go to school, Dimitrov was despised by his companions for being the son of a Macedonian and a workman. He learnt early to know injustice. His mother who read life aright and as few read it, did not wish her son to be a workman and to suffer as his father had done. She, who could neither read nor write, desired that her son should study and that through education the doors to a fuller and freer life would be opened to him. But eight hungry young mouths had to be fed, so at the age of thirteen Georgi Dimitrov went forth into the world. He started work as a printer's apprentice.

He worked a twelve-hour day and then, by the dim light of an oil lamp, sat up far into the night hours at study. Self education and contact with the printers, the *élite* of the working class in Bulgaria, opened a new world to Dimitrov. His first conceptions of political and economic development were formed in the atmosphere of the struggle in which he and his workmates were themselves engaged. Before he had been many months at his work a strike broke out. It was the first active struggle in which he took part and as such gave direction to his whole life and work. At the age of sixteen he wrote his first revolutionary pamphlet and was one of the founders of the Printers' Union.

In 1903 Dimitrov founded the United Printers' Association, a revolutionary trade union, and in the same year he became a member of the Bulgarian Social-Democratic Party of whose left wing he was long the most prominent member. In 1904 he collaborated in the foundation of the Federation of Bulgarian Trade Unions and was elected to its governing committee. The reliance of the rank and file of Bulgarian workers was displayed in his election to the position of General Secretary in 1907. In this capacity Dimitrov commenced a long experience of strikes and working-class activity. He conducted a vigorous campaign against the reformist official elements in the trade unions which succeeded in stamping out the bulk of their influence. He produced many articles and pamphlets. His repute and fame grew and in 1913 he was elected to the Bulgarian Sobranje as the representative of the workers of Sofia where for ten years he protected and furthered their interests. His voice was ever raised against war. He urged the Government to accord humane treatment to war prisoners. He waged an unremitting struggle against Bulgarian participation in the world war of 1914-18, an activity which eventually led him into prison where he was held for two years without trial. The period of his incarceration Dimitrov employed to widen his knowledge of history and politics and to learn German. Forced in the end by the pressure of the working class to give Dimitrov his freedom, the Government released him. He was welcomed by a mighty demonstration of workmen and workwomen. The next four years, until 1923, were crowded with working-class activity. Strike followed strike, the transport workers, the railwaymen and the miners one after another downed tools. Dimitrov was constantly at the head of their struggles.

In 1920 Dimitrov was sent with a companion, Kolarov, to represent the Bulgarian Communist Party at the second World Congress of the Communist International. Barred from the usual ways of crossing frontiers, Dimitrov and his colleague took ship on a small sailing-vessel on the Black Sea to sail to the shores of the Soviet Union. Their vessel was overtaken by a Rumanian warship. They were arrested and thrown into prison in Rumania on the charge of being 'emissaries of Moscow.' The combined pressure of the working-class movements in the various Balkan countries secured their release and rescued them from the fate awaiting them in the obscure gaols of Rumania.

The year 1923 saw the murder of Stambuliski and the military *coup d'état* which brought about the establishment of the Fascist Tsankov Government. Dimitrov and his colleague Kolarov took their places at the head of the workers' and peasants' insurrection which ensued. Not until the risings had been stamped out in rivers of blood did Dimitrov seek his own safety, by escaping from Bulgaria at the head of a small band of his most faithful supporters. The Bulgarian Courts condemned the absent Dimitrov to life imprisonment and later to death.

For the next ten years Dimitrov occupied himself with the re-organisation of the Bulgarian working-class movement. Although in exile, Dimitrov whether he was in Vienna, Moscow or Berlin never ceased to work in the interests of the Bulgarian Communist Party and its adherents. Though himself in serious financial straits he never forbore to help those whose position was worse than his own. The other political exiles from his land looked upon him as their mentor and their father in adversity. He cared for them and he shared his humble possessions and means with them regardless of himself. They lived frugally and modestly. Dimitrov himself had owned for six years the suit in which he conducted his defence before the Supreme Court. In his Bulgarian days Dimitrov had always given of his possessions to those whose needs were greater than his own. His political adversaries, a group of whom communicated to the Supreme Court to this effect, all acknowledged his high personal qualities, his integrity his honesty and his altruism. Shining above all his other qualities was Dimitrov's intelligence which he displayed so strikingly in his trial. Always resourceful, always resolute and always unafraid, he drew forth the admiration of all those who saw and heard him.

Ljubov Dimitrova

This short account of Dimitrov's life would be incomplete without reference to his wife. In 1905 Dimitrov married Ljubov Ivoshevitch, the daughter of a Serbian peasant. Just as her husband, Ljubov knew the darker side of life. Left an orphan when four years old, she had lived with an aunt who eked out a meagre living as a seamstress. Ljubov commenced her life of toil when she was six. Her aunt had fallen prey to alcoholism; she wasted Ljubov's earnings and beat her almost daily to make her work harder. After some years of this treatment, when she was ten, Ljubov ran away from her home and for the next four years eked out a hard and precarious existence as a waif, sleeping on pavements, under bridges and in cellars, earning a few meagre coins at casual tasks. At the age of fourteen she was fortunate enough to find permanent work as a seamstress. It was this which for the first time brought her into contact with the members of the industrial working class. She became a member of the Serbian Workers' Party. Three years later, attracted by the better conditions and higher wages of workers in Bulgaria she wandered across the frontier and found work as a laundry-hand in Ruschuk. Later she went to Sofia where she quickly began to take part in the Bulgarian working-class movement. A tireless worker in the Tailors and Seamstresses Union she became editress of their journal. She got to know Georgi Dimitrov and became his wife. They worked together constantly. Ljubov Dimitrova became a prominent figure in Bulgarian politics as well as a poetess of distinction. The poems and songs contained in her four volumes of verse, written in Serbian, Bulgarian and Russian, are sung to this day by the Balkan workers and peasants. She had left Bulgaria when Dimitrov was forced to flee and had lived for the greater part of her exile in the Soviet Union where she was when the news of her husband's arrest reached her. Her strength and health had been undermined by the deprivations which she had suffered and the hard life which she had lived. She was not able to bear the blow which the news of the arrest and charges against her husband struck her. She died early in the summer of 1933. Her political work and her poetry remain as monuments to her memory.

The Witnesses against Dimitrov

The tactics and tools of provocation, the 'framing-up' of evidence and the bribery and corruption of witnesses, were well known to Dimitrov from his experiences in Bulgaria. No different were the methods and the witnesses by which he was attacked in the Reichstag fire trial.

The chief witness incriminating him was, of course, the National-Socialist waiter Helmer, who alleged having frequently seen him in the Bayernhof restaurant, where he was employed, with Popov and van der Lubbe during the summer of 1932 and with Popov, Tanev and van der Lubbe in 1933, the last occasion being February 27th. Helmer's testimony gradually fell into disrepute with the production of proof that neither van der Lubbe nor Popov could have been in Germany much less in the Bayernhof in Berlin at the times when he alleged that he had seen them there. The last shred of credibility was removed when in face of Dimitrov's incontrovertible alibi Helmer stood firmly by his statement that he had seen Dimitrov with van der Lubbe and the others in the restaurant on the afternoon of the fire, when indeed Dimitrov was hundreds of miles away in Munich. When Helmer came to be discredited in the Court, Dimitrov pointed out that the incredibility of his statements, and their obvious inaccuracy could have been easily established during the preliminary investigations. The proceedings had made this abundantly plain, not only by the alibis of the accused men but also by an abundance of evidence easily accessible to the police. Only Helmer of all the employees of the restaurant recognised van der Lubbe, the remainder including the manager himself were not only sure that van der Lubbe had never been a client there but that he would not even have been admitted. Of Helmer's evidence, the very basis of the accusations and charges against the three Bulgarians, there remained nothing which the Court could accept save the fact that Dimitrov and Popov had taken occasional meals there, as they admitted themselves. Nevertheless Helmer though an exposed liar left the Court without a stain on his character.

Two other 'witnesses,' Anna Meyer and Thael, were spared a similar fate. The former declared that she had seen Dimitrov together with van der Lubbe in a café on the Düsseldorferstrasse on February 26th; the latter, that he had seen Dimitrov engaged in close conversation with van der Lubbe at 7 o'clock on the evening of the fire in the neighbourhood of the Reichstag building. As the evidence of these two witnesses would have been demonstrably false in the face of Dimitrov's alibi, the Public Prosecutor passed over them with some regrets. Dimitrov's application that to elucidate the methods and value of the preliminary investigation these two witnesses should be summoned was rejected by the Court.

The National-Socialist, Dröscher, a journalist who under the pseudonym of Zimmermann had been writing articles in the *Völkischer Beobachter* attacking Dimitrov, was summoned as a witness. It was he who had identified Dimitrov as one of the men responsible for the blowing up of Sofia Cathedral, his identification resting on nothing more substantial than the recollection of a post card which he had been shown some eight or so years previously. It was upon Dröscher's evidence that Vogt, the Examining Magistrate without further check or inquiry, had issued the statement that the Bulgarians had been involved in and been sentenced for the Sofia outrage. To this 'identification' Dröscher added in Court that he had seen Dimitrov in the Reichstag the day before the fire. He was the associate of Weberstedt, who had given evidence incriminating Tanev and van der Lubbe. Dimitrov asked Weberstedt whether he had discussed his evidence with Dröscher.

"*Weberstedt:* Naturally!

"*Dimitrov:* Weberstedt and Dröscher have discussed the matter, Weberstedt saw Tanev, Dröscher saw Dimitrov. I am my own defender in this Court. At the risk of expulsion I desire that the following question should be put. 'Have these two witnesses divided the work between themselves?'"

The question was not permitted; but its answer was none the less clear.

One of the porters of the Reichstag surpassed Dröscher. He declared with a certainty that Dimitrov had been in the Reichstag on the afternoon of the fire and had passed close to him. As he passed, Hornemann, the witness, heard him mutter:

"The whole Reichstag will blow up into the air within fifteen or twenty minutes!"

It was Hornemann too who supplied one of the points which the Public Prosecutor used for the purpose of incriminating Torgler. This was the allegation that Koenen had passed the

porter on the afternoon of the fire with his coat collar up-
turned, and averted gaze. Towards the end of the day's
proceedings Dimitrov put the decisive question to Hornemann:

"Who has put all these things in your head?"

The President forbade Dimitrov further questions, none
indeed were necessary.

The old woman who had given evidence incriminating
Popov and Tanev, Frau Hartung, also, after some delay,
produced evidence involving Dimitrov. She declared that
when the "Red Aid" was applied to by any Bulgarian for
relief payments, the matter had always been referred to
Dimitrov. This Dimitrov denied and his denial was supported by employees in the former office of the "Red Aid,"
but even had Frau Hartung's evidence been correct it is
difficult to appreciate how it would have done more than
corroborate Dimitrov's assertion that he occupied himself
with matters of Bulgarian politics during his stay in Berlin.

Beyond these witnesses there were one or two other persons
such as the convict Krause who told the Court how Dimitrov
had turned pale in prison when he read of the arrests of certain
German Communists. There were also the 'map,' which
beyond all doubt had been tampered with by the police, and
the two post cards which were all that remained of the seven
or eight in Dimitrov's possession. During the course of the
proceedings Dimitrov deprived all these pieces of incriminating
evidence of their value by his incisive questioning.

Counter-Attack!

Dimitrov alone amongst the accused had a perfect alibi,
an alibi so unchallengeable that the Public Prosecutor had
jettisoned the bulk of the witnesses who alleged having seen
him in Berlin on February 27th. From a lawyer's viewpoint
Dimitrov's best course might have been to content himself
with the acceptance of his alibi by the prosecution and to
remain largely silent and undemonstrative during the proceedings. But as a politician and a revolutionary it was
impossible for Dimitrov to confine himself to such a passive
defence. The President asked him on the first day of the trial:

"For what reason do you imagine you have been really brought here?"

To this he gave the reply which explains the major content of his defence:

"To defend Communism and to defend myself!"

Dimitrov's questions and his tactics were determined by these aims, to defend Communism, to defend his Party and to defend his comrades whom circumstances had made practically defenceless; these aims, only to be secured by the relentless exposure of National-Socialism and its part in the Reichstag fire, determined the questions which lit up the trial like flames and which shone not seldom upon the face of the truth.

From the first Dimitrov appreciated the political character of the proceedings, it was not long before the precise intentions of the German Government were revealed to him. He lost no time in opposing them and countering them effectively despite the opposition and obstruction of the Court. The circumstances which made his task harder, the sufferings which he had undergone, the foreign tongue in which the trial was conducted, the opposition and obstruction which he experienced both from the Court and indeed from his own 'official' counsel, only served to make his questions the more incisive, his conduct of the defence the more brilliant. That his applications for the summoning of witnesses should be so uniformly rejected, that he should be deprived of knowing what facts in the favour of himself and his colleagues had been adduced in the Brown Book or the Commission of Inquiry did not stay him from the effective defence of his comrades in adversity and of his Party. Alone and unaided he carried on his task, he captured the attention of the world, drawing it to the salient points in the case and exposing the political intentions of the prosecution before all. He dominated the proceedings. He became a hero for the whole world.

Since his release Dimitrov has revealed the manner in which he formulated his famous questions:

"My colleagues and myself were isolated, almost hermetically sealed off from the world. The bulk of the letters addressed to us were not handed to us. We were allowed to read only National-Socialist newspapers. We had thus to rely almost exclusively upon our political intelligence. The test which I adopted was the attitude of the Fascist press to my conduct. I always bore in mind Bebel's adage: 'If my enemies praise me, I know then that I have done something foolish.' Throughout the case, when I suspected that I had made a false move I used to turn to the *Völkischer Beobachter*, the official paper of the Nazi Party.

When I read that paper's report of the trial I was able from its reaction to my questions, from the stress which was laid upon certain points and from the disparaging comments which were aimed at me, to judge whether or not I had shot straight with my questions. If I had misjudged a point then, through the foolishness of this newspaper, I was able the next morning to shoot again and to shoot straight!

"It is absolutely fallacious to imagine that an accused man can hope for a better outcome from the trial for himself if he behaves 'correctly' in the Court, if he imposes restrictions upon himself and if he hesitates to attack the prosecution. On the contrary, the more strongly, fearlessly and determinedly a Communist defends himself, the more difficult it becomes for a Court to convict him if he is innocent. It is right to make no concessions, not only from the viewpoint of Communism, but also from the stand of the accused man himself."

In this manner Dimitrov constructed, day by day, the line of his defence and directed his questions more and more to the vital points in the case, the facts and motives through which the truth about the Reichstag fire was necessarily to be revealed. Space does not permit an exhaustive examination of the points which Dimitrov was able in this way to elucidate, a selection of the most important must, therefore, suffice.

Footsteps in the Night

Dimitrov was the first to raise the question of the use of the underground passage leading from the Reichstag to the Palace of the Reichstag President before the Court. On October 16th, 1933, the lamplighter Scholz, who had glanced into the passage at about 8.30 p.m. on the night of the fire, gave evidence. Dimitrov put the question:

"Is it possible that the incendiaries entered the Reichstag through the underground passage?"

The question was disallowed, although as was revealed later the use of the underground passage by the incendiaries asserted by Göring, even in Court, and by the official bulletins was a vital factor in explaining the fire and identifying the culprits.

The importance of this matter raised by Dimitrov in his question to Scholz became apparent to the world with the examination two days later of the witness Adermann, who told the Court of the noises which he had frequently heard in the underground passage during the nights up to some ten days before the fire and of the experiment with paper and cotton which had definitely proved that the passage was being secretly used. Adermann alleged that he had informed the

Inspector of the Reichstag, Scranowitz, of his strange experiences. Dimitrov asked:

"What steps did Scranowitz order you to take?"

Adermann replied:

"He told me to keep a careful watch"!

Thus by the answer to a single question, without knowing of the allegations of the Brown Book or the evidence called before the Commission of Inquiry, Dimitrov was able to establish before the world that the secret use by night of the underground passage was known to the official in control of the Reichstag, politically a supporter of the National-Socialists, who failed to take effective steps to solve the puzzle. Dimitrov's further question:

"Could people make use of the passage without being seen?"

was frustrated by the intervention of the President who said:

"The witness has already explained that this could not have occurred on the night of the fire."

By questions to a further witness, Weber, head of Göring's S.S. bodyguard, Dimitrov was able to establish that on the orders of Göring's adjutant an inspection of the passage was carried out shortly after the fire had begun. Despite Dr. Sack's attempts to deal with this inspection as 'official,' Dimitrov was able definitely to reveal that it was entrusted to Weber in his capacity as S.S. man, that the policemen who accompanied him did not do so at his request and that while the policemen together searched one part of the passage, he alone searched the other and vital part, that which ran between the Reichstag and the Reichstag President's Palace. Through his clear-sighted questioning Dimitrov has provided the world with the essential facts, examined in detail in a later chapter, from which the truth of the Reichstag fire can be elucidated.

Lubbe in Henningsdorf

Despite the statement in the indictment stressing the importance of van der Lubbe's movements on the last day before the fire the Prosecutor and the Court constantly passed over this vital question. Dimitrov incessantly pressed the Court to summon witnesses from Henningsdorf and elsewhere to establish the details of van der Lubbe's movements. The fact, which emerged, that neither the police, nor Judge Vogt, nor the Prosecuting officials had thought it necessary to make inquiries there or to obtain witnesses only made Dimitrov's application more insistent. Eventually the Court had to give way. The result of this was to establish that van der Lubbe had spent the day preceding the Reichstag fire largely in the company of National-Socialists. Dimitrov's persistence was justified by its results, as with the underground passage.

Exposing the Prosecution

One of the earliest and most striking encounters in which Dimitrov was engaged during the trial was his attack upon Judge Vogt, who had been responsible for putting him in fetters. Vogt was exposed as a deliberate liar, having been forced into the admission that Dimitrov had made proper written application for their removal, which he had received, despite his former denial that any application had been made. Vogt's treatment of the engagement card and his official statement connecting Dimitrov and the others with the Sofia cathedral outrage sufficed to complete his exposure. Dimitrov was able not only to expose the tactics of the Examining Magistrate and the police to the Court and the world, he went further and destroyed much of the value of the evidence given in support of the prosecution by asking simple questions which though obviously elementary to the elucidation of the truth were neglected by the Court. Most pointed, in view of the conflicting statements as to van der Lubbe's knowledge of German and his apparent incoherence and inability to understand it in Court was the question which Dimitrov put to Heisig:

"Did van der Lubbe with his own lips and mouth speak the fluent German of which you have told the Court?"

Neither the counsel nor the Court ever commented upon the obvious point that a common language is usually necessary to enable persons to engage in any detailed and fluent conversation. To Kroyer and Frey who alleged having seen Torgler and Popov in deep and excited discussion in the Reichstag on the afternoon of the fire Dimitrov put the simple question:

"In what language?"

Neither of them was able to reply!

He took advantage of the presence of Kroyer, an Austrian National-Socialist to ask him:

"Are your activities on behalf of Austrian National-Socialism not just as illegal as mine, on behalf of Bulgarian Communism? Do not the Austrian Nazis have newspapers and pamphlets printed outside Austria and then sent into the country? Does the witness know that Austrian National-Socialist officials and deputies live in Germany and work here in the interests of National-Socialism in Austria?"

Before the President, angered by this question, was able to intervene Kroyer answered that there was a difference. Dimitrov retorted:

"Yes! I know that. The difference between my Communism and your National-Socialism is like the difference between Heaven and Hell."

The President then forbade Dimitrov to put further questions; too late! Questions framed with a view to elucidating the political past of the National-Socialist deputy Karwahne, expelled from the Communist Party some eight years previously, were also disallowed, but Dimitrov parried with the ironic comment:

"I much regret not having the opportunity of an open discussion with this witness!"

The Guilt of the Communists

To the expert Dr. Schatz whose opinion that the fire in the Plenary Sessions Chamber had been caused by a secret auto-inflammable fluid was designed to incriminate Torgler, Dimitrov put the decisive question:

"If I have correctly understood your interesting explanations, those persons who made use of the substance which you describe, so successfully, must have been possessed of a certain technical knowledge?"

Schatz in his answer sought to avoid the question by replying:

"People who occupy themselves with such matters always have a perfect knowledge of them."

151

But this deliberate attempt to side-track the question made it clear to every impartial person that to employ the secret fluid with success, technical knowledge such as Torgler did not possess was essential.

Count Helldorf whose evidence is described at greater length elsewhere, did not escape being exposed to Dimitrov's relentless interrogation. He was asked:

"What reason had you for believing that the incendiaries were either Communists or Socialists?"

Helldorf weakly answered:

"We are firmly convinced that the criminal element of society is in general Marxist. I had not the least doubt but that the criminals on this occasion were to be found in the Marxist ranks."

This reply revealed to all those seeking enlightenment the exact circumstances in which the responsibility for the crime was laid at the door of the Communists.

National-Socialist Deputies, Journalists and Thieves

When on October 31st the Public Prosecutor called the much-convicted Lebermann before the Court as a witness of truth, Dimitrov remarked:

"The last link in the chain of witnesses for the prosecution is supplied by this witness. It began with National-Socialist deputies, went on to National-Socialist journalists and is now completed with this thief."

Examination of the numbers of witnesses summoned by the Prosecutor will show how fully justified was this comment of Dimitrov's. The main points of the case against the four Communists depended on the evidence of Karwahne, Frey, Kroyer, Weberstedt, Dröscher and Helmer, all National-Socialists and all mistaken, to put the kindest construction upon their assertions; for the rest there were the criminals Kunzack, Lebermann, Krause, Bannert and many others. On November 14th another much-convicted man, Kämpfer, was summoned as a witness. Dimitrov referred to his record. To the retort of the Assistant Prosecutor, Parisius, Dimitrov replied with dignity that his own previous convictions were political and not convictions for theft.

In Grothe, the Prosecutor's star witness against the Communists and particularly strong on the political aspects of the

GEORGI DIMITROV ADDRESSING THE COURT

fire, Dimitrov was quick to recognise a mental case. He forthwith applied for an examination into Grothe's mental condition. Although the Court declined this, subsequently as Grothe's evidence became daily more incredible, they had no option but to obtain a pyscho-pathologist's report. The contents of this report read to the Court on December 6th strikingly demonstrated the correctness of Dimitrov's rapid deductions and the propriety of his application. Grothe turned out in fact to be mentally defective, subject to hallucinations and delusions and with a previous history of treatment in mental institutions.

The real weakness of the case against Dimitrov and his colleagues was revealed by the type of evidence and witnesses called to support it. The appearance of the charwoman Anna Schrieber on October 20th with her allegations that Dimitrov had attempted to violate her drew forth a scathing comment by Dimitrov on the methods of the Prosecutor.

"This testimony is deliberately false. It is only given to puff out the baseless accusations of the indictment."

Such methods were again illustrated by an attempt made by the Public Prosecutor, even while the proceedings were on foot, to get evidence against the accused. He sent an alleged law student, Wolff, into the prison on the pretext that he was studying the psychology of criminals, for the purpose of inducing the fellow-prisoners of the accused men to give evidence against them. Wolff went so far as to visit the accused men in their own cells to get material, allegedly for his book, from them. His researches had at least one concrete result. A criminal obtained by Wolff appeared to testify against Popov, basing his evidence on facts which he alleged had been told him by Popov in confidence. Dimitrov commented upon the appearance of the witness:

"The preliminary inquiry lasted seven months, the trial has already lasted two months. Has the prosecution so little material against us that they are reduced to having recourse to such methods as these?"

The Public Prosecutor answered with a confession of failure:

"Whenever and however I get material against you, even to the last day of the trial, I shall use it!"

153

All the attempts made by the prosecution effectively to use their selected criminals and mental defectives against the accused men were brought to naught. Towards the end of the trial, on December 6th, 1933, when the official records and experts' reports on numbers of the prosecution's witnesses were read Dimitrov requested that Heisig should be asked how he came to accept the statements of Grothe without first making investigations into his character and his history. The President interrupted. The following dialogue ensued:

Dimitrov: "You are very nervy to-day, Mr. President, I cannot imagine the cause."
President: "I am never nervy."
Dimitrov: "I must ask your pardon, but I must defend myself. It is doubtless bad luck for the prosecution that numbers of its chief witnesses are mental defectives, drug addicts and thieves."

Van der Lubbe's Condition

The Court did not share the universal interest in seeking an explanation of van der Lubbe's demeanour and condition during the trial. Where judges and counsel all regarded van der Lubbe as perfectly fit and normal, even when he heard voices in his body, not so Dimitrov. When on December 6th, 1933, Professor Bonnhöfer repeated his opinion on van der Lubbe's condition to the Court, Dimitrov pressed him cogently and closely for an accurate explanation.

"Van der Lubbe says that he has heard voices in his body. I for myself am amazed that the experts have paid no attention to this symptom. Does it not indicate hallucinations? Have I rightly understood that Professor Bonnhöfer describes this individual as normal and fully responsible for his actions?"

Without knowing of the interest which it had raised abroad, Dimitrov thus put his finger on the central point in van der Lubbe's condition and definitely exposed Bonnhöfer as a witness who aimed at the suppression and not at the elucidation of the truth.

The Last Witness

On December 6th, 1933, House Inspector Scranowitz was recalled. Dimitrov's expulsion from the Court had saved Scranowitz from close questioning on the occasion of his former appearance. He was recalled in order that the allegation that he had seen the three Bulgarians in the Reichstag, which he had made to Judge Vogt should be dealt with. Dimitrov inquired why the matter had not been raised before. Scranowitz, the picture of confusion, tried to evade the question. He said that he had seen people in the Reichstag who had reminded him of the Bulgarians. He indicated that he was no longer able to support his former statement. Dimitrov despatched him with a shrewd thrust:

"When I saw Scranowitz for the first time I mistook him for a Bulgarian terrorist who has the murders of ten Communists on his conscience and who looks exactly like Scranowitz. Not until later did I learn that he was an honoured government official."

Scranowitz made his way stealthily out of the public laughter.

The Armed Insurrection

However brilliant, however incisive his attacks upon the prosecution's evidence, Dimitrov kept constantly before his eyes the political issues of the trial. He fought incessantly for the elucidation of the political situation in February 1933. He seized every available opportunity to illume and enlarge upon the political significance of the Reichstag fire and the part which it played in the campaign leading to the National-Socialist hegemony. He made application for the summoning of Thälmann, the leader of the German Communist Party, General von Schleicher, von Papen, Hugenberg, Brüning and Duesterberg, amongst others, as witnesses. The Court had heard the statements of Göring and Goebbels on the political situation, which had painted a picture of one colour. Dimitrov grounded his application that light should be thrown from other quarters on the state of affairs with reasons:

"I am making this application so that the political situation as it really was in the early months of this year may be described to the Court and thus that it may be ascertained whom the Reichstag fire could really have benefited, the Communists or other persons."

The Court rejected his application. It did not desire to get a picture painted by less partial, less interested hands than those of the two National-Socialist leaders.

But this refusal did not serve to sway Dimitrov from his purpose. He continued the pursuit of the political issues, he strove for the elucidation of the political situation in February 1933. His duel with Göring and Goebbels, examined in detail in a subsequent chapter, demonstrates the significance and the importance of this matter.

While continuing to indicate the importance of the Reichstag fire to the National-Socialists and the uses to which they put it, Dimitrov did not cease to demonstrate at every available moment the fallacy of the theory advanced by the prosecution that the Communists had designed the fire as the 'beacon' for their planned armed insurrection. His question to Helldorf and the negative response which it drew forth were significant:

"Did you observe anything whatever from which to draw the conclusion that the Communists had prepared an armed insurrection to break out in the night of February 27th?"

A similar question was put to Heller, who had charge of the supervision of Communist activities in Germany. To the inquiry whether he possessed the smallest fact or scantiest document indicating that an insurrection had been prepared by the Communists for February 27th, a negative answer was forthcoming. Dimitrov pressed Heller further:

"Is it not a fact that towards the end of 1932 the National-Socialists threatened Reichschancellor Schleicher with an armed revolt unless he surrendered power to Hitler?"

Heller weakly replied that that matter was outside his official cognisance. But Dimitrov pursued the matter with a further question, which the President disallowed:

"Early in 1933 was there not a danger of an armed struggle between the National-Socialists on the one side and the supporters of von Papen and Hugenberg on the other?"

To Brösig, a high official of the Düsseldorf police force he put the question:

"Was the Reichstag fire not in actual fact the signal for the destruction of the working-class parties and a means of resolving the differences within the Hitler Government?"

This pertinent question, pointing directly at the purposes of the fire, was disallowed by the President. Dimitrov followed it by asking:

"Is it not a fact that in January 1933 the relations between the National-Socialists and the Stahlhelm were so strained that open conflict between them was imminent? Did this tension not continue after Hitler's nomination to the Reichschancellorship? Is it not true that local sections of the Stahlhelm joined with Reichsbanner units in order to undertake common measures against the Nazis?"

The Public Prosecutor intervened before the witness could reply to point out that it was quite irrelevant whether such differences had existed or not. Dimitrov's reply exposed the fallacy of the Prosecutor's argument.

"From a purely legal standpoint that may be so. But this, let me remind you, is a political trial and the truth can only be discovered if the political situation of February 1933 is elucidated in all its aspects. You wanted a political trial. Well so be it! let us have a really political trial. *A la guerre comme à la guerre! Wenn schon, denn schon!*"

This retort of Dimitrov's expresses forcibly and succinctly the answer to the allegation of 'irrelevance' used by both the Prosecution and the Court to hamper the defence. The trial, as the judgment indeed amply testifies, was a trial with a political motive and a political object. Whenever the accused men tried to introduce matters of political import they were restricted by the weapon of irrelevance, whenever the prosecution introduced matters of politics then it was relevant. The Court thus avowed itself as the instrument of the Government. The National-Socialists desired and attained a verdict against the Communists which would achieve the twofold purpose of sheltering themselves from suspicion and of justifying the dictatorship in its origin and its manifestations. The Court was subservient to these ends. Questions directed by Dimitrov seeking to reveal the differences and intrigues within the ranks of the reactionary alliance, questions which turned upon the identity and adherence of the real incendiaries were almost without exception disallowed by the Court. The prosecution was frankly political in its methods, its direction and its aim, while the defence, the accused men themselves, were bound hand and foot with restrictions aimed at preventing them from answering the political allegations so vital for their fate, if not indeed from defending themselves.

With the eyes of the world upon him, in the hands of the most relentless enemies Dimitrov avowed himself a revolutionary. In the course of his first examination by the Court he said:

"I am an ally of the Soviet Union and am proud to be a member of the party of Stalin."

He acknowledged the part which he had played in the Bulgarian working-class movement and in the rising of 1923. He told them:

"I believe in the overthrow of capitalism through the proletarian revolution."

He castigated Fascism and Fascist rule. He declared:

"Certainly Fascism in Bulgaria is barbarous, but what Fascism is not so?"

His voice spoke with the authority of the thousands of murdered and imprisoned victims of National-Socialism, he stood before the world and before the German people as the representative and embodiment of that international solidarity, that world-wide brotherhood of the working class which Hitler and his colleagues abhor and abnegate. Dimitrov was an accuser and not an accused. In his own words to the Court:

"I am not a debtor but a creditor here!"

IX

VAN DER LUBBE

MARINUS VAN DER LUBBE, an unemployed and vagrant Dutchman was arrested at about 9.25 p.m. on the night of the fire in the burning Reichstag. His arrest was carried out by Pöschel, a police officer and by the Inspector of the Reichstag, Scranowitz. He offered no resistance, nor did he attempt escape.

He was the first of the accused to be led into the Court when the trial opened on September 21st, 1933. He appeared then to have completely collapsed. He walked as if he were asleep. His head was bowed. The expression on his face was set; his eyes unseeing. When in his place amongst the accused his head was bent over his breast. He appeared to take no notice of those around him. He was almost unaware of the proceedings. When he was made to answer questions he rose slowly and awkwardly, without raising his head. The answers he gave were most of them mere unrelated expressions—'Yes,' 'No,' 'Perhaps,' 'I don't know.' Frequently he answered both 'Yes' and 'No' to the same question. Often he replied to the Presiding Judge's questions and efforts to make him speak with a low and indistinguishable murmur which, to the amazement of the journalists present, the interpreter put into comprehensible language.

The two policemen stationed at his side did not budge from their position. When he was called upon to stand facing the judges one of them always accompanied him. Arthur Garfield Hays, the American member of the International Commission of Inquiry, who attended the greater part of the trial, early expressed his view: "Any American or English lawyer would have applied for an adjournment of the trial for an investigation to be made into van der Lubbe's mental condition."

The foreign press were almost unanimous in expressing the view that a doctor would be a more fitting companion for van der Lubbe than a policeman.

Van der Lubbe's official lawyer did not trouble the Court with any application for the investigation of his client's condition. In fact Dr. Seuffert had very little to do at all during the trial. For days at a time van der Lubbe appeared so stupefied and apathetic that he could not wipe his own nose. This was the major activity of Dr. Seuffert, who, armed with paper handkerchiefs, fulfilled this function for his client. Little else did he do to aid his client whom the death penalty threatened.

The Brown Book Confirmed

During the first and second days of the trial the Presiding Judge endeavoured to draw from van der Lubbe a description of his life and movements. Van der Lubbe's replies were mere low murmurs, it seemed doubtful whether he understood what was required of him. So Dr. Bünger furnished an account of van der Lubbe from the indictment, from which that accused did not appear to dissent.

The statements in the Brown Book anent van der Lubbe were strikingly confirmed. His gravely-impaired eyesight, his ambition and thirst for notoriety, his attempt to swim the Channel, his wanderings over Europe, his stay in Munich, his stay in Sörnewitz, Saxony, which is dealt with more fully in a later chapter, all these facts stated in the Brown Book found their confirmation within the Court. Further the Brown Book's proof that van der Lubbe had left the Dutch Communist Party in 1931 was admitted by the Presiding Judge, who declared however, that his secession from the Party was purely a matter of form, and that van der Lubbe did not thereby cease to be an intellectual adherent of Communist doctrines—therefore a Communist. The Dutch police report upon van der Lubbe which was later read in Court also confirmed the statements of the Brown Book on the point of his membership of the petty "Rade-Communist" group. It ran:

"Van der Lubbe was always ambitious of being a leader but was wanting in every quality necessary for leadership. He was filled with an avid thirst for notoriety, almost amounting to an obsession. In 1931 he left the Dutch Communist Party. From this time onwards his influence amongst the unemployed declined; he joined the insignificant group of 'International-Communists' whose numbers throughout Holland are only twenty."

The statements of the Brown Book went no further than this except to bring out the sharp opposition of van der Lubbe and of his new group to the Dutch Communist Party. The characteristics of this group, which came to the surface in the so-called *Red Book on van der Lubbe* published by some of his Dutch political associates, were described in the report of the sub-commission of the International Commission of Inquiry which, consisting of the three lawyers, Dr. Betsy Bakker-Nort, Senator Branting and M. Vermeylen, was sent by the Commission to make inquiries in Holland concerning the character, activities and associates of van der Lubbe. Concerning the "Rade Communists" the report stated:

"It was established beyond doubt that the circle in which van der Lubbe pursued his activities during the last two years, the 'Rade' or 'International' Communists, was in fact a group of anarchistic tendencies who strongly opposed the industrial and political organisations of the Dutch working class, particularly the Dutch Social-Democratic and Communist parties."

It is notorious that van der Lubbe consistently denied membership of the Communist Party and, contrary to the statement in the official bulletin, had never admitted it to anyone. Even under strong pressure from the Presiding Judge, who warned him "to distinguish between membership of a political organisation and adherence to the ideological aspect of Communism," van der Lubbe was not to be moved from his denials. Neither this fact nor the truth about the Rade-Communists, which was well known to the Court, prevented the Presiding Judge from elevating van der Lubbe's petty anarchist circle into an important political party, assimilating it to a Communist Party and stating, at a very early stage in the trial:

"I am quite clear in my mind that you are a Communist."

The revelation made in the Brown Book of van der Lubbe's homosexuality was something which the Court at Leipzig passed over in silence, although in his concluding speech the Public Prosecutor declared it to be an invention. The sub-commission of the International Commission of Inquiry took advantage of their visit to Holland to receive statements from the closest of van der Lubbe's friends upon this point and as a result reported that van der Lubbe's homosexuality was established beyond contradiction. The indications of a connection between van der Lubbe and Roehm, present commander of Storm Troops and Cabinet Minister, contained in the Brown Book were further supported by the evidence of a German journalist, a former acquaintance of the murdered Dr. Bell, given before the Commission of Inquiry. Further evidence was made available upon this point by the statements of Freek van Leeuwen, the Dutch writer, and a member of the circle to which van der Lubbe adhered in Holland. Abundant proof of van der Lubbe's homosexuality has been assembled by the Dutch judge, de Jongh, in his work on the Reichstag fire case, where amongst other sources of information he quotes a close friend of van der Lubbe to the effect that: "He was long friendly with van der Lubbe and their relations together were like those of a youth and a girl."

This feature of van der Lubbe's character was nowhere raised idly, or with the desire to foment scandal, its importance lies in the fact that, in conjunction with the many statements made by van der Lubbe to his Dutch friends about the events of his travels in Germany, it furnishes strong indications of a connection existing before the Reichstag fire between van der Lubbe and certain leading National-Socialists, amongst them the notorious Roehm.

Faced with these indications the Court ignored the point. It would have been a simple matter to call Roehm, together with his colleagues Goebbels and Göring, before the Court and to ask him for a complete denial of the suggestions. This course for some reason was not taken, although the Court made it its business to see that other, less vital, points in the Brown Book were 'contradicted' by witnesses summoned for the purpose.

Twelve Missing Days

In elucidating van der Lubbe's movements in Germany the Presiding Judge again followed the indictment closely, breaking off his repetition now and then to draw a nod or murmur of assent from that accused. It emerged that van der Lubbe left Leyden on February 3rd or 4th and crossed the Dutch frontier into Germany on February 5th or 6th. He did not arrive in Berlin until February 18th. For twelve days, then, van der Lubbe was at large in Germany and no light was thrown on his movements. The police and prosecuting officials who in other matters had made the most searching and detailed inquiries and had never been at a loss to reveal facts pointing in a certain direction, either could not or would not produce any evidence or explanation of van der Lubbe's movements during these twelve days.

From the time when he entered into conversation on February 22nd with a group of unemployed on the street in front of the Neukölln Welfare Bureau until the night of February 25th, just after van der Lubbe had attempted to set on fire the Welfare Office in Neukölln, the Town Hall and the Palace in the Lustgarten, van der Lubbe's movements about Berlin were traced down to the last detail. But with the morning of February 26th the close investigation of his movements ended. During the next twenty-four hours it was barely recounted that van der Lubbe had walked by way of Charlottenburg to Spandau and thence to Henningsdorf where he passed the night. The detailed story was again resumed on the morning of February 27th as van der Lubbe began his journey back on foot from Henningsdorf to Berlin. Despite the importance laid on van der Lubbe's adventures in Spandau and Henningsdorf in the indictment, which alleged that there was no doubt but that the threads between van der Lubbe and those who had planned the arson were woven there, no exact account of his movements during the twenty-four hours between the morning of February 26th and the following day was offered. The police had not troubled to make any inquiries. The Court, too, would have allowed the matter to be passed over but for Dimitrov's reiterated insistence that there, at least, was something which it was essential to clear up from the viewpoint of both the prosecution and the defence. The results of the belated investigation into van der Lubbe's movements on February 26th, when it was established that during that time he had been with National-Socialists, can only lend a deeper significance to the omissions of the police, the prosecuting officials and the Court.

Setting the Reichstag on Fire

Whether or not van der Lubbe had ever given a consistent or intelligible account of the manner in which he set fire to

163

the Reichstag is a matter which is now unlikely to be elucidated. The geography of the Reichstag building is extremely
complicated, as anyone who has had occasion to wander
through its intricate corridors, lobbies and passages will
testify. The detective Zirpins no doubt had this in mind
when he told the Court that van der Lubbe, on his first
interrogation, had appeared to him to be a "mathematical
genius" from the accurate plans and sketches of the interior
of the Reichstag which he had produced to illustrate to the
wondering police the route which he had taken within the
building. Unfortunately none of these plans so obligingly
made by the accused had been deemed worthy of preservation,
or if they had the Court was not vouchsafed a glance at them.
Zirpins it was who described van der Lubbe as talkative and
boastful, and as having command of the German language.
Heisig, while less certain of van der Lubbe's perfect German
or fluency in conversation, was able to tell the Court how
van der Lubbe, with occasional hesitation retraced his route
in the Reichstag building.

This, of course, was absolutely contrary to the statement
of Judge Vogt, that it was quite impossible from van der
Lubbe's statements to get a picture of his movements inside
the Reichstag. But yet the indictment contained a detailed
description down to the most minute points of van der Lubbe's
course in the building. This account has been examined at
some length in an earlier chapter. It will suffice at this point
to indicate the two things which make it most improbable.
Firstly, there is no indication of the quarter from which the
account emanated and secondly, if the account be genuine,
then it is impossible that the movements contained in it, some
hundred and sixty-seven in all, could have been carried out
by a normal man, be he well acquainted with the geography
of the building, in the fourteen short minutes between 9.8
and 9.22 p.m.; much less would it be possible for a half-blind
stranger like van der Lubbe. The Court, however, was
content with van der Lubbe's murmured or nodded acceptance
of the mysterious account contained in the indictment. In
order to give it a semblance of reality it was arranged to hold
a reconstruction of the crime on October 12th, 1933.

The Reconstruction

The walls of the Reichstag were lit up with searchlights. The curious crowd was held back at a distance by a treble cordon of police. The accused, with the exception of Dimitrov to whose all-seeing eyes the appreciation of this comedy was denied, the Court and a variety of officials and politicians met before the Reichstag.

One of the mysteries connected with the entry of van der Lubbe into the Reichstag was how he with his bad eyesight had managed to clamber unobserved up the façade of the Reichstag, which was far too slippery for the firemen to climb without a ladder, without leaving any marks whatever. Although the weather conditions of February 27th—when the walls were covered with a glaze of ice—could probably not have been duplicated, it would nevertheless have been possible for some athlete to demonstrate how van der Lubbe was able to perform the feat which brought him on to the restaurant balcony without leaving any traces of his progress. This had not occurred to those who arranged the reconstruction, which accordingly opened at the point when van der Lubbe, carrying a light, or perhaps two van der Lubbes, without lights, were seen on the restaurant balcony, trying to break the window, the one of them by Flöter, the two by Thaler.

After several attempts the three chief actors in the reconstruction, the police sergeant Buwert, Thaler and Flöter, managed to get their movements to accord with their evidence. The fatal flaw in the statements of these three, who none of them recognised the others as having been the actual persons concerned, was happily forgotten. The result of the reconstruction was conclusively to prove that two minutes five seconds (at the third or fourth attempt) elapsed between the time when Flöter made his first observation of the man with the light on the balcony and the time when Buwert fired into the Reichstag at the moving lights. According to the account of van der Lubbe's movements in the Reichstag, during this hundred and twenty-five seconds, he had already performed the first ninety-seven actions in the complete list; not only a mathematical genius but a marvel of velocity!

Van der Lubbe and the Communists

The proof of van der Lubbe's connection with the Communist Party rested firstly upon Heisig's statement, strongly shaken by the widely-published denials of his alleged informants, and secondly upon the alleged effects of a conversation between that accused and some unemployed in front of the Neukölln Welfare Office on February 22nd, 1933. The most important witness of this conversation was the Nationalist workman Panknin, who had been kept in a concentration camp pending the trial. Panknin's first statement to the Court raised a new point, he alleged that van der Lubbe had produced a Communist membership card. Unfortunately for Panknin, his political experiences were as limited as those of the average rank and file, dyed-in-the-wool Conservative. When asked how he was able to identify the card as being Communist he replied, somewhat naturally:

"Well, because it was red!"

This hardly suited the prosecution because it was notorious that the only Party who had ever used red cards was the National-Socialists. The cards of the German and Dutch Communist Parties were black and blue-black respectively.

But Panknin hastened to retrieve his error. He stated, again making a new point, that van der Lubbe had asked his way to the Communist headquarters of Berlin.

The sting of Panknin's evidence was that Zachow, a Communist sympathiser declared to the Court that as a working man he would vote Communist to-day; he said, "Everything must be destroyed, first of all public buildings." This allegation was followed by a duologue between Panknin and the Presiding Judge:

Panknin: "Bienge (another man present) said that all public buildings must be set on fire."
President: "Formerly you said that Zachow stated that."
Panknin: "Yes, that was so."
President: "Good, Zachow said that. Then what?"
Panknin: "Then they said when we come to power we shan't need the Reichstag."
President: "Who said that?"
Panknin: "Zachow."
President: "Formerly you said that Bienge said that, who was it really?"
Panknin: "Bienge."

President: "Why then did you tell me that Zachow said it."
Panknin: "I made a mistake. Bienge said that but it was Zachow who talked about arson in the Palace and the Reichstag."
President: "Who talked about that?"
Panknin: "Zachow."
President: "But you formerly said that Bienge said that."
Panknin: "Yes, Bienge did say it."

While the Court and the lawyers passed over these contradictions in silence, the German press stressed the clarity and importance of Panknin's evidence. Consider the comment of the Wolff Bureau:

"The strenuous efforts of the President, Dr. Bünger to reconstruct this conversation as nearly as possible word for word were powerfully assisted by the memory of the witness Panknin and by his clear and definite statements."

Panknin was followed in the witness box by Zachow and Bienge, brought from concentration camps. They both contradicted Panknin's account of the conversation, denying that there had been any mention of burning public buildings or of the Communist headquarters. They were in accord with Panknin on one fact only, that van der Lubbe's German had been halting and difficult to understand. It was Zachow who first forcibly reminded the Court and the members of the public of the conditions prevailing outside the Court-room.

"I have been punished enough already: I come from the concentration camp!"

Brave in demeanour before the Court was the workman Jahnecke who drew attention to the activities of a certain police spy Hintze, who provoked the unemployed to a raid on the welfare office and to whose influence Panknin had probably been subjected. Hintze was a well-known figure in Neukölln, had created much trouble there and may even have come into contact with van der Lubbe during the first three days of his known stay in Berlin. Jahnecke, having spoken out boldly what he knew, returned to a concentration camp. With the conclusion of his evidence, failed the attempt of the prosecution to connect van der Lubbe with the German Communist Party.

Simulation?

Apart from the defects in his eyesight, due not to idiopathic disease but to accident, van der Lubbe was physically a healthy and even a strong man before the Reichstag fire. He was hardened to a rough life, and so bodily powerful that his friends had been in the habit of calling him 'Dempsey.' His mental condition was not abnormal. The detectives Heisig and Zirpins described him as intelligent. The witnesses from Neukölln were united in agreeing that he did not seem to be a fool. Judge Vogt declared that he was a cunning person; while the Public Prosecutor in an interview which he gave to the Swedish press in August 1933 painted van der Lubbe as a man of intelligence above the normal.

The impressions of those witnesses who were in contact with van der Lubbe before or shortly after the Reichstag fire of his physical and mental soundness, were borne out by the examination conducted into van der Lubbe's condition by Professor Bonnhöfer of the Berlin Charité Hospital in March 1933, shortly after his arrest. Bonnhöfer then found van der Lubbe to be healthy and bodily strong.

Very different from this young 'Dempsey' was the van der Lubbe led into Court on September 21st, 1933. This was the wreck of a man. So apparent was his indifference and apathy, so obvious the signs that all was not well with him, that from the first day of the trial his condition was the subject of constant discussion and conjecture. To foreign observers it was doubtful whether van der Lubbe understood what was happening around him and, in any case, whether he was in a fit condition to be tried.

It was against these suggestions that the Court in an effort to justify the trial of van der Lubbe, sought the opinions of experts—some more and some less qualified to judge—upon van der Lubbe's condition. Bonnhöfer appeared to communicate the results of his investigations which were made in March 1933 and possibly, though this is by no means clear, after that date. Another medical expert, Dr. Schütz, made a brief examination of van der Lubbe on the evening of September 25th and the morning of the following day. As the consequence of these short investigations Dr. Schütz found no difficulty in stating that van der Lubbe fully understood the proceedings and was perfectly capable of giving replies if he cared to do so. Schütz concluded by saying:

"His whole conduct is deliberately designed. The mode of his defence has been chosen with a deliberate purpose. He is following the precepts of the German Communist Party to its members upon their conduct in court."

Bonnhöfer and Schütz found themselves in agreement upon van der Lubbe's normality in Court. Their conclusions, one of them only by inference alleging simulation, the other directly attributing van der Lubbe's conduct to that cause, had been based upon short examinations. Neither of them undertook periodical observation of the case from a medical standpoint, no chemical analyses were made, nor was his dietary investigated.

The Court could not help but notice the limitations to the effect of the opinions of these two experts and accordingly summoned foreign assistance the more easily to justify their treatment of van der Lubbe as sane in the eyes of the world. It was not surprising that the two foreign experts selected for the purpose were able to conclude that van der Lubbe was quite normal in every way. The first of these men was a Swedish criminologist, one Södermann, an expert on fingerprints, without medical experience or academic qualification. Södermann, who allowed it to be understood and announced that he was a medical expert, visited van der Lubbe in his cell and there examined him for marks of ill-treatment. Södermann told van der Lubbe that he was making his examination because of allegations of ill-treatment in the foreign press, at which van der Lubbe laughed. All, he stated, was in good order. Van der Lubbe was being well treated. His body bore no marks of ill-usage of any kind. In answer to his inquiries van der Lubbe informed Södermann that he was well physically and mentally.

During his evidence Södermann made a curious remark upon which he was later questioned by Dr. Sack. This remark was to the effect that in the matter of food van der Lubbe was being treated far better than the other prisoners. Dr. Sack pursued this point with the question:

"It is further stated that he is being fed with slow poisons?"
Södermann: "I also asked van der Lubbe if he at any time had felt anything strange after eating or drinking. This he emphatically denied."

This point of van der Lubbe's diet was not concluded with Södermann's reply. His original statement that van der Lubbe was being subjected to preferential treatment as far as food was concerned is strikingly confirmed by reliable information from a fellow-prisoner that van der Lubbe's meals were served separately from those of the other inmates of the prison. From the medical experts' evidence it was known that van der Lubbe had many months before gone on hunger strike for a short period. Since then he had been well and abundantly fed, but despite this his physical condition had seriously deteriorated and he had lost many pounds in weight. Van der Lubbe himself later provided abundant corroboration of the unusual attention which was being paid to his diet. On November 23rd he told the Court that he was tired of the continuous struggle which he had to go through in prison, that he did not desire to be forced to eat five or six times a day and always to be asked how his food was tasting. The Court forbore from following up the implications of this protest. No inquiry was made into its accuracy or as to the possible reasons which there might be for such treatment.

The second foreign expert upon whose assistance the Court relied was the Dutch journalist Lüger. The results of Lüger's visit to van der Lubbe were less fortunate than those of Södermann's. Although a compatriot Lüger was not able to extract more than bare affirmations and denials from him, while his demeanour was the same as in Court. Lüger's observations thus made it certain that van der Lubbe was not conducting himself differently during the times when he was actually before the Court. His picture was rather different from that painted by Södermann and even by the expert Schütz, it is decidedly opposed to the simulation theory advanced by Schütz and adopted by the Public Prosecutor.

It is indeed difficult to appreciate how the simulation theory came to command the acceptance of the Court, as it appears to have done. To begin with it was built up on very slender ground. Despite Schütz's positiveness, Bonnhöfer only gave the theory very slight support and in the end appeared to differ from it entirely. Södermann's observations were indifferent for any theory, while Lüger's report was decidedly adverse to Schütz's views. Even had the medical opinion been based upon sufficient and proper materials, a careful and prolonged observation, coupled with the necessary examinations and analyses, it is difficult to see the purpose or reasons which could have actuated van der Lubbe in 'simulating' to the extent which he did. Even if he were the consummate actor which the course of such simulation would have demanded, what gain would it serve him? He had already confessed to the crime and he steadfastly asserted his guilt. The Prosecutor suggested that he was simulating in order to shield his accomplices—but if he had really desired to shield his accomplices he would surely have taken a more active and intelligent interest in the proceedings, he would have concentrated upon proving that he did and could have done the act alone. He would certainly not have allowed indications of accomplices to slip from his lips, or proofs of accomplices to pass unchallenged. Can the suggestion of Schütz that he was employing 'Communist' tactics in Court be supported for one moment in the light of the tactics which the avowed Communists, his co-prisoners, employed. The theory of simulation is indeed so contrary to the medical evidence, so contrary to the facts, and so contrary to the probabilities that it cannot be regarded for one moment as bearing impartial investigation, much less acceptance.

The striking contrast between the facts of van der Lubbe's case, made apparent to the world by his demeanour in the Court, by his tragic indifference and bewilderment, roused interest amongst medical and juristic circles all over the world. One of the most eminent of French psychiatrists, Dr. Toulouse, wrote to Dr. Seuffert, van der Lubbe's counsel, suggesting that the opinion of a foreign medical expert should be obtained upon van der Lubbe's condition and that if his views should differ from those of the two German experts already heard, the difference should be decided by a further impartial expert to be officially summoned. To this letter a copy of which was forwarded to the Court, no reply was vouchsafed. Dr. Toulouse's letter was by no means the only quarter in which the view was expressed that van der Lubbe was mentally disordered. That view, together with the opinion that van der Lubbe's condition was attributable to some external influence was expressed in letters written by experts of all nationalities and throughout the world's press.

The famous psychopathologist, Dr. Magnus Hirschfeldt,

described van der Lubbe's case as almost exceptional in a thirty-years' experience of criminal cases. He regarded van der Lubbe's indifference coupled with his physical weakness and decrepitude as paralleled within his experience of criminal psychopathology only by the case of Prince Eulenburg, in his perjury trial, who

> "was led into the court in a similar condition of total mental and physical collapse. It was however quite clear in this instance that the condition had been brought about by the prisoner's own excessive use of narcotics. It is clearly possible than van der Lubbe's condition in the present case is not natural, but is the result of external factors."

To choose between the conflicting views of the Court and the foreign experts is a difficult but yet a necessary task. This might have been avoided but for the attitude of the German Government in strenuously declining permission for van der Lubbe's body to be transmitted to his relatives for burial. The conducting of an autopsy would have at least removed, or confirmed, certain doubts and fears as to van der Lubbe's physical condition and its causes. But since the German authorities have deliberately made this impossible, one may only go upon such materials as are available for all the world, the symptoms which van der Lubbe was observed to display during the proceedings.

The most prominent features of van der Lubbe's mental state were these: a continuous apparent bewilderment and indifference, spasms of empty and unprompted laughter and hallucinations (the celebrated passage in which van der Lubbe spoke of the "voices in his body" was a clear indication of this, as Dimitrov indicated to Bonnhöfer). The physical indications of his condition appeared in the obvious difficulty which he experienced in moving, his slow and shuffling gait, the manner in which his head sunk lower and lower on his chest and his insensibility to the mucus discharges from his nose. The way in which he awoke from his seeming trance to the sharp strident command of Count Helldorf on the twenty-first day of the trial, the weakened mind imposed upon by a normal will, is also not without importance in a consideration of the cause of van der Lubbe's condition.

All these symptoms point emphatically in one direction— to an external influence so strong that it can make the wreck of a man otherwise mentally and physically healthy and strong.

Just as the typical case of poisoning can in the absence of an autopsy be best judged by the symptoms displayed by the victim, so is it with van der Lubbe. There is one poisonous drug with such qualities that comparatively minute doses will produce symptoms exactly similar to those displayed by van der Lubbe. Such is scopolamin. Its effects can be produced, as was stated by an eminent toxicologist in an article in the *Neue Tagebuch* on October 28th, 1933, "by a daily dose of from a quarter to a half milligram of the drug, the effect of which will be to reduce a normal man, in physical and mental health, to a state of complete indifference and passivity."

In this connection one is forcibly reminded of the passages in the proceedings, described above, in which the question of van der Lubbe's feeding was discussed. The five or six meals a day of which van der Lubbe complained, his special treatment in the matter of feeding, his separate meals and the questions which followed them can be reasonably explained only on the assumption that drugs were being administered to him. This assumption, too, would also furnish a reason for the German Government's refusal of the simply human request of van der Lubbe's relatives. One would otherwise have supposed that his dead body was harmless enough to the Government which by the decision of the Supreme Court he was adjudged to have attempted to overthrow.

There is more in support of this theory, for it is no more than a theory which is now beyond the bounds of proof or rebuttal, than against it. The facts are consistent with the assumption that van der Lubbe's condition was brought about by the administration of drugs; the medical evidence summoned by the Court, in the absence of the necessary observations and examinations, cannot be regarded as excluding the assumption. Moreover, the theory coincides far more with all the probabilities of the case than any other which has been advanced, nor is it wanting in reason.

Did van der Lubbe act alone?

The facts relating to the fire are the most eloquent testimony that van der Lubbe had accomplices; a brief allusion to them will suffice. The findings of the International Commission of Inquiry, based on the observations of eye-witnesses, that van der Lubbe could not have acted alone, were supported by all the facts adduced in the proceedings at Leipzig. A torch was found in the corridor of the Reichstag, petrol was found, both in a spitoon and upon the carpets, heaps of newspapers were seen. It was nowhere alleged that van der Lubbe had used or carried such materials into the building. The fire experts summoned before the Court unanimously rejected the theory that the fire, above all in the Sessions Chamber, could have been the work of one man, or could have been caused by such materials as firelighters, cloths and towels which van der Lubbe was said to have employed. The improbability of his alleged statement, contained in the indictment, has already been referred to; it indicates no less than van der Lubbe's partial blindness and lack of knowledge of the complicated geography of the Reichstag building, that it would have been impossible for van der Lubbe to have set the Reichstag on fire unaided in the short time available, much less to emerge from his work unscorched and unscathed.

Against this overwhelming evidence that van der Lubbe had accomplices, the opposing theory, that he acted alone was maintained by van der Lubbe solely. But he was not entirely consistent in these assertions for on three occasions he let slip phrases strikingly indicating their untruth.

Heisig during his evidence as to van der Lubbe's first interrogation told the Court that "he first stuck to it that he had acted alone." This was followed by Judge Vogt's statement that on one occasion during his inquiries van der Lubbe had remarked to him that "the others must have done that." This statement it may be mentioned was nowhere embodied in Vogt's records of the interrogations, but the Judge was quite emphatic that it had been made. Lastly, before the Court itself van der Lubbe, replying to the suggestion that he could not have laid the inflammable materials on the seats in the Sessions Chamber, said:

"Then the others must have done that"!

It is surprising that the Court did not endeavour to elucidate from van der Lubbe or any other source who these 'others' three times referred to by him, could have been. At such moments the Court appears, indeed, to have underlined the theory, which can be little supported by the facts, that van der Lubbe did cause the fire unaided.

Did van der Lubbe know he was not alone?

The weight of the evidence and probabilities is so contrary to the theory that van der Lubbe carried out the arson alone that it can for practical purposes be ignored. It rests almost solely on the inconsistent assertions of van der Lubbe made at a time when his mental condition was, to say the least of it, of doubtful quality.

The unchallengeable assumption that van der Lubbe had accomplices gave rise to a theory finding acceptance in certain quarters that van der Lubbe was ignorant of their presence and identity.

This theory is contradicted by the bulk of the facts and probabilities. In the first place its accuracy is absolutely dependent upon the accuracy of the description painted in the indictment of the means by which van der Lubbe obtained access to the Reichstag. How doubtful is the truth of his alleged climb up the façade of the Reichstag is demonstrated by the fact that the firemen, men of normal eyesight and considerable experience, had to obtain a ladder to mount on to the balcony, so slippery had the walls been made by the frozen snow: while van der Lubbe left not a mark, not a trace behind him. Nor was the climb ever repeated, even during the reconstruction, to show how it could have taken place unobserved. The contradictions in the evidence of the two eye-witnesses who alleged seeing one or two men on the balcony have been mentioned earlier. More significant is the fact that van der Lubbe, who was wearing shoes sadly worn and out at the toes, was apparently able to batter in a thick glass pane and enter the restaurant without cut or scratch. It was never established by expert evidence, an easy matter if it were true, that the pane had actually been smashed by physical force or by blows with an instrument, or whether it was smashed from without or within.

If it is doubtful whether van der Lubbe made his entrance into the Reichstag in this manner, an abundance of evidence from within the building points against the suggestion that van der Lubbe did not know he had accomplices. Inflammable materials were found, a torch, papers and traces of petrol, in the corridors outside the Sessions Chamber. These must have been employed by the 'other' incendiaries who therefore did not confine their work to the very interior of the building. During the course of his wanderings, indicated by positive clues, the presence of his clothes in various places and the like, van der Lubbe must have come across any other persons engaged in setting fire to the building.

In conclusion, the theory that van der Lubbe acted alone, or that he did not know he had accomplices cannot be supported by the facts or by the testimony, even of van der Lubbe himself. It is extremely unlikely that he gained access to the Reichstag in the manner suggested in the indictment and accepted by the Court, or that he executed the fire in the manner described in the circumstantial account furnished from some unknown and mysterious source in the indictment.

In fact van der Lubbe's presence in the Reichstag and his activities there can be more easily explained, having regard to the facts brought out in Court, by his having been brought by some other devious means into the building and left there to be found by the police when the others had done their work and made their escape. To this assumption van der Lubbe's physical disability, his ignorance of the interior of the building, and his unscorched, unscathed condition lend an almost irresistible weight. Nor is it contradicted by any of the proved facts.

To the question of the identity of the persons who accompanied van der Lubbe a subsequent chapter is devoted.

X

TWO MINISTERS OF THE REICH

GERMAN law provides a procedure whereby persons who have been accused of having committed crimes or against whom allegations of criminal activity have been made may institute criminal proceedings against themselves in order to obtain a judicial decision of their innocence. This procedure is well known and is used not rarely. The Supreme Court seems, however, to have used the Reichstag fire trial as an opportunity whereby it could invite all and sundry before it to speak themselves free of any accusations and join to their testimony abuse and even threats against the prisoners under trial. It was in this situation that the two Ministers of the Reich, Göring and Goebbels, were summoned as witnesses before the Supreme Court on November 4th and 8th, 1933, respectively.

On November 4th, 1933, the stage in the Budget Committee Room in Berlin was set as for a gala day. The police patrols in the neighbourhood were strengthened. The Reichstag was packed with police. The ordinary cards of admission for the trial had been cancelled, whosoever desired to hear Reichsminister Göring testify had to provide himself with a special ticket. Members of the Diplomatic Corps were present in Court, other Ministers, Secretaries of State and high officials of the Reich were present. The audience and the world outside were anticipating with curiosity what statements the General would make in reply to the allegations and accusations which were so widely entertained against him; they were eagerly awaiting the combat which must ensue between the irrepressible and dauntless Dimitrov and the irascible, bombastic Minister. When Göring entered the Court with a train of followers Dimitrov was in the course of making an application for the admission of certain evidence. The President interrupted Dimitrov, bade him be silent and proceeded forthwith with some words of introduction to give the freedom of the

177

Court to the General, who aping his leader had for once abandoned his more magnificent uniforms for the simple garb of an S.A. man.

The exact purpose for Göring's appearance in the trial was doubtful, for whereas the Minister himself declared that he came as an ordinary witness of the crime itself and that he would not bother to deal with the allegations made against him by propagandists, the Court itself seems to have taken quite a contrary view. The President introduced Göring's harangue with the following remarks:

> "Herr Prime Minister, in naming you and Herr Reichsminister Dr. Goebbels as witnesses whom he desired to summon before the Court, the Public Prosecutor stated that you could not be deprived of the right to express yourselves under oath concerning accusations and slanders which have been directed against your Excellencies from certain quarters, particularly in the so-called Brown Book, regarding the subject matter of this trial. The Supreme Court desires to express its concurrence in this statement."

In introducing Göring's 'testimony' in this manner the Court omitted to carry out the formalities which prescribe that before a witness is called upon to testify, he shall be told of the subject of the charges under trial and of the persons of the accused. This fact, together with the President's intimation of the purpose of Göring's appearance, indicates that he was not summoned as a witness to testify as to the fire itself, although Göring took care to point out at the commencement of his statement that he was definitely not there to deal with the slanders made against him. How consistent he was with this avowal was soon revealed.

The attitude of the Court towards the all-powerful Minister was not merely displayed in the manner in which the President, presumably with a view to humouring him, characterised the accusations against Göring as 'slanders' before he had opened his mouth to refute them. Throughout Göring's presence in Court the President and his colleagues demonstrated their subservience and exerted themselves to remove any suspicions as to their independence and impartiality which might hitherto have been entertained. In violence to the rules of procedure Göring was permitted to give his testimony in the form of a lengthy peroration, rambling and confused in nature, a mixture of hearsay, opinions, rumours, abuse, accusations, presumptions and personal knowledge—a form which pre-

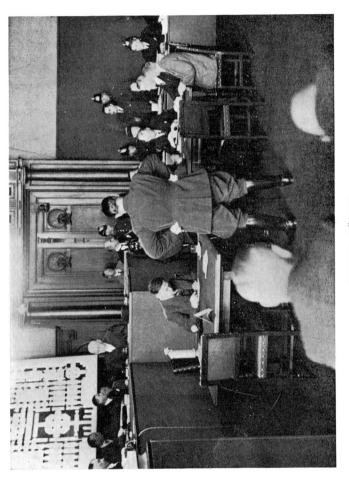

GENERAL GÖRING

To Dimitrov:—" I am not afraid of you, you crook! You belong to the gallows! Wait until I get you outside the power of this Court!"

cluded any objective valuation of his testimony and indeed rendered difficult any questioning. That it should have been possible to Dimitrov to formulate clear and specific questions to submit to Göring upon the basis of such a statement does him great credit, for many a lawyer would have been puzzled as to where to begin when confronted with 'evidence' like Göring's. The acceptance of evidence in such form was little calculated to assist the Court in the elucidation of the truth, or the conduct of the defence.

Other instances of the Court's fawning upon Göring are to be found in its apparent imperviousness to the threats which he made against Dimitrov, in his permitted abuse of their powers, by refusing to answer questions and eventually in ordering Dimitrov from the room—for the words "Out with you" can hardly be interpreted otherwise than as a command; it was certainly as such that they were regarded and obeyed. It was significant that the Court should allow a witness, however great his title, to say as Göring did:

"Although it is the task of the Court to find the culprits I must affirm that it is my task to ascertain the instigators of the whole terrible agitation. Let the trial end as it will, I will find the culprits and lead them to their punishment."

Typical of the tribunal's whole attitude to the witness was indeed the little incident which occurred in the middle of Göring's speech when the President addressed him with the following words:

"At eleven o'clock I usually have a five-minute pause. Do you mind if I make one now?"

This deserves to be remembered as perhaps the most unusual request which a Court has ever made to a witness summoned before it.

As has been remarked, Göring's statement was long and rambling, by no means easy to analyse or to comment upon. Yet it is possible to divide it into three rough sections, corresponding with the matters with which he dealt.

Despite the words with which he had commenced Göring began with a long-winded attack on the Brown Book and the findings of the Commission of Inquiry. It is not surprising in view of the Court's own treatment of the contents of the Brown Book, which will be later referred to, that Göring was permitted to give and to deny his own version of that work's contents while the substantial and undeniable allegations concerning him were ignored. Thus Göring said:

> "It is stated that I looked on while the fire was being prepared. I think it says that I was dressed in a blue silk robe, a toga. The only thing that is missing is an allegation that like Nero, I was playing the violin. . . . The Brown Book is a work of incitement and provocation which I have destroyed wherever I see it. It says that I am a complete idiot, that I have escaped from an asylum and that my skull has collapsed in several places."

One may or may not, according to one's political adherence, be amused at Göring's sallies or the picture which he endeavoured to give of himself, as his enemies see him. What is serious, however, is the fact that the General should have chosen to ignore the actual facts recorded in the Brown Book, if in truth he regarded them as slanders, that he had been adjudged unfit to have the custody of his stepson, concerning his confinement in asylums in Sweden and his morphiomania. Many of the representatives of the foreign press in Berlin on this day were hoping that the General would have some information to vouchsafe on these matters, that he would be able to contradict the statements of the Brown Book. But he saw fit to ignore them, because he could not deny them and, instead, to controvert facts which the Brown Book, at least, had never stated. He displayed just as little attention to the actual contents of the findings of the Commission of Inquiry.

Göring's next line of attack was upon the methods through which the facts recorded in the Brown Book and elucidated in the Commission of Inquiry had been obtained. After asserting that an office had been set up to organise the bribing of persons to make false statements and give untrue information he went on:

> "I know from what my confidential agents have told me that any red wastrel who is needing money can find easy well-paid work any day by writing something about imaginary atrocities or suggestions implicating me in this matter of the Reichstag fire. We know that offices were established in Germany and that recruiting officers were sent out to find persons amongst the scum of the underworld who would be willing to be trotted out prominently as credible witnesses in that grotesque affair in London concerning this case."

Had Göring even troubled to find out who were the witnesses at the London session of the Commission of Inquiry he must have found it a little difficult to describe them as the scum of the underworld. Although his political adversaries, although many of them had been forced by the policy of him and his leaders to flee abroad, accusations of bribery, lying and vileness made in these general terms can hardly be taken seriously. From this statement of Göring one suspects that he as well as some of his colleagues would like to deny that there had been a single murder, a single beating or a single act of violence committed against the political opponents of the National-Socialists or even against the most humble and unoffending folk, Christians as well as Jews. But if his statement might for some minutes have borne this interpretation, have indicated that despite the admitted excesses of the Storm Troopers, the atrocity stories were all so much baseless propaganda, Göring soon indicated that it was not to be so construed. He spoke of the acts of violence which had preceded and accompanied the National-Socialism attainment of power.

"Amongst the terrorist activities which are described in the Brown Book are some of those which were committed by Communists in disguise. The larger part of the atrocities attributed there to National-Socialists were actually committed by Communist spies."

Until Göring made this statement to the Supreme Court the Hitler Government has always maintained that the records of atrocities collected in the Brown Book and elsewhere were so many fables, so much anti-German propaganda. The official attitude is indicated in the statements of both Hitler and Goebbels that "not a single hair of a Jew's head has been harmed." But it has taken Göring to reveal the truth. Henceforward every proved atrocity, every known murder, beating, torture and assault wherever it takes place, in the prisons, in the concentration camps, in the Brown Houses, in the secret places of the Gestapo, must be regarded as the act of Communists in disguise.

The rapidity and ease with which the Court accepted Göring's explanation of the 'atrocities' is the more extraordinary in that it directly conflicted with his allegation, made but a few minutes before, that the 'atrocities' were the products of the imaginations of the corrupted scum of the underworld.

The next main subject of Göring's peroration was the accusation made by the National-Socialist leaders and sustained by the Prosecution, that the Communist Party had prepared an armed insurrection to break out on the night of February 27th, the signal for which was to be the blazing Reichstag. He told how the Communists put in serious straits by his policy and by the growing power of the National-Socialists had to do something, that it was "now or never." In these circumstances, what could they do but make a last bold bid for power, plan an insurrection to be followed by such a terror as would extirpate their opponents. Göring described the plans which the Communists had made for this purpose, for the poisoning and murder of thousands of people and of prominent National-Socialists. He described the system of 'hostages' which was apparently to accompany the Communist terror, in just the same way as it has accompanied the Nazi terror. This opinion that "the Communists were forced to do something" together with these terroristic plans Göring produced solely from his imagination. He did not refer to one existing document, not to a single specific instruction, he quoted from no written or printed page, he produced not a letter and not a line in support of his allegations. He referred to the finds in the Karl Liebknecht House which, *were they revealed*, would suffice to convince the public. He repeated in substance the contents of the first official bulletins and the allegations made from the date of the fire onwards in the speeches and writings of National-Socialist leaders.

This would of course be a plausible theory, if it were borne out by some demonstrable facts or some authentic documents. Upon it, upon the assumption that in the sudden and immediate urgency of the Communists' position, the burning of the Reichstag was designed as a beacon to set the insurrection ablaze, the indictment was conceived. It was upon this basis too that the National-Socialist leaders, alluding to the 'finds' which supported their allegations, proceeded to the extirpation of Marxism. It is interesting to compare this attitude, supported by Göring in his evidence, with what he has to say about the Reichstag fire and the insurrection which was to follow it in *Germany Reborn*. One reads:

"I have been reproached for publishing old instructions as the Communist orders for civil war. Does anyone really think that an order is less dangerous because it was issued years before? Does anyone think that we must judge the Reichstag fire more leniently because it had already been planned by the Communists several years before?"

This is an entirely new theory and although it appears to be unsupported by evidence of any kind, has this importance, that it deftly takes away the basis for the 'fanal' theory which was built up upon the sudden emergency in which the Communists "had to do something." It also assumes that the Communist leaders were gifted with amazing foresight, if this had been the case then it must be as incredible to Göring as to anyone else that they could have set the Reichstag on fire. It is curious that in *Germany Reborn* there is no allusion to the still unpublished finds in the Karl Liebknecht House. Apparently the old story is getting a little worn and Göring is looking about for something new. If it is true that the Reichstag fire had been planned years before, then that assertion must be capable of proof, otherwise whence comes Göring's knowledge? One can, however, no more expect the production of this material than one can look forward to the publication of the finds in the Karl Liebknecht House, upon the announcement of which the National-Socialists so largely attained their political paramouncy.

Having dealt with the insurrectionary preparations of the Communists and indulged in a violent attack upon Communism and Socialism in such terms as to produce diplomatic protests to the German Government from at least two quarters, Göring went on to make his assertions directly concerning the fire. He announced that the Communist Party was responsible for the fire, that there had been a number of incendiaries and that all of these save van der Lubbe had escaped through the underground passage connecting the Reichstag with the engine house and with his, Göring's, Palace. From the pronouncement concerning the use of the underground passage the Court violently dissented in its judgment; its importance will be demonstrated later. In view of Göring's long account of the insurrectionary plans of the Communists, of the position in which they were forced to light a 'beacon' to announce the uprising, of his new assertion that these things had been planned for years and of his statement that in any case he was fully aware, again through the finds, of the Communists' intentions, it is interesting to see exactly upon what basis Göring first recognised the Reichstag fire as the work of the Communists. If the story of the plans of insurrection be true then Göring must have known of them, for the finds were reported to him two days at least before the fire, yet he took no steps to guard the Reichstag or any other public building which was to be the central point of the Communist onslaught. So much for the vigilant guardian of the safety of the Third Reich! But even more surprisingly when Göring first heard the news of the fire on the telephone "at about 9 o'clock," it "never entered my head that it had been set on fire." Not until:

"an official mentioned the word incendiarism did the curtain fall from my eyes. At that moment I knew that the Communist Party was guilty of the fire. I could only wish that the outer world had seen it just like that!"

If it was true as Göring has indicated that the Communists had planned the fire as a 'fanal' whether a month or several years beforehand, then it was extraordinary that he should not have recognised the 'fanal' when it was given: even more so, since the nature of the 'fanal' had been revealed through the discoveries which had been announced. In the absence of publication of any of this material one must therefore attribute the theory of the 'fanal,' that deft announcement to the Government of an impending insurrection, to the intuition of Göring. He may well say that "he wished the outer world had seen it just like that!"

Having explained the impending insurrection and the purpose which the Reichstag fire, according to intuition, was to serve, Göring then went on to explain, as he necessarily must, how the insurrection had been averted. He referred to the five thousand arrests on the night of the fire. The arrested men he described as Communist leaders, deliberately passing over the fact that not a single member of the Central Committee of the Communist Party and not a single district or sub-district secretary was arrested during the night of February 27th, and that very few even of the hundred odd Communist deputies fell into the hands of the police until a later date. The five thousand unhappy victims were in fact largely ordinary workers, Social-Democrats as well as Communists, who had incurred for some reason or other the enmity of the local Storm Troopers, with an upper sprinkling of pacifist, Marxist and internationalist intelligentsia. Not a single report of rising or attempted rising anywhere in Germany; despite Hitler's strange announcement to the

New Yorker Staatzeitung, not a mention of other acts of violence attempted or averted. Never before, in truth, had a threatened insurrection taken place so peacefully, never had it been defeated with so little trouble.

By now, needless to say, the Court accepted whole all of Göring's strange and even contradictory statements. Having exhausted his vocabulary and store of epithets upon the Communists, having thoroughly denounced and exposed their insurrectionary aims, he went on to extol his own virtues, to laud himself as the saviour of Germany, of Europe, from the Bolshevist menace. After having painted the fate which apparently awaited the peaceful German people in the most lurid colours, he proceeded to sing a hymn of praise to his own perspicacity, vigilance and quickness in action. "I was awake while the others slept," said Göring. If the German citizen now slumbers peacefully at nights, then he has only him to thank for it; that his womenfolk can walk abroad without fear of outrage and assault, Göring too be praised; that the water which the peaceful drink, even the very air they breathe is free from the most subtle and deadly poisons, is due to the commendable foresight of the General.

Göring declared that the Leader on the night of the fire entrusted him with the task of extirpating Marxism. He had indeed worked at the reorganisation of the police for the whole of February. Seeking as he did to find a method whereby the force of the National-Socialist Storm Troops could be used against the Government's political opponents and the working class, his most obvious course was to fill the ranks of the police with numbers of newly-appointed Storm Troopers. He not only carried out a replacement of the personnel on a large scale, but he took steps to tighten up the discipline of the whole body. In the course of his evidence he stated:

"The first thing was to bring the whole machinery of the State to grips with the enemy . . . . I had to point out that the sole responsibility for their actions lay on my shoulders. I had to make it plain to them. 'When you shoot, then I am shooting! When a man lies dead there, then I have shot him.'"

Simultaneously with this reconstruction of the police force and the new spirit which was infused into them, typified, for example, by the replacement of truncheons with revolvers on the grounds that it was undignified for Germans to use truncheons, Göring had actual preparations for his St. Bartholomew's night set afoot. Lists of names and addresses were collected. Warrants of arrest were prepared. The orders to the Storm Troops were made ready. The police were urged to be 'ruthless,' the carrying out of the more delicate tasks, like policing Communist meetings, was entrusted solely to the Storm Troops.

Then came the Reichstag fire. Göring, despite Helldorf's assertion that he acted on his own responsibility, set the Storm Troops in motion for the activity which was to secure them political hegemony in Germany. To them was the work of arrest entrusted, to their hands was most of the ill-treatment and torture wreaked on the unfortunate captives attributable. The night had come when the National-Socialists' ambitions were fulfilled. The Storm Troops became the arm of the nation, they became the warriors of the Third Reich upon whose backs the Leader and his clique climbed to power. Göring concluded his long speech with an expression of his achievements. He had, as he declared—only to contradict himself within the near future—succeeded in uprooting Marxism.

Göring had spoken for several hours. He had been alternately naive and cunning, he had mixed fact with opinion, with rumours and ravings of his wildest imagination. His statements had enlightened many of the real truth about the use of the Storm Troopers on the night of the fire, namely that they had been an instrument made ready specifically and sharpened for use in the manner in which they were actually employed. Göring's statement of his preparations, coupled with his openly avowed intention of prohibiting the Communist Party, had left many people to believe that the Reichstag fire was not unexpected for him, that it was less intuition which told him where to look for the culprits, than political expediency. The deft and thorough use of the expediency could not be passed over without raising suspicions that instead of awaiting a psychological moment for its initiation, the occasion had been carefully chosen with a view to producing measurable and immediate effects. His statements concerning Oberfohren, examined in another context, had made it quite clear that Oberfohren had been guilty of indiscretions

186

in collecting material relating to the National-Socialists, that Göring had been extremely interested in his activities; what then more likely than his having composed and distributed the Oberfohren Memorandum. Göring also revealed his responsibility for the direction and contents of the official bulletins relating to the fire and the "impending insurrection." As part of his task he had thought it necessary to give explicit instructions "upon the manner in which the eyes of the people were to be opened." There was no doubt that from the first the purpose of the press bulletins was clear in the minds of the National-Socialist leaders and that no opportunity was neglected to exploit the fire to the full against the Communists, accuracy and truth being cast aside in the process.

Dimitrov Cross Examines!

At length Göring's peroration ended. Anticipation of the coming duel between the Minister of the Reich and the leader of the Bulgarian Communists, the avowed and dauntless representative of the Communist International, grew more intense. The Court-room was silent with expectation. A few questions put apologetically by the President of the Court to Göring. Then Dimitrov rose upon his feet. All eyes were turned upon him. Revolution and reaction stood face to face embodied in the persons of their respective champions. Worker faced ex-officer. Fascism was confronted with Communism. The duel began.

"Herr Prime Minister Göring stated on February 28th that when arrested the 'Dutch Communist van der Lubbe had upon him his passport and a membership card of the Dutch Communist Party.' From whom was this information derived?"

Göring sought to avoid the question, he replied:

"The police search all common law criminals and report the result to me."

Bünger, the President, hastened to Göring's side, but Dimitrov pursued the question:

"The three officials who arrested and examined van der Lubbe all agreed that no membership card of the Communist Party was discovered on him. I should like to know where the report that such a card had been found came from?"

187

The answer was a blatant confession:

"I was told by an official. Things which were reported to me on the night of the fire, particularly those which were made in the course of explanations by officials, could not all be tested and proved. The report was made to me by a responsible official and was accepted as a fact, as it could not be immediately tested it was announced as a fact. When I issued the first report to the press on the morning after the fire the interrogation of van der Lubbe was not concluded. In any case I do not see that anyone has anything to complain about because it seems to have been proved in the trial that van der Lubbe had no such card on him"!

Thus Göring confirmed what the world, through the press, what the Brown Book and the findings of the Commission of Inquiry, had asserted, that the contents of the official press bulletins which were never officially contradicted at any time before the trial were a mass of falsehoods and inaccuracies. The kernel of the accusation against the Communists, van der Lubbe's Communist card and his alleged confession of membership of the Communist Party were thus both acknowledged falsehoods, not to mention the statements concerning Torgler the 'finds' and the rest. Göring personally saw to the issue of the first bulletin and gave directions as to "how the eyes of the world were to be opened." There is not a single statement in the first bulletin, mentioned by Göring in his reply, which can be pronounced true. But where would the National-Socialists' propaganda have been without these falsehoods? How could Marxism be successfully extirpated by telling truths about it?

Dimitrov's next question bore on the important question of van der Lubbe's movements at Henningsdorf:

"I would like to ask the Minister of the Interior what steps he took to make sure that van der Lubbe's route to Henningsdorf, his stay and his meetings with other people there were investigated by the police in order to assist them in tracking down van der Lubbe's accomplices?"

Again Göring's reply came as a confession:

"As I am not an official myself but a responsible Minister it was not important that I should trouble myself with these petty, minor matters. It was my business to point out the Party and the mentality which were responsible for the crime."

The facts indeed bear out Göring's reply. He was not interested in the real clues, they were a petty and minor matter beside the attribution of guilt to the proper 'Party responsible.' It was certainly in this sense that the contents of the bulletins were directed; to indicate the 'Party and mentality responsible.' That the bulletins had another, a more sinister purpose and that Göring was not so disinterested as he affected in the inquiries of the police and in the clues which were to be revealed was shown by his reply to a further question of Dimitrov's:

"If the police and judicial investigations were allowed to be influenced in a particular direction (by the official bulletins.—*Ed.*) then in any case they were only influenced in the proper direction."

Göring's reference to criminal mentality of the Communist Party evoked a vigorous and provocative question from Dimitrov:

"Is Herr Reichminister aware of the fact that those who possess this alleged criminal mentality are to-day controlling the destinies of a sixth part of the world, namely the Soviet Union?"

Göring appeared to lose his self-control:

"I don't care what happens in Russia. I know that the Russians pay with bills and I should prefer to know that their bills are met. I care about the Communist Party here in Germany and about Communist crooks who come here to set the Reichstag on fire."

The duel was nearing its climax. Dimitrov's voice sounded in icy clearness above the applause of the audience at Göring's outburst. He posed his next question:

"This criminal mentality rules the Soviet Union, the greatest and best land in the world. Is Herr Prime Minister aware of that?"

Göring displayed most open anger and shaking both fists shouted:

"I will tell you what the German people know. They know that you are behaving in a disgraceful fashion. They know that you are a Communist crook who came to Germany to set the Reichstag on fire. In my eyes you are nothing but a scoundrel, a crook who belongs to the gallows!"

The President intervened to point out that Dimitrov must not make propaganda and to excuse Göring's rage, whereat Dimitrov pointed out that Göring's peroration was nothing but propaganda from beginning to end, and in any case that he was not put out by Göring's rage, that on the contrary he was quite satisfied with the answers. But he knew that he would not be permitted to remain in the Court longer. His

189

few questions had already produced such an effect upon Göring and such an attitude in the Court that his continued presence was clearly an embarrassment if not a danger to them. It was thus that Dimitrov prepared a question which he knew would be his last to Göring:

"You are very afraid of my questions are you not, Herr Minister?"

Like an arrow, this question reached its mark. The oft-vaunted dignity of the Court was shattered, the limitations of its forms were thrust aside. Impartiality and objectivity were forgotten. Göring literally danced with rage. Fury had overcome him. A stream of abuse and slander issued from his lips. Threats, vilification left Dimitrov unmoved. Then came the command:

"Out with you, you crook!"

The police seized Dimitrov and led him from the Court, as he went the Court hastened to give judicial effect to the order pronounced by Göring and already executed by his minions. As Dimitrov was forced, reluctant to the door, Göring shouted after him:

"You wait till I get you out of the power of this Court!"

Thus ended the appearance of the great Göring as a witness. The newspapers the world over discussed the events of November 4th with the closest interest. Dimitrov was everywhere pronounced to be the victor. Göring was everywhere taken to task for his answers, his threats and his behaviour. The German Government had suffered a serious reverse. Even Göring's own pride was somewhat downcast. His megalomania must have suffered a little when he read the official announcement of the Wolff Telegraph Bureau issued on the following morning:

"In connection with the false and tendentious statements made in connection with the evidence of Prime Minister Göring in the Reichstag fire trial, it is officially announced that all the obligations to date of the Soviet Union in Germany have been promptly met and discharged."

The Minister of Propaganda

While the damage which Göring had done to the case of the prosecution concerning the Reichstag fire trial and the alleged insurrection was irreparable, the harm which his appearance had worked in foreign quarters was not beyond recovery. It was to this end that Goebbels appeared to testify on November 8th, 1933. His demeanour and the effect of his evidence was vastly different from that of the bombastic and conceited Prime Minister. Göring's rage was replaced by the suave tones of diplomacy, his wild outbursts with curt and sardonic answers. Goebbels made no long speech to the Court and the public but contented himself, for the most, like an ordinary witness, with replying to questions addressed to him by the Court. However remarkable the differences in tone and manner, the effect of Goebbels' speech nevertheless was not dissimilar to that of Göring's.

The first news of the Reichstag fire he took as a bad joke. A second telephone call was necessary to convince him. Although taken by complete surprise, from the first he had entertained no doubt that the fire was the work of Communists and no doubt that a Communist insurrection was to be evoked by the appearance of the fire as a beacon. He endeavoured to explain that the presence of himself, Hitler and Göring in Berlin on the night of February 27th was due to a meeting of the Cabinet in Berlin that evening. He omitted to mention that no such meeting had in fact taken place and he forgot that four days earlier, on November 4th, Göring had dated the Ministerial discussions as taking place upon February 28th and March 1st. Which of these two contradictory assertions is accurate will probably never be known, for although no Cabinet Meeting did in fact take place on the evening of February 27th, arrangements had been made for Hitler to speak at Leipzig on the evening of February 28th, and at Breslau the following day, facts which make Göring's statement of doubtful accuracy.

This did not end the contradictions between the statements of the two Ministers of the Reich. Goebbels told the Court that he and Hitler met Göring at the entrance to the Reichstag, a statement which is borne out by Hitler himself in his account of the night of the fire. Göring on the other hand did not recall this meeting, he placed his encounter with Hitler in his room (the Speaker's room) in the Reichstag. This contradiction is not so important in itself but merely as indicating the degree of accuracy which the Ministers observed in their statements. What followed is, however, of more consequence. Whereas Goebbels declared in accordance with Hitler's statement to the American press in August 1933 that:

"Upon our (Goebbels and Hitler's) arrival we were immediately informed by the Prime Minister Göring that it was a Communist outrage."

Göring, on the other hand, in describing the circumstances in which the Leader entrusted the task of 'extirpating Marxism,' said:

"The Reichschancellor had the same impression as myself. I had not even spoken so much as a word to him. But he expressed his convictions as to who was responsible for the outrage. He said: 'this is the beacon (fanal) lit by the Communists.'"

Putting aside the rival claims for the first use of the word 'fanal' in its political significance, it was obviously important to establish from whom the idea that the fire was a Communist 'beacon' first emanated. Göring attributed it to his intuition and expressed the wish that the world had seen it in the same light. Whether or not Hitler and Goebbels were favoured with the same intuition (which as will be seen also visited Helldorf) the Court did not trouble to find out. The contradictions between the Ministers were by no means negligible, but the President saw fit entirely to ignore them. Since no clarity was forthcoming it is impossible to say whether these points were passed over in the interests of truth or not. Their neglect certainly left much relating to the fire and its immediate results unexplained.

Dimitrov and Goebbels

Goebbels desired at all costs to avoid a repetition of anything approaching Göring's behaviour before the Court. He sought also a personal triumph over his rival (anent this rivalry it is interesting to note that Göring's work *Germany Reborn* nowhere mentions the name of Goebbels!). He wanted to demonstrate his superiority and thus, if possible, win back the world's Press to the side of the German Government.

To an early question relating to the murders of Erzberger and Rathenau, Goebbels replied that:

"National-Socialists had nothing to do with those murders."

This despite the fact that the crime and its authors had been incessantly lauded in the National-Socialist press and that a few days before Goebbels appearance in Court a monument dedicated to the murderers had been unveiled and a day of thanksgiving had been appointed by the Government for Rathenau's murder. The Court did not regard these as sufficient reason to challenge Goebbels' statement.

Dimitrov then asked questions relating to murders by National-Socialists. The Public Prosecutor protested against them but Goebbels anxious to demonstrate that he was not afraid of Dimitrov intervened:

"I will answer this question, not because it will have any effect upon the elucidation of the truth but in order that neither Dimitrov nor the world's press shall be able to say that in the face of his questions I remained downcast and silent. I have given reason and answer to greater men than this little Communist agitator."

This reply left Dimitrov completely unruffled:

"Are you aware, Herr Reichsminister, that your spiritual brothers, the National-Socialists in Austria and Czechoslovakia have also to work with illegal methods, with false addresses and false signatures?"

Goebbels who a moment before had pronounced so magniloquently that he would reply to questions now retorted:

"I will answer you with Schopenhauer; every man deserves to be looked at but not to be spoken to!"

Where Göring had taken refuge in anger and abuse, Goebbels covered his silence with a philosopher. He too had met his match.

He concluded his evidence with a direct appeal to the foreign press:

"Herr President, I have been at the greatest pains to contradict the accusations which are made against the German Government and the National-Socialists with minute scrupulosity. On behalf of the German Government I express regret that the lying accusations made in the Brown Book are still being circulated abroad. I ask the foreign press to report fully and faithfully the detailed account of the facts which I have given in this connection."

For the most part the foreign press was not satisfied with Goebbels' real account of the facts. His appearance before the Court was received with as little favour as his colleagues had been. In his foreword to Dr. Sack's book on the trial Professor Grimm openly expresses regrets that despite

Goebbels' appeal the results in the foreign press were and remain unfavourable. He particularly pointed at the treatment of Göring's evidence by the foreign press and complained that instead of being accepted as contradicting the accusations of the Brown Book it was largely taken as confirming them!

Typical of Goebbels' reception may be taken two extracts from the foreign press:

"His evidence did not throw much light on the subject." (*Manchester Guardian*.)

"He asked that every one of his words should be repeated in the foreign press. They were certainly interesting, considered, sometimes ironic and sometimes clever, but the Minister of Propaganda is mistaken if he imagines that he has thrown any light whatsoever on the whole trial and its subject matter." —(*Le Temps*.)

While Goebbels' evidence failed to enlighten the inquirer upon any point, that of Göring was, as has been shown, strikingly consistent with the bulk of the allegations made against the German Government in the Brown Book. He publicly avowed that the contents of the official bulletins, to that time firmly upheld, were a mass of falsehoods and that he himself was responsible for the most serious of them.

XI

"GERMAN JUSTICE"

"Remember that amongst the fallen, there numbered jurists too. . . . I am thinking of Horst Wessel and others." (Dr. Hans Frank, Reichskommissar and Minister of Justice, addressing a gathering of Judges on October 1st, 1933, in Leipzig.)

AS has been shown, the propaganda machine of Dr. Goebbels was exerted to its utmost in spreading far and wide the impartial composition of the Fourth Criminal Court of the Supreme Court, before whom the Reichstag fire trial was to be enacted. This campaign, bruiting abroad the impartiality and 'objectivity' of the judges, did not cease with the opening of the trial, nor did it fail to cross the threshold of the Court itself. Judge Bünger, the President, in declaring the trial open stressed the impartial qualities of himself and his colleagues. The Ministers of the Reich, Hitler, Goebbels, Göring and Frank raved in their speeches of the objectivity of the Court—a raving which, at least in Göring's case turned somewhat with the tardy realisation that, no thanks to the impartiality of the Court, an acquittal for the majority of the accused was unavoidable. In their final speeches, as they had done throughout their defence, the counsel representing the accused men congratulated the Court on its impartiality. The Court in its own judgment solemnly sought to set any remaining doubts at rest by proclaiming that it had heard the case impartially and with 'objectivity.'

One might not be justified in regarding these repeated protestations as issuing from a guilty conscience if a survey of the events of the trial bore out the Court's estimate of its own qualities. But the continued repetition of these self-appraisements and the manner in which the Court used them to excuse conduct little objective or impartial in appearance only lends weight to the grave conclusions which cannot but be drawn from closer examination.

The jurisprudence of civilised lands is in general agreement that certain standards are to be observed in the conduct of a criminal trial. It is difficult exhaustively to formulate these conditions, but one may briefly indicate at least the most important of them. As principles commanding common acceptance may be enumerated: the free choice of counsel; that the proceedings should be within the comprehension of the accused men; that in hearing the evidence the Court should exclude the use of any methods which are calculated to prejudice its validity, that, from the other standpoint, the witnesses should be able to testify without fear or favour; that no obstacles should be placed in the conduct of the defence; and lastly, that the Court should conduct an impartial investigation into the true facts.

To the first of these points no further allusion need be made as the subject has been dealt with in a preceding chapter.

The second proposition, that the proceedings should be within the comprehension of the accused, involves several factors; primarily, that the accused shall, as far as the proceedings are concerned, be *compos mentis*, shall be able to understand the nature and effect of the proceedings, the charge and the evidence. Secondly, that for the hearing of a grave charge, the accused shall either be or have the opportunity of being present.

The Triability of van der Lubbe

German law accords with the body of civilised law in making the trial of a person accused on a criminal charge conditional upon his ability both to comprehend the proceedings and to defend himself to the full extent of his rights.

Actually two days before the proceedings at Leipzig opened there appeared a revised edition, edited by men in the foremost ranks of their profession, of the classic German authority on criminal law and procedure, *von Löwe-Rosenburg*. The text of *von Löwe-Rosenburg* might almost have been penned to describe the apparent condition of van der Lubbe throughout the trial. The points which that authority indicates as decisive for the 'triability' of an accused are these: his ability to make comprehensible to other persons points which he desires to make during the proceedings; ability to comprehend and appreciate the nature and effect of the evidence against him;

ability to understand the charge and to make full use of the rights given to him to defend himself. That the Court should itself, at every stage of the proceedings, take cognisance of the 'triability' of the accused according to these tests is laid down in the Court's own decisions and rulings, if not dictated by the elementary canons of jurisprudence.

Any indication that van der Lubbe's condition precluded him from being tried in accordance with the law and justice should have sufficed for the Court to adjourn the proceedings in order that a thorough investigation of that accused's mental and physical condition should be undertaken. It was for the Court to take notice, unprompted, of van der Lubbe's condition and to adjourn the proceedings against him until it was satisfied upon the most detailed and precise materials, that he was capable of being tried. This course would not have involved any necessary delay in the pursuit of the charges against van der Lubbe's co-accused. The Criminal Procedure Code permits of the cases against persons charged together being separated at any time before or during the proceedings if the Court so orders. It would have been an easy matter for the Court to separate the case against van der Lubbe from that against the four accused Communists. Such a proceeding would have involved no danger of injustice, specially having regard to the different nature of the separate charges and to the nature and quality of the evidence in general.

That the Court was fully aware of the initial incompetence of the proceedings against van der Lubbe is shown by the fact that it sought protection for carrying on the proceedings against him in expert opinion. Though ostensibly designed to remove the least doubt of van der Lubbe's physical and mental normality and to quiet the rumours and accusations widely made by the world's press on the basis of the reports from Leipzig, there is little doubt that in truth the Court sought the opinions of Bonnhöfer and Schütz in order to justify the pursuit of the case against van der Lubbe. Upon the basis of these opinions formulated as has been shown on scanty material and wholly inadequate investigations, the Court pronounced van der Lubbe a completely normal man, attributed his conduct from the beginning to the end of the trial to 'simulation' and thus ended the matter. That the Court appreciated the insufficiency of the results of the medical experts' opinions, it hastened to indicate by seeking to bolster up the simulation theory with the accounts of two foreign 'experts'—one the Swede, Södermann, of elusive qualifications, the other a Dutch journalist, Lüger.

The haste with which the Court accepted the unlikely theory that van der Lubbe was wholly normal is only paralleled by the aptitude which it displayed for neglecting any further inquiry into van der Lubbe's condition, even when he spoke of the "voices in his body" or of his "fight in prison" over the frequency and amount of his meals. The facts upon which it was alleged to be based and the whole probabilities speak absolutely against the simulation theory. To the observer it was painfully obvious that van der Lubbe was abnormal; that his mind was deranged; that his physical condition was extraordinary; and that his ability to understand the proceedings or to defend himself was highly questionable, to say the least. All these things the Court chose to pass over, and to cover its attitude with the tendentious, improbable and unfounded theory of 'simulation.'

The Provision of Interpreters

As one of its grounds for excluding non-German lawyers from participation in the defence the Court relied on their alleged lack of knowledge of German. While it is important that the lawyer of an accused man should possess mastery of the tongue in which the proceedings are being conducted, it is even more essential that the utmost possible care should be taken to see that the accused himself, should he speak the language imperfectly or not at all, is made fully cognisant of the charge and the content of the evidence against him.

In the Reichstag fire case the Court did not limit itself to refusing the assistance of Bulgarian lawyers to Popov and Tanev who knew no German, a piece of strange inconsistency for the Court was prepared to admit a Dutch lawyer to assist van der Lubbe. It was not thought necessary that the evidence or other parts of the proceedings should as a whole be translated to them. That accused men, specially on a grave charge, one involving the infliction of the death penalty, should thus be cut off from the bulk of the proceedings and should be deprived of understanding evidence, even though it inculpated them personally, is a proceeding which must astonish any lawyer and amaze any thinking man. The fact that the men concerned were acquitted deepens rather than lightens the gravity of the estimate which must be formed of the Court's conduct on this score.

The Court saw that the accused men were provided with interpreters, Dutch and Bulgarian. Had they been lacking, the trial would have lacked even the outward appearances of a judicial proceeding. Indications that the Court was less interested in the purpose of the interpretation than in its appearance are not lacking. The first interpreter employed to assist van der Lubbe was a Dutch woman of integrity and ability. When she declined on the grounds of its inaccuracy to sign the translation of one of van der Lubbe's early interrogations she was dismissed and her place taken by a Dutch-speaking German. Incidentally, the fact that it was thought necessary to provide van der Lubbe with an interpreter seems to contradict the Court's acceptance of the evidence of the two detectives Heisig and Zirpins who testified as to his fluency in German and the 'flowers of speech' which he employed in expressing his ideas.

The interpreter employed to assist Popov and Tanev, as has been remarked, was officially requested to translate but little of the evidence to them. Although he was observed of his own accord to make whispered translations to them of occasional parts of the evidence, the Court did not concern itself with making the bulk of the proceedings comprehensible to them. It was openly stated by Dimitrov on several occasions when the interpreter was translating publicly at the Court's request, that he was consciously omitting some passages and misconstruing others. Far from denying these charges, in several encounters the interpreter admitted them, either changing his translation when challenged or stating that in his view the translation of several passages was unnecessary. The Court at no time indicated to the interpreter the solemn nature of his duties, nor reproved him for omission or error, conscious or otherwise.

The assumption which one can scarcely refrain from making, that the Court was interested only in the appearance and not in the object of interpretation is supported by the manner in which the non-German speaking accused were made aware of the contents of the lengthy indictment. While van der Lubbe had the document in his possession without being able to read more than half of it and without understanding it at all, Popov and Tanev had to rely upon their recollection of the hasty oral translation of the document to them. One is not therefore unjustified in concluding that to the principle that the proceedings should be made comprehensible to the accused the Court paid but lip service.

The Exclusion of Dimitrov

To a lawyer brought up in the traditions of the English Common Law it is incomprehensible that the trial of an accused man on a grave charge, more on a charge involving the death penalty, should be conducted or continued in his absence. While such a course is not unknown in other quarters of the globe, for example in British India, it is impossible in England. Obvious reasons, even apart from considerations of justice, dictate that the accused should be present at his own trial.

The unusual methods employed by the police and examining officials in the preliminary investigations, examined in detail in an earlier chapter, were little calculated to win the confidence of the accused. Much of the evidence adduced in Court against them was dependent for its veracity upon circumstances by no means unimpeachable. At a very early stage in the trial Dimitrov challenged the methods of the Examining Magistrate, and demonstrated openly in the eyes of the Court and the world that Judge Vogt had lied and had attempted to mislead the Court and the accused. The very essence of the defence was an attack on the bulk of the 'incriminating' evidence coming from the hands of the police and the other officials.

It was Dimitrov's attack on the police, an attack which as the facts showed was amply justified, which brought about his first exclusion from the Court. On October 6th, 1933, he was ordered out of the Court on the grounds that he had slandered officials. How it was possible to challenge the accuracy of evidence resting only on the statements of officials without attacking their veracity the Court did not indicate. True, Dimitrov had been a thorn in their side, true he had drawn their attention to matters which they would fain have passed over, yet to exclude him from the proceedings for attacking officials, by impugning their good faith, in a case where there was no alternative and he was demonstrably in the right was a course inconsistent both with the dignity and with the impartiality of a court of justice. To justify a ruling excluding an accused in such circumstances from his own trial upon the grounds of 'Beamtenbeleidigung'—slandering officials, is to open the door to fabricated evidence.

On October 11th, the fourteenth day of the trial, Dimitrov was excluded from the proceedings for stating that he was "not only Dimitrov, the accused, but also my own defender." His expulsion, justified in the Court's view by this statement, was continued to prevent him from being present at the reconstruction of the fire, enacted on the following night. The omissions and defects of this reconstruction have already been dealt with, it seems curious that Dimitrov should have been deprived of the opportunity of appreciating them. His first expulsion prevented him from being present during the examination of Popov, not unimportant because he had already successfully challenged the interpreter and he was the only other person present understanding both languages. The second expulsion not only excluded him from observing the reconstruction but also from hearing the evidence of Lateit, the first police official to enter the burning Reichstag; of Scranowitz, the much-suspected House Inspector; of the porter Wendt who saw the National-Socialist deputy Albrecht leave but not enter the Reichstag on the night of the fire; of the Air Ministry expert Lepsius who conducted an unusual interrogation of van der Lubbe and followed it by a tour of the Reichstag in his company; of the Fire Director Wagner and the Fire Chief Gempp, who both testified as to the alarming of the fire brigade. Much of this evidence was vitally important. Not only was Dimitrov deprived of his right to examine them on their statements, but he was prevented from hearing even what they had got to say concerning the fire.

On October 31st Lebermann, the much-convicted thief who had given evidence implicating Torgler, collapsed under examination by Dimitrov and drew from him the scathing observation that "the chain of witnesses for the prosecution against us Communist accused, which began with Nazi deputies and Nazi journalists is now completed by this thief."

On the morning of the following day the *Völkischer Beobachter* appeared with a reproach against the President and the Public Prosecutor for their toleration of Dimitrov:

"We National-Socialists hope that the Court will in future find the means to repress such filthy outbursts from a Communist criminal against a National-Socialist witness."

The proceedings of the Supreme Court opened on the morning of November 1st with the President ordering Dimitrov to be excluded for a remark which had passed unreproved but not unnoticed early in the course of the preceding day! As he went Dimitrov remarked aloud, to the anger of the President, "now the *Völkischer Beobachter* can be satisfied!"

Dimitrov was admitted to the trial on the next day but he did not long survive. Witnesses from Russia as to Popov's sojourn there in 1932 were being heard by the Court when the Public Prosecutor accused one of them, a woman called Weiss of giving evidence under a false name. She explained that Weiss was the name which she went under in Russia and refused for political reasons to give her husband's former Bulgarian name. Dimitrov intervened to explain that by Soviet law, as indeed in English law, persons can change their name at will. He accompanied his information by declaring that he was surprised that the Prosecutor should be so ignorant of questions of Soviet law. Called to order by the President, Dimitrov remarked to the Prosecutor that "he had a lot to learn!" For this the Court ordered Dimitrov to be excluded from the trial for three days. During the remainder of November 3rd, the day of his fourth expulsion, the evidence of witnesses inculpating the three Bulgarians was proceeded with.

On November 4th, the following day, the exclusion order was suspended to allow Dimitrov to be present upon Göring's appearance before the Court. It would be no exaggeration to say that the world was waiting with expectation to see the consequences of the encounter between the fearless Communist and the proud and boastful General. Dimitrov was quick to appreciate the importance of Göring's presence. His first two questions to Göring brought to light the fact that the story of van der Lubbe's being in possession of a Communist membership card was not only completely false, but also that the official statement embodying it emanated from Göring himself. Göring, in excuse, and even justification of the falsehood, stated that mistakes were bound to happen in such matters and that, in any event, no harm had been caused!

Dimitrov's next question drew from Göring the admission that the investigation and pursuit of 'minor clues' was a matter to which he paid no importance, that his interests were centred on proclaiming the guilt of the Party and of the mental outlook of Communism, to which the crime was attributable.

Upon the traces of this admission there came the encounter which led to the lodging of diplomatic protests by the Soviet and Spanish Ambassadors in Berlin, Göring lost his self-control, commenced a violent attack upon the Soviet Union and culminated by vilifying Dimitrov in the lowest terms. It was obvious that Göring's rage would prevent Dimitrov from receiving further replies to his questions, the duel between them reached its climax when, overcome with rage at Dimitrov's rapier thrusts, Göring ordered him from the Court. The last stages in this encounter which ended in torrential abuse and the Court's belated confirmation of the Minister's orders have already been described.

Some general observations as to the nature and consequences of the incidents leading to Dimitrov's exclusion from the Court are not inapposite. To expel an accused man from his own trial is a measure of such severity that it can be justified, if at all, only by the most grave misconduct or contempt. The orders of expulsion against Dimitrov, where indeed any reason was advanced for them at all, were made upon grounds of the most trivial character. This fact considered together with the result of his absences, that vital evidence was withheld from his scrutiny and attack, makes it permissible to challenge the good faith of the Court responsible for a course so prejudicial to the interests of all the accused and to justice.

Without Fear or Favour!

Reference in an earlier chapter has been made to the courage of certain witnesses who, brought from police prisons or concentration camps, nevertheless spoke the uncoloured truth even to the point of denying the accuracy of statement previously extorted from them. Again there was the journalist Oehme, who informed the Court that he had deliberately made a misstatement to the investigating officials in order to remain free to testify truly at the trial. The striking conduct of these witnesses, their courage and disregard for what might happen to them subsequently, is by no means to be attributed to the impartial attitude of the Court.

The President of the Court who had opened the proceedings by announcing that the trial would conclude with a sentence did not refrain from attempting to threaten and intimidate the accused. On the twenty-ninth day of the proceedings Dimitrov was warned by the President that "his words would be remembered and accounted for in his treatment at a future time." On the same day Torgler was told that "he would be dealt with in a different fashion." Almost at the opening of the trial the President reproached Dimitrov for his conduct during the preliminary proceedings and warned him to behave himself with propriety before the Court. Almost daily were rebukes addressed to Dimitrov for his impertinence and his 'shamefacedness.' Little wonder that Dimitrov threw back his classic answer: "I am neither a criminal, nor am I on the parade ground. I am a political prisoner and I shall defend myself as such."

The Court did not reserve to itself a monopoly of threats against the accused. Göring's harangue to the Court was a mass of threats, accusations and imprecations. The President remained silent. What was good enough for Göring was no less permitted to Heines, who commenced his evidence by informing the Court, unrebuked, that he and the Storm Troopers were dissatisfied with the conduct of the trial. Heines declared to the Court that it was untrue that Torgler, as Göring had declared, was conciliatory.

"Torgler is a cynic whom I consider fully capable of having taken part in the arson. . . . I am absolutely convinced that he did so."

The President hastened to excuse Heines, saying:

"Yes, yes, you have of course the right in your capacity of Chief of Police (in Silesia) to make such statements."

No less designed to influence the evidence given in the proceedings was the treatment meted out to those witnesses who testified for the defence. One indication, strikingly contrasting with the freedom with which police witnesses and the strange crew from the underworld were allowed to give obviously false and even contradictory evidence was found in the summary arrest for perjury of the little workman Sonke who was so frightened at being dragged into the case that he made up a story of previous acquaintanceship with Tanev to explain why Tanev was staying in his house. The story did no harm to anyone. It was irrelevant to the proceedings but as Sonke was called in support of Tanev's statements the Court treated him with the utmost rigour. The harshness of the examination of the Russian witnesses called in support of Popov's alibi furnished another example of the Court's attitude. Its demeanour in face of Göring and Goebbels, little indicative of its independence or impartiality, is discussed elsewhere.

Obstruction of the Defence

The indications previously discussed of an absence of 'objectivity,' were all of them little calculated to assist the conduct of the defence. Forcibly excluded from the Court or unable to follow the proceedings the accused Bulgarians, more even than Torgler round whose neck the defence of Dr. Sack hung like a millstone, were subjected to heavy initial disadvantages.

As the most vigorous of the defendants, whose right to defend himself was ultimately conceded by the Court, Dimitrov experienced the full weight of the President's intransigence. Far-reaching as was the virtual prohibition upon questions impugning the statements of officials, enforced by Dimitrov's exclusion for 'Beamtenbeleidigung,' its effect was exceeded by the free use which the President made of the ruling that questions proposed were irrelevant to the case. The exact manner with which this powerful judicial weapon was wielded is best seen from an example which occurred at an early stage during the trial. Five questions which Dimitrov desired to put to van der Lubbe were ruled 'irrelevant' by the President. These were:

"Has he ever in his life heard my name?"

"Why does he say merely 'yes' or 'no' now? Did he merely say 'yes' and 'no' in the preliminary investigation, or did he tell his story in his own words?"

"Has he read and signed the records of the preliminary examination?"

"Why and with whom did he commit this crime?"

"Has he spoken with anyone other than the examining officials about the three fires?"

Having regard to the charge against van der Lubbe's co-accused and the evidence called in support of it, it is indeed difficult to appreciate how exactly the President was able to justify to his colleagues and to himself the ruling that these five questions were irrelevant. This instance is merely typical, the total number of questions put by Dimitrov to such witnesses as he was permitted to examine and disallowed by the President would fill many pages.

The Court's attitude to Dimitrov in this connection reached its climax during the political stage of the trial when after a long-continued fight by Dimitrov to have his questions answered the Court took the step of forbidding Dimitrov to question the witnesses separately at all. Not only did this ruling stretch the weapon of 'irrelevance' to the furthest interpretation, but it appears to have been in clear violation of the Penal Code which gives an accused the right to formulate and submit questions to be put to each witness as he is called. That the Court should have seen fit to take this course during the political stage of the trial is not without significance in determining the exact degree of its 'objectivity.'

The part played in the proceedings by the Brown Book—the sixth accused, as it has been styled—is well known. Witnesses were specially summoned to refute statements alleged to have been contained in it. The defending counsel joined with the Court and the Prosecution in denouncing the work and its allegations. Yet despite this, despite the fact that days were filled with references to it, the Court from beginning to end denied Dimitrov the right to a copy. Examples will later be given to show exactly how the Court treated the allegations of the Brown Book, it may be that in these the explanation of its denial to Dimitrov may be found. It is in any event quite obvious that without the Brown Book in his hands Dimitrov would be seriously hampered in examining those witnesses called to refute it. It thus seems impossible to find any explanation of the Court's conduct in this point other than that such obstruction was deliberate.

A number of witnesses whose evidence was important, particularly to Torgler, had succeeded in escaping abroad in the early days of the terror. Although German law permits the taking of evidence on oath abroad for use in German courts, the Court refrained from taking any steps to obtain their testimony. Had these witnesses been accorded safe conducts they would have been willing to go to Leipzig to testify, but in the absence of these they could hardly be expected to do so. The Court refused to take any step in this direction. This attitude was further confirmed in its refusal to summon to Leipzig the two Dutch acquaintances of van der Lubbe, Albada and de Vink who had accused Heisig of falsifying their statements and both of whom had expressed their willingness to attend the trial. There were many other witnesses whom the Court either refused or neglected to summon including those whose names were proposed by Dimitrov to testify to the actual political situation in February 1933, an account of which had been given only in the statements of Göring and Goebbels.

Searching for the Truth

From the commencement of the trial the task of elucidating the truth about the Reichstag fire had been made more difficult by the political issues which were at stake. As much by this as by the doubtful course pursued by the police and investigating officials the proceedings were initially hampered. Hard as the search for truth had been made by the politicians with their 'official bulletins,' by the detectives and judge with their preliminary investigations, and by the Prosecutor with his impossibly long and misbegotten indictment, a truly impartial and objective Court would have succeeded in revealing much of what is shrouded in mystery and silence.

The methods adopted by the Court in setting about their task were scarcely calculated to evoke confidence. The scant consideration which appeared to be paid to the serious problem of van der Lubbe's condition, to making the proceedings comprehensible to the accused and to the adduction of unbiased and credible testimony, laid only too well the foundations upon which the obstruction of the defence was based. It is not surprising that this edifice was completed with methods from which it is almost impossible to deduce any conclusion short of deliberate partiality and prejudice actuating the Court. It is to the examination of this point that the remainder of this chapter will be devoted.

The Commission of Inquiry and the Court

Although the Court's own refusal to admit foreign lawyers as co-defenders in the trial and the other unsatisfactory circumstances connected with the case had, in a strong sense, brought the Commission of Inquiry on to the heads of the Court, the fact that the Court was injured in its dignity and repute in Germany, even incommoded in its work, would not serve to justify the attitude which the Court adopted in relation to the Commission's work. Had the Court, as indeed many judicial organisms similarly placed would perhaps have done, chosen to ignore the Commission's existence that might have been understood, though not excused.

But the Court chose, indeed in the circumstances it had little choice, to acknowledge the work of the Commission of Inquiry at the outset. Albeit in denouncing and traducing its members and their work, the Court recorded the fact that neither its own members nor the German Government could ignore the Commission's findings, which the world had thrown down as a challenge to 'German justice.' As the accuracy of the Commission's findings became more and more unimpeachable in the light of the proceedings at Leipzig, as their soberly recorded sentences gained daily confirmation, the more vehement grew the abuse showered upon the Commission in the Court at Leipzig.

The Court's omission to refer to the careful qualification with which the Commission's findings was prefaced and concluded may or may not have been conscious. The reproach continuously flung in the face of the Commission at Leipzig, that its materials were incomplete, does seem to indicate that the Court was not merely negligent. There could, however, be no such doubt about the Court's acceptance of Dr. Sack's statement that the findings of the Commission were valueless because they were based on two false premises; that the giving of the 'highest alarm' to the fire brigade was postponed and that the Reichstag employees had been dismissed earlier than usual on the day of the fire. Dr. Sack's statement went unchallenged and was accepted by the Court when the fact was that the Commission's findings expressly in black and white referred to both these assertions and declared that the evidence before it did not support either of them. A further example of the manner in which the Commission's work was attacked is to be found in the junior Prosecutor's assertion that in London Kühne had stated that the trams were still running when Torgler decided to stay the night of February 27th in his flat. This assertion was accepted by the Court as contradicting Torgler's evidence before it, that the trams had stopped running when he decided to stay that night with Kühne. Yet at that very moment the complete transcript of the proceedings before the Commission in London was in the hands of the Public Prosecutor. The inaccuracy of this assertion in no way invalidates a denunciation of the aptitude of the Court to make use of a document which they had themselves condemned as valueless, in an attempt to discredit one of the accused men.

The Court and the Brown Book

No different in method was the use made by the Court of the Brown Book. The Court commenced its attack on that work on the very first day of the trial. This opening was greeted by the German press as the "exposure of the Brown Book lies." The examination of the Brown Book's allegations concerning van der Lubbe's alleged stay at Sörnewitz in Saxony was begun by the President of the Court reading an extract which he alleged to be contained in it.

THE PRESIDENT'S VERSION

Page 5 of the Brown Book states:

"According to an announcement of the Saxon officials van der Lubbe is said to have spoken of the coming revolution. It is established beyond doubt that van der Lubbe stayed in Sörnewitz in June and was there looked after by the National-Socialist Sommer. Witnesses have also made sworn statements proving that van der Lubbe was an active National-Socialist. Information to this effect was furnished to the Saxon Minister but the further investigation of the matter was forbidden by the Reich Government."

THE ACTUAL BROWN BOOK

"He passed the night of June 1st-2nd at Sörnewitz where he was seen together with the local councillor and with Schumann, a market gardener. Both are National-Socialists. After the Reichstag fire Councillor Sommer reported van der Lubbe's visit to the Mayor of Brockwitz.

"These facts were recorded in a sworn statement which was sent to the Saxon Minister of the Interior, who notified the Reich Minister of the Interior, Frick, of these facts in a memorandum. They became public as the result of an interpellation by a Social-Democratic deputy in the Saxon Diet. They have not been denied by anyone."

Actual reference to the Brown Book, as the above contraposed statement indicates, shows that it nowhere alleges that van der Lubbe had spoken of the coming revolution, nor that he was active as a National-Socialist, nor that he was looked after by Sommer. Where the President obtained his extract one is at a loss to imagine. The assertion that the facts stated in the book had been embodied in a sworn statement made to the Saxon authorities and communicated by them in a memorandum to the Reich Government after the Reichstag fire had taken place was not denied, and the fact of the interpellation in the Saxon Diet was well known. The Court had to content itself with contradicting something which, for some reason or other, it chose to attribute to the Brown Book. If it had not appeared that the Court was in possession of the Brown Book and that copies were in the hands of all the counsel engaged in the case the mistake could perhaps have been attributed to a simple accident.

As it was the Court contented itself with the summoning of two witnesses, Sommer, a National-Socialist, and Keil, the Social-Democratic Mayor of Brockwitz, brought from a concentration camp, where he was doubtless confined for his part in the matter. Although Keil's broad Saxon accent made it difficult for the foreign press representatives to understand the effect of his evidence, it did appear that he was most reluctant to deny the fact that van der Lubbe, who had admittedly been in Sörnewitz at the time, had been in touch with National-Socialists there. The embarrassed Sommer denied that he had ever looked after van der Lubbe, but agreed that a Dutchman of similar appearance had stayed with him for a short time later in the summer. In view of the fact that van der Lubbe was actually in Sörnewitz on the date stated in the Brown Book, and that while the relevant documents from the Reich and Saxon Ministries of the Interior were not produced, the interpellation went unanswered it cannot be said that the Court's first day's work was particularly convincing.

The Oberfohren Memorandum

When the Court furnished Göring and Goebbels with the occasion to contradict and denounce the slanders of the 'foreign press' and the 'Judo-Marxists' it neglected the very existence of important evidence which supported the alleged slanders. This was the Oberfohren Memorandum.

While the Government's declarations as to the cause of the Reichstag fire and the guilt of their political opponents were received with a good deal of scepticism in Germany, the rest of the world received them with general disbelief. Certain German newspapers expressed doubts, which were quickly stifled by their suppression, but foreign newspapers were not slow to print the words 'provocation.' The suggestion, indeed the accusation, against the National-Socialist leaders was not slow to appear. Many indications of their own complicity in the fire had become known during March and the discoveries brought to light within Germany through various sources added weight to the accusation against the Government.

It was to a bulk of already existing material implicating the National-Socialist Party in the fire that at the end of April appeared the now celebrated Oberfohren Memorandum. Prepared by Dr. Oberfohren, the Chairman of the Parliamentary Group of the German-Nationalist Party and a close colleague of von Papen, the Memorandum contained a vivid picture of the inter-Cabinet disputes between the National-Socialist and the Nationalist Ministers both before and after the Reichstag fire. It contained detailed and graphic information concerning the *coup d'état* planned for early March by the Nationalists against their restless bed-fellows, concerning the way this plan was circumvented by Goebbels and Göring and the manner in which the Reichstag fire, planned by them for this purpose, was executed. On May 6th shortly after the existence of the Memorandum had been made known to the world, through the columns of the *Manchester Guardian*, Dr. Oberfohren 'committed suicide' in Kiel.

The Oberfohren document would have constituted valuable material for the purposes of the trial not only in the account which it gave of the actual burning of the Reichstag but also for the light which it cast upon the tense political situation of February and March 1933. The relevance of the latter to the issues of the trial emerged both from the statements made by Goebbels and Göring and from the judgment of the Court itself. It was not thought necessary to examine the authenticity of the Memorandum, despite the fact that both Göring and Goebbels attacked it, or indeed to summons any witness of non-National-Socialist views. Dimitrov's application for the summoning of von Papen, Seldte, Hugenberg and Duesterberg as witnesses was rejected. Their absence is the more significant from the fact that they were all colleagues of Oberfohren and could easily have contradicted the contents or impugned the authenticity of the Memorandum.

Actually the Court contented itself with a picture of the political situation preceding the Reichstag fire from the ingenuous Göring and the subtle Goebbels, whose combined efforts did not fail to produce something which, if not tendentious, was at the least highly coloured. As for the Oberfohren Memorandum, Goebbels' opinion of its falsity was taken for gospel, while Göring's false statement that the document was never heard of until after Oberfohren's death was accepted as true. The striking confirmation of the Memorandum's authenticity which Göring actually furnished in Court, which is later fully examined, was entirely passed over by the judges.

National-Socialist Alibis

Accused in the Brown Book of direct complicity in the Reichstag fire was the notorious National-Socialist Heines, now Police President of Breslau, formerly a Vehme murderer sentenced for the brutal killing in cold blood of a 'traitor,' a crime which he acknowledged to the Supreme Court on November 6th, 1933, as "sending a traitor to the place where all traitors belong." The accusation in the Brown Book was based upon the account given in the Oberföhren Memorandum and it was in answer to this that Heines was summoned to testify in the Reichstag fire trial. With him there came Bonn, proprietor of a hotel in Gleiwitz, Silesia, and the hotel porter, Bammert.

The President introduced the evidence of these witnesses with a statement calculated to instil confidence:

"Since this accusation emanates from a book which is a libel on Germany and on the German nation, as to which I can say, without prejudicing my impartiality, that it is completely at variance with the true facts, I have pleasure in calling upon these witnesses. . . ."

DR. GOEBBELS DICTATES

"I have given reason and answer to bigger men than this little Communist agitator!"

Although thus assured that the allegation which they were being called to contradict was false and baseless, the witnesses did not succeed too well in their allotted tasks.

The hall porter stated that Heines left the hotel in Gleiwitz at 7.30 in the morning and returned at 10 or 10.30 p.m. Heines declared that he had spoken in an election meeting in Gleiwitz at 8 p.m. that evening and produced newspapers and photographs to support his statements.

The interest of the National-Socialist Party and its leaders in air communications is well known. It is notorious that during their election campaigns the more important of its leaders were provided with private National-Socialist aeroplanes to facilitate their progress in the country. Heines is and was an important member of that Party, he was in constant touch with the National-Socialist Cabinet Ministers. Gleiwitz is three or so hours flight from Berlin. Nothing in the world could have prevented Heines from flying to Berlin in a National-Socialist 'plane in the morning for a Party Conference in Berlin and returning the same evening in time to resume his election campaign. Even excluding the possibility of an error of date on the part of the hall porter, there was nothing to stop Heines from going to Berlin in connection with the fire and returning in time to provide himself with a convenient alibi.

That this possibility did enter the mind of Heines, to say the least of it, is indicated by his own statement that he did not leave the hotel until the late afternoon. Not only was this statement at variance with the hall porter's, but also with the hotel proprietor's who declared that Heines had left the hotel at about midday! There must have been an abundance of witnesses who could have proved the truth of Heines' movements on February 27th in Gleiwitz, had he actually been there, but none of them was summoned. It would have been just as easy to bring from the hotel waiters who had served Heines with lunch or early supper, chambermaids who had tidied his bedroom and many others, but none appeared. The Court had to content itself with the three statements, all at variance, against which stood a possibility which had entered the mind of at least one of them.

Count Helldorf's Exciting Evening

If Heines' alibi was not too happily proved, the evidence adduced to contradict the allegation of the Brown Book and the Oberfohren Memorandum against Count Helldorf served to accumulate suspicion against him. Like Heines, Helldorf was notorious amongst the National-Socialist minor leaders. In the old bad days of 'Judo-Marxist' rule, Helldorf, levered into some prominence through his associations with Roehm, had led an anti-Semitic riot on the Kurfürstendamm in Berlin. He was a close friend of the medium Hannussen, who through his clairvoyance had been able to predict the Reichstag fire, but not apparently his own murder, in mysterious circumstances, which followed it. On account of suspicions entertained against Helldorf of a hand in that business he had been removed from his position in the National-Socialist hierarchy and relegated to the position of Police Chief of Potsdam.

Helldorf's evidence is best appreciated in his own words:

"I think it would be best for me to describe my movements on February 27th. Until 7 p.m. I worked in the office. I was at that time leader of the S.A. for Berlin. Sometime between 7 and 7.30 p.m. I went out to supper with the former Chief of Staff of S.A. for Berlin-Brandenburg District, Professor von Arnhim. While we were having dinner the S.A. Headquarters telephoned to say that a fire had broken out in the Reichstag. *That must have been at about* 8.30."

The President interrupted him at this point and pointed out that the Reichstag was not on fire at that time. Helldorf continued:

"Oh, well! *It must have been at about 9 p.m. then!* We were in the Klinger Restaurant. There is a fire station opposite and we had already remarked that fire engines were passing along the street outside. I then asked Professor von Arnhim to go at once to the scene of the fire and if my presence were needed, to telephone me at my flat in the Nurnburger Strasse. Myself, I went straight back to my flat and about 10 p.m. received a telephone call from Professor von Arnhim that my presence was not necessary, and that the Reichstag had been cordoned off. About one hour later, at 11 p.m., I returned to my office and held a meeting in which the Reichstag fire was discussed. Group Leader Ernst and Commander Pretzel were present. Early the following morning a large number of Communist and Social-Democratic officials were arrested on my orders."

Helldorf's two errors in the time at which he received his telephone message are quite inexplicable. He could hardly have been told upon the telephone of the Reichstag fire nearly an hour before it actually broke out. Curious, too, was Helldorf's deliberate absence from the Reichstag. One would have thought that Helldorf's place at such a moment, for he too was gifted with the same providential faculty for discerning the red hand of Communism as the Leader and his lieutenants, would have been at the Leader's side in the burning edifice. But Helldorf, if his story be true, ignobly or perhaps through cowardice stayed away and sent a subordinate. The Court made no comment upon Helldorf's curious errors about times and made, indeed, no effort to clear them up.

If the effect of Helldorf's statements so far had been dramatic, if they had given rise to spontaneous suspicions, the conclusion of his evidence furnished one of the most dramatic scenes of the whole trial. He was to be confronted with van der Lubbe in order finally to dispose of any suggestion that he had seen or met him before. One may picture the scene. Helldorf had already drawn more suspicion upon himself than he had explained away. The atmosphere was tense. The attention of everyone in the court-room was drawn upon the domineering Helldorf and the bowed inanimate van der Lubbe. The shorthand report of the proceedings runs:

President: "Accused van der Lubbe, step forward! Raise your head, Lubbe! Look at the witness in the face. Come, Lubbe, raise your head, like this! Look at the witness!"
Interpreter: "You must look at the witness."
President: "Now, come! Hold up your head!"
Dr. Seuffert: "Raise your head, Lubbe!"
Interpreter: "You must look at the witness, raise your head."
President: "Come now, hold your head up! Head up, van der Lubbe!"

Then came suddenly the parade-ground voice of Helldorf:

"Man, hold your head up, quick!"

A miracle happened. Van der Lubbe raised his head and looked with vacant expression and blinking eyes at Helldorf. Why? Had the shrill command penetrated through the mists of van der Lubbe's memory: had it cleaved the fog in his brain for one transient second? Van der Lubbe, who might have given the answer to this question, no longer lives. But the fact remains that for some reason he who had been impervious to the frequent exhortations of the President, to the urgings of his counsel and to the shouts of the Prosecutor reacted to the sudden sharp command of Helldorf's voice.

With this sudden gleam of light a rare opportunity of penetrating van der Lubbe's silence presented itself. The Court refrained from taking the situation in hand. Some searching questions might have been addressed to van der Lubbe, a few minutes only might have enabled the Court, and the world, to lay bare the heart of the mystery which enveloped him. But this moment of lucidity was allowed to pass by, other moments were to occur later during the trial, but they too were no differently treated, at no time did the Court profit from them.

Helldorf or Göring

To the three points of suspicion produced through Helldorf's appearance in Court, his mistakes as to the time of his telephone message, his deliberate absence from the Reichstag and his amazing effect on van der Lubbe, a further point came to be added fourteen days later. Göring, outlining to the Court on November 4th the steps taken by him following the Reichstag fire to suppress the armed insurrection, the imminence of which had been so suddenly revealed to him, stated:

> "I ordered Helldorf to come to me. Although he stated in his evidence that he had made the arrests entirely on his own responsibility, I must make a minor qualification. While I left him a free hand in matters of detail, I definitely instructed him immediately to use all the forces at his disposal to seize and arrest all those on whom he could lay his hands."

The conflict between Göring, whose evidence is at least clear upon this point, and Helldorf, who denied having seen Göring on the night of the fire and who asserted that he had carried out the arrests entirely on his own responsibility, is by no means elucidated by the claim which Herr Hitler himself has made to be credited with giving direct orders for the arrests. Göring's statement on the point does, however, appear more consistent, having regard to the known facts, and is probably accurate. If this be the case, the whole of Helldorf's evidence is suspect. If he did see Göring on the night of the fire and before the arrests commenced, the meeting must have taken place either in the Reichstag or the nearby Ministry of the Interior, and Helldorf's statement of his movements on the night of the fire must be a complete fabrication. In any case Helldorf's denial is directly contradictory of Göring's assertion

216

which the Court accepted. Yet Helldorf has not been charged with perjury and remains to-day in his honoured official position.

Stones Unturned

German law provides that the judgment of the Court must be based upon a complete investigation and elucidation of the whole series of events composing the deed with the consideration of which the Court is entrusted. By the written law and by the practice and decisions of the Supreme Court, that tribunal is obliged to make its own fresh investigations where those undertaken by the police and examining authorities have been inadequate, or where the materials furnished to the Court are insufficient to elucidate the whole circumstances of a matter under trial.

The defects and omissions of the police and judicial preliminary investigations in the Reichstag fire case have been dealt with at some length. Opportunities came to the Supreme Court almost daily of repairing these defects and supplying these omissions by posing questions to witnesses before the Court, which were left unasked, by summoning witnesses to the Court, who remained away, or the discovery of material which was left unsearched for.

One of the interesting points relating to the fire which was left entirely in obscurity, was the fact that whilst the fire was raging a drunken chimney-sweep was arrested near the building on account of his suspicious conduct. So seriously was his presence taken by the police in the early stages that the first statements taken from the firemen dealt almost entirely with his arrest. His existence was known to the Court, for on the sixteenth day of the trial the President commenced to read out a statement which commenced with the words: "A chimney-sweep was arrested." Here he stopped. He then read the sentence a second time in a low voice, and said: "Ah! that has nothing to do with it." Thus the shadow of the chimney-sweep passed across the trial and was gone. Similar was the transitory emergence in the proceedings of a young man, clad like the S.S., in black high-boots and a black cloak, who gave the first warning of the fire to the nearby police post in the Brandenburger Tor and then vanished. No effort was made to seek him out or to identify him. The mysterious black-cloaked young man remained undiscovered.

The allegation contained in the Brown Book that the employees of the Reichstag had been dismissed earlier than usual on the day of the fire was much discussed in Court. The chief witness relied upon to contradict it appeared himself to have left the building at the unusually early hour of 3 p.m. and thus could have had no first-hand knowledge of the facts to which he was summoned to testify. That the Brown Book's allegation had some basis in fact emerged during the evidence of the Director of the Reichstag, Herr Galle, who stated that an employee of the Reichstag had been dismissed for making a communication to that effect to the press. This admission, coupled with the departure from the building of Scranowitz, the previous witness, at the early hour of 3 p.m., seems to lend some colour to the Brown Book's allegation. The Court, however, did not see fit to summons the dismissed employee to obtain a denial from him of his former communication.

While the Court did with some reluctance summon the National-Socialist deputy Albrecht before it, it was not seen fit to require the presence of Hanfstaengl, the Party press-chief, who had been an early spectator of the fire and had been the author of the 'joke' which was played on Goebbels over the telephone. The treatment of Albrecht's evidence, which will be later dealt with, was peculiar. The Court accepted without question his extraordinary story about family papers being kept in the Reichstag—where exactly the deputy did not explain. It did not call evidence from the boarding-house where Albrecht was staying in order to test his statement of his having been roused from a sick-bed by a chambermaid. Most unusually it obtained no explanation from Albrecht as to how, when the fire was blazing, the Reichstag was beset with police and the doors were either locked or closely guarded, he had managed to enter the building without being seen.

Van der Lubbe in Spandau and Henningsdorf

Although the indictment stressed Spandau and Henningsdorf as the probable places where the link between van der Lubbe and the arson conspiracy was forged, neither the Court nor the Prosecutor seemed to regard his movements there as a matter of practical relevance. The detail with which van der Lubbe's movements had been traced from February 22nd to the morning of February 26th made it more surprising that no attempt was made by the Court to elucidate fully his movements on February 26th. It was content with knowing that van der Lubbe walked to Charlottenburg, then to Spandau, and then further out, to Henningsdorf where he passed the night. Following upon repeated applications by Dimitrov the Court eventually, on the twenty-seventh day of the proceedings, decided to cause inquiries to be set on foot with a view to summoning witnesses as to van der Lubbe's movements on February 26th. Fourteen days later the first witness, a police officer, was called to state that it was impossible to ascertain why van der Lubbe had gone to Henningsdorf and to indicate that it was now too late to search for important witnesses. One or two witnesses were then heard. The effect of their evidence was that van der Lubbe had begged food and money from them. It also emerged that he had gone to the police at Henningsdorf and had been sent by them to a night shelter where he passed the night with another man, one Waschinski.

The matter was carried further, in a dramatic manner on November 13th, a day which foreshadowed surprises. For the first time van der Lubbe seemed to have cast his cloak of apathy and indifference away from him. He held his head up. He looked about him. He returned audible answers to the President's questions. If Helldorf had unwittingly supplied one of the sensations of the trial, van der Lubbe on this occasion did so deliberately when he replied to the question of the President: "With whom were you at Spandau on February 26th?" with the answer: "With the Nazis."

It appeared that van der Lubbe had gone to Spandau in order to attend a certain meeting of Nazis and that he had spoken after the meeting to a young man about National-Socialism and its aims, and amongst other things "about the Reichstag." (*Vossiche Zeitung*, November 14th, 1933.)

Not unnaturally Dimitrov, hot on the scent, hastened to ply van der Lubbe with searching questions. It seemed that the Court was on the brink of further revelations, when the President intervened to silence Dimitrov. At this he protested: "I cannot be silent as long as this trial is the trial of van der Lubbe and his accomplices and I am supposed to be one of them!" The President again silenced him and explained that in his view, as van der Lubbe had at last broken his silence, he should be humoured and not pressed with questions. He went on to say:

"If one addresses him as you are doing the success in bringing him out will be set at naught. It is most inappropriate that you should ply him to-day with unnecessary questions."

Thus was Dimitrov silenced. Van der Lubbe must be humoured and it was inappropriate that he should be questioned. That the Court should have seen fit to refrain from making any searching inquiries of van der Lubbe on this occasion as well as to prevent Dimitrov from questioning him was the more extraordinary in that they could hardly expect van der Lubbe's abnormality not to recur. In fact within a few hours van der Lubbe had sunk back into his old condition. His mouth was again silenced.

Neither Waschinski, van der Lubbe's comrade in the night shelter, nor the young Nazi with whom he conversed at Spandau were summoned before the Court. No inquiries were made by the Court as to what steps had been undertaken to identify or discover them. In fact, the police had not searched. It is not unimportant at this juncture to mention the extreme comprehension of the police investigations upon some points. No pains had been spared to produce witnesses with whom van der Lubbe had come into contact in 'red' Neukölln on February 22nd to 25th. The police net had been cast sufficiently wide to catch the two tramps with whom van der Lubbe had discussed politics in Germany a year and more before, to find a red-haired girl who had visited the cinema at which Popov and Tanev were present on the evening of February 27th and to discover many other persons the thread of whose lives had for an instant crossed those of van der Lubbe's or the Bulgarians'. This indicates that the police had an apparatus sufficiently powerful and intricate to enable them to search for witnesses with the most minute care. Yet it was impossible for them to find Waschinski, to find the young Nazi, to find the mysterious young man who gave the alarm to the police or to trace van der Lubbe's movements during the first twelve days of his stay in Germany. Is it not reasonable to suppose that if these missing witnesses had been Communists, they would have been produced, perhaps trembling perhaps courageous before the Court, or even if they were ordinary, non-party men suspected of intercourse with Communists?

Is it not, in conclusion, possible to state that if the preliminary investigation was conducted improperly and with gross disregard for the demands of the law, of justice and of truth, the conduct of the proceedings in the Supreme Court was little better. Was that Court not tendentious to a degree verging upon a breach of its own binding regulations, and partial to an extent that it placed every conceivable obstacle in the path of the defence? How, in the light of this investigation into the cold facts, the records of the proceedings, is it possible to regard the Court as impartial, as objective? The leading Ministers of the Third Reich are united in proclaiming that 'objectivity' has no place in the new, the true 'German justice.' The decision of the Court, which will be analysed in detail in a subsequent chapter, must sweep the last illusions aside.

XII

DIMITROV'S FINAL SPEECH

Dimitrov: "By virtue of Article 258 of the Criminal Procedure Code I am entitled to speak both as defender and as accused."
President: "You have the right to the last word and you can make use of that right now."
Dimitrov: "By virtue of the Criminal Procedure Code I have the right to argue with the prosecution and then to deliver my final speech."

MY Lords, Judges, Gentlemen for the Prosecution and the Defence! At the very beginning of this trial three months ago as an accused man I addressed a letter to the President of the Court. I wrote that I regretted that my attitude in Court should lead to collisions with the judges, but I categorically refuted the suggestion which was made against me that I had misused my right to put questions and my right to make statements in order to serve propagandist ends. Because I was wrongly accused before this Court I naturally used all the means at my disposal to defend myself against false charges.

In the letter I acknowledged that several of my questions had not been as apposite from the point of view of time and formulation as I could have wished. May I explain this by referring to the fact that my knowledge of German law is but limited and further that this is the first time in my life in which I have played a part in judicial proceedings of this character. If I had enjoyed the services of a lawyer of my own choice I should doubtless have known how to avoid these misunderstandings so harmful to my own defence. Permit me to recall that all my requests for the admission as my defending counsel of MM. Detcheff, Moro-Giafferi, Campinchi, Torres, Gallagher and Lehmann were one after another rejected by the Supreme Court for various reasons. I have no personal distrust of Dr. Teichert either as a man or as a lawyer, but in the present conditions in Germany I cannot have the necessary confidence in his official defence. For this reason I am attempting to defend myself, a course in which I may have been sometimes guilty of taking steps legally inapposite.

In the interests of my defence before the Supreme Court and also, as I am convinced, in the interests of the normal course of the trial, I now apply to the Court for the last time to permit the lawyer, Marcel Willard, engaged by my sister, to undertake my defence in conjunction with Teichert. If the Court also rejects this application, then the only course remaining open for me is to defend myself as best I can alone.

.   .   .   .   .   .

Now that the Court has rejected my last application, I have decided to defend myself. I want neither the honey nor the poison of a defence which is forced upon me. During the whole course of these proceedings I have defended myself. Naturally I do not feel myself in any way bound by the speech made by Dr. Teichert in my defence. Decisive for my case is only that which I say and have said myself to the Court. I do not wish to offend my Party comrade Torgler particularly as, in my opinion, his defending counsel has already offended him enough, but as far as I am concerned I would sooner be sentenced to death by this Court though innocent, than be acquitted by the sort of defence put forward by Dr. Sack.

President (interrupting Dimitrov): "It is none of your business to make criticisms of that nature here."

I admit that my tone is hard and sharp. The struggle of my life has always been hard and sharp. My tone is frank and open. I seek to call things by their correct names. I am no lawyer appearing before this Court in the mere way of his profession. I am defending myself, an accused Communist; I am defending my political honour, my honour as a revolutionary; I am defending my Communist ideology, my ideals, the content and significance of my whole life. For these reasons every word which I say in this Court is a part of me, each phrase is the expression of my deep indignation against the unjust accusation, against the putting of this anti-Communist crime, the burning of the Reichstag, to the account of the Communists.

I have often been reproached that I do not take the highest Court in Germany seriously. That is absolutely unjustified.

It is true that the highest law for me is the programme of the Communist International; that the highest Court for me is the Control Commission of the Communist International. But to me as an accused man the Supreme Court of the Reich is something to be considered in all seriousness—not only in that its members possess high legal qualifications, but also because it is the highest legal organism of the German State, of the ruling order of society; a body which can dispose of the highest penalties. I can say with an easy conscience that everything which I have stated to this Court and everything which I have spoken to the public is the truth. I have always spoken with seriousness and from my inner convictions.

President: "I shall not permit you to indulge in Communist propaganda in this Court. You have persisted in it. If you do not refrain I shall have to prevent you from speaking."

I must deny absolutely the suggestion that I have pursued propagandist aims. It may be that my defence before this Court has had a certain propagandist effect. It is also possible that my conduct before this Court may serve as an example for other accused Communists. But those were not the aims of my defence. My aims were these: to refute the indictment and to refute the accusation that Torgler, Popov, Tanev and myself had anything to do with the Reichstag fire.

I know that no one in Bulgaria believes in our alleged complicity in the fire. I know that everywhere else abroad hardly anyone believes that we had anything to do with it. But in Germany other conditions prevail and in Germany it is not impossible that people might believe such extraordinary things. For this reason I desired to prove that the Communist Party had and has nothing whatever to do with the crime. If the question of propaganda is to be raised, then I may fairly say that many utterances made within this Court were of a propagandist character. The appearance here of Goebbels and Göring had an indirect propagandist effect favourable to Communism, but no one can reproach them on account of their conduct having produced such results.

I have not only been roundly abused by the press—something to which I am completely indifferent—but my people have also, through me, been characterised as savage and barbarous. I have been called a suspicious character from the

Balkans, and a wild Bulgarian. I cannot allow such things to pass in silence.

It is true that Bulgarian Fascism is savage and barbarous. But the working class, the peasants and the culture of Bulgaria are neither savage nor barbarous. True that the level of material well-being is not so high in the Balkans as elsewhere in Europe but it is false to say that the people of Bulgaria are politically or mentally on a lower scale than the peoples of other countries. Our political struggle, our political aspirations are no less lofty than those of other peoples. A people which lived for five hundred years under a foreign yoke without losing its language and its national character, a people of workers and peasants who have fought and are fighting Bulgarian Fascism—such a people is not savage and barbarous. Only Fascism in Bulgaria is savage and barbarous. But I ask you, Mr. President, in what country does not Fascism bear these qualities?

President (interrupting Dimitrov): "Are you attempting to refer to the situation in Germany?"

At a period of history when the 'German' Emperor Karl V vowed that he would talk German only to his horse, at a time when the nobility and intellectual circles of Germany wrote only Latin and were ashamed of their mother tongue, Saint Cyril and Saint Methodius invented and spread the use of the old Bulgarian script.

The Bulgarian people has fought obstinately and with all its strength against foreign oppression. Therefore I protest here and now against these attacks on my people. I have no cause to be ashamed of being Bulgarian, in fact I am proud to say that I am the son of the Bulgarian working people.

I must preface my discussion of the main issues with this statement. Dr. Teichert has seen fit to accuse us of being responsible for our own plight and position here. In reply I must say that much time has elapsed from March 9th, 1933, when we were arrested, to the beginning of this trial. Any suspicious circumstance could have been thoroughly investigated during that period. During the preliminary inquiries I spoke with officials, members of the investigating authority, concerning the Reichstag fire. Those officials assured me that we Bulgarians were not to be charged with complicity in that crime. We were to be charged solely in connection with our false passports, our adopted names and our incorrect addresses.

President: "This is new matter. It has not been mentioned in the proceedings hitherto and therefore you have no right to raise it at this stage."

Mr. President, during that time every circumstance could have been invesitaged in order promptly to clear us of any charge in relation to the fire. The indictment declares that "Dimitrov, Popov and Tanev have alleged that they were mere political fugitives from Bulgaria but that it must be considered as proved that they were in Germany for the purpose of illegal political activities." They are, as the indictment further declares, "emissaries of Moscow sent to Germany to prepare an armed insurrection." Page 83 of the indictment points out that "although Dimitrov declares that he was not in Berlin from the 25th to the 28th of February, this does not materially affect the position and could not free him from the charge of being implicated in the burning of the Reichstag." Complicity, continues the indictment, is proved not only by the evidence of Helmer but by other facts. . . .

President (interrupting): "You must not read the whole of the indictment here. In any case the Court is quite familiar with it."

As far as that goes, I must state that three-quarters of what the counsel for the prosecution and defence have said here was generally notorious long ago. But that fact did not prevent them from bringing it forward again. (Laughter in Court.) Helmer stated that Dimitrov and van der Lubbe were together in the Bayernhof restaurant. Now permit me to refer again to the indictment which says: "Although Dimitrov was not caught red-handed at the scene of the crime, he nevertheless took part in the preparations for the burning of the Reichstag. He went to Munich in order to supply himself with an alibi. The Communist pamphlets found in Dimitrov's possession prove that he took part in the Communist movement in Germany." That is the basis of this precipitate, this aborted indictment.

(The President here interrupted Dimitrov again and warned him not to refer disrespectfully to the indictment.)

Very well, Mr. President, I shall chose other expressions.

President: "In any case you must not use such disrespectful terms."

I shall return in another context to the methods of the prosecution and the indictment.

The direction of this trial has been determined by the theory that the burning of the Reichstag was an act of the German Communist Party, of the Communist International. This anti-Communist deed, the Reichstag fire, was truly blamed upon the Communists and declared to be the signal for an armed Communist insurrection, a beacon fire for the overthrow of the present German constitution. An anti-Communist character has been given to the whole proceedings by the use of this theory. The indictment runs: ". . . The charge rests on the basis that this criminal outrage was to be a signal, a beacon for the enemies of the State who were then to commence their attack on the German Reich, to smash the existing constitution on the orders of the Third International and to set up in its place the dictatorship of the proletariat, a Soviet State."

My Lords, this is not the first time that such an outrage has been falsely attributed to Communists. I cannot here enumerate all the instances, but I would remind you of a railway outrage committed at Juterbog in Germany some time ago by a certain mentally-deranged adventurer and agent provocateur. For weeks the newspapers declared both in Germany and abroad that the outrage had been committed by the German Communist Party, that it was a terroristic act of Communists. Then it transpired that a mentally-afflicted adventurer, Matushka, was the author of the crime. He was arrested and convicted. Let me recall yet another instance, the assassination of the French President by Gorgulov. In this case too the press of many lands proclaimed for weeks that the hand of Communism had shown itself. Gorgulov was pronounced to be a Communist and emissary of the Soviet. And what was the truth? The outrage was the work of Russian white-guardists, Gorgulov was an agent provocateur who aimed at destroying the friendly relations between France and the Soviet. I would also remind you of the outrage in Sofia cathedral. This incident was not organised by the Bulgarian Communist Party, but the Bulgarian Communist Party was persecuted on account of it. Under this false accusation two thousand Bulgarian Communists, workmen, peasants and intellectuals were murdered. That act of provocation the blowing up of Sofia cathedral was actually organised by the Bulgarian police.

President (interrupting): "That has nothing to do with this trial."

The police official Heller, spoke in his evidence of Communist propaganda for arson. I asked him whether he had ever heard of arson having been committed by capitalists in order to get insurance monies and of Communists having been blamed for them. On October 5th, 1933, the *Völkischer Beobachter* wrote that the Stettin police . . .

President: "The article in question was not referred to at any time during these proceedings."
Dimitrov attempted to continue referring to the article.
President: "Do not dare to refer here to matters which have not been previously referred to in the course of the trial."
Dimitrov: "A whole series of fires. . . ."
President again interrupts.

It was dealt with during the preliminary proceedings, because the Communists were accused of having been responsible for a whole series of fires which turned out to have been committed by the owners of the buildings themselves "in order to make employment." I should like also for a moment to refer to the question of forged documents. Numbers of such forgeries have been made use of against the working class. Their name is legion. There was for example the notorious Zinoviev letter, a letter which never emanated from Zinoviev, and which was a deliberate forgery. The English Conservative Party made effective use of the forgery against the working class. I would like to remind you also of a series of forgeries which have played a part in German politics. . . .

President: "That lies outside the scope of these proceedings."

It was alleged here that the burning of the Reichstag was to be the signal for the breaking out of an armed insurrection. Attempts were made to justify this theory after the following fashion: Göring declared before the Court that the German Communist Party was compelled to incite the masses and to undertake some violent adventure when Hitler came to power. He proclaimed, "The Communists were forced to do something, then or never!" He stated that the Communist party had for years been appealing to the masses against the National-Socialist Party and that when the latter attained power the

Communists had no alternative but to do something immediately or not at all. The Public Prosecutor attempted more clearly and ingeniously to formulate this hypothesis.

(President again interrupted Dimitrov.)

The statement which Göring as chief prosecutor made was developed by the Public Prosecutor in this Court. Dr. Werner declared "that the Communist Party had been forced into a situation in which it must either give battle or capitulate without even making preparations for a fight; that in the circumstances was its only alternative; that it had either to surrender its aims without a struggle or take a risk, dare a hazard which might alter the circumstances in its favour. It might fail, but its situation then could be no worse than having surrendered without firing a shot!" This hypothesis presented by the prosecution and laid at the door of the Communists is certainly no Communist hypothesis. It shows that the enemies of the Communist Party do not know much about Communism. He who desires to fight his enemy well, must learn to know him. Prohibition of the Party, dissolution of the mass working-class organisations, loss of legality are serious blows indeed for the revolutionary movement. In February 1933 the Communist Party was faced with the threat of suppression, the Communist press had been prohibited and the destruction of the Party as a legal organisation was momentarily expected. These things the Communist Party knew well. They were pointed out in pamphlets and newspapers. The German Communist Party was well aware of the fact that although the Communist Parties of many other lands were illegal they nevertheless continued to exist and to carry on their activities. Such is the position in Bulgaria, Poland, Italy and many other lands. From my own experience I am able to speak of the position in Bulgaria. The Communist Party there was prohibited after the insurrection of 1923, but has nevertheless continued to exist and to work. Despite great sacrifices it has in time become more powerful than in 1923 prior to its suppression.

Anyone with a critical faculty can appreciate the importance of this phenomenon. Given the necessary situation the German Communist Party can still carry out a successful revolution. The experience of the Russian Communist Party proves this. Despite its illegality and the violence of the persecution to which it was subjected, that Party won over the working class in the end and came to power at its head. The leaders of the German Communist Party could not possibly think that with the suppression of their Party all would be lost; that at any given moment the question was now or never; that the alternative was insurrection or extirpation. The leaders of the German Communist Party could not have entertained such foolish thoughts. Naturally they knew perfectly well that illegality would mean tremendous losses, that it would mean self-sacrifice and heroism, but they also knew that the revolutionary strength of the Party would increase again and that one day it would be able to accomplish its final tasks successfully. For these reasons the possibility of the Communist Party seeking to indulge in any hazards at any moment must be rigorously excluded. The Communists fortunately are not so near-sighted as their opponents; neither do they lose their heads in difficult situations.

It must be added that, like every other Communist Party, the German Communist Party is a section of the Communist International. What is the Communist International? Permit me to quote from its programme: "The Communist International, an international association of workers, is the association of the Communist Parties in individual lands; it is a united world Communist Party, the leader and organiser of the universal revolutionary movement of the proletariat, the bearer of the principles and aims of Communism. Therefore the Communist International fights to win the majority of the working class and the broad sections of the peasantry for the establishment of the world dictatorship of the proletariat, for the creation of a world union of Socialist Soviet Republics, for the complete abolition of classes and for the setting up of Socialism as the first stage towards a Communist society."

In this world Party of the Communist International, which numbers millions of members all over the world, the Communist Party of the Soviet Union is the strongest single unit. It is not a party in opposition, but the governing Party of the Soviet Union, the largest State in the world. The Communist International, the world Communist Party, judges the political situation together with the Communist Parties of all countries. The International to which all its sections are directly respon-

SAFE IN MOSCOW

Left to right:—Knorin; Molotov; Popov; Kuibischev; Tanev; Ordschonikidse; Dimitrov; Stalin; Voroschilov; Manuilski and Kaganovitch

sible is a world Party, not a mere organisation of conspirators. Such a world Party does not play with insurrection and revolution. Such a Party cannot officially say one thing to its millions of adherents and at the same time in secret do exactly the opposite. Such a Party, my dear Dr. Sack, does not go in for double book-keeping. . . .

Dr. Sack: "All right! Carry on with your Communist propaganda!"

Such a Party proceeds with all seriousness and with a full awareness of its responsibility when it approaches the millions of the proletariat and when it adopts its decisions concerning tactics and immediate tasks. It does not go in for double book-keeping. Permit me to quote from the decisions of the Twelfth Plenary Session of the Executive Committee of the Communist International, for these decisions were quoted in Court and I therefore have a right to read them out. According to these decisions the chief tasks of the German Communist Party were: "to mobilise the masses of the toilers in defence of their day to day demands, against the robber offensive of monopoly capital, against Fascism, against the emergency decrees, against nationalism and chauvinism and for the development of political and economic strikes and, by the struggle for proletarian internationalism and by demonstrations, to bring the masses to the point of a political general strike: to win over the main sections of the Social-Democratic workers by overcoming the weakness in the trade union activity of the party. The slogan which the German Communist Party must put in the forefront, against the slogan of the Fascist dictatorship, the Third Reich and the slogan of social democracy "the Weimar Republic," must be the slogan of the workers' and peasants' republic, "Soviet Germany," which in itself contains the possibility of the voluntary adherence to such Soviet Republic of Austria and other German districts."

Mass work, mass activity, mass opposition and the united front—no adventurism—these are the elements of Communist tactics.

A copy of the appeal of the Executive Committee of the Communist International was found in my possession, I take it that I may read from it. Two points in it are of particular importance. The appeal speaks of demonstrations in various countries in connection with the events in Germany. It further speaks of the tasks of the Communist Party in Germany in its fight against the National-Socialist terror and for the defence of the organisations and the press of the working class. (Dimitrov then read the appeal.)

This appeal contains no mention of any immediate struggle for power. Such a task was put forward neither by the Communist International nor by the German Communist Party. It is of course true that the appeal of the Communist International does not preclude the possibility of armed insurrection. From this the Court has falsely concluded that the question of armed insurrection was an immediate one and that, having an armed insurrection as one of its aims, the German Communist Party must necessarily have prepared for an insurrection and worked for its immediate outbreak. But that is illogical, it is untrue, to use no stronger expression. Naturally the struggle for the dictatorship of the proletariat is the task of all Communist Parties the world over. That is our principle; that our aim. But the achievement of that aim is bound up with a process and a stage of development. It does not depend exclusively upon the forces of the working class, other sections of the toilers are necessary to its accomplishment. Everyone knows that the German Communist Party was in favour of the dictatorship of the proletariat, but that is by no means a point decisive for these proceedings. The point is simply this: was an armed insurrection aimed at the seizure of power actually planned to take place on February 27th, 1933, in connection with the Reichstag fire?

What, my Lords, have been the results of the legal investigations? The legend that the Reichstag fire was a Communist act has been completely shattered. Unlike some counsel here, I shall not quote much of the evidence. To any person of normal intelligence at least this point is now made completely clear, that the Reichstag fire had nothing whatever to do with any activity of the German Communist Party, not only nothing to do with an insurrection, but nothing to do with a strike, a demonstration or anything of that nature. The legal investigations have proved this up to the hilt. The Reichstag fire was not regarded by anyone—I exclude criminals and the mentally deranged—as the signal for insurrection. No one observed any deed, act or attempt at insurrection in connection with the Reichstag fire. The very stories of such things expressly appertain to a much later date. At that moment the working class was in a state of alarm against the attacks of Fascism. The German Communist Party was seeking to organise the opposition of the masses in their own defence. But it was shown that the Reichstag fire furnished the occasion and the signal for unleashing the most terrific campaign of suppression against the German working class and its vanguard the Communist Party. It has been proved beyond refutation that the responsible members of the German Government did not in the least consider the possibility of a Communist insurrection on February 27th or 28th. Upon this point I put many questions to the witnesses who appeared here. In particular I asked Heller, the notorious Karwahne, Frey and the police officers such questions. Despite other contradictions in their evidence they were all agreed on one thing, that they neither knew nor had heard anything about a threatening Communist insurrection. That indicates that the Government had taken no measures of any kind against the possibility of such an insurrection.

The President then pointed out that the Police Chief of the Eastern Command had given such evidence.

That official said no more than this: that he was summoned to Göring who gave him verbal instructions concerning the fight against Communism, that is to say, for the suppression of Communist meetings, strikes, demonstrations, election propaganda, etc. But his evidence mentioned no measures to be taken against the threat of an imminent Communist insurrection. Yesterday Dr. Seuffert dealt in his speech with the very same point and arrived at the conclusion that no governmental authority was anticipating the outbreak of any insurrection. He referred also to the evidence of Goebbels who stated, whether truly or not is another question, that when he first heard the news of the Reichstag fire he did not believe it! To this point the Government's emergency decree issued on the morning after the fire provides further proof. Read the decree—what does it say? It announces the suspension of various articles of the constitution, particularly those guaranteeing the inviolability of the person, the freedom of organisation and the press, the immunity of domicile and so forth. That is the essence of the emergency decree, its second paragraph.

President again interrupts Dimitrov accusing him of wandering from the point.

I should like to point out that under this emergency decree not only Communist, but also Social-Democratic and Christian workmen were arrested and their organisations suppressed. I would like to stress the fact that although this decree was directed chiefly against the Communist Party, it was not directed solely against them. This law which was necessary for the proclamation of the state of emergency was directed against all the other political parties and groups. It stands in direct organic connection with the Reichstag fire.

President: "If you attack the German Government I shall deprive you of the right to address the Court."

. . . One question has not been in the least elucidated, either by the prosecution or by the defending counsel. This omission does not surprise me. For it is a question which must have given them some anxiety. I refer to the question of the political situation in Germany in February 1933—a matter which I must perforce deal with now. The political situation towards the end of February 1933 was thus, that a bitter struggle was taking place within the camp of the "National Front."

President: "You are again raising matters which I have repeatedly forbidden you to mention."

. . . I should like to remind the Court of my application that Schleicher, Brüning, von Papen, Hugenberg and Duesterberg, the Vice-Chairman of the Stahlhelm organisation should be summoned as witnesses.

President: "The Court rejected the application and you have no right to refer to it again."
Dimitrov: "I know that, and more, I know why!"
President: "It is unpleasant for me continually to have to interrupt you in your closing speech, but you must respect my directions."

. . . This struggle taking place in the camp of the "National Front" was connected with the struggle which was being waged behind the scenes amongst the leaders of German economy. On the one hand was the Krupp-Thyssen circle, which for many years past has supported the National-Socialists, on the other hand, being gradually pushed into the background were their opponents. Thyssen and Krupp designed to establish absolutism, a political dictatorship under their own personal direction; it was to this end that the crushing of the revolutionary working class was necessary. At the same time the Communist Party was striving to establish a united working-class front and so consolidate all forces in resistance to the National-Socialist attempts to destroy the working-class movement. The need for a united front was felt by many Social-Democratic workers. The meaning of the united front in February and March 1933 was the mobilisation of the working class against the principle of brutal absolutism established by the National-Socialists, it meant neither insurrection nor preparations for insurrection.

President: "You have always implied that your sole interest was the Bulgarian political situation. Your present remarks however show that you were also keenly interested in the political situation in Germany."

. . . Mr. President, you are making an accusation against me. I can only make this reply: that as a Bulgarian revolutionary I am interested in the revolutionary movement all over the world. I am, for instance, interested in the political situation in South America and, although I have never been there, I know as much about it as I do of German politics. That does not mean that when a Government building in South America is burned down I am the culprit! I am interested in German politics, but I do not intermeddle in German political affairs.

During these legal proceedings I have learned much, and thanks to my political capacity for appreciating things much has become clear to me. The political situation at that time was governed by two chief factors: the first was the effort of the National-Socialists to attain power, the second, the counter-factor, was the efforts of the German Communist Party to build up a united working-class front against Fascism. In my view, the accuracy of this has been made abundantly clear during these proceedings. The National-Socialists needed something which would both divert the attention of the people from the differences within the national front and, at the same time, break up the unity of the working-class front. The "National Government" needed a passable excuse for issuing its emergency decree of February 28th, 1933, which abolished the liberty of the press and of the individual and introduced a system of police persecution, concentration camps and other measures against the Communists.

> *President:* "Now you have reached the limit, you are making suggestions."
> *Dimitrov:* "My only desire is to explain the political situation in Germany on the eve of the fire as I understand it to have been."
> *President:* "This court is no place for unwarranted suggestions against the government and for statements long since refuted."

. . . The attitude of the working class at this time was a defensive one, the Communist Party was, therefore, doing its best to organise a united front. . . .

> *President:* "You must proceed to your own defence if you want to, otherwise you will not have sufficient time."

. . . Once before I stated that I was in accord with the indictment on one point, and now I am compelled to reaffirm my agreement. I allude to the question whether van der Lubbe acted alone in setting fire to the Reichstag or whether he had accomplices. The junior prosecuting counsel, Parisius, declared that the fate of the accused depended upon the answer to the question whether van der Lubbe had accomplices. To this I answer, no, a thousand noes! Such a conclusion is illogical and does not follow. My own deduction is that van der Lubbe did not set fire to the Reichstag alone. On the basis of the experts' opinions and the evidence which has been submitted I conclude that the fire in the Plenary Sessions Chamber was of a nature different from that in the restaurant, the ground floor, etc. The Sessions Chamber was set on fire by other persons, employing other means. Although coincident in time with the fires caused by van der Lubbe himself, the fire in the Sessions Chamber is fundamentally different. Van der Lubbe has by no means told the truth in this Court and he remains persistently silent. Although he did have accomplices, this fact does not decide the fate of the other accused. Van der Lubbe was not alone, true; but neither Dimitrov nor Torgler nor Popov nor Tanev was in his company. Is it not probable that van der Lubbe met someone in Henningsdorf on February 26th and told him of his attempts to set fire to the Town Hall and the Palace? Whereat the person in question replied that things such as those were mere child's play, that the burning down of the Reichstag during the elections would be something real? Is that not probably the manner in which through an alliance between political provocation and political insanity the Reichstag fire was conceived? While the representative of political insanity sits to-day in the dock, the representative of provocation has disappeared! Whilst this fool, van der Lubbe, was carrying out his clumsy attempts at arson in the corridors and cloak-rooms, were not other unknown persons preparing the conflagration in the Sessions Chamber and making use of that secret inflammable liquid of which Dr. Schatz here spoke?

(At this point van der Lubbe began to laugh silently. His whole body was shaken with spasms of laughter. The attention of everyone, the Court and the accused included, was directed upon him. Dimitrov resumed, pointing at van der Lubbe.)

The unknown accomplices made all the preparations for the conflagration and then disappeared, without a trace. Now this stupid tool, this miserable Faust is here in the dock, while Mephistopheles has disappeared. The link between van der Lubbe and the representatives of political provocation, the enemies of the working class, was forged in Henningsdorf.

The Public Prosecutor declared that van der Lubbe was a Communist. He went further, he asserted that even if van der Lubbe was not a Communist he carried out his deed in the interests of and in association with the Communist Party. That argument is entirely false. What is van der Lubbe? A Communist? Inconceivable! An anarchist? No! He is a declassed worker, a rebellious member of the scum of society. He is a misused creature who has been played off against the working class. No Communist, no anarchist anywhere in the world would conduct himself in Court as van der Lubbe has done. Anarchists often do senseless things, but invariably when they are haled into Court they stand up like men and explain their aims. If a Communist had done anything of this sort, he would not remain silent knowing that four innocent men stood in the dock alongside him. Van der Lubbe is no Communist. He is no anarchist; he is the misused tool of Fascism.

The Chairman of the Communist Parliamentary Group and we Bulgarians accused alongside him have nothing in common, nor any connection with this creature, this poor misused scapegoat. Permit me to remind the Court that on the morning

237

of February 28th Göring issued a statement on the fire, declaring that Torgler and Koenen had together fled from the Reichstag at 10 o'clock the previous evening. This statement was broadcast all over Germany. In the same statement Göring declared that the Communists had set the Reichstag on fire. Yet no attempt has been made to investigate van der Lubbe's movements in Henningsdorf. No search is made for the man with whom van der Lubbe passed the night there.

President: "When do you intend to conclude your speech?"
Dimitrov: "I want to speak for another half-hour. I must express my views on this question."
President: "You cannot go on for ever."

Mr. President, during the three months this trial has lasted you have silenced me on many occasions with the assurance that at the conclusion of the trial I should be able to speak fully in my defence. The trial is drawing to a close now, but contrary to your assurance you are now limiting me in my right to address the Court. The question of what happened in Henningsdorf is indeed of importance. The man with whom van der Lubbe spent the night there, Waschinski, has not been found and my suggestion that the police should search for him was rejected as useless. Had van der Lubbe met Communists in Henningsdorf the question would have been gone into long ago, Mr. President! But no one is interested in finding Waschinski. The young man who brought the first news of the fire to the police at the Brandenburger Tor has not been searched for, his identity remains unestablished, he is still unknown. The preliminary examination was conducted in a false direction. Dr. Albrecht, the National-Socialist deputy who hurried out of the Reichstag after the fire had begun was hardly interrogated. The incendiaries were sought where they were not to be found, in the ranks of the Communist Party, rather than where they would have been found. Thus the real culprits were permitted to disappear. As the real incendiaries could and durst not be found, other persons were taken in their stead.

President: "I forbid you to make such statements and I give you another ten minutes only."

I have the right to lay my own reasoned proposals for the verdict before the Court. The Public Prosecutor stated that all the evidence given by Communists was not worthy of credence. I shall not adopt the contrary view. Thus I shall not declare that all the evidence given by National-Socialist witnesses is unreliable. I shall not state that they are all liars for I believe that amongst the millions of National-Socialists there are some honest people.

President: "I forbid you to make such ill-intentioned remarks."

. . . But is it not remarkable that all the chief witnesses called in support of the prosecution are National-Socialist deputies, journalists or hangers-on? Karwahne declares that he saw Torgler with van der Lubbe in the Reichstag! Frey declares that he saw Popov with van der Lubbe in the Reichstag. Helmer declares that he saw Dimitrov with van der Lubbe! Weberstedt asserts that he saw Tanev with van der Lubbe! All National-Socialists! Is this a mere accident? The witness, Dr. Dröscher, known under the name of Zimmermann to contribute to the National-Socialist *Völkisher Beobachter*, declares in Court that Dimitrov was responsible for the Sofia cathedral outrage, which was completely disproved, and alleges that he has seen me with Torgler in the Reichstag.

Heller, the police official, read in Court a Communist poem out of a book published in 1925 to prove that the Communists set the Reichstag on fire in 1933. Permit me also the pleasure of quoting a poem, a poem by the greatest German poet, Goethe:

> "Lerne zeitig klüger sein.
> Auf des Glückes grosser Wage
> Steht die Zunge selten ein;
> Du musst steigen oder sinken,
> Du musst herrschen und Gewinnen
> Oder dienen und verkieren,
> Leiden oder triumphieren,
> Amboss oder Hammer sein."

Victory or defeat! Be hammer or anvil! The German working class did not realise the truth of this either in 1918, or in 1923 or in 1933. . . .

Much has been said here about German law and I should like to express my views on the matter. Undoubtedly the political constellation ascendant at any particular moment affects the decisions of a Court of law. Let me refer to an authority whom this Court will doubtless accept, the Minister of Justice Kerrl. This gentleman has expressed his views in an interview on the subject of Prussian justice published in the press. He refers to the liberal prejudice that objectivity should be the fount of justice. "Objectivity," he declares, "has no worth in the struggle of a people for existence. It is a dead principle which must be abandoned once and for all. There must be only one judicial criterion: that which will nourish the nation, that which will succour the people!" Justice is a relative conception.

President: "Doubtless! But you must now bring forward your final proposals."

The Public Prosecutor has proposed that the Bulgarian accused should be acquitted for lack of proof. I dissent from that proposal. It is not enough; it would not completely clear us from suspicion. The truth is that this trial has proved absolutely conclusively that we had nothing whatsoever to do with the fire and that there is not the slightest ground to entertain further suspicions against us. We Bulgarians, and Torgler too, must all be acquitted, not for lack of proof, but because we, as Communists, neither have nor could have anything to do with an anti-Communist deed.

I therefore propose the following verdict:

1. That Torgler, Popov, Tanev and myself be pronounced innocent and that the indictment be quashed as ill-founded;

2. That van der Lubbe should be declared to be the misused tool of the enemies of the working class;

3. That those responsible for the false charges against us should be made criminally liable for them;

4. That we should be compensated for the losses which we have sustained through this trial, for our wasted time, our damaged health and for the sufferings which we have undergone.

A time will come when these accounts will have to be settled, with interest! The elucidation of the Reichstag fire and the identification of the real incendiaries is a task which will fall to the people's Court of the future proletarian dictatorship.

When Galileo was condemned he declared:

"e pur si muove!"

No less determined than old Galileo we Communists declare to-day: "E pur si muove!" The wheel of history moves slowly on towards the ultimate, inevitable, irrepressible goal of Communism. . . .

(The Court forbade Dimitrov to speak further.)

XIII

THE LEIPZIG JUDGMENT

THE interest of the world in the proceedings at Leipzig grew from day to day. As the weeks dragged by the comments and tone of the world's press grew in sympathy towards the four accused Communists and in adversity to the German Government. The speeches of the counsel and accused ended on December 16th. The Court adjourned for a week. During this week a bitter struggle took place within the Reich Government, but the anti-fascist movement without Germany doubled, nay trebled, its forces and efforts to show that the world would never accept a verdict of guilty against Torgler, Dimitrov, Popov and Tanev. Gigantic meetings of protest were held all over the world. The German Embassies were again besieged by deputations and demonstrations. To the Supreme Court itself, to the German Government and its responsible Ministers there came thousand upon thousand of letters, telegrams and resolutions all protesting against any conviction and urging the acquittal and liberation of the four Communists. The foremost names in art, science and literature the world over were joined in aiding to thwart the designs of the German Government and the prosecution in Leipzig.

The warning of Heines, the Vehme murderer, given in the Court:

"I am here as the representative of the S.A. and as such I will say that we S.A. men cannot understand why the accused men are being treated so leniently."

was well within the world's memory, as were the menaces of Göring and his concluding threat:

"Whatever the verdict of this Court, I shall know how to deal with the guilty."

That Göring had by no means retracted his fulminations was

242

made clear by his public statement made on December 12th, 1933:

> "I hope that the Leipzig trial which has greatly disappointed the German people will soon come to an end. It has shown that it is impossible to adhere to abstract paragraphs when an infamous political crime is to be adjudged, such a course leads to an impossible position. . . . The attack on the Reichstag . . . was a political attack upon the German people to bring about a Bolshevist Revolution. For that the accused are responsible. . . . It is deplorable that nine months after the deed this crime is still not expiated and that this long-winded trial is still going on."

This statement was widely interpreted as a flagrant attempt to influence the decision of the Court.

It was in these circumstances that the date for the verdict approached. Although the Public Prosecutor had seen fit to drop his demands for the death sentence against the Bulgarians, this by no means precluded the Court from passing sentence upon them. The bitter struggle between the individual Members of the Cabinet, the open attempts by one side to influence the Court, the conditions in which the Public Prosecutor had formulated his demands, all these things conspired to perpetuate the atmosphere of uncertainty with which the verdict was surrounded.

Two days after the close of the speeches at Leipzig the Commission of Inquiry met for its second full session in London. Since the publication of its first findings and their confirmation, almost to the letter, in the proceedings at Leipzig, the weight of the Commission's authority had vastly grown; its concluding deliberations were followed with attention in the press of the world.

In its final session the Commission occupied itself with two matters of paramount importance, the case against Torgler and the fate of van der Lubbe. Upon a comprehensive review of the whole proceedings of the Supreme Court, the Commission confirmed its previous findings. It then examined in detail the case against the accused men, particularly against Torgler, and came to the conclusion that the charges against them as laid in the indictment and as supported in the Court could not be sustained. In connection with the fate of van der Lubbe the Commission considered the position in German law which had been created by the passing by a subservient Reichstag on March 23rd, 1933 of the so-called Lex Lubbe, which imposed a retrospective death penalty upon high treason and arson committed from political motives. Article 2 of the German Penal Code which is still in force provides that:

"Acts are only punishable when committed contrary to an existing law making them punishable. Should a law in force at the time the act was committed make different provision for punishment of the offence than the law in force at the time when sentence is passed upon the act, then the more lenient penalty is to be imposed."

The Commission had therefore to resolve the apparent contradiction between the effect of the Lex Lubbe on the one hand and the unambiguous provision of the Penal Code, on the other. The foremost consideration in this connection was that the principle *nulla poena sine lege*, is not only an elementary principle of the jurisprudence of all civilised nations ranging from France to Liberia, and all codes of justice, written and unwritten, but also that, expressly embodied in Article 2, it forms one of the fundamental principles of German criminal law. The application of the ordinary canons of interpretation to the apparent antithesis produced the result, that the Lex Lubbe should be regarded only as amending and supplementing the Criminal Code, not as repealing its provisions, and that despite the terms of the later enactment the provisions of Article 2 of the Code probably remained effective.

The Commission accordingly embodied the results of its considerations in the following final conclusion:

"That the retrospective application of the penal law of March 29th imposing the death sentence in cases of arson or high treason would constitute a monstrous violation of one of the principles of justice most universally recognised among all civilised nations.

"That the conviction of the accused Torgler, the accusation having been withdrawn against the three accused Bulgarians, will doubtless and rightly give rise to universal protest.

"That bound by its terms of legal reference the Legal Commission is not in a position to give expression to that protest in this report,

"BUT that it considers it its duty to proclaim that in these circumstances the sentencing to death of Torgler would constitute a judicial murder."

The final conclusions of the Commission of Inquiry found as wide publicity throughout the world's press as had its first findings, no less because they reflected the opinions which the world itself had entertained and expressed with increasing force.

December 23rd, 1933

The environs of the Supreme Court building presented the same picture two days before Christmas as they had done on September 21st, three months before. The streets and open spaces near the Supreme Court were heavily picketed with police. The interior of the building swarmed with their uniforms.

For the last time the accused were led into the Court. They were marshalled in the same order as on the opening day of the trial, van der Lubbe at the front, his expression vacant, his face blank; Dimitrov and his colleagues pale but composed; Torgler anxious yet determined. Their entrance was followed by the appearance of the same nine red robes and the array of arms raised in the Hitler salute. The President's voice rang through the silent Court-room:

"Let the accused stand up!
"In the name of the Reich I pronounce the following verdict.
"The accused Torgler, Dimitrov, Popov and Tanev are acquitted.
"The accused van der Lubbe is found guilty of high treason, insurrectionary arson and attempted common arson. He is sentenced to death and to the perpetual loss of civil rights.
"The costs of the trial will fall, according to the verdict upon the convicted man, the remainder will be borne by the Treasury of the Reich.
"In the name of the law."

Hardly were the words of the President concluded than the wires were humming with the news of the acquittals. The tape machines in all the cities of the world ran out the information. Within a half-hour special editions of the newspapers were being sold on the streets of the capitals of Europe. Posters proclaimed to the world the acquittal of the four Communists, newsvendors shouted them to the winds. The world echoed with the names of the innocent men. There was jubilation at the victory of the anti-fascist armies, a note of triumph at the reverse suffered by the present rulers of Germany.

There remained only the reading of the grounds of the Supreme Court's verdict. The Court's reasoning was the inevitable outcome of a trial prepared and conducted with the methods which have been fully discussed above. Forced by the pressure of world opinion to pronounce the acquittal of the four innocent Communists, the Court was nevertheless bound not to speak them free of guilt. It had been made clear to the judges by the Ministers of the Reich what task was entrusted to them; the statements of Goebbels and Göring had indicated precisely the political issue upon which the Court was to pass and the form in which its conclusions were to be embodied. It is in the light of these matters that the grounds furnished by the Court for its verdict have to be considered.

The Brown Book and the Commission of Inquiry

The first of the four sections into which the Court's judgment falls dealt with the 'lies' and 'slanders' concerning the Reichstag fire published abroad. Without entering into a detailed consideration of these allegations the President expressed the opinion of the Court that they were "absolutely contradicted" in precisely the same terms as those with which he introduced the evidence of Göring and Goebbels. Amongst these matters he gave some instances of what had been contradicted; the allegation that van der Lubbe met National-Socialists at Sörnewitz or Henningsdorf; the suggestion that van der Lubbe's passport had been forged by German officials, which incidentally emanated from the Ministry of Propaganda and was neither made in the Brown Book nor in the Commission of Inquiry; the accusation that leading members of the Government, German statesmen, had been implicated in the burning of the Reichstag; the statements that the incendiaries had made use of the underground passage, which Göring himself had never ceased to repeat, even before the Court itself; that Göring's bodyguard had access to the Reichstag President's Palace, in connection with which the President must have forgotten the evidence of the head of the bodyguard S.S. man Weber; that the work of the fire brigade had been impeded. All these points are discussed in detail in a following chapter. It therefore suffices at present to say that the Court was easily satisfied on each one of them, for the real outcome of the proceedings, as will be shown, was to bring to light an abundance of evidence in support of the majority of the instances which the President referred to as amply contradicted.

The first part of the Court's judgment thus furnished the fiat for the refutations made by Goebbels and Göring of the allegations in the Brown Book and the findings of the Commission of Inquiry—the bulk of which were actually confirmed by the evidence before the Court.

Van der Lubbe

The second part of the judgment dealt with the accused van der Lubbe. At the outset one may remark that it is indeed extraordinary that the Court did not trouble to deal in its judgment with van der Lubbe's mental and bodily condition during the proceedings. The Criminal Procedure Code in so many words imposes upon the Court an obligation to discuss the question of 'triability' in its judgment and fully to set forth its conclusions upon that issue whenever any point involving the 'triability' of the accused has been raised or has arisen during the proceedings. At the outset of the trial the Supreme Court had gone to the length of summoning witnesses, including two medical experts, to testify as to van der Lubbe's mental and physical condition. These witnesses had reappeared towards the end of the proceedings for the same purpose. Their evidence was, of course, solely directed at the issue of van der Lubbe's 'triability,' doubts of which had been widely expressed within and without the Court-room. Despite this and despite the clear obligation imposed upon the Court by the law, the judgment entirely neglected the question. Nowhere were the grounds stated upon which the Court decided that van der Lubbe was 'triable,' that he fully understood the nature and effect of the proceedings and was fully capable of exercising all the rights accorded to him for his defence. That the Court should deliberately choose to ignore one of the points which played so large and important a part in the whole proceedings is explicable only on one assumption.

The Court's failure to express its decisions concerning van der Lubbe's physical and mental condition necessarily went a long way towards vitiating the conclusions which it did express concerning him. For example, the acceptance accorded in the judgment to van der Lubbe's account of the manner in which he set fire to the Reichstag is worthless without an examination of the circumstances in which that account, contained in the indictment and adopted by nods and murmurs from van der Lubbe at the trial, was obtained from him. The Court did not see fit to enter into any discussion of this point although it was confronted with conflicting statements about the lucidity of van der Lubbe's accounts of his movements.

The views of the fire experts that van der Lubbe did not set fire to the Reichstag alone are, as they necessarily must be, accepted. The Court accepts the view that van der Lubbe had accomplices, but the judgment in no way examines the question as to how these accomplices obtained access to or departed from the Reichstag. That the Court was not oblivious to the thorny problem which confronted it once the theory of accomplices was accepted is apparent from the probability expressed that the stranger whom Boghun saw emerging from the Reichstag must have been one of the accomplices. What happened to the others the Court does not indicate, it must deliberately have turned a blind eye to the matter. The existence of accomplices necessarily involves the whole question of ways and means of access and escape, the transport of the incendiary material, the short period of time available for the preparation of the fire, and the knowledge of the precise movements of the Reichstag employees; with none of these matters the Court saw fit to occupy itself. That in the absence of such considerations it adopted the view that van der Lubbe had accomplices and then, in a later part of the judgment as will be shortly shown, went on to indicate where those accomplices were to be found, makes this part of its judgment unworthy of the least consideration.

Not Innocent—Not Proved Guilty

The third part of the Court's judgment may be treated with the contempt it deserves. Forced after the manner in which it had conducted the trial, after its threats, its hindrances and obstruction of the defence, in the face of its serious infractions of its own binding rules and regulations, to acquit the four Communists because the world would not have tolerated a conviction, so demonstrably clear and unchallengeable was their innocence, the Court sought to leaven the bitter bread of defeat. The assumption, drawn unavoidably after an exhaustive discussion of its methods, that the Court desired to furnish a precedent for the "German justice" of the Third

Reich in the conviction of the innocent accused is fully borne out by the terms and methods employed in grounding its grudging acquittal. Every sentence in this part of the judgment teems with suggestions, every phrase is tendentious. Consider these few examples:

"The Court holds that the grounds of suspicion *so far brought forward* or pressed against Torgler are either not proved *or else inconclusive*."

"The fact that Torgler left the Reichstag with Koenen is *suspicious but not conclusive*."

"It has not been established that Dimitrov visited the Reichstag but *it remains unexplained why* he had made crosses against the Palace and the Reichstag on the map of Berlin which was found in his possession."

"*There remain suspicions* against him (Dimitrov) that he was occupied with the affairs of the German Communist Party."

"*There are suspicions* that he (Popov) occupied himself with matters other than the welfare of the Bulgarian emigrés."

"*Absolute proof* that Popov was seen with van der Lubbe was not forthcoming."

"The Court orders the acquittal of the four remaining accused on the grounds that the offence charged is *not proved* against them."

In this language the Court expressed its reasons for the acquittal of the four innocent Communists.

It dealt more kindly with the National-Socialist witnesses for the prosecution. Of the star witness against the Bulgarians, Helmer, it said little. But it administered a compliment to the three witnesses against Torgler, the notorious Karwahne, Kroyer and Frey. Whilst indicating that their identifications of van der Lubbe and Popov were lacking in reasonable or convincing grounds, the Court hastened to point out that this by no means reflected on the veracity, integrity or the honour of these three. Their part in the case was, declared the President, due to righteous indignation, that notorious seducer of the recollection!

In rejecting the evidence of the three witnesses Lebermann, Kunzack and Grothe, concerning whose antecedents and sanity Dimitrov had expressed himself in scathing terms, the Court displayed its disgust at the manner in which the police and investigating officials had failed in their duty. Upon this point, as upon the question of identification, the President laid down a series of observations, intended without doubt to guide the future conduct of such cases. Latent in the President's words can be descried the message— "You have let us down badly, don't do it again!" One may anticipate that with this object lesson the officials will be a little more careful in the future.

The Reichstag Fire—A Communist Signal

The fourth and concluding part of the Court's judgment is occupied with the anticipated proof that, as the German Government had so convincingly stated, the Reichstag fire was the work of Communists, that it was the signal for an armed insurrection, and that the National-Socialists were in fact and in law what they had proclaimed themselves to be, the saviours of Germany from Bolshevist chaos. At first blush it is apparent how closely this thesis corresponds with the attitude exploited by Herr Hitler and his colleagues in their speeches from the night of the fire onwards. These statements were always based upon the alleged discoveries in Karl Liebknecht House but since not a shred of this material was produced or even referred to before the Court, different reasons had to be found to support it.

The fourth part of the judgment is important, therefore, not only because on the basis of it van der Lubbe was sentenced to death on account of high treason and insurrectionary arson, but also in the justification, which it somewhat belatedly furnishes, for the acts and speeches of the National-Socialist leaders and for the Hitler terror. Supported by the terms of this judgment the rulers of Germany have altered the grounds of their self-appreciation. The judgment states:

> "It is established that van der Lubbe's accomplices are to be found in the Communist Party of Germany, that Communism is equally guilty of the Reichstag fire, that the German people stood in the early part of the year 1933 on the brink of chaos into which the Communists sought to lead them, and that the German people were saved at the last moment by men of reliability."

In order to sentence van der Lubbe to death the Court proved his connection with the Communists in two ways; firstly in assuming that, as the Reichstag fire was an act of the Communists destined as a 'beacon' to their supporters, it could only have been carried out by a Communist; secondly in declaring that:

> "The assertion that van der Lubbe's accomplices are to be found in the ranks of the Communist Party of Germany is reinforced by the fact that van der Lubbe is himself a Communist. This has hardly been contested."

A glance will show that these two lines of reasoning are mutually exclusive. It is impossible to prove anything with logical force by stating firstly, that van der Lubbe was a Communist because his deed was a Communist action and secondly, that van der Lubbe's deed was a Communist action (that is, his accomplices were Communists) because he is a Communist. The Court does not appear to have seen the illogicality of this process.

The grounds upon which the Court could pronounce van der Lubbe a Communist were scanty indeed. It was, of course, true that he had once been a member of the Dutch Communist Party; it was true that he adhered to the "International Communist" Group, with its score or so of members throughout the world. Yet it was never stated to the Court that van der Lubbe was still a Communist in 1933. Indeed, even with their willingness to supply evidence, the two detectives Heisig and Zirpins could rely upon nothing more concrete than their 'impressions.' These facts the Court suppressed, and by elevating van der Lubbe's "International Communist" Group into the level of a political party, identical in some way with the Communist International and its affiliated parties, grounded the reasoning that van der Lubbe was a Communist.

As far as the assertion that his accomplices were to be found in the ranks of the Communist Party went, the Court did not trouble itself to name or indicate a single Communist to whom the crime was attributable—not even the 'suspicious' Koenen. It did not occupy itself with the troublesome question of the means by which the accomplices had entered and left the Reichstag unobserved, a matter absolutely fundamental to the assumption that van der Lubbe had accomplices. It was, in fact satisfied to base its indication of the party adherence of van der Lubbe's accomplices solely upon the thesis that the fire was an act of Communism and a signal for a Communist armed insurrection.

The grounds furnished in the judgment for the last mentioned thesis are truly extraordinary. They commence:

"Since the accused maintain that the Communist Party rejects the methods of individual terrorism, it is necessary to declare that the burning of the Reichstag was not an act of individual terror, but an act of mass terror which was to be the occasion for a general strike leading to insurrection."

Thus has judicial sanction been given to a new theory of political science conceived by the National-Socialist leaders, the 'fanal,' the beacon theory! That there can be found persons sufficiently ingenuous to give it credence is truly a credit to their methods of propaganda. In future one will be able to forestall revolution by watching for a beacon, for the signal which the plotters will give to their supporters, by setting fire to a building to show that the hour has struck.

But what are the facts upon which the Court based its pronouncement? During the political stage of the trial, when the prosecution's case called aloud for some proof, some witness of insurrectionary plans or activities, there came no one but police officials with long reports of 'subversive' activities. Not a line and not a sentence to indicate that the Communists had prepared an insurrection! As Dimitrov indicated in his speech, it would have been folly and worse for the Communists at that time to entertain such ideas. Not only this, but all the police officials of whom Dimitrov asked the question whether they knew or had heard anything of a Communist insurrection planned for February 27th or 28th denied any such knowledge. The Government itself, indeed, despite the 'finds' in the Karl Liebknecht House which should have put it on its guard had taken no measures to protect the foremost of the public buildings which were to be attacked. Neither Göring nor Goebbels at first believed the news of the fire, it was only when Göring had had his divine inspiration concerning its cause that the word 'fanal' became current. The fact that none of the important leaders of the Communist Party and not a single district secretary was amongst the men arrested on the night of the fire, coupled with the complete absence of any reported acts of violence or attempts at uprising on the night of the fire or the next day can only indicate one thing, that the Communists had nothing to do with the fire and that there exist no grounds in fact upon which the Court could seriously pronounce the fire to be either a signal for insurrection or an act of Communism.

That the Supreme Court could, in the face of the proved facts, have based its judgment upon such a collection of wild improbabilities, deliberate omissions and false assumptions, fully justifies the criticisms directed against it in the preceding chapter. It is only possible to conclude that the Court desired at all costs to furnish the German Government with a judicial basis and justification for all its misdeeds, all its acts of terror and oppression. The sentencing to death of van der Lubbe in violation of the express terms of Article 2 of the Penal Code was the logical culmination of this motive, and, at the same time, a demonstrable service to the Government, which desired to rid themselves of an incubus potentially dangerous. The judgment indeed is a triumph of 'German justice' written in the terms of 'Blood and Honour' and conceived in the 'warrior spirit!'

XIV

THE TRIAL IN THE NEWS

THE Propaganda Ministry maintains a strict and constant control over the contents of the National-Socialist and the politically co-ordinated press. In this way the reports of the Reichstag fire trial given in the German press were under the censorship of the Ministry of Propaganda which issued instructions as to what was to be reported, what was to be omitted and what was to be invented concerning the proceedings.

The comparison which will be found in the following pages of extracts from the German and the foreign press will suffice to present a picture of the whole reports of the trial contained in the Hitler press. The most important events during the proceedings were either suppressed or reproduced in a totally different complexion. There were no prosecution witnesses who were not depicted as worthy of credence. The readers of the Hitler press never got to know that there were many convicted criminals amongst the witnesses tendered by the Public Prosecutor. No information as to the ill treatment of witnesses was recorded. Contradictory statements were represented as confirming one another. The rage, threats and complete lack of self-control manifested by General Göring were elevated to dignified conduct for the edification of the German public.

The following extracts are of course by no means complete. They cover only some of the more prominent incidents of the trial. But they are enough to demonstrate the character of the reports of the trial contained in the Hitler press. The fact that the major part of the extracts from the German press emanate from non-National-Socialist papers further shows that between the latter and the 'politically-co-ordinated' press there is not the slightest difference. The hand of the Propaganda Ministry is equally firm.

VAN DER LUBBE

"The fact that Professor Bonnhöfer in his opinion asserts without reserve that van der Lubbe is absolutely *compos mentis* effectively blunts the edge of all the attempts which have set afoot in certain quarters to apply Paragraph 51 to his case.

"According to the opinion of this expert, van der Lubbe is fully responsible for his actions."

(*Angriff*, September 22nd.)

"One question stands out above all others. If van der Lubbe is not a madman then who is responsible for this terrible change in his mental condition?

"What has happened to him to make him appear as he did to-day? Is he simulating mental or bodily illness? Yesterday and the day before one might have been disposed to support such a view. . . . But it is difficult to believe that any man would be able to enact a part as van der Lubbe is doing. His groans, his cretinous laughter, his profound apathy seem to-day to express the feelings of a man who is really suffering and who seems to have lost all his contact with the world of living things."

(*Excelsior*, Paris, September 24th, 1933.)

DIMITROV

"His whole appearance and behaviour give the impression of a criminal on a large scale."

(*Deutsche Allgemeine Zeitung*, September 24th, 1933.)

"The trial deepened in its dramatic excitement to-day through the ardent and dominating personality of the Bulgarian Communist Dimitrov. . . . There was an air of sincerity about this outburst. . . . Dimitrov gave the impression that acts of terrorism were genuinely repugnant to his nature."

(*News-Chronicle*, September 25th, 1933.)

TORGLER IN CHAINS

"Before the accused gave details concerning himself he declared that he would take the first opportunity of declaring before the public of the world that he was completely innocent and that he had absolutely nothing to do with the burning of the Reichstag."

(*Frankfurter Zeitung*, September 26th, 1933.)

"The *Ère Nouvelle* is deceiving its readers with the allegation that the accused were kept in fetters for five months."

(*Angriff*, September 28th, 1933.)

"Reuter telegraphs: 'In connection with Torgler's dramatic declaration of innocence at to-days' hearing in the Leipzig trial, the German newspapers have been instructed not to publish his declaration textually but to summarise it by saying that he proclaimed his innocence.'

" 'Papers accordingly do not tell their readers that Torgler described the Reichstag fire as a crime with which neither he nor the Communist Party was in the slightest degree connected. Neither do they mention that he has been in chains for five months, a fact which has always been officially denied.' "

(*Manchester Guardian*, September 26th, 1933.)

255

THE EXAMINING MAGISTRATE

"The most important events of to-day were provided by the examination of the Magistrate, Judge Vogt who supplied valuable detailed descriptions of the psychology of the accused men and who indicated some important points bearing on the political aspect of the case.

"It is tremendously important, amongst other things, that the protocols were recorded at the verbal dictation of the accused."

(*Deutsche Allgemeine Zeitung*, September 28th, 1933.)

"The examination of Judge Vogt brought forth many sharp exchanges. It would be untrue to say that they were always resolved in the favour of the Examining Magistrate.

"Dr. Vogt appeared in a very bad light when the accused Bulgarian reproached him with having himself supplied the vacancies in the record of the Examination."

(*Journal*, September 28th, 1933.)

DIMITROV EXCLUDED FROM THE COURT

"Dr. Bünger took the only possible course. He had the phrasemonger removed. This action will be enthusiastically received, at least in Germany. Such delirium has nothing to do with his defence. But in any case Georgi Dimitrov's loud mouthed talk has not made his LIES the more credible."

(*Leipziger Neueste Nachrichten*, October 7th, 1933.)

"To-day's proceedings have shown more than ever in how false a position a judge is put who is obliged to act as counsel for the prosecution and to cross-examine prisoners. The President more than once suggested that Dimitrov was not telling the truth, although his evidence seems to have rung true to those who heard it and there was nothing improbable in it."

(*Manchester Guardian*, October 7th, 1933.)

A REICHSTAG PORTER'S FAIRY TALES

Under the caption:

"Dimitrov Again Identified!"

"The witness Hornemann further stated that several gentlemen went out through the doorway . . . one of the gentlemen made some such remark as that the Reichstag would probably blow up shortly. The witness turned to the accused Dimitrov. 'That one of them I recognise. I think that he is the one who said that the Reichstag would blow up in twenty minutes."

(*Völkischer Beobachter*, October, 25th, 1933.)

"A Reichstag porter Hornemann, to-day made the surprising statement in his evidence at the trial of 'van der Lubbe and associates' that he had seen Dimitrov leave the Reichstag on the afternoon of the fire, February 27th, and that Dimitrov in broken German said 'The Reichstag may go up in the air in fifteen or twenty minutes.' The faces of Dimitrov and his counsel Dr. Teichert were not dismayed at this damning statement but were wreathed in smiles, while the public broke into a roar of laughter which was an appropriate comment on this evidence."

(*The Times*, October 25th, 1933.)

HELLDORF'S INACCURACIES

" . . . While we were dining there was a telephone call. If I am not mistaken it came from the office of the S.A. group to say that fire had broken out in the Reichstag. It must have been at about nine o'clock. '
(*Deutsche Allgemeine Zeitung*, October 21st, 1933.)

"Count Helldorf declared that he was informed that the Reichstag was on fire by a telephone message which he received at about 8.30 p.m., which he believed came from the S.A. offices. The President than reminded him that the Reichstag was not yet on fire at 8.30 p.m."
(*Le Temps*, October 21st, 1933.)

TORGLER IN THE REICHSTAG WITH VAN DER LUBBE

"One cannot illustrate the present position better than by the metaphor that Torgler is at last in a trap of steel. What has happened then? No more and no less than this, that a witness has categorically and unhesitatingly declared under oath that he saw Torgler together with van der Lubbe on the afternoon of February 27th in the Reichstag in the ante-room before the Budget Committee Room.

"At last actual complicity in the crime has been brought home to Ernst Torgler.

"The afternoon session produced another severe blow for the accused. The witness Frey has seriously incriminated the accused Popov."
(*Leipziger Neueste Nachrichten*, October 26th, 1933.)

"One is brought to wonder that Karwahne and Frey have so neatly divided up their work as witnesses. The one noticed only van der Lubbe, the other only Popov—and at one and the same encounter with Torgler."
(*Le Temps*, October 27th, 1933.)

"It seems strange that as Karwahne and Frey were together on both occasions when they saw Herr Torgler in the Reichstag one of them was able to identify only van der Lubbe and not Popov and the other to identify only Popov and not van der Lubbe."
(*Manchester Guardian*, October 26th, 1933.)

SIGNS OF MUCH SUFFERING

"The next witness was the former member of the Reichstag, Dr. Neubauer. He was not able to remember with certainty whether he could have been seen together with Torgler on the sofa in the ante-room to the Budget Committee room."
(*Leipziger Neueste Nachrichten*, October 28th, 1933.)

"Herr Neubauer, who was brought to the Court from a concentration camp testified that it was he who was with Herr Torgler in the Reichstag on February 27th at the time when the witness Frey said that Popov was with Herr Torgler. . . . The witness looked terribly haggard and bore the trace of much suffering in his face and manner."
(*Manchester Guardian*, October 28th, 1933.)

THE REICHSTAG FIRE TRIAL

GÖRING BEFORE THE COURT

"The world must not have the slightest doubt but that the whole German people has testified on this memorable thirty-first day of the trial against the Reichstag incendiaries through the mouth of the Prime Minister of Prussia, Hermann Göring. What this man and leader declared was not merely the result of his private opinion but the conviction of the whole German people. One conviction is that at last we have triumphed over the frame of mind into which the Communists for so many years have drilled us.

"To-day when these dangers have been banished pledges have once more the worthy content of their original meaning. Special joy and pride filled our hearts at seeing that upright and noble man to whom the German people is largely indebted for this victory, taking his place before the bar of the Court and hearing him speak of the mighty struggle in our internal political history in which he ultimately triumphed and emerged victor over the most dangerous enemies. The whole world must know that all Germany stood as one man united behind Hermann Göring on November 4th, 1933."

(*Leipziger Neueste Nachrichten*, November 5th, 1933.)

"No counsel in a Law Court worthy of the name would be allowed such licence as was given to Herr Göring. He was allowed to make *ex parte* statements for which no evidence was or can be offered, and was treated in general as though he was a sort of demi-god whose statements it would be sacrilege to question.

"The proceedings were an illuminating revelation of the character of the present German regime. Dimitrov on the other hand was treated with great injustice.

"It is to be hoped that a completely reliable verbatim report of the trial will be published. It will then be seen that nothing could be more damaging to the Nazi case than some of the words uttered by General Göring at yesterday's proceedings."

(*Manchester Guardian*, November 6th, 1933.)

CULTURE'S ADVOCATE

"But no one is so well fitted to sift all these problems, to breathe a new individuality into them so that they may present an historical precedent for the instruction of future generations as the present Reichsminster, Dr. Josef Goebbels. Dr. Josef Geobbels aged six and thirty years, head of Propaganda in National-Socialist Germany is of those rare leaders who have it in their power to change the face of the world by the magic and force of their word. It is through his participation that we are able for the

"In his evidence yesterday in the trial against the alleged incendiaries of the Reichstag Dr. Goebbels appears to have addressed himself to the foreign press. He requested that his statements should be fully reported. The Minister of Propaganda is deceiving himself if he imagines that he has contributed anything new to the content of the trial. The pronouncment that Communism is terrorist in nature and that the leaders gave to their troops the slogan 'Strike the Fascists wherever you see them,' do

CULTURE'S ADVOCATE—*continued*

first time correctly to realise the meaning of this great trial for the world. In him spoke the advocate of culture and of every human civilisation, a conscious outpost, clear upon the goal of the completely new mental attitude for which his Leader, Adolf Hitler stands. . . . Truly German's mouthpiece to the world!

"And thus November 8th was one of the high points in the spiritual significance of the trial, it emerges predominatingly from the broad review of the mighty struggle between the two opposing mentalities whose conflict was in danger of being sidetracked or relegated to disputes around minor points. Dr. Goebbels unravelled the threads which seemed to have become entangled; with sensitive fingers he drew the principal ones forth again; he did not so much simplify the difficult situation as bring forth its underlying clear principles once more. Dr. Goebbels again set the trial in the right direction. That is his perpetual service in its history."

(*Leipziger Neueste Nachrichten,*
November 9th, 1933.)

not add in the least to the proofs of guilt against the accused."

(*Le Temps,* November 10th,
1933.)

VAN DER LUBBE AND THE NAZIS

"The President posed a series of questions to the accused van der Lubbe which the latter answered haltingly and with contradictory replies. From his answers it appears to be established that he did not know the people who were standing on the landing in Grawe's establishment; he went into the house because he wanted to get some food. He was given something to eat there. He could not say why he had gone to Henningsdorf."

(*Frankfurter Zeitung,* November 14th, 1933.)

"Van der Lubbe said that he had simply begged food there from people he had never seen before and to the general question, 'Where were you on the day before the fire?' answered, 'With the Nazis.' Further questions elucidated that he had followed a Nazi procession for some distance, attended a Nazi demonstration in Spandau and talked with a young man. . . ."

(*The Times,* November 14th,
1933.)

DIMITROV'S CHARACTER

"The examinations of the witnesses to-day completed the picture of the accused Dimitrov. It was indeed quite a different picture than that accused has sought himself to furnish

"A roar of laughter greeted the answer to a question of Dimitrov's as to whether Frau Schreiber did not leave Fraulein Kaspiezer's service because the latter was dissatisfied with

259

DIMITROV'S CHARACTER—*continued*

by his wild speeches and attacks in the manner of the 'grand revolutionary' before the Bar of the Court. It was the picture of a disgusting swindler, a criminal who passed in society as a doctor, a scientist and God knows what else, a man who sought amatory adventures, who tried even to lay his hands upon a charwoman, a member of that class for whose salvation he pretended that he had so strenuously fought. In truth, the hero of the Hate press had been thoroughly shown up by the facts which have emerged, above all from the many trustworthy statements of credible witnesses, for what he really is; as a crook and a criminal who deserves not the slightest patience or consideration from the Court."

(*Völkischer Beobachter*, November 10th, 1933.)

her work. In a state of great excitement Frau Schrieber replied that the reason for her leaving was the fact that Dimitrov tried to ravish her."

(*The Times*, November 10th, 1933.)

"Frau Schrieber's testimony has not the slightest claim to credibility."

(*Republic*, November 10th, 1933.)

A CRIMINAL TESTIFIES

"The witness Oskar Kämpfer stated that the accused Popov had frequently stayed in his flat in Zechlinger Strasse 6, during the summer of 1932 at intervals of several weeks. Thus the statement of Popov that he was in Russia from May to November 1932 are once more and finally proved to be lies; thus also the statements of the witnesses from Russia with which we have dealt ourselves the week before last are exposed as fabrications. From the manner in which it was adduced in Court there cannot be the slightest reason to doubt the accuracy of Kämpfer's statements."

(*Völkischer Beobachter*, November 15th, 1933.)

"Amongst the witnesses who appeared to-day in the trial of the alleged incendiaries of the Reichstag, was one Kämpfer in whose flat both Tanev and Popov are alleged to have been seen. . . . The President stated that Kämpfer had received sentences for theft totalling more than six and a half years' of imprisonment."

(*Le Temps*, November 15th, 1933.)

MALTREATED WITNESSES

"The examinations of the workman Jaschke, from Zinzendorf near Frankfurt am Oder, of the workman Hieske and the agricultural labourer Noske produced no results. All three of them tried to withdraw from the statements made by them during their earlier examinations and pretended that they could not recollect the important information which they had given to the police."

(*Frankfurter Zeitung*, December 5th, 1933.)

"The workman Jaschke was most convincing. Despite all the attempts of the President to force him to allege that the question of outrages such as the blowing up of the electric station and the disarming of the local police had been discussed at secret meetings of Communists, the witness did not allow himself to be led astray. He plainly stated two things, that he had been maltreated by S.A. men and that he had been forced by the police to answer 'yes' to all the questions they put to him.

" 'Were you beaten by the police?' asked the Public Prosecutor.

" 'I was badly enough treated by the S.A.' replied the witness.

"The Public Prosecutor: 'Why did you sign the record of your examination?'

"The witness: 'I had been so ill-treated, and my head was hurting me so much that I no longer knew what I was doing. I answered all the questions which they put to me with "yes."

"Dr. Teichert, counsel for the Bulgarians asked the witness to furnish actual details.

" 'I was afraid,' answered the witness, 'the police threatened me and I had been beaten.' "

(*Le Temps*, December 5th, 1933.)

The Reichstag Fire Trial in Headlines

The National-Socialist and politically co-ordinated press sought from the very night of the fire onwards, to the end of the trial, to induce their readers to believe that the guilt of the German Communist Party and of the four accused Communists had been proved up to the hilt. The following collection of headlines taken intact from the National-Socialist press gives a picture of the means whereby it was sought to inculcate the belief of Communist guilt. The bulk of the examples are culled from the three most important National-Socialist newspapers, the *Völkischer Beobachter*, the *Angriff* and the *Rote Erde*.

261

AFTER THE FIRE

February 28th, 1933.
"A Communist Arson in the German Reichstag."
"Communist Incendiary arrested in the Reichstag."
March 1st, 1933.
"Communist Torgler—the Reichstag Incendiary."
"Communist Torgler Set Fire to the Reichstag."
March 3rd, 1933.
"On the Brink of Blood and Fire Communism."
March 15th, 1933.
"Communist Reign of Terror Narrowly Averted."
"Astounding New Plans of Terrorist Gangs Discovered. Planned Preparations for Arson, Explosions and Murder of Hostages—Hoards of Weapons and Dynamite Revealed."
March 17th, 1933.
"Van der Lubbe's Communist Accomplices Arrested."
"Three Bulgarians implicated in the Reichstag fire."

BEFORE THE TRIAL

August 18th, 1933.
"No Longer shall the New Germany be Suspect."
"The Public Prosecutor's Move in the Reichstag Fire Case."
August 20th, 1933.
"Branting Evades the Point."
August 25th, 1933.
"All Cards on the Table in the Reichstag Fire Trial!"
"The Public Prosecutor Despatches Foreign Lies."
August 26th, 1933.
"The First Five Accused in the Reichstag Arson Trial."
September 6th, 1933.
"Einstein's Bad Business with the International Brown Book."
September 11th, 1933.
"Einstein's Brown Book, an Evil Communist Farrago of Nonsense."
September 13th, 1933.
"Germany on the Verge of an Attempted Communist Coup on the Eve of the National Revolution."
"The Planned Communist Coup of February 1933."
September 15th, 1933.
"Breitscheid, Georg Bernhard, Grzesinski Appear in Disguise before the International Reichstag Fire Court. The Jewish Communist Comedy in London."

THE TRIAL

September 22nd, 1933.
"Van der Lubbe Testifies against the Swindle of the Brown Book."
"The Solution to the Riddle of van der Lubbe."
September 23rd, 1933.
"A Monster in Disguise."
"Van der Lubbe Feigns Idiocy."
September 25th, 1933.
"Van der Lubbe's Accomplices Examined."
"Dimitrov Tries to be Clever."
September 26th, 1933.
"The Preparations for the Reichstag Fire Elucidated."
"Torgler Lies!"
September 27th, 1933.
"The Incendiaries Run to Earth."
"Participation of Communists in the Crime of the Burning of the Reichstag Definitely Proved."

September 28th, 1933.
"The most public Trial in the History of the Reich!"
"Van der Lubbe Absolutely Sane and Healthy."
"Van der Lubbe and Torgler were by Entrance No. II."
September 29th, 1933.
"The Brown Book Pronounced a Tissue of Falsehoods from Abroad."
October 3rd, 1933.
"Dimitrov, the Communist with Scruples!"
October 5th, 1933.
"Torgler's False Testimony Concerning his Movements in the Reichstag."
October 6th, 1933.
"Torgler Irrefutably Incriminated."
"Torgler Completely Nonplussed."
"Torgler's Fairy Tales."
October 7th, 1933.
"Long standing Connections between Lubbe and the Bulgarians."
"Torgler's Attempts to Exculpate himself Shattered."
"The Vital Point in Torgler's Attempt to Exculpate himself Proved False."
"Dimitrov, a Raging Devil."
October 9th, 1933.
"Where were the Bulgarians on the Night of the Fire?"
"Attempts at Deception Frustrated."
"Dimitrov Defence Tactics Thwarted."
"Dimitrov's Romancings."
October 11th, 1933.
"Fresh Incriminating Evidence against the Reichstag Incendiaries."
"The Rabid Dimitrov Quenched."
October 12th, 1933.
"Dimitrov at Last Excluded for the Second Time."
"The Manœuvres of the Bulgarian Dimitrov."
"A Propagandist Slanderer at Work."
October 16th, 1933.
"The Lies of the Ordered Delaying of the Fire Alarm Collapse."
October 17th, 1933.
"More Deception from the Brown Book."
"Not a Single Fact to Support the Romances of the Brown Book."
"Behind the Scenes of the Red Arson."
October 18th, 1933.
"Göring and Dr. Goebbels will Contravert the False Slanders of the Fleeing Traitors."
"Two More Falsehoods from the Brown Book Exposed."
"Fairy Stories about the Reichstag President's Palace."
October 19th, 1933.
"Torgler Used Portfolios to Bring in the Inflammable Materials for the Fire."
"Popov Identified by the witness Boghun."
"The Chain of Proof at last Completed."
October 21st, 1933.
"Count Helldorf Makes van der Lubbe Speak."
"The Atrocity Propaganda concerning the Reichstag Fire Completely Collapses."
October 23rd, 1933.
"Connections of Lubbe with Leading Communist Circles Proved."
"The German Communist Party Always behind the Scenes."
October 24th, 1933.
"On the Tracks of Van der Lubbe's Accomplices."
"Torgler Gravely Incriminated."

October 25th, 1933.
"More Damning Evidence against Dimitrov and Torgler."
"Torgler's Part in the Arson."
"Dimitrov Again Identified."

October 26th, 1933.
"The Noose Tightens."
"Torgler seen in the Reichstag with van der Lubbe."
"Torgler Entrapped!"
"Popov there Too."

October 27th, 1933.
"Torgler Caught!"

October 28th, 1933.
"The Connection of Torgler and van der Lubbe Further Proved."
"Lubbe was in the Reichstag with Torgler."

October 29th, 1933.
"More Serious Evidence against Torgler and Tanev."
"Now for Tanev!"

October 30th, 1933.
"Lubbe and Tanev with a Box."
"The Conspiracy Hatched in the Communist Group Rooms."
"Torgler and Tanev Run to Earth."

October 31st, 1933.
"Defence Witnesses Completely Contradicted."

November 1st, 1933.
"Secret Courier of German Communist Party Incriminates Torgler."
"Sensational Developments in the Reichstag Fire Trial."
"Torgler Offers 14,000 Marks for Burning the Reichstag in Autumn 1932."

November 2nd, 1933.
"Cornered, the Vermin Try to Bite."
"Impudence of the Accused in the Reichstag Fire Trial."
"Dimitrov the Incendiary in a Corner."

November 3rd, 1933.
"The Secret Threads of the Third International."
"Tanev Confesses he Lied."

November 4th, 1933.
"The Propagandist Inciter Dimitrov Excluded for Three Days."

November 6th, 1933.
"The Prussian Prime Minister Accuses."
"Lies Laid Bare."
"Dimitrov Excluded Every Day Anew."
"Communism the most Pronounced Sadism ever sprung from Human Mind."
"Dimitrov Tamed!"
"You are a Crook; you Belong to the Gallows."
"Torgler an Inciter in the Background."
"The Brown Book Lies."

November 7th, 1933.
"The Bulgarians Caught in the Net."
"Popov's Complete Fabric of Lies Collapses."
"Popov and Tanev were there too."
"Error Impossible; It Was Popov."
"Popov Seen by Seven Witnesses."

November 8th, 1933.
"The Conspirators' Table in the Bayrnhof."
"Van der Lubbe with Dimitrov."
"Bolshevist Manœuvres for the Defence Fail."

November 9th, 1933.
"Dr. Goebbels Flays the Communist Lies."
"Dimitrov Completely Extinguished."
"Dr. Goebbels Exposes the Red Worthies!"
"Foreign Recognition at Last."
"After the Lex Lubbe van der Lubbe cannot be an Agent Provocateur."
November 10th, 1933.
"Dimitrov, a Chartered Libertine."
November 13th, 1933.
"The Bulgarians Emissaries of the Third International."
November 14th, 1933.
"Lubbe's Communist Abettors in Henningsdorf."
November 15th, 1933.
"Popov's Alleged Alibi Completely Collapses."
"What now—Herr Popov?"
November 16th, 1933.
"The Communists have Weak Memories!"
"Torgler Gave the Password."
November 18th, 1933.
"A Beacon for the Whole World."
" Popov's Rule."
November 25th, 1933.
" Popov was in the 'Red Aid.' "
November 26th, 1933.
"The Guilt of the German Communist Party."
November 27th, 1933.
"Popov Involved in a Tissue of Lies."
November 28th, 1933.
"The German Communist Party had made all Preparations for Civil War."
November 29th, 1933.
"The Organised Plans of Murder by Poisoning made by the German Communist Party."
"The Poison Squad of the Communist Party in Düsseldorf."
"The Communists' Plan to Poison 18,000 People."
December 3rd, 1933.
"Hand Grenades to Attack Torchlight Processions."
"The Impudence of Dimitrov the Incendiary."
December 6th, 1933.
"How the Communists Hoped to Save Torgler's Head."
December 10th, 1933.
"Communist Origin of the Crime Proved."
December 15th, 1933.
"Torgler Guilty and Brought to Reckoning."
"Death Sentence Demanded against Torgler and Lubbe."
"The Setting on Fire of the Reichstag was a well-prepared blow on the part of the Communists."
December 17th, 1933.
"Dr. Sack's Speech: Exposure of the Traitorous Propagandists Abroad."
December 24th, 1933.
"Torgler and the Bulgarians Acquitted."
"The Acquitted Men Taken into Protective Custody."

XV

AFTER THE VERDICT

THE Judgment of the Supreme Court had been spoken. Its effect and content were discussed with the same interest with which the whole course of the proceedings had been followed. Thanks to the force of world opinion the four accused Communists, Dimitrov, Torgler, Popov and Tanev, had been acquitted. But they were immediately re-arrested in the very Court-room.

The threats to which the enraged Göring had given vent during his encounter with Dimitrov were not forgotten. An international delegation had journeyed from London and Prague to Leipzig on the day of the judgment in order to make arrangements for the future safety of the prisoners should they be acquitted. Dimitrov's mother was still in Leipzig and had expressed her determination to stay as near to her son as possible until he was got to safety. With the closing of the prison doors again behind the acquitted men, the worst fears to which the pronouncements of the leaders of the German Government had given rise were justifiably entertained.

A new campaign began throughout the world for the liberation of the acquitted man. Mass meetings were held, demonstrations passed by the German Embassies and consulates, the diplomatic representatives of the Hitler Government were besieged by deputations of every type, they were overwhelmed by letters, telegrams and telephone inquiries. All over the world the columns of the press were thrown open to letters and articles demanding the release of the acquitted men. This time the campaign was so strong, so forceful, that no elements could hold back from supporting it, no section of the press from giving it publicity.

In Germany the letters and telegrams received by the Reichschancellor and the Minister of the Interior grew mountainous in their respective offices. The Gestapo Secret Report of March 1934 testifies to the enormous effect of these protests from within Germany and abroad upon the minds of the leaders of the German Cabinet. The French savant, Professor Prenant, hastened to Berlin to request the release of the acquitted men in the name of the scientists of France. Two of the most distinguished French men of letters, André Gide and André Malraux journeyed to Berlin to protest to the Minister of Propaganda against the continued imprisonment of the innocent men. Lawyers from abroad, particularly Douglas Benabue of London and Leo Gallagher of California remained in Berlin working for the liberation of the prisoners. Eventually Gallagher was expelled from the country by order of the Minister of the Interior, but others remained in Berlin and continued the work. Dimitrov's mother stayed behind first in Leipzig and then in Berlin, ill with anxiety and strain, often deprived of the opportunity to see her son and turned back disappointed from the prison doors. Her interpreter, the only medium through which she could communicate with those, both friends and adversaries, about her was expelled from Germany on the grounds that he had 'interfered' in German politics. Yet she remained, despite the restrictions which her age, her ill health and her ignorance of German imposed upon her. Even in the face of threats of expulsion, threats against her son and his colleagues, rebuffs and official insolence of the grossest character she stood by her post.

While millions demonstrated their solidarity with the acquitted men and worked for their liberation, their 'defending' counsel stood aside. Dr. Teichert, who had refused to assist Dimitrov's mother, gave an interview to the press enlarging upon the good treatment which was being meted out to the Bulgarians during their confinement. Dr. Sack remained silent. It was he who had applied for Torgler to be taken into protective custody and thus furnished the German Government with a specious justification for the decree ordering his re-arrest.

Several weeks after their acquittal the four Communists were transferred from Leipzig to Berlin and thus came again under the jurisdiction of General Göring. In an interview Dimitrov has described the treatment which was meted out to them in the Gestapo prison. While the subordinate officials both in the S.A. and in the police treated the prisoners in a humane manner on the whole, the more responsible officials particularly the doctors were inexcusably cruel. During the few weeks immediately preceding their release the Ministry of Propaganda sent a number of doctors to examine the Bulgarians. It will be remembered that photographs of the acquitted men 'enjoying themselves' in the cells were taken for propaganda purposes in face of their own protests. The object of the visits of the medical men, S.A. men and others, was similar. Reports confirming that the Bulgarians were in good health were published. The exact truth about their condition was revealed by the thorough medical examination to which they were subjected on arrival in the Soviet Union which disclosed that all three of them were seriously ill. Dimitrov has furnished an account of the manner in which the German medical reports were obtained. None of the doctors sent into the prison conducted any physical examination of the prisoners, none of them made any diagnosis, none of them prescribed remedies. To Dimitrov's reproaches concerning the manner in which they were carrying out their functions they either made evasive answers or else retorted with cynical gestures or laughter.

The success in the foreign political sphere which the German Government had hoped to achieve with the acquittal of the four Communists was brought to naught by their re-arrest and continued incarceration. These facts gave rise to a new campaign against the German Government far more powerful than that which had preceded the verdict. The foreign apologists of Hitler and his colleagues, those who had hailed the Leipzig verdict as a "victory for German justice" now kept silent. On January 18th the *Manchester Guardian* wrote:

"If little has been said since the Leipzig trial about the fate of Dimitrov and the other two Bulgarians, it has not been because public opinion outside Germany is unconcerned about them. It is because public opinion desired to assume that the German Goverment would do the just thing and put them over its frontier. . . . If new misgivings arise it is because the prisoners have been kept in prison for almost a month since the verdict, because we remember General Göring's brutal, frenzied threats of what he would do to Dimitrov when he had him outside the Court, and because a high official of the Ministry of the Interior had just said openly that the Government may keep the Bulgarians indefinitely under protective arrest. That might mean in prison, with a treatment that was comparatively humane; it might also mean in a concentration camp with Dimitrov at the mercy of General Göring and his like."

And as the days went by the danger in which the acquitted men lay grew. Dimitrov made this clear to the world's press in an interview which he had with the *Daily Express* correspondent in Berlin on February 6th in the presence of Heller, a high official in the secret police. Dimitrov declared:

> "But what I want to know is: Why am I not let free? I can understand that the Germans want to execute a man whom they consider dangerous to their country. I can understand that Göring would like to execute me. I would feel like him if I were a member of the German Government; but to keep a man hanging about in captivity after acquittal—that I cannot understand. I protest against it, and I hope you will protest for me too."

The Hitler Government sought to excuse the continued imprisonment of the acquitted men with the most diverse reasons. They announced for example, that Dimitrov, Popov and Tanev could not be taken over the frontiers because no other country would allow them to pass through its territory. This statement was untrue, for both the French and the Polish Governments had informed the German Government that they were prepared to grant the Bulgarians permits to pass through their countries.

With the brief announcement made on February 15th, 1934, that the Soviet Government had conferred Soviet citizenship upon Dimitrov, Popov and Tanev, the anti-fascist movement for the liberation of the acquitted men received an enormous impetus. The following day saw the intervention of the Soviet Ambassador in Berlin with the German Government. According to the *Manchester Guardian* he called upon the German Government immediately "to take the necessary steps to see that these Soviet citizens who had been acquitted by the highest Court in Germany should be able to return to their country in the shortest possible time." On the same day there appeared an interview with the Reichschancellor published in the London *Daily Mail* in which Hitler gave his personal assurance of the release of the three Bulgarians. But two days afterwards General Göring moved to a counter-attack in an interview published in the same newspaper, which clearly indicated a serious dispute:

> "Questioned concerning Dimitrov Göring said:
>
> "Dimitrov may not have set the Reichstag on fire perhaps but he did his best to set the German people in a blaze. He was the most active Bolshevist agent in Germany. I told him in Court that he deserved the gallows if only for his criminal and seditious work in Germany before the fire. That is still my private opinion. If his side had won they would have hanged us without mercy, I see no reason why I should be more indulgent. Well, he is safe under lock and key now. He will remain there for the present at any rate. He is best where he is. Such a man is too dangerous to release on society."

On February 23rd there ensued a further intervention by the Soviet Government requesting in more forcible terms the immediate liberation of the acquitted men. Four days later, on February 27th, Dimitrov, Popov and Tanev were taken by aeroplane to the Soviet Union. Freedom had been accorded to them as the result of the united international campaign and the action of the Soviet Union.

Göring had to justify their liberation to the German press whom he had so recently fed with stories of his intentions. In absolute contradiction to his recent statement in the *Daily Mail* there appeared the following official announcement:

"At Reichsminister Dr. Goebbels' reception of the Diplomatic Corps and foreign press, Prime Minister Göring appeared and made use of the occasion together with Dr. Goebbels in disposing of the legend that there had been differences of opinion between the Leader and himself or other quarters concerning the liberation of the three Bulgarians. He stated most definitely that there had been no such difference between the Leader and his subordinate leaders, and that the most perfect unanimity had reigned amongst them on the question of the Bulgarians as upon all other matters. The cause of the delay were the demands which had been formulated in certain sections of the foreign press in such a way as to seek to bring a pressure to bear upon him to which he would never in any circumstances have submitted.

"There had never been any question but that the Bulgarians would be released eventually. The only question was when they should be released and upon this he refused to be influenced by any pressure from abroad. When the hostile statements and tone of a section of the foreign press had somewhat diminished, he had decided that the moment was opportune to expel the Bulgarians to Russia. In order to prevent demonstrations of triumph before their release or a welcome being accorded them in Moscow he had liberated them without notice and sent them by aeroplane."

Göring made a further statement to the effect that the date of the release of the Bulgarians, already decided upon, was delayed pending a reply from the Bulgarian Government. This was denied by an official statement circulated by that Government to all the press, contradicting reports which had appeared in German newspapers.

Dimitrov's first statement to the press took the form of the expression of the thanks of his comrades and himself to all those who had supported the campaign for their acquittal and their release, the workers and intellectuals of all lands and the Soviet Government. He then declared:

"In the name of my comrades in the trial and myself I must declare that had not the mighty world-wide mobilisation of opinion and activity against German Fascism sprung into being we should not be here to-day, free in Moscow. The Fascists wanted to the very last moment to hold fast to us, to avenge themselves upon us, to destroy our bodies and our minds. They designed that we should pay for the fiasco of the Reichstag fire trial with our lives and our reason.

"Unfortunately my comrades and myself were not aware until a late stage of the united campaign of the whole world outside Germany. We were isolated. We received no news. We were not even allowed to receive things from our own families. We were quite cut off from the world. We have learnt for the first time of much which concerned us only to-day. Such a campaign, I am firmly convinced is the means of freeing hundreds and thousands of revolutionary workers from their chains. Besides us, as Göring stated during his evidence, hundreds of others were destined for the hangman."

Torgler Imprisoned

Much of the hatred of the National-Socialists is now centred upon the unfortunate Torgler who has been in the hands of Göring and his police for five months since the acquittal. From the hell of the concentration camp in which he is confined, scanty news penetrates now and then to the outside world which indicates that Torgler is bearing manfully and courageously all the tortures which are being wreaked on his mind and body. From Göring's own statements to the press it is well known that Torgler is the object of special interest and attention. The National-Socialists have refused to make known their intentions in relation to him. Conflicting statements have emanated from various high officials. It has even been suggested that he has renounced Communism. If this be the case, and there is no doubt that the National-Socialists have constantly entertained the hope that Torgler could be induced to abandon his political faith, one must perforce inquire why he has not been released, for the world has always been led to understand that when a prisoner in protective custody renounced Communist activities his release automatically followed. The movement for the liberation of Torgler is not yet ended, for his courage and his sufferings will never be forgotten.

The Execution of van der Lubbe

The death penalty pronounced on the basis of retro-active legislation and contrary to Section 2 of the German Penal Code upon van der Lubbe drew forth universal disgust and abhorrence. The removal of van der Lubbe would secure the disappearance of the one man who would some day be likely to tell the truth concerning the Reichstag fire. But van der Lubbe's silence will be everlasting. His head has fallen and even his body which could have told the truth concerning him was secreted and shielded from investigation.

The world did not know of van der Lubbe's execution until it had been carried out. He was beheaded by the hand axe in the courtyard of Leipzig prison on January 10th, 1934. The execution was carried out in the strictest privacy. Only the twelve members of the community whose attendance is legally requisite were present beside the members of the Court, the lawyers and the prison officials.

While the official report of the execution announced that van der Lubbe listened calmly to the reading of the sentence and mounted the scaffold quietly and unaided, other reports have reached the world. One of the witnesses of the execution has described the horrible scene which was in fact enacted. Van der Lubbe emerged from the prison accompanied by warders. When he set eyes on the scaffold his expression changed to one of the uttermost fear; he seemed to realise for the first time that this was in earnest. His eyes opened wide with fright and horror. When the reading of the sentence was commenced he broke out in piercing shrieks. He was dragged to the scaffold by the headsmen, struggling all the time and his screams continued to the very moment of his decapitation. This eye-witness was only able to make out a few of the phrases which van der Lubbe was uttering in his last despair. Several times he appeared to shout: "Let me speak! Not alone! Not alone!" One of the witnesses fainted. Another has said that he can still hear van der Lubbe's cries ringing in his ears.

These statements from witnesses furnish confirmation of the report which appeared in the *Prager Montagsblatt* shortly after van der Lubbe's execution:

"Accounts which have reached us paint a vastly different picture of the tragic drama of the execution of the alleged Reichstag incendiary, van der Lubbe, than that furnished in the official German report. . . . When he was led into the courtyard he shrieked and cried and had to be dragged step by step to the scaffold. Even at the last moment he succeeded in freeing himself from the four attendants who were holding him down for a few seconds. . . . He was shouting the whole time and making accusations, as the account runs, 'against several prominent members of the German Government.'"

The official announcement stated that President von Hindenburg had refused to exercise the prerogative of clemency. It is, however, indicated by reports which found their way into the *Neuer Vorwärts* and the English press shortly after the execution and which have not been denied, that this is incorrect and that it was actually Hitler who gave the order for van der Lubbe's execution without Hindenburg's knowledge. If this be correct then this is a factor which cannot be regarded otherwise than as gravely incriminating to the German Government.

The Havas Telegraph Agency coupled with the report of van der Lubbe's execution the statement that the Supreme Court had decided to accede to the request of van der Lubbe's relations that his body would be handed them for burial in Holland. On January 12th, 1934, the Public Prosecutor issued an official announcement that van der Lubbe's body would not be handed over to his relatives but would be interred in Leipzig. Van der Lubbe's step-brother was permitted to attend the interment only on condition that he agreed to waive all rights to the surrender of the body. Van der Lubbe's grave in the cemetery at Leipzig is constantly under guard. The German Government seem even to be afraid of the dead body of their poor victim. If the widely-published theories that van der Lubbe had been drugged or poisoned were entirely lacking in foundation it would have been easy to deprive them once and for all of any strength. Now the evidence which both van der Lubbe and his body could have furnished are put beyond human ken.

A New Reichstag Fire Trial

The result of the trial at Leipzig dealt the German Government a heavy blow. Its members cannot forget their bitter reverse. Despite the statements of Göring and Goebbels, the speeches of counsel and the pronouncement of the Court, the proceedings resulted in establishing that the Communists and their Party were completely free of guilt of the fire. Not a witness, not a document, was produced to indicate the contrary. The false accusations of the National-Socialist Party against the Communists, formulated on the very night of the fire were exposed in their naked untruth and Göring's responsibility for them established. The results of the trial were powerfully to fortify the suspicions hitherto entertained against the National-Socialists themselves.

It is thus that the Hitler Government aspires a second time to that which they failed to attain at the first Reichstag fire trial. The leader of the German Communist Party, Ernst Thälmann, has been in their hands since March 3rd, 1933. The Hitler Government is preparing to try him in a second Reichstag fire trial which will be accompanied by a large-scale political trial of the whole Communist Party.

The preparations which have so far been made, the spies, provocateurs and the perjured witnesses have already been sought out. Confessions inculpating Thälmann have been sought and found in the police prisons and concentration camps by methods even more brutal than those used in the first Reichstag fire trial. One of these witnesses, Kattner, a former Communist, was destined to be the star witness of the prosecution against Thälmann. When after his release from the concentration camp he withdrew some of the statements which had been forced out of him, he was found 'shot' in his dwelling.

The preparations for the monster trial against Thälmann and the German Communist Party have been recently intensified. The stage has now been set with the issuing of the new decree affecting the trial and punishment of offences against the State. Thälmann is destined to be the first victim of the new Court composed of a majority of laymen specially appointed by the Government for their "experience in the suppression of subversive activities." The ordinary legal procedure is to be dispensed with. No evidence will be collected by means of a preliminary examination. The accused will be deprived of knowing of the substance and content of the charges against him except as and when they emerge during the course of the proceedings. The last pretence of 'free representation' so sedulously kept up by the Supreme Court and the lawyers in the Reichstag fire trial is removed for cases coming before the new tribunal, formed to administer 'Blood-justice.' Lastly, it is probable that the proceedings may be conducted in secrecy.

In the face of this new decree expressly directed to the case of Ernst Thälmann as is now openly stated in the German

ERNST THÄLMANN

Leader of the German Communist Party. Arrested March 3rd 1933. Not yet brought to trial

press, it cannot be denied that he and hundreds of other prisoners of the Hitler Government stand in the direst and most imminent peril. Their safety, their freedom can be secured only by another such international campaign as rallied to the acquittal and the liberation of the Reichstag fire trial prisoners.

XVI

WHO BURNT THE REICHSTAG?

DESPITE the fact that the trial of the five accused men before the Supreme Court was concluded with the judgment of December 23rd, 1933, the question "Who Burnt the Reichstag?" is as important to-day as ever it was. The Reichstag fire was the occasion and pretext for the loosening of the Hitler terror, for the suppression of the working class, international, intellectual and pacifist organisations in Germany and for the propaganda against the Jews.

Step by step the Hitler Government was compelled to give way. Under the mighty pressure of the universal anti-fascist movement, under the moral force of the revulsion and abhorrence of the world at its methods, the German Government was forced to bring the men accused of burning the Reichstag to public trial. The trial itself which stayed the hand of Nazi 'justice' furnished a forum for Dimitrov and produced a devastating exposure of the methods of the present rulers of Germany and their willing underlings. Dimitrov took on the role of an accuser. The pursuit of the guiltless men before the Leipzig Court was halted. Even the Public Prosecutor was forced to demand that the Bulgarians be acquitted.

But the Reichstag fire did not lose its vital significance with the pronouncement of the verdict in Leipzig. On the contrary the Court's judgment brings out more clearly than ever before the political importance of the fire, its significance for the present regime. It is these facts which justify the pursuit of the real culprits, which make it necessary to carry further the investigation and the search for the guilty.

276

Could it Profit the Communists?

In the light of events it is unnecessary to inquire whether the Communist Party of Germany did in fact profit by the Reichstag fire, or whether they did plan or instigate an insurrection for which it was to be the signal. The known facts on the one hand, and the absence of any proof whatever on the other, render it superfluous to pursue the matter any further than has so far been done.

But the inquiry whether the Communists could possibly have benefited from the Reichstag fire has an importance because it furnished the Public Prosecutor and the Court with the main reasons for laying the guilt of the arson at the door of the Communists. Disregarding the pertinent observation that the best method of measuring possibilities is to read the facts, it is not difficult to meet the National-Socialists on their own chosen ground.

The Public Prosecutor and the Court formulated the position as follows:

"That after the accession of the National-Socialists to power through the 'National Government' the Communists were faced with the moment of crisis and the last possible chance under the prevailing conditions of victory. The Communist Party must have been and was in fact clear that unless it seized this precise moment to act, the movement would be so shattered that its recovery could only be reckoned upon after several decades had passed, if ever at all."

The question then, as formulated by the Public Prosecutor, was whether in February 1933 the conditions in Germany were such that the Communist Party should have found the moment a proper one for insurrection. It is widely known, notorious indeed amongst students of politics, that the Communist Party nowhere "plays with insurrection." The only conditions upon which an armed insurrection can be productive of success and thus form a stage on the path towards Socialism have been laid down for all the world to read in the following passage from Lenin's works, which strangely enough was quoted in the Communist pamphlet *The Armed Insurrection* used in the Reichstag fire trial as evidence against the Communists.

"One must make sure firstly, that all the class forces hostile to us have fallen into complete enough confusion, are sufficiently at loggerheads with each other, have sufficiently weakened themselves in a struggle beyond their capacities to endure, to give us a chance of victory; secondly, one must ensure that all the vacillating, wavering, unstable, intermediate elements—the petty bourgeoisie and the petty-bourgeois democracy in contradistinction to the bourgeoisie—have sufficiently exposed themselves in the eyes of the people, have disgraced themselves through their material bankruptcy; thirdly, one must have the feeling of the masses in favour of supporting the most determined, selfless, resolute, revolutionary action against the bourgeoisie. Then indeed revolution is ripe; then, indeed, if we have correctly gauged all the conditions briefly outlined above, and if we have chosen the moment rightly, our victory is assured."

Never has it been, nor could it be suggested that the Communist Party of Germany departed from the observance of these factors. At no time did the German Communist Party regard the necessary conditions for a successful insurrection as being present. At its Plenum in November 1933 the Executive Committee of the Communist International discussed the events of the preceding February and March in Germany and unanimously agreed that the conditions for the carrying through of a Communist revolution in Germany at that time were not present. Their views were expressed by Manuilski, one of the leading theorists as:

"There is not the slightest doubt but that the line of the German Communist Party and of our comrade Thälmann of avoiding an open armed struggle against the Fascist hordes was absolutely correct. The Reichstag fire trial has revealed that the Fascists actually designed to provoke such a struggle in order to be able physically to exterminate the whole advance guard of the German working class. . . . It would have been suicidal for the German Communist Party, supported as it was by only a part of the working-class proletariat, whose ranks had been split by the Social-Democrats, and a part of the poorest peasantry but which was completely isolated from the petty bourgeois of the towns, to provoke or enter an armed struggle with the swarming gangs of the Fascists and the Reichswehr; such a course would have been the purest Putschism."

These few quotations, coupled with the facts that the German Communist Party undertook no plans or preparations for an insurrection, issued no call to arms, and continued despite the most grave provocation and the heavy restrictions which were daily placed upon it, to work for the creation of the united front of the working class against Fascism, indicate that the reasoning of the Public Prosecutor and the Court is not only fallacious, but conditioned by their ignorance of the actual situation. This Dimitrov pointed out in his final speech to the Court.

But one may nevertheless be permitted to pursue the argument of the Public Prosecutor further. The failure of the

Communists successfully to grasp their last chance, to seize the critical moment, would mean their destruction, or at least their decisive defeat for many years. The falsity of this argument is demonstrable. The current reports of the Gestapo (State Secret Police) are all in accord on the fact that the Communist Party is alive to-day, and that though it works underground it constitutes a grave and growing menace to the Government and the political aspirations of the National-Socialists. Amongst other things the secret police report for March 1934 states:

"The fact that the Gestapo has intentionally refrained from publishing announcements in the press concerning repressive measures against the Communists during the last few months, furnishes no grounds for optimistic estimates of a considerable diminution much less any suppression of illegal Communist activities. . . . There are indications that in certain parts of Germany, particularly in the thickly-populated and industrial centres a rising curve of Communist activity is to be observed particularly in the most recent days. It is further announced that Berlin, West Germany and Silesia are flooded with Communist propagandist literature brought in from abroad. . . ."

Göring himself in an interview with the press at the end of April 1934 declared that the Communist danger within Germany was acute and that Communist activity had increased. The increasing daily number of arrests of workmen from all political parties, the growing violence of the pronouncements of the leaders of the Government and the recent severe measures introduced in the endeavour to quell oppositional activity testify to the accuracy of the statements of the Gestapo and of Göring. Far from being shattered beyond recovery by the failure of its alleged insurrectionary plans, the German Communist Party, despite illegality and the most severe repression, remains a living and vital force in Germany, in Göring's own words "an acute danger." The falsity of the Public Prosecutor's prophecies, taken almost word for word from the lips of Göring, is thus demonstrated within a year from the burning of the Reichstag.

In the absence of a single piece of evidence the German Government, no less than the Prosecutor and the Court, holds fast to the theory that the burning of the Reichstag was a Communist act and a signal for insurrection. It matters nothing to them that in the prevailing conditions it would have been madness, a crime, for the Communist Party to contemplate such action, that had they contemplated such action then surely their fate would have been sealed for ever. They ignored the fact that not only did the Communists suffer the heaviest losses from the results of the fire, but their circumstances were such that they had nothing to gain and everything to lose from its occurrence. The National-Socialists deliberately misrepresented the facts from the very night of the fire, suppressed what was actual and real while they relied upon and promulgated proofs which had no existence and statements which were false and baseless.

But if the Communists had nothing to gain from the Reichstag fire, the position of the National-Socialists was exactly the reverse. The elections were approaching and the whole propaganda apparatus of the country was in their hands, Goebbels at the head. Göring and Goebbels had gone as far as they dared with the employment of the Storm Troops, using them to police Communist meetings, to the exclusion of the proper police force, elevating them to the position of auxiliary police. Despite all the initial repressive measures of the National Government, the suppression of the Communist press, the veto of Communist election meetings and propaganda, yet the National-Socialists could not be sure of their position. They were perfectly aware as Göring states in his ingenuous work *Germany Reborn* that:

"There remained the Storm Troops as an instrument of power. We know to-day that the middle-class Cabinet would never have tolerated the slightest use of the Storm Troops as a political instrument of power."

It was necessary for them to create a situation in which the use of the Storm Troops as a political instrument of power would command the consent and approbation of the German middle classes. It was essential, at the same time, that the policy of the National-Socialists should gain the widest possible success at the forthcoming elections, that the masses of the bourgeoisie and petty bourgeoisie whose support Hitler feared to be losing should be rallied once more to the rescue of 'German culture.' It was necessary to provide a justification for the intended cancellation of the Communist mandates, foreshadowed by Göring in a conference of Prussian Provincial Governors in the middle of February 1933 and since proclaimed openly by him before the Supreme Court at Leipzig. Göring, indeed, had spent the month of February in re-organising the police in preparation for the specific task of uprooting Marxism, a task which had to be initiated in some manner which would permit the free use of emergency decrees and the Storm Troops.

The immediate aims of the National-Socialists at the end of February 1933 were thus the flooding of the middle classes with unscrupulous anti-Socialist propaganda, the creation of sentiments and conditions amongst the petty-bourgeoisie upon which the pogroms loosened against the enemies and the scapegoats of the National-Socialists could be effectively based and the furnishing of pretexts permitting the free use of the Storm Troops. These immediate results having ensued, the National-Socialists could look further ahead, to the attainment of sole power in Germany, to the surrender of the representatives of the German Nationalists within the Cabinet, to the handing over of Germany to the Junker landlords and barons of heavy industry and finance for whose interests the National-Socialist Party stood and whose dictates the Leader and his henchmen obeyed.

The very events of the night of the fire furnished indications that it was the moment waited for by the National-Socialists for the launching of their campaign for sole power. How else can be explained the false official bulletins, the immediate and extensive illegal use of the Storm Troops, the execution of the multitude of arrests, the spate of violent anti-Marxist, anti-Semitic, anti-democratic propaganda suddenly let loose with the force of the whole official apparatus behind it. The desired immediate results were largely forthcoming. After the cancellation of the Communist mandates, the basis for which had been provided in the official bulletins, the National-Socialists disposed of a majority in the utterly subservient Reichstag sufficient to attain any purpose. The holy 'German' crusades against the working class, progressive intelligentsia and Jews went forward with unslackening fury. The Storm Troops were effectively embodied in the state machine. From these achievements the National-Socialists went on to the attainment of their ultimate ends. Within four months of the fire their Party was the sole legal political force in Germany. The Nationalist direction of the Cabinet was slowly but surely yielded to them, the unco-ordinated representatives of the German upper classes were squeezed out of office and power.

The Storm Troops became the forces of the State. The greedy hands of 'Gleichschaltung', political co-ordination, foraged everywhere. Twelve months or so after the fire they were laid even upon the Reichswehr itself, that former stronghold from which National-Socialism had formerly retreated.

'Gleichschaltung' brought many advantages in its train. The hierarchy of the National-Socialists ceased to be a burden on the funds of that party, the Storm Troops are subsidised by the Government from the spoils got from the German workers and taxpayers, instead of by the private purses of the barons of industry. The Reichstag fire, indeed, with the consequent confiscation of the property of every working-class political and economic organisation, produced the wherewithal for the remuneration of the incendiaries!

Who are the Terrorists?

Ever since there has been a revolutionary working-class movement the use of individual terrorist methods has formed the subject of discussion in its ranks. From the time of the Communist Manifesto, Communists have ever "scorned to conceal their views and aims." They, and indeed the whole of the progressive working-class movement have declared openly their rejection of methods of individual terror as a means of struggle for the attainment of power or as a means of winning power itself. Marx and Lenin, the founders of present-day Communism constantly voiced their renunciation of any resort to methods of individual terror, denounced those who employed or approbated such means as the enemies of the working class and warned their followers of the dangers inherent in such means.

The history of the Communist International and of all its component parties shows that they have ever relentlessly and vigorously opposed individual terrorism. Under the leadership of their respective Communist Parties the working class of many lands have waged hard struggles rich in sacrifices. But in every case their method of combat was mass action. These struggles have never been ushered in nor accompanied by arson, bomb or poison outrages, nor other acts of individual terrorism. True that many such acts have been laid at the door of the Communists by their enemies, but this is no indication of the truth, on the contrary when the authors of such acts have been tracked down they have invariably been proved to be madmen or police agents.

For these reasons and in this wise the German Communist Party since the date of its foundation has waged a continual and vehement struggle against the adoption or approbation of methods of individual terrorism. At a time when the feeling of the German working class against the elements of reaction was at its most bitter on account of the provocative and terrorist onslaughts and attacks of Nazi bands, the German Communist Party expressed its attitude towards individual terrorism in a declaration of November 1931 which may be taken as typical of many:

"The Central Committee of the German Communist Party again recalls to the memories of all party members and revolutionary workers the fact tested and proved beyond doubt by seventy years' experience of the Marxist revolutionary movement that anarchistic and terroristic acts and attempts serve only one end, that of distracting the working class from the real class struggle, that of alienating the masses from revolutionary leadership, of facilitating the vile work of provocation of all kinds and of furnishing easy and cheap grounds to the bourgeoisie for the campaign aimed at the annihilation of the Communist Party."

Upon this declaration of the Central Committee, Ernst Thälmann commented in an article in the current issue of the *International* as follows:

"The principal reason for this exceptionally serious and meaningful decision of the Central Committee of the German Communist Party was its conviction that any departure from the Bolshevist, the mass methods of struggle against individual terrorism, any reconciliatory attitude towards it, would only facilitate the manœuvres of the National-Socialists, and through them of the bourgeoisie in endeavouring to distract the working class from the decisive revolutionary tasks of the mass struggle."

The decisions and the attitude of the German Communist Party did not vary after Hitler's attainment of power. That party as its whole history shows, not to speak of the declarations, spoken and written, of its leaders has ever renounced and combated recourse to methods of individual terrorism. The Reichstag fire was an act of individual terrorism, par excellence; its very consequences, its very context were fraught with disaster for the German working class; it demonstrated to a nicety the accuracy of the condemnations made by the Communist Party's leaders. It is thus inconceivable both from the nature and from the circumstances of the Reichstag fire that the party of revolutionary mass action could have ushered in an armed struggle, which nowhere, in any case, took place, by a terrorist outrage exactly calculated to bring down the full and waiting wrath of their sworn enemies on their heads.

The National-Socialists and Terrorism

How different from the words and deeds of the Communist Party are the pronouncements and actions of the National-Socialists, even of the leaders amongst them. It is an easy task to prove that terrorism is one of the methods selected and nursed tenderly by the National-Socialist Party. One would indeed be surprised if the facts proved that the Party which for years has fed its deluded adherents with the vision, by no means Messianic, of the Night of the Long Knives, of Blood and Honour, of the physical extirpation of Marxists and Jews, possessed a record free from the stains of blood and violence of every degree. In truth, the climb of the National-Socialist Party to power has been accompanied by an unbroken chain of murders, outrages, and other acts of terrorism. Some of these have been collected by Professor Gumbel in his work *Verräter verfallen der Feme*. The leaders of the National-Socialists have consistently exhorted their followers to resort to violence and terror against their political opponents. They have always approbated the use of terrorist methods of the most bloody kind. One need do no more than refer to the telegram sent by Hitler to the National-Socialists sentenced to death for the most brutal and cold-blooded murder of a workman in Silesia, in which he greeted them as his 'comrades' and lauded their action as a part of the struggle for liberation. No different from this action of the present Reichschancellor have been his own pronouncements and those of his colleagues.

The wave of terrorism, officially sanctioned, on the part of the National-Socialists grew with each year; it rages even now, as the record collected.in the concluding pages of this work will testify. While each day during the year preceding the National-Socialists' attainment of power cost one victim to the working class, the spate of murders has proceeded unabated since Hitler was nominated Reichschancellor. Built upon blood and violence in word and action, the National-Socialist power has now come to its terrible realisation. The exhortations of its leaders have brought forth a daily crop of murder and unrestrained brutality.

National-Socialist terrorism does not confine itself within the boundaries of the Reich, it is waged in every land where its satellite parties exist, secretly or openly. A few instances will suffice. Professor Lessing, whose murder was openly incited in the Nazi classic *Juden Sehen Dich An*,* perished from the bullets of National-Socialists in his study in Marienbad, Czecho-slovakia. In Austria the terrorist acts of the National-Socialists have been legion, dynamite outrages, murder and attempted murder of their political opponents of all parties, violent assaults forming a daily accompaniment to the repressive acts of the Dollfuss Government against the organised workers of Austria. Violence by National-Socialists is no less rife in Rumania, where the Prime Minister was murdered by members of the "Iron Guard," supported by Hitler, at the end of 1933. Most typical perhaps, is the position in the Saar, where the League of Nations Governing Commission has frequently reported with anxiety upon the terrorist activities of the German National-Socialist Party, masquerading under the guise of the "German Front" and supported by the German Government. Card indexes are kept of the opponents of the National-Socialists, such have been discovered at Ottweiler and St. Wendel; terrorist outrages are planned and executed against anti-fascists, particularly those of German blood, daily assaults upon unarmed workers, especially those occupying official positions in the trade unions, are organised and carried through. Opponents of fascism are threatened, when not actually maltreated. They receive letters and circulars in which they are reminded of what will happen to them in 1935, after the plebiscite.

* The passage is as follows:—

Theodor Lessing
Professor in Hannover, hetzte gegen das Deutschtum. Schrieb u. a. eine lügenhafte Schändung Schopenhauers, Wagners und Nietzsches. Wurde auf Druck der deutschen Jugend entfernt, worauf ihm das sozialdemokratische Kultusministerium einen „Studienauftrag" gab. Lügner und Hetzer im Hintergrund. (Ungehängt).

The relevant words have been removed as also from the part dealing with Einstein in subsequent editions. This is a trick common to National-Socialist works. It accounts for the scarcity of the first edition of *Mein Kampf* which has in the same way been rendered fit for the consumption of civilised minds.

These methods, so disturbing to the Governing Commission of the Saar, are the means whereby the National-Socialists seek to spread their power over Europe. They are but a mere fragment of the methods and acts of terrorism which National-Socialism fosters and by which it prospers within and without Germany. But they are sufficient to reveal that theoretically and practically the National-Socialist Party supports and propagates the doctrine of individual terrorism, in its worst and most cruel form and that it is ready and prompt to reap every advantage which can be gained thereby.

So must it be in the case of the Reichstag fire. Not only was it the National-Socialists solely who could and did profit by the burning of the Reichstag, but that crime was one by no means foreign either to their teaching or their practice. As adherents to and exploiters of the policy of individual terrorism it is in the camp of the National-Socialists that the Reichstag incendiaries should be primarily sought. The fact that the fire is an integral part of their climb to power, an essential element in their present position renders the initial suspicions of their guilt even more pointed.

Van der Lubbe and the National-Socialists

In support of van der Lubbe's connection with the German Communist Party, the very basis of the Reichstag fire trial, the two pieces of evidence offered by the prosecution, the conversations in Neukölln and the 'impressions' of Heisig, collapsed in the face of examination and could not be sustained. The other allegations widely published during the first days following the fire proved to be untrue. The suspicions that van der Lubbe had connections with National-Socialists before the fire, widely entertained both in Germany and abroad, on the other hand received much support through matters disclosed during the proceedings. It is to these suspicions that attention is now directed. As against the complete absence of any proof or suggestion of connections between van der Lubbe and Communists, there are six definite clues indicating his association with National-Socialists.

The first of these is van der Lubbe's stay at Sörnewitz on June 1st, 1932, in Saxony, first revealed to the world by the Brown Book. The fact that he did stay at Sörnewitz on the date alleged was established in Court. In order to disprove the suggestion that van der Lubbe had been in touch with National-Socialists there the Court had to identify him with another alleged Dutchman of similar appearance named Barge. Barge, it was said, had actually imposed upon the National-Socialist councillor Sommer early in August 1932, two months after van der Lubbe's stay. For this reason it would have been important that the records of the Saxon Ministry of the Interior, where the sworn statements concerning the matter were deposited, should be produced. Neither this, however, nor the record of Barge's alleged conviction for false pretences were revealed to the Court. In face of van der Lubbe's admitted stay in Sörnewitz in June, the abortive effort to identify him with the mysterious visitor of August was unconvincing. It is indeed curious that the *Völkischer Beobachter* of February 28th should have reproduced the name of the arrested incendiary as 'van Bergen' when the second visitor to Sörnewitz was alleged to be called Barge. The allegation that van der Lubbe met National-Socialists in Sörnewitz therefore remains.

The second clue is the fact of van der Lubbe's homosexuality, which suggests a connection with leading National-Socialists. This matter has been discussed at length in Chapter IX, it is not, therefore, thought necessary to enlarge further upon it.

The third clue points directly to Count Helldorf, who following upon the two significant mistakes in his evidence, stated that he did not know and had not seen van der Lubbe ever before. Yet within a few minutes of this avowal he succeeded in producing a reaction in van der Lubbe which the collective exhortations and imprecations of Court, counsel and interpreter had not been able to evoke.

The fourth clue points to the unknown S.A. man who was seen in conversation with van der Lubbe on the bridge over the Spree at the end of the Königstrasse. This fact is proved by an affidavit sworn before Vald Huidt, the Danish member of the Commission of Inquiry, on December 13th, 1933, and accepted by the Commission upon due proof of the deponents identity. The statement runs:

"I had to go to the Post Office in the Königstrasse in Berlin two days before the Reichstag fire in order to collect some money. In front of me in the queue there was a very shabby young man. When he went up to the counter he gave

287

the official a name which sounded something like 'Vanderlohe.' The young man held out his passport and took away some 16 marks which were handed to him. I was standing sufficiently close to him against the counter that I could see he had a Dutch passport. He put the money in his pocket and went out of the office.

"I left the building a few moments afterwards and went over the bridge at the end of the Königstrasse when I saw the same badly-dressed young man on the bridge talking to a man in S.A. uniform. The two went away together over the bridge. When I saw van der Lubbe's picture in the papers after the Reichstag fire I recognised him without hesitation or doubt as the same young man whom I had seen in the Post Office and on the bridge."

The encounter spoken of between van der Lubbe and the S.A. man thus took place on the very day when van der Lubbe made his infantile attempts at arson in the Neukölln Welfare Office and the Town Hall and Palace in Berlin. Although the effect of this sworn statement was communicated to the Court by telegram and letter, the Court refrained from investigating it or inquiring into its veracity.

The fifth clue leads to Spandau. Van der Lubbe revealed to the Supreme Court that he had gone specially to Spandau to attend a National-Socialist meeting. With whom he had made any such arrangement was not elucidated, nor the purpose of his visit. It is not improbable that the conversation with the National-Socialist which followed had some bearing on the purpose of van der Lubbe's trip to the west end of Berlin away from the 'red' East to the reactionary quarters of Charlottenburg and Spandau. That van der Lubbe should have gone there for a purpose, and should in fact have discussed 'the Reichstag,' amongst other things with a National-Socialist whom he met there throws a strange light upon the statement in the indictment that:

"The police have received reliable confidential information that the threads connecting van der Lubbe with the affair were woven at Spandau."

Although the Court did nothing to throw light upon the identity of the young National-Socialist concerned and even intervened to prevent Dimitrov from questioning van der Lubbe during the short period of lucidity which followed his revelations, there is a short passage in van der Lubbe's examination which throws a little light upon the matter. On November 14th that accused was examined by Dr. Teichert upon the events of February 26th. The report of this examination from the *Vossische Zeitung* runs:

Teichert: "You formerly stated that you always became angry at the sight of National-Socialists. Did it have the same affect upon you on this Sunday?"

Van der Lubbe: "No!"

Teichert: "When you saw the demonstrations on the Sunday were you not moved to exclaim: 'Something must be done to stop them'?"

Van der Lubbe (answering quickly): "No! That was in front of the Welfare Office."

The importance of these replies of van der Lubbe does indicate one thing, that he had undergone a change of attitude towards the processions of National-Socialists during the time between his conversation with the unemployed on February 22nd and his discussion with the National-Socialist at Spandau on February 26th. One may only speculate as to the cause of this. Taken in connection with the indictment's statement concerning Spandau, the acknowledged meeting and discussion with the National-Socialist and the other proved circumstances, it is not difficult to imply from van der Lubbe's answers the probability that he had been in touch with National-Socialists in the intervening time and had been favourably impressed by them.

The sixth clue connecting van der Lubbe with the National-Socialists leads to Henningsdorf, where van der Lubbe went "because he wanted a good sleep!" That van der Lubbe begged food and money there was proved, it was also admitted that he reported himself to the police and was sent by them to the shelter where he passed the night. In the absence of the mysterious Waschinski, for whom the police made no search or inquiry, it is difficult to say more of what passed with van der Lubbe in Henningsdorf. Had Waschinski been a 'Marxist' is it not unreasonable to suppose that the police, with their excellent machinery, would have been able to trace and identify him, if not to track him down. But with him the police adopted the same methods as with the National-Socialist from Spandau and several other 'unknowns,' they failed to search for him.

Together with the above six indications of a connection between van der Lubbe and National-Socialists there must be considered the omission of the police either to clear up the events of van der Lubbe's stay in Germany between February 6th and February 18th, when he is said to have arrived in Berlin, or to establish in detail his movements on February 26th, while almost every hour of his activities during February

22nd and the following three days was exhaustively investigated. Again although his movements on the morning of February 27th up to the time when he was seen at about 2 p.m. in front of the Reichstag are set out in the indictment in full, what happened to him between that hour and the time when he is alleged to have entered the Reichstag was left and still remains a complete mystery. In view of the obvious importance of the few hours immediately before his crime the omission of the police to uncover any clue to his movements is no less surprising than their omission to investigate the events of February 26th. Had van der Lubbe's movements between 2 p.m. and 9 p.m. on the afternoon of the fire been inquired into by the Court, the same strange revelations, as with February 26th, might have occurred. In the absence of judicial curiosity upon the point, the record remains blank. A page, an important page, is missing.

Van der Lubbe—An Embryo Fascist

The report of the Dutch police upon van der Lubbe which was read by the Court has already been quoted. This report agreed with the Commission of Inquiry's Dutch investigators, whose conclusions are particularly valuable inasmuch as they were based upon the examination of a large number of actual friends and acquaintances of that accused. The picture they painted was of a man "vain, magniloquent, ego-centric, easily led and actuated by an acute thirst for notoriety; one whose personal weaknesses rendered him easy to be exploited by unscrupulous persons for their own ends and marked him out as a tool for others."

The results of the Commission of Inquiry's investigations threw some light on van der Lubbe's political activities in Holland late in 1932, after he emerged from prison. A Fascist meeting was held in Amsterdam in October which van der Lubbe attended. It was proved by several members of the audience that he had spoken in the meeting in support of the principal speaker and that after the meeting was over he had argued with two witnesses in favour of Fascism. This furnishes some indication that at the time when he entered Germany in February 1933 he was already a sympathiser with Fascism. Such sympathies nourished by a man of so weak a character as van der Lubbe would indeed furnish a valuable breeding ground for provocative suggestion. A seed sown in van der Lubbe's confused mind would fall on fertile soil.

In Disguise?

Photographs have made the world aware of the shabbiness of van der Lubbe's clothing. One of the minor mysteries is where these clothes came from. His friend Harteveld has asserted that van der Lubbe had never in his life owned a coat like the one which he wore on the night of the fire. In fact, when van der Lubbe left Leyden early in February 1933 he was wearing a new suit with which his brother had presented him. Like other things in the case, this new suit has vanished from the face of the earth and its place was taken by old, shabby garments which, at least in the photographs supplied by the German authorities, make van der Lubbe appear to belong to the criminal classes.

It is well known to those who have studied National-Socialist political methods that in the days before their achievement of power it was a common practice for groups to disguise themselves as workmen of Communist or Social-Democratic leanings and dressed in old shabby clothes to attach themselves to "left" political meetings and processions in order to promote disorder and violence. Interesting instances of these methods are to be found in the diary of the National-Socialist prototype, Horst Wessel, published by his sister in her story of his life. It is further not unlikely that Göring's ingenuous explanation of National-Socialist atrocities is inspired by the recollection of these now obsolete campaigning methods of his party. That it was in the minds of the authorities to make van der Lubbe look as much like a Communist, in the middle class conception, as possible can be guessed, but it is more difficult to establish that in fact he was provided with the 'disguise' thought necessary for this purpose. The disappearance of his own clothes and the mysterious appearance of shabby garments raises a problem which it would be difficult, in the absence of any investigation, to elucidate. Together with the matters already discussed it does add, if a little, to the probability of a previous association between van der Lubbe and the National-Socialists.

The final indication of a connection between van der Lubbe and the National-Socialists is furnished by a letter which was produced before the Immigration Committee of the American House of Representatives in the course of the Inquiry into Nazi activities within the U.S.A. Not only has this letter been published in the Minutes of that Commission's sessions but it has also appeared in the American press without contradiction or denial. Since the contents of the letter are so grave it is only right and proper at the outset and before setting them out to indicate the evidence of the letter's genuineness and authenticity. It is typed upon the notepaper of the "Friends of New Germany." The letter bears the signature of Haag, the second-in-command, and the initials of Spannknoebel, the head of the organisation. Both the signature and the initials have been compared with originals known to emanate from these respective persons. Those on the letter are exactly similar in appearance and in the opinion of handwriting experts the signatures emanate from the same persons. The letter was actually typed, as experts proved, upon a typewriter which was in use at the time when it appears from its date to have been written in Haag's own office or in the office of the Efende Publishing Company at the same address. The letter bears also at its foot a stamp similar in appearance to that which appears on other letters known to have emanated from the office of the "Friends of New Germany." There seems thus to be serious ground for accepting the letter as genuine. It is addressed to a National-Socialist organisation in Berlin. The relevant part of the letter runs:

"I cannot get rid of van der Lubbe over here, so the best thing would be to send him by ship somewhere else and have him thrown overboard on the way. By the way, whom do you intend to hang in his place in Germany? I quite agree with your idea that it would be a good thing to innoculate those confounded Communists in Leipzig with syphylis. Then we can say that Communism comes from syphylis of the brain!"

The remainder of the letter is made up with requests for literature for a new code and for spies to be sent out from Germany, matters which preclude the letter being regarded as a joke, assuming it to be genuine. The evidence summarised above lends substantial support to the theory that the letter is a genuine document. It is unnecessary to comment on its statements, which speak for themselves. If this letter is indeed authentic, it forms one of the most damning points indicating National-Socialist complicity in van der Lubbe's deed.

The Oberfohren Memorandum

References have been made in the earlier chapters of this work to the Oberfohren Memorandum. In view of the importance of the contents of this document, not only as gravely implicating prominent National-Socialists amongst them Goebbels, Göring, Heines and Helldorf, in the burning of the Reichstag, but also as presenting a valuable picture of the dissensions between the National-Socialists and the Nationalists within the 'National' Cabinet—it is necessary carefully to examine the question of its authenticity.

As is now well known Dr. Oberfohren was the Chairman of the German-Nationalist Parliamentary Group and in that capacity enjoyed the confidence of von Papen and Hugenberg, with whom he was well acquainted. A long extract from a document emanating from Oberfohren, later styled the 'Memorandum,' was published in the *Manchester Guardian* of April 26th, 1933. The newspaper indicated the source of the document but not the name of its author. The exact date of the first publication of extracts from the document is important not only as absolutely contradicting Göring's unchallenged statement to the Supreme Court that:

"The so-called Oberfohren Memorandum must have been written by Oberfohren after he had died."

but also as throwing light on the events which followed.

On May 7th Dr. Oberfohren who had in the meantime resigned his appointment, 'committed suicide' at Kiel. That he had fallen under serious suspicion was made clear beyond a doubt by Göring's evidence; it was also established that he had been put under surveillance and that his house was visited by Storm Troopers. Some light has been thrown on the manner of Oberfohren's suicide by Walter Tschuppik, formerly editor of the *Münchner Sonntagspost*, and a confidant and trusted friend of the former Bavarian royal house. Tschuppik was confined from March to November 1933 in the police prison at Löwengrube in Munich, amongst his fellow-prisoners was a National-Socialist Captain Roehrbein, leader of an S.A. "Roll-kommando." Roehrbein, who had been thrown into prison on account of some dispute with Roehm, confided in Tschuppik that he and his band of S.A. men had been instrumental in Oberfohren's death and that their instructions to act in the matter emanated from Göring himself. This information was communicated by Tschuppik after his release to the Commission of Inquiry which after careful investigation and taking into consideration his character and repute immediately communicated it to the Supreme Court. The Court did not investigate the matter although it would have been a simple matter to summon Roehrbein before it to explain his alleged statement to Tschuppik.

The findings of the Commission of Inquiry were important in establishing the authenticity of the Oberfohren Memorandum. That the opinions expressed in the document on the association between the Nationalists and their restless allies were in conformity with the views held by Oberfohren personally was established by the evidence of prominent German politicans, amongst them Professor Bernhard, personally well acquainted with him. It was further proved that Oberfohren possessed the ear of the Nationalist Cabinet Ministers and enjoyed their confidence, and thus it seemed probable that the account of the dissensions within the Cabinet emanated from inspired sources.

More important for the authenticity of the Memorandum than its political accordance with the views of Oberfohren and his circle was the evidence heard by the Commission of Inquiry which established beyond doubt the manner in which the Memorandum was prepared and circulated. The draft was prepared on Oberfohren's instructions by a journalist who frequently collaborated with him. The draft was submitted to Oberfohren who corrected and revised it. The document bearing Oberfohren's handwritten corrections was then retyped at his orders in a number of copies by the witness whose evidence was received by the Commission. These copies were distributed to reliable Nationalists of the von Papen circle from one of whom an 'original' copy was obtained by a well-known journalist. In addition to the hall mark of a most reliable newspaper, the genuine character of the Memorandum was thus proved beyond doubt by the careful inquiries of the Commission.

The German Government, to the heads of which the contents of the Memorandum were so gravely incriminating, was highly alarmed by the growing belief in its authenticity. Goebbels loosened a wave of propaganda directed at disproving the genuineness of the document and at demonstrating the falsity of its contents. While the account of the Reichstag fire contained in the Memorandum must necessarily have been second-hand, and thus made room for error, its genuine character presented quite a different problem, and one which it was found difficult to tackle.

When the Court came, as it had perforce to do, to deal with the question of the Oberfohren Memorandum, several of its members were placed in a dilemma. Some of them had been political associates of Dr. Oberfohren, others were near in sympathy to the Nationalists. The Court passed over the Memorandum in silence. The President refrained from entering into any inquiry as to its authenticity or the accuracy of its contents. The requests made for the summoning of von Papen, Hugenberg and Seldte, all of whom could have thrown light upon the Memorandum were ignored. But the proceedings nevertheless cast some light on the subject.

While Goebbels was content to leave the dangerous matter after expressing his view that it was impossible that Oberfohren had anything to do with the Memorandum, Göring went into the matter in more detail. It was obvious that Göring was very interested in Oberfohren's activities. He told the Court:

"I was personally informed on the telephone by a watcher that Oberfohren had just previously been speaking with a lady in a hotel and that during their conversation he had asked her to give him the incriminating material which she had against the National-Socialist leaders. . . .

"It was clear to me that this incident meant that Oberfohren had been offering to buy incriminating material against the National-Socialists from someone. I sent the police at once to make inquiries and it was established that the lady in question was Oberfohren's secretary."

Göring went on to tell of a search carried out in Oberfohren's house and the discovery there of letters allegedly betraying the leader of his party, Hugenberg. He concluded his harangue on the Oberfohren matter by stating:

"One may still recollect that it was announced that Oberfohren had resigned from his chairmanship for reasons of ill-health. In fact he was compelled to resign. There was no alternative. His treachery had been discovered and that was the reason why he shot himself."

It clearly emerges from these statements that Göring at least was closely interested in Oberfohren. It is plain that he knew that Oberfohren had collected material, which was designed to be used against him and his colleagues, that he had actually committed 'treachery,' that he had been discovered, his house searched for documents, which were found, and that his resignation was forced by the National-Socialist members of the Cabinet. One could hardly require a more lucid explanation of the reasons for Oberfohren's death than was furnished by Göring, nor a more frank avowal of his dangerous activities.

Had Göring revealed to the Court the exact nature of Oberfohren's treachery or chosen to produce for inspection the documents which were discovered in the search of his house, or the materials which he had collected against the National-Socialists, or had the Court chosen to require explanations upon these points, then there might have been room for some doubt. But in the absence of these one may regard as entirely legitimate the conclusion that Göring's evidence amounted to a complete confirmation of the authenticity of Oberfohren's Memorandum. This assumption would indeed explain why Oberfohren was under surveillance, why it was necessary to raid his house and in what, finally, his treachery consisted.

With the establishment of the fact that the Oberfohren Memorandum is a genuine document, borne out as it is by the evidence of the persons who co-operated in its production, on the one hand, and the statement of Göring on the other, the suspicions of guilt against the National-Socialist leaders are strengthened to the point of gravity. Nor, in the light of the Court's attitude towards it, can these suspicions be regarded as one whit abated.

A National-Socialist Conspiracy

Although Goebbels, Göring, Heines and Helldorf swore to the Supreme Court that their hands and consciences were free of guilt, the effect of their evidence was rather to confirm and enlarge the suspicions entertained against them than otherwise. The fortuitous presence of the three leading National-Socialists in Berlin on the night of the fire, the surprise which they all avowed at the fire, notwithstanding the alleged 'discoveries' made days before in the Karl Liebknecht House, the deliberately false statements of the A.P.P.D., the immediate political advantages accruing to them from the fire and the savage suppression unloosened against their opponents, all these are important in weighing the case against the National-Socialists. To the three men, Hanussen, Bell and Oberfohren, whose deaths may be laid at their door there has been added a fourth, van der Lubbe, who has taken his secret and his knowledge to the grave with him. But while the ranks of the non-National-Socialists who knew of the mystery of the Reichstag fire have been thus thinned, the circle of members and adherents of the National-Socialist Party against whom suspicions of complicity in the fire may justifiably be entertained has widened. Others have now entered the ranks of the suspected, besides Göring, Goebbels, Heines and Helldorf. To these names may now be added those of Daluege, Hanfstaengl, Scranowitz and Albrecht.

Göring's Police Chief

The position of Daluege in the National-Socialist Party and the administration has been referred to in an earlier chapter. It was to Daluege in his character as Police Chief that the control and supervision of the official inquiries and investigations fell. His hands, partly responsible for the production of the 'treasonable' material alleged to have been discovered in the Karl Liebknecht House, were capable enough for his new task. He was responsible under Göring's direct orders for the issue of the first official bulletins and the false statements which were contained in them. He was present at the first interrogation of van der Lubbe. It was he who invented the story of van der Lubbe's confession of membership of the Communist Party. He too was the first official to talk to the three National-Socialists Karwahne, Frey and Kroyer who since four o'clock in the afternoon of the fire had been waiting in a restaurant conveniently near to the Ministry of the Interior where Daluege and Göring were 'working.' It was after seeing Daluege that these three famous witnesses went to the police headquarters, viewed van der Lubbe and made their false statements against Torgler. Daluege's responsibility is no light one.

Hanfstaengl Sees the Fire

Not until the thirty-fourth day of the proceedings was the name of Hanfstaengl, the National-Socialist Press Chief, mentioned in the trial. Hanfstaengl, who also happened to be in Berlin in the middle of the most vital election campaign ever waged by his party in Germany, was the first person to communicate the news of the fire to Goebbels, who, as he said, took the message as a bad joke. Hanfstaengl was placed conveniently near the fire, in no less a building t..an the Palace of the Reichstag President, directly opposite. The Court did not see fit to summon Hanfstaengl to give evidence although his observations, made from so close a vantage point and at an early stage of the fire, would assuredly have been of great interest. His absence from the Court-room deprived the world, not only of the opportunity of following his observations, but also of obtaining any explanation of what he was doing in the Reichstag President's Palace at the date and time in question.

House Inspector Scranowitz

The suspicions against this official, of decided National-Socialist leanings, were shortly indicated in the Brown Book. The chief point made against him was based on uncontradicted newspaper reports which alleged that he had dismissed the Reichstag employees earlier than usual on the afternoon of the fire. Scranowitz's denial in Court cannot be regarded too seriously in as much as he stated that he himself had gone home at 3 p.m., which was not his usual hour. That the allegations had some basis was revealed by the evidence of Galle that the employee from whom the press statements had emanated had been dismissed. The truth about the matter was thus by no means made clear.

It is not unimportant, specially in view of what follows, that Scranowitz lodged in the building in the grounds of the Reichstag President's Palace. In his custody also were the keys of the underground passage leading from the engine house and the Reichstag President's Palace to the Reichstag itself. Although Scranowitz took some part of his duties extremely seriously, for example, the unauthorised searches which he frequently conducted of the rooms and lockers of the Communist and Social-Democratic deputies in their absence, others he appeared to regard rather more lightly. The most significant instance of this was that revealed to the Court by the Porter Adermann, stationed in the Reichstag President's Palace, who, having heard footsteps one night in the underground passage, pasted strips of paper and cotton over the doors which led into it, and on several occasions found them broken the next morning. Adermann reported his experiences to Scranowitz who was satisfied with instructing Adermann to keep a close watch and neglected any further precaution. Nothing was done to clear up the mystery of the nocturnal visitors. No doubt Scranowitz passed on Adermann's account to the proper quarter for from about ten days before the fire onwards Adermann heard no more noise. This of course was no proof that the passage was not being used secretly by night by persons clad in felt slippers or rubber-soled shoes.

Scranowitz was extremely unnerved on the night of the fire. He himself described the arrest of van der Lubbe made by him and a policeman, Pöschel, when in his excitement he struck van der Lubbe several times. The state of his mind displayed itself a second time when, at about 10.30 p.m. he came face to face with a party of foreign journalists who were being led by Gempp, the responsible Fire Chief, over the Reichstag. Scranowitz forbade them to enter the building and ordered the two policemen stationed nearby to make use of their firearms should anyone try to enter against his directions. This display of his excitement is the more extraordinary in that Göring was alleged to have given Gempp sole authority over the building, and that in the exercise of his powers the latter had expressly permitted the journalists to enter.

Scranowitz was an old and a tried official. It is a little hard to conceive why he should become so excited, unless thoughts of a doubtful nature were passing through his mind. In his evidence Scranowitz stated that he was in his lodging at 9.15 p.m. and also that he was called by Wendt to the scene of the fire. Wendt, however, stated that he telephoned Scranowitz at about that time but obtained no reply. Although he did not communicate with Scranowitz the latter appeared shortly afterwards at the entrance to the building. The discrepancy between these two statements was not cleared up by the Court.

But Scranowitz was guilty of even more astonishing things on that fateful night. On arriving at the Reichstag building he met police-officer Lateit and a policeman Losigkeit, together with whom he entered and searched the building. They had passed by the Sessions Chamber when Scranowitz exclaimed to Losigkeit:

"Come with me! I can hear noises in the cellar."

They did not, however, inspect the cellars. Scranowitz who had been informed of the use of the underground passage by Adermann shortly before the fire and to whose mind the noises which he apparently heard must have recalled the possibility of its having been used did not regard it as necessary to search the passage. It may also be recalled that Scranowitz was the first and staunchest adherent to Göring's theory of a multitude of incendiaries. He even declared to a meeting of journalists shortly after the fire that the remainder of the incendiaries had escaped from the Reichstag by means of the underground passage. To the Court he maintained that he had the impression of there having been at least seven or eight accomplices with van der Lubbe.

The suspicions which were entertained against Scranowitz at an early stage have been powerfully reinforced by the facts which have since come to light and not least by his own evidence and the statements of the porters Adermann and Wendt and the policeman Losigkeit.

The Deputy Albrecht

Amongst the many surprises which the trial had in store was the revelation of the hasty exit from the burning Reichstag of a scantily-dressed, excited National-Socialist deputy. It will be recollected that the first official bulletin spoke of deputies leaving the Reichstag in flight at about 10 p.m. While the bulletin attributed this to Torgler and Koenen, the facts corresponded almost exactly with Albrecht's conduct. Albrecht's story that he lay in bed in his boarding-house near the Reichstag when the chambermaid informed him of the fire, at which he hastily rose, threw on a few clothes and hurried to the Reichstag to save some important family papers, must be regarded with some scepticism for several reasons; no witness was produced in support of any part of it, he did not inform the Court where the family papers, of an undisclosed character, were kept and no one saw him enter the Reichstag. It was true that Albrecht had hurried out of the burning building at 10 p.m. He had been at once seized by the vigilant porter who allowed him to go only after Albrecht's identity had been satisfactorily proved. The mystery was how Albrecht had managed to pass through the police cordons, the guards at the only entrance open and the porters, and to run through the building to the safe place where his papers were kept without being seen by a soul. The Court saw fit neither to inquire more closely into his account of the incident nor to establish the precise reasons for his presence in Berlin at a time when his election campaign was under weigh in Thuringia. All these circumstances cannot but give rise to suspicion against Albrecht.

Unknown Accomplices

The list of suspected persons does not close with the names of Daluege, Hanfstaengl, Scranowitz and Albrecht. There are other shadows, of bodies substantial enough, which passed over the proceedings. One would have asked for more of that droll figure, the drunken chimney-sweep. Certainly one would have desired to search out and identify the National-Socialist with whom van der Lubbe was seen in converse in Berlin on February 25th and the other with whom he discussed "the Reichstag amongst other things" at Spandau on February 26th. A third unknown was the mysterious stranger whom Boghun saw pass through door Number 2 of the Reichstag, left locked at 8.15 p.m., and found locked at 9.20 p.m., and whom he mistakenly identified, in a manner which has been discussed, as Popov. A fourth unknown was the young man in the black high boots and black cloak who first brought the news of the fire to the police post at the Brandenburger Tor at 9.15 p.m., returned with Lateit to the Reichstag and then vanished without leaving his name or address with the police.

Perhaps he was the mysterious stranger whom Boghun had seen emerging stealthily from the Reichstag. It is curious too that he should have conveyed the news to the police when Buwert had sent a Reichswehr soldier, who never appeared to have arrived, to the police on the same mission. The shadows of these unknown men passed bat-like over the proceedings. There was no attempt to search for them, none of them came forward during the trial, their part in the mystery of the fire is unsolved.

Gempp—Ex-Director of Fires

The Saarbrücken *Volksstimme* on April 24th, 1933, published a long and detailed account of a meeting of fire brigade officers held in Berlin early in March. It was alleged that Gempp, then Director of Fires for Berlin, chief officer of the fire brigade, had addressed the meeting on the subject of the Reichstag fire. The effect of his statement, as reported in the Saarbrücken paper and later reproduced in the Brown Book was that:

> "The highest alarm had been given too late . . . that Göring had forbidden him at first to circulate a general call . . . and that large quantities of unused inflammable materials were found lying about in the undestroyed parts of the Reichstag."

It was established by the evidence of the firemen before the Supreme Court that the first two fire-engines arrived at the Reichstag at 9.18 p.m. and 9.19 p.m. At this time the Sessions Chamber of the Reichstag was still free from flames and only two small indications of smouldering substance were seen there by Lateit and Losigkeit. When the fire brigade arrived they turned to the small fires in the restaurant and the west corridor, though had their attention been drawn to the beginnings of the fire observed in the Sessions Chamber it would have been possible to save it from serious damage. Not until nearly 9.30 p.m. was the attention of the fire brigade drawn to the fire in the Sessions Chamber, and by that time the flames had attained considerable dimensions.

Not only did it appear at the trial that the firemen's attention had not been drawn to the Sessions Chamber on their arrival, when its condition was already known, but it was also established that the highest stage of alarm was not given to the fire brigade until half an hour too late. Lateit, the police lieutenant, gave the order for the highest alarm shortly after his arrival at the Reichstag, at about 9.17 p.m., but not until 9.42 p.m. was the alarm communicated to the fire brigade. No explanation of this admitted delay was vouchsafed at the trial. The lost half-hour was the more extraordinary in view of the fire regulations for the government quarter of Berlin, introduced in 1931. These required that in the event of any fire taking place in that quarter of Berlin the highest alarm was automatically to be given, unless a specific order was issued to the contrary. The effect of these regulations was confirmed by the statement of the former Berlin police chief and ex-Minister of the Interior, Grzesinski. The delaying of Lateit's specific directions for the giving of the highest alarm, coupled with the non-compliance with the fire regulations was responsible for the disastrous effects of the fire in the Sessions Chamber, the devastation in which was made good use of by the National-Socialist propagandists. It was not surprising that credence should thus be given to the report of Gempp's speech to the fire-brigade officials alleging that Göring was directly responsible for the delay. Although Gempp in his evidence to the Court denied the accuracy of the report the reasons both for the delaying of the alarm and for the failure to observe the regulations were not elucidated.

The third suggestion contained in the *Volksstimme* report was directly confirmed by the evidence of a foreign journalist received by the Commission of Inquiry. With his statement that he had seen a quantity of newspapers strewn about near the Sessions Chamber on the night of the fire, the evidence before the Court of the policeman Losigkeit was exactly in accord. Herr Gempp denied the truth of the journalist's statement, but Losigkeit was not challenged on the point and even Herr Gempp himself found traces of inflammable liquid on the carpet in the Bismarck Hall. Another official of the fire brigade spoke too of finding petrol poured into a spitoon in a corridor. There was in fact abundant evidence that unused inflammable material was lying about the Reichstag building, yet Gempp, under the strong persuasion of the Prosecutor denied this was the case.

It is not necessary to look far for an explanation of Gempp's denials of the allegations reproduced in the Brown Book from the *Volksstimme*, the accuracy of two of which, at least, was established. On March 24th, shortly after the meeting of fire-brigade officials, Gempp was removed from his office and disciplinary proceedings were commenced against him on the ground that he had permitted Communist propaganda amongst the fire brigade. On April 29th, five days after the report appeared in the *Volksstimme* a charge was laid against him under the Penal Code on the grounds of breach of official secrecy. It was in these circumstances that Gempp appeared as a witness in the Reichstag fire trial. Before the trial, at the end of June 1933, an official denial of the *Volksstimme* report was issued. Gempp explained in his evidence the way in which this came about:

"One day I received a telephone request to call at Commissioner Lippert's office. I went there and was taken to see Lippert. I was shown the report which had appeared in the *Volksstimme*. I was asked to state that it was complete nonsense. This was issued as my démenti."

It is not difficult to picture that interview between the National-Socialist officials and the discharged and suspected Gempp over whose head serious charges were impending. Neither is it unreasonable to suppose that Gempp appeared to testify under pressure. The press representatives present were almost unanimously struck by his nervous demeanour on the witness stand.

The Secret Inflammable Liquid

Mention has already been made of the theory of the expert Dr. Schatz that the fire in the Sessions Chamber was caused by means of a secret inflammable liquid, for the employment of which the possession of chemical knowledge was essential. There is some possibility that such a liquid might have been available or accessible to persons other than those belonging to the Reichswehr, the Air Ministry, or the technical and transport sections of the Storm Troops, quarters in which it would indeed be possible to find those with the necessary technical knowledge; but in the case of the Reichstag fire this possibility can be almost excluded. Possession of such inflammable liquid, otherwise than in the quarters indicated, could only have been brought about by theft, in which case it is highly probably that some notification from the factory, depot or laboratory at which the theft was committed, would have reached the police. This was not the case. A further indication of the source of liquid actually used was given by the Air Ministry expert Lepsius, who was aware of its qualities and constituence from his work at the Ministry. The fact that those who carried out the burning of the Sessions Chamber had access to this secret liquid is not without importance in the search for the real incendiaries.

The Underground Passage

Throughout the discussion of the Reichstag fire, in the Brown Book, in the Commission of Inquiry and, to a lesser extent, in the Supreme Court, it has been recognised that the clearing up of the means of ingress and egress used by van der Lubbe's accomplices would furnish a valuable clue as to their identity. The two main factors which fall for consideration in this connection are the nature and quantity of the inflammable material used, and the number of the persons whose assistance was required in the preparation of the fire. At this stage it will suffice briefly to indicate the facts which a long, exhaustive analysis has brought to light on both points.

Shortly before 9 p.m. all was well in the Reichstag. There were no sounds in the building. The lamplighter and postman had noticed nothing whatever unusual even in passing through the Sessions Chamber. There were certainly no inflammable materials lying about anywhere. Since it was impossible to accumulate such things secretly in the Reichstag and more to smuggle them in unnoticed, it may be taken as highly probable that the materials which were used in the fire were brought into the Reichstag between the time when the postman and lamplighter completed their rounds, shortly before 9 p.m. and the time when the fire broke out. As a considerable quantity of such material was used, upon which all the witnesses were in agreement, there must have been a store nearby from which it could all be brought in the short time available. The quantity of the material, the shortness of time and the widespread nature of the fire, particularly in the Sessions Chamber, dictated in their turn the participation of a number of persons —put in the official statements at seven to ten, estimated by Göring at about ten, and by Scranowitz at eight. These persons must have been ready to carry out their work rapidly, both the bringing in of the material and the preparation of the fire within the Sessions Chamber. They must not only have been well acquainted with the movements of the staff within the Reichstag but also with the complicated geography of the building.

Early in the trial one of the National-Socialist witnesses advanced the interesting theory that the incendiaries had escaped by means of ladders through the upper storey of the Reichstag on to the roof. When this theory was greeted with general amusement by the foreign press who pointed out that in such a case the incendiaries must have been transported thence by secret areoplanes the theory was abandoned. In truth the question of the route used for the transport of the materials into the building and the entrance and exit of the body of accomplices was narrowed within a small compass. After 8 p.m. only one door of the building (Door No. 5) remained open, the others being all locked. The open door was guarded all the time by Wendt, who locked it after the fire had broken out, before the arrival of the main body of police. The various sides of the Reichstag building were regularly patrolled and the neighbourhood was strongly policed. With the exception of the mysterious stranger who was observed stealing out of Door No. 2 (left locked after 8 p.m. and found locked shortly before 9.20 p.m.) no person was seen to enter or leave the building between 9 p.m. and the commencement of the fire. A thorough search of the Reichstag revealed only van der Lubbe. The number of incendiaries must therefore have made use of some means of ingress and egress which permitted them to enter the Reichstag, with the material for the fire, and to leave the building after laying and starting the fire entirely unobserved.

Only one means of entering the Reichstag presents these possibilities, this is the underground passage which runs between the Reichstag President's Palace and the Reichstag and to which there are only three entrances, one in the engine house, the second in the hall of the Reichstag President's Palace and the third in the Reichstag itself. Despite the fact that there are only three doors to it, it must by no means be imagined that the passage itself is a simple straight tunnel. Its true nature is indicated by Torgler's statement:

THE UNDERGROUND PASSAGE

It was through this passage connecting Göring's Palace with the Reichstag that the
incendiaries made their way

"The inspection of the passage showed what a labyrinth it was in fact. One would have to know one's way about it very well in order to get through. Myself I felt absolutely lost."

The doors to the passage were kept locked and the keys were in Scranowitz's custody. The evidence of Adermann had proved that shortly before the fire the passage was being used secretly during the night, the persons who had used it must have obtained the keys from someone. The Court's inspection of the passage demonstrated that while it was possible for a person shod in heavy boots to wander in the various offshoots of the passage without being overheard by anyone outside, yet the sound of such a person's footsteps could be distinctly heard in the hall of the Reichstag President's Palace but nowhere else. A person shod in rubber-soled shoes or slippers could pass through the passage without any noise at all.

Although the use of the underground passage by the incendiaries was rejected as impossible by the Prosecutor and the Court, neither of them saw fit to provide an alternative explanation of the means of entrance and exit of the incendiary gang. Göring had never ceased to maintain, even in the Court, that the culprits had made use of the underground passage, in this he was strongly supported by Scranowitz. One might ignore the comment that Göring, as Reichstag President and Reichscommissar, and Scranowitz as Inspector of the Reichstag and custodian of the keys of the passage, were both surely in a position to know best, were it not for the fact that all the probabilities point most strongly to the assumption that the underground passage was in fact employed and that no other suggestion has been brought forward.

The assumption made by Göring and Scranowitz and produced in the official bulletins was given further support by the conclusion of the Commission of Inquiry after a painstaking investigation into all the available facts and probabilities that:

"It is highly probable that the incendiaries made use of the subterranean passage leading from the Reichstag to the house of the President of the Reichstag."

On February 28th there had as usual been numbers of S.A. and S.S. men in the Reichstag President's Palace and grounds. The porters employed in the Palace gave evidence before the

Court which confirmed Torgler's own observations and the evidence of witnesses before the Commission of Inquiry to this effect. Scranowitz went back to his lodging in the grounds early in the afternoon, how long he remained there or what he did was not elucidated, in any case he failed to answer a telephone call at about 9.15 p.m. At 7 p.m. the men employed in the engine house went off duty. Shortly before 8.30 the lamplighter Scholz looked into the Reichstag end of the underground passage and saw nothing unusual, he locked the door again.

Then came the fire. At about 9.18 p.m. Scranowitz, excited as he was, told Losigkeit the policeman that he heard noises of people running about in the cellars. At about 9.30 p.m., upon the orders of Göring's adjutant Jacoby, apparently given before the receipt of the divine revelation, S.S. man Weber, curiously enough a chemist, head of Göring's body-guard, conducted a search of the underground passage. There were several interesting features about this search. Although three policemen attached themselves to Weber, when they had unlocked the door and entered the passage the party split into two, the three policemen searched the passage between the Reichstag President's Palace and the engine house while Weber alone searched the passage leading to the Reichstag. This curious division of forces, unexplained to the Court, is rendered the more extraordinary in that although Weber professed it to be his first experience of the passage he was able to find his way without the slightest difficulty and to inspect the 'labyrinth' thoroughly in the short space of seven or eight minutes. There are serious reasons to doubt the truth of Weber's statement that he had never been in the passage before, and the suspicion which must be aroused by the fact that he, a chemist and the head of Göring's personal body-guard, was regarded as a suitable person to conduct the inspection of that portion of the passage communicating with the Reichstag, therefore the most important for the incendiaries, which was unknown territory to him, alone and unaided, is fortified by the fact that he failed to explain where he received his orders, or how he obtained access to the Reichstag President's Palace.

The suspicions of the guilt of National-Socialists can only be strengthened by these facts. The Reichstag President's

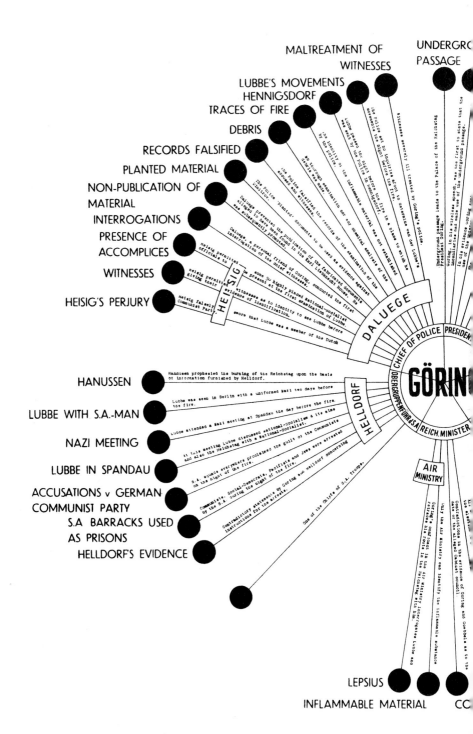

MALTREATMENT OF WITNESSES

UNDERGRO PASSAGE

LUBBE'S MOVEMENTS HENNIGSDORF

TRACES OF FIRE

DEBRIS

RECORDS FALSIFIED

PLANTED MATERIAL

NON-PUBLICATION OF MATERIAL

INTERROGATIONS

PRESENCE OF ACCOMPLICES

WITNESSES

HEISIG'S PERJURY

HEISIG

DALUEGE

CHIEF OF POLICE PRESIDEN

OBERGRUPPENFÜHRER S.A REICH.MINISTER

GÖRIN

HELLDORF

HANUSSEN

LUBBE WITH S.A.-MAN

NAZI MEETING

LUBBE IN SPANDAU

ACCUSATIONS v GERMAN COMMUNIST PARTY

S.A BARRACKS USED AS PRISONS

HELLDORF'S EVIDENCE

AIR MINISTRY

LEPSIUS

INFLAMMABLE MATERIAL

CO

THE THREADS LEAD T

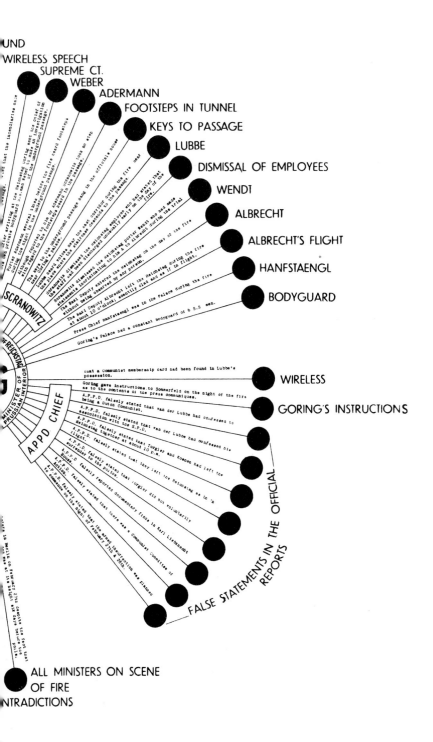

UND

WIRELESS SPEECH

SUPREME CT.

WEBER

ADERMANN

FOOTSTEPS IN TUNNEL

KEYS TO PASSAGE

LUBBE

DISMISSAL OF EMPLOYEES

WENDT

ALBRECHT

ALBRECHT'S FLIGHT

HANFSTAENGL

BODYGUARD

SCRANOWITZ

REICHSTA

MINISTER OF PRUSSIAN INTERIOR

APPD CHIEF

WIRELESS

GORING'S INSTRUCTIONS

FALSE STATEMENTS IN THE OFFICIAL REPORTS

ALL MINISTERS ON SCENE
OF FIRE

NTRADICTIONS

GÖRING

that the inconsist… sta…

Porter Adermann arriving at the Reichstag sent the chief of his own private bodyguard during the night to make an inspection of the underground passage.

Although Goring reported that 2-3 men had seen footsteps with regard to the footsteps heard in the passage.

The man sent to die by Adermann ousted… Goring a false… ideas before for fire heard footsteps.

Lubbe heard voices near the east corridor during the fire.

There were more in the underground passage came to the officials above.

Scranowitz dismisses the reloading employee who had made the statement with regard to the footsteps heard in the passage.

Scranowitz dismissed the reloading porter Wendt who had made the statement incriminating to him & to Albrecht during the trial the day of the fire.

Statements incriminating to him & to Albrecht during the fire.

The Nazi Deputy Albrecht left the Reichstag during the fire without being observed by any person.

The Nazi Deputy Albrecht left the Reichstag in flight at about 10 o'clock; possibly Glad and as if in flight.

Press Chief Hanfstaengl was in the Palace during the fire

Goring's Palace had a constant bodyguard of 6 S.S men.

that a Communist membership card had been found in Lubbe's possession.

Goring gave instructions to Sommerfeld on the night of the fire as to the contents of the press communiques.

A.P.P.D. falsely stated that van der Lubbe being a Dutch Communist.

A.P.P.D. falsely stated that van der Lubbe had confessed to association with the S.P.D.

A.P.P.D. falsely stated that Torgler and Koenen had left the Reichstag together at about 10 p.m.

A.P.P.D. falsely stated that they left the House surrender to the police.

A.P.P.D. falsely reported documentary finds in Karl Liebknecht House.

A.P.P.D. falsely stated that Torgler did not voluntarily… to…

A.P.P.D. falsely stated that there was a Communist Committee of… police…

A.P.P.D. falsely stated that the present insurrection was planned on the… of February 27th & 28th.

Palace and grounds, to which Storm Troopers had habitual access, were the only places from which access could be got to the underground passage. By means of the underground passage materials stored in the Reichstag President's Palace could be quickly and safely transported into the Reichstag and the numbers necessary for the preparation and starting of the fire could gain speedy entrance and exit. To employ the passage with safety only the keys and a knowledge of the movements of the Reichstag officials were necessary. To these Scranowitz provided the solution. The execution of the work necessitated a thorough knowledge of the twists and turns of the passage and of the geography of the Reichstag, rehearsals carried out secretly by night in the passage assured the smooth working of the scheme and the rectification of mistakes, such as noisy footgear. As an additional safeguard a subsequent check of the passage was necessary, who more likely for this than the head of Göring's bodyguard. Hanfstaengl directed operations within the Palace, the propaganda apparatus stood ready, and the leaders of the Storm Troopers were in their places. With the official bulletins planned in advance, the orders of arrest prepared, Karwahne, Frey and Kroyer waiting patiently in their café, the preparations were complete, the scheme almost perfect.

The use of the underground passage, with all its complications, was possible only to National-Socialists, the advance and escape of the incendiary gang was feasible only with the connivance of highly-placed employees of the Reichstag. Every clue, every probability points damningly in one direction, to the conclusion that the burning of the Reichstag was the work of National-Socialists.

A National-Socialist Jacket in the Underground Passage

One last, but by no means least important, piece of evidence has come to light to indicate that the underground passage was used by National-Socialists on the day of the fire. The Secretariat of the International Commission of Inquiry has come into possession of the following sworn statement:

"On the day after the Reichstag fire I was arrested and taken to Spandau Prison. During my imprisonment there I struck up an acquaintance with another prisoner whose father was employed in the Berlin fire brigade. This prisoner told me that his father along with two other firemen was arrested early in March for the following reason: these three firemen had taken part in the work of putting out the fire in the Reichstag. After entering the burning building at about 9.30 p.m. they passed by the door of the underground passage. They saw a Nazi jacket hanging on the corner of the door. They left it there and pursued their way through the building. When my fellow prisoner's father returned to the door about an hour and a half later the jacket had disappeared. The three firemen made a written report of this incident on the next day, so I was told. Shortly afterwards the father of my fellow prisoner was arrested. His wife and family were unable for many weeks to ascertain his whereabouts, but in May 1933 they learned that he had been placed in a concentration camp together with the two other firemen. Up till August 1933 at least my informant's father had not been released. The latter had been, as I was told, very impressed by the discovery and disppearance of the Nazi uniform and had talked much of it at home."

The deponent of the affidavit which is reproduced above is known to the Secretariat of the Commission of Inquiry as a thoroughly reliable person. His name cannot be disclosed for obvious reasons as long as he has close relations living in Germany. It is impossible not to connect up the effect of this information with the extraordinary behaviour of Scranowitz and Albrecht in the Reichstag on the night of the fire. Although the information is not first-hand, it does seem to present the features of authenticity and, in any case, provides information which can be easily checked and if it be untrue, disproved. Coming as it does to add to the large number of other points implicating the National-Socialists of complicity in the fire it is impossible to ignore this information. It furnishes merely one link more in a long and unbreakable chain leading to the true explanation of the burning of the Reichstag.

The Nazis Burnt the Reichstag

Because of the importance of the Reichstag fire as the pretext and justification for the terror in Germany, because of the trial at Leipzig and the events which unrolled themselves about it, because of the fate which hangs over the heads of thousands of anti-fascists both within and without prison in Germany, it would be leaving a duty unaccomplished to conclude this work without grounding an accusation against the National-Socialists. The political implications of the deed together with the gravity of the suspicions which have everywhere been conceived and expressed against leading personalities in the German Government make it essential, at this stage, to furnish the fullest reason for the propriety of these suspicions, to give line and letter for the accusation.

Nor should it be thought that the accusation is made without due sense of responsibility. Knowing as they do, that they are at one with the heroes of the fight against Hitler in Germany, with the sentiments and aspirations of the most progressive elements of all classes throughout the world, the compilers of this work ground their accusation with the fullest sense of responsibility to their supporters. It is in these circumstances and for these reasons that the Reichstag fire is pronounced to be the work of National-Socialism.

1. National-Socialism has elevated and promoted acts of individual terrorism, murder, arson, outrage with explosives and provocation to be the decisive methods of their political aspirations. The Reichstag fire was an event well in accord with this aspect of National-Socialist policy.

2. National-Socialism alone could derive advantages from such an act of arson, and in fact did derive advantages from it. The Reichstag fire aided the National-Socialist Party to become the sole wielders of the power of the Fascist state.

3. Through their control of the Prussian police the National-Socialists secured the pursuit of false clues and the suppression of accurate ones.

4. Through the Official Prussian Press Service the National-Socialists broadcast false information concerning the Social-Democratic Party and lies and unrestricted slanders against the Communist Party relating to the Reichstag fire. The effect of this, directly attributable to Göring and his immediate subordinates, was to cover the tracks of the real incendiaries.

5. The National-Socialists used the Reichstag fire as the pretext for the suppression of the whole Communist and Social-Democratic press, thus rendering insuperably difficult the exposure to the German people of the deliberate falsehoods broadcast through the Official Press Service.

6. The National-Socialist leaders, Hitler, Göring and Goebbels together with the high National-Socialist officials, Daluege, Hanfstaengl and Albrecht, happened to be present in Berlin on the day of the fire, despite that the election campaign was at its highest pitch throughout Germany, six days before the poll. Göring and Goebbels, under oath, furnished contradictory explanations for their 'fortuitous' presence in Berlin with Hitler on that day.

7. The National-Socialist Hanfstaengl, as Göring's 'guest,' was present in the Palace of the Reichstag President, immediately adjacent to the Reichstag, at the time when the fire broke out although his 'host' was not there at that time.

8. The National-Socialist Daluege, appointed Director of Police, after the fire, was present in the Ministry of the Interior, three minutes away from the Reichstag, at the time when the fire broke out.

9. The National-Socialist Albrecht emerged from the Reichstag during the fire, at about 10 p.m., scantily clad and in great haste. No one saw him enter the building.

10. The National-Socialist Heines, accused of complicity in the fire in the first Brown Book, was unable to furnish a satisfactory alibi covering his movements on the day of the fire.

11. The National-Socialist Helldorf, accused of complicity in the fire in the first Brown Book, was unable to furnish a satisfactory alibi covering his movements on the day of the fire, specially during the evening. Through his perjuring statements concerning the mobilisation of the S.A., the arrests on the night of the fire, and the inaccuracies in the times furnished by him to support his evidence Helldorf has greatly reinforced the suspicions hitherto entertained against him.

12. The National-Socialist Göring, despite the promises made by himself and by Hitler and Goebbels in their speeches and press interviews to give the material over to immediate publication, has not published the alleged documents found in the Karl Liebknecht House.

13. The National-Socialist Daluege procured the fabrication of documents alleged to have been found in the Karl Liebknecht House. He also was present in an official capacity at van der Lubbe's first interrogation in which it was falsely alleged that van der Lubbe had confessed to membership of the Communist Party and to association with the Social-Democratic Party. The written record of this first interrogation was never produced before the Court.

14. The National-Socialist Daluege was the first to interrogate the three National-Socialists Karwahne, Frey & Kroyer, whose false statements were so highly incriminating to the innocent accused Torgler and Popov.

15. The National-Socialist Göring failed to take any measures to protect the 'threatened' government buildings, *inter alia* the Reichstag, from attack or outrage, although he had been informed, according to an official announcement of the Berlin police, on February 26th by the Police President of the substance of the alleged finds in the Karl Liebknecht House which were stated to furnish proof of the intended burning of government buildings.

16. The National-Socialists were accused of guilt of the Reichstag fire by the German-Nationalist Deputy Dr. Oberfohren, a confidant of von Papen and Hugenberg. The authenticity of the Oberfohren Memorandum was established by numbers of witness' statements. Even the National-Socialist Göring admitted in his evidence before the Supreme Court that Oberfohren was in possession of material incriminating the National-Socialists, and that his activities were regarded as dangerous.

17. The three National-Socialists Levetzow, Berlin Police President Lippert, State Commissioner for Berlin, and Göring, Prussian Police Minister, were responsible for the delaying of the highest alarm to the fire brigade by half an hour and so prevented the saving of the Sessions Chamber from destruction.

18. The National-Socialist Göring, in his capacity as President of the Reichstag, controlled the Reichstag and the Reichstag President's Palace. The incendiaries made their entrance into and their escape from the Reichstag through the underground passage which runs between these two buildings.

19. National-Socialist Storm Troopers keep the Reichstag President's Palace and its grounds under constant observation. It was thus only possible for National-Socialists to make a base there for the carrying out of the operations in connection with the Reichstag fire.

20. The National-Socialist Göring is the superior of Scranowitz, Inspector of the Reichstag, Scranowitz controls the keys to the Reichstag. He left the Reichstag building officially, at three o'clock in the afternoon, and did not reply to a telephone call made to his flat when the fire broke out although he alleged before the Court that he was at home at that time. Scranowitz prevented the proper and immediate search of the underground passage being carried out by the police after the outbreak of the Reichstag fire.

21. The jacket of a National-Socialist uniform was observed by three firemen hanging on the door into the underground passage when they entered the building. These men reported their observation and were subsequently arrested.

22. The National-Socialist, S.S. man Weber, head of Göring's personal bodyguard, was the first and only person to conduct a search of the underground passage between the Reichstag and the President's Palace during the fire.

23. National-Socialists alone had the possibility of obtaining and making use of the self-inflammable substance which, according to the opinions of the experts, had been employed in setting fire to the Sessions Chamber.

24. The National-Socialist Police President, von Levetzow, had ready prepared by the night of the fire no less than five thousand completed and signed warrants of arrest (some of them furnished with photographs) in order after the execution of the prepared act of provocation, immediately to set afoot the campaign of suppression against the 'Marxists' and progressive elements in the intelligentsia.

25. The National-Socialist Storm Troops were mobilised for action in Berlin on February 27th, 1933. They cordoned off the burning Reichstag. According to the statement of Helldorf, they made arrests on the night of the fire. From 10 p.m. on the night of the fire onwards S.A. squads were at work in the streets and cafés describing the Reichstag fire as the work of the Communists.

26. The National-Socialists were responsible for the murders of Dr. Georg Bell (killed in Austria by assassins who escaped in a motor-car bearing the number plate of the Chief of Police of Munich, then the National-Socialist Himmler) and of the clairvoyant Hanussen, both of whom knew too much about the Reichstag fire. There are further, serious grounds, for suspecting them of responsibility for the death of Oberfohren who was under surveillance for 'traitorous activities,' whose house was searched, and some of whose papers were seized.

27. National-Socialists were associated with the incendiary van der Lubbe. It was proved before the Supreme Court that van der Lubbe had, as alleged in the Brown Book, visited Sörnewitz in Saxony in June 1932.

28. There are strong grounds for suspecting that van der Lubbe was connected with high Officials in the Storm Troops, in particular with the Chief of Staff and present Minister Roehm.

29. A National-Socialist was seen conversing with van der Lubbe on a bridge in Berlin two days before the fire, on February 25th.

30. A National-Socialist spoke with van der Lubbe at a National-Socialist meeting in Spandau a day before the fire on February 26th. Amongst other things they had talked of the Reichstag.

31. The National-Socialists alleged that they were unable to find van der Lubbe's companion in the night refuge at Henningsdorf on February 26th, 1933. They had omitted for eight months to attempt to do so.

32. The National-Socialist Lepsius, a chemical expert employed in the Air Ministry under Göring, according to his own statement, on the day after the fire retraced with van der Lubbe the latter's path in the Reichstag. He thus had the opportunity of refreshing van der Lubbe's memory concerning the account which he was to give of his movements in the Reichstag.

33. National-Socialists were in control of the prison within which van der Lubbe was confined. It was possible only for them by means of the administration of poisonous drugs to reduce him to such a condition of mental and physical apathy and indifference as would secure his silence.

34. The National-Socialists used van der Lubbe as their tool. It has been established beyond doubt that he was not a member nor a sympathiser of the Communist Party, but its opponent; that he sympathised with Fascism, that he was easily influenced and was thus marked out as an instrument of provocation.

35. The National-Socialists conceived and passed into law the Lex Lubbe, which through its retrospective enforcement of the death penalty permitted the sentencing of van der Lubbe to death.

36. National-Socialists forbade the handing over of van der Lubbe's body to his relatives in order to prevent the carrying out of an autopsy and the consequences which would ensue therefrom.

37. National-Socialists guard the grave of van der Lubbe in order to prevent the removal of his body.

38. National-Socialists falsified evidence. National-Socialists extorted confessions from witnesses. National-Socialists perjured themselves before the Supreme Court.

39. National-Socialists have failed to produce any evidence of whatsoever nature in support of the allegation, formulated and sustained only by them, that the Communists burned the Reichstag.

40. For the foregoing reasons, there can be only one conclusion, that the burning of the Reichstag was designed and executed by the National-Socialists as an act of provocation.

Let the accusation be plainly published to the whole world
The National-Socialists burned the Reichstag!

APPENDIX

MURDER IN HITLER GERMANY

THE principles upon which National-Socialism is based are force and lies. Force and lies are not only means used for the achievement of its ends, but are in themselves constituent parts of the organism of National-Socialism.

Convinced that the telling of lies in the interests of the National-Socialist Party is the highest social duty, the Government of the Third Reich has built up an apparatus for the propagation of falsehoods more comprehensive and more technically perfect than the world has ever known. This apparatus for the dissemination of falsehoods is the one constructive achievement of the National-Socialists. Thanks to them the German Reich has been, as it were, hermetically sealed off from the rest of the world, so that it is defenceless against the falsehoods which are disseminated many million-fold daily by the special Ministry founded for the express purpose, through the loudspeaker and the printed page.

One can understand that the civilised world should express its indignation in the strongest terms at the monstrous audacity of this system for the dissemination of falsehoods. But indignation leads nowhere. The only way in which the National-Socialist propaganda machine can be fought with the slightest possibility of success is by simple, restrained and constant reference to the proved facts.

In the following pages there are set forth some eight hundred cases of murders committed by National-Socialists. It can with certainty be said that these constitute only a fraction of the deaths which have been brought about by the rulers of the Third Reich. Even according to the official statistics, under National-Socialist rule the population of Germany has fallen by some four hundred thousand. The conjecture that murders committed by the National-Socialists have contributed towards this fall in the population is justified.

The contents of the following pages are not, however, founded upon mere conjecture. They contain little more than an enumeration of the names of the murdered men, with

the date and place of their death. It is an unemotional reckoning and makes dreary reading. Contrasted with the pretentious
and glittering torrents of lies to which the enemy gives
utterance our truths seem indeed crude and reticent. No
high-sounding tumultous words, but bare facts, figures and
dates are to be found in the following pages. But the vital
difference between them is that while the assertions of the
National-Socialists represent, at the very best interpretation,
a Utopia, the data which are presented here are capable of
actual proof.

Herr Hitler has, for example, stated that in no other country
in the world is the individual as secure as in Germany. He
has asserted that the whole National-Socialist 'Revolution'
was attained at a cost of only fifty-one lives, and that the
fifty-one who laid down their lives were only scoundrels.
But in the pages which follow there will be found a list of
nearly eight hundred men with the places and dates of their
deaths. The German Government is invited to explain how
it is that of these eight hundred murders only fifty-one
were known to Herr Hitler, and upon what facts Herr Hitler
relied in styling the fifty-one victims as scoundrels. The
German Government is invited to examine the details of the
list, to investigate the cases of murder which it recites and to
submit each one by one to the examination of impartial,
uncorrupted judges. The German Government will, of
course, be very careful not to do any such thing. It is
fully conscious of the fact that in a civilised country any single
one of these murders would suffice to kindle the flame of
revolution. It realises that, were these murders known to
them, the German people even from their deep present
humiliation would rise and sweep away Herr Hitler and his
associates with anger and abhorrence. The German Government is able to maintain itself in power solely and simply by
constant and systematic lying: without the apparatus for the
dissemination of these lies it would collapse in a night.

To National-Socialism it must be conceded that their
apparatus for lying is extraordinarily good, fashioned with an
almost loving care it works flawlessly down to the smallest
detail. Every means is used to sustain the illusion of peace
and good order. No one who walks along the Kurfürstendamm in Berlin, the Jungfernstieg in Hamburg, or the Höhe-

strasse in Cologne, no one who goes to ski in the Garmisch-Partenkirschen sees anything but peace and good order. But this good order is maintained only through the deeds of violence perpetrated in the concentration camps, only by the commission of more murders like those which may be found listed in the following pages. The peace and good order of Germany are false appearances. The deeds and the omissions of the rulers of the Third Reich are both falsehoods. False are their spoken words and their silences. They rise with falsehood in the morning and lay themselves down with falsehood at night. False is their good order, false their justice and their judgments, false are their language, their science, their laws and their creeds, their Nationalism, their Socialism are falsehoods. Only these—their rapacity, their lust for revenge and their brutality—are true.

Because this is so, because the very ground upon which these creatures, the rulers of Germany, stand is falsehood, it is doubly necessary to sap the foundations of their edifice and ceaselessly to oppose the glittering falsehoods of National-Socialism with the sordid truth, the bloody and bestial reality.

Despite the power of their propaganda apparatus, the present rulers of Germany will not succeed for ever in hiding the face of truth. The civilised world has already awakened to the reality which is veiled by the cloak of the Third Reich.

LION FEUCHTWANGER.

London, March, 1934.

MURDER BY NATIONAL-SOCIALISM

"The whole German revolution cost only 50 lives and those 50 were scoundrels." (Hitler in the *Sportpalast*, Berlin. October 25th, 1933.)

"What are the facts? The total of our opponents killed in riots has been 27 and the number of wounded 150. Amongst them was not a solitary woman or child, nor has any house been destroyed or shop plundered." (Hitler to the *Daily Mail*. February 17th, 1934.)

LATE at night on August 9th, 1932, a motor-car containing five National-Socialists drove into the little village of Potempa near Moslowitz in Silesia. They came to a house where the door stood open. The five Nazis entered. They walked into the bedroom where the widow Pietcuck and her two sons Alfons and Konrad lay sleeping. They went to the brothers' bed and flashed on their torches. The men were awakened with cries of "Get up! you cursed Communist swine!"

Konrad was seized by the Nazis. He tore himself away and made for the door. One of the gang, Kotesch, drew his revolver and fired. Konrad fell mortally wounded, they trampled him to death with their heavy boots.

Eleven days later the Potempa murderers appeared before the Special Tribunal. The facts were clear. The deed was one of disgusting and cold-blooded bestiality. The victim was poor, innocent and defenceless. The Court must sentence the murderers to death. However clear the facts, however beastly the deed, however poor and defenceless the victim Adolf Hitler expressed his solidarity and sympathy with the Potempa murderers. He telegraphed to them assuring them as his comrades of his own and his Party's support. The Potempa murderers were reprieved and subsequently amnestied. To-day they walk abroad honoured and free men. To-day when he is Chancellor of the Reich and ruler of sixty-five million Germans, Hitler no longer telegraphs his support to murderers in the Storm Troops. Murder is one of the rungs in the ladder of a successful Storm Trooper's career. Promotion to a higher rank in the S.A. hierarchy is the more concrete reward afforded to the murderer. Murder is accorded official sanction and official blessing. Hitler himself, not to speak of his immediate colleagues, has demanded that summary vengeance be wreaked upon his political opponents. Deeds of violence have indeed been erected into a political method of the first importance.

But the leaders of Germany to-day speak with two voices. Hitler, in the passages quoted at the head of this chapter, refers contemptuously to the petty number of dead men, a number which he himself has reduced by a half in the course of three months. To the world outside, the Reichschancellor and his associates lose no opportunity of stressing that peace and order prevails in Germany, and that nowhere else in the world are the lives and property of peaceful citizens so secure. These protestations made by broadcast, speech and writing, form a great part of the material circulated by the terrorist department of the Ministry of Propaganda. To their own followers the National-Socialist leaders speak often with a different voice. Albeit less commonly in public than before, the masses of Storm Troopers are goaded into blind fury and hatred, are prepared for the blood baths in which their leaders aim, from time to time, to plunge them. No one is now unaware of the bloodthirsty anti-Semitic campaign waged with the Government's sanction by Streicher, the editor of *Der Stürmer* and a prominent National-Socialist governing official. Typical of the methods adopted is the following secret command issued by the Cabinet Minister and S.A. Commander Roehm, to his underlings:

To Head S.A. Leaders
Ch. Nr. xxxx/33
Reference: Discipline
Division 1 III   Munich. 31st July, 1933.
"I have done my utmost to secure and protect the rights of the S.A. in every direction as the legally recognised army of the National-Socialist revolution. The decree dealing with the jurisdiction of the S.A. furnishes a legal basis for these efforts. I will protect and willingly answer for every action of S.A. men which serves exclusively the interests of the S.A., even though it may not comply with the legal limitations imposed. For example, when an S.A. man has been killed, any number up to twelve of the members of a hostile organisation responsible for the death may be tried as a reprisal by a competent S.A. leader. The tribunal will be presided over by the leader and its proceedings will be conducted in a brief and soldierly manner. . . ."

The barbarity of the practices exercised by the German Government on its political opponents and its scapegoats, revealed by the two above examples, is fully confirmed by the representatives of the foreign press, by letters smuggled out of the country, by the accounts of those who have escaped from concentration camps and prisons and even between the lines of the politically co-ordinated press within Germany. These sources are supported by the results of the International Inquiry Commission which sat in Paris in December 1933 under the chairmanship of Lord Marley and Professor Lahy, the members of which examined witnesses and documents brought before it, which established beyond a doubt that the National-Socialists have revived all the methods of the Inquisition and that their prisons, barracks and concentration camps are veritable hells on earth.

Consider for a moment upon whom the vengeance of National-Socialism wreaks itself. Trade union officials, whatever their political adherence, are marked out for special attention. Although their arrests are no longer announced in the press, as was the case until September 1933, their obituaries or the police announcements of their deaths, usually from 'suicide' or from 'being shot whilst attempting to escape,' may be read from time to time.

The blindest and most undiscriminating force of the terror has fallen on the heads of the people of Jewish race in Germany. The publication of Dr. Goebbels' Diary has made it plain to the world that the anti-Jewish excesses of the Storm Troopers, the whole campaign indeed, was conceived and deliberately set afoot by Goebbels with Hitler's approval. Yet in the face of this, and in the face of the recent article in his newspaper the *Angriff* and his speech in the Berlin Sportpalast in May 1934, Goebbels has the impudence to maintain to the world that "not a hair on a Jew's head has been harmed." The facts, which are only too well known, belie this and similar statements of Hitler and Göring, as much as they justify the credit which Goebbels deserves for the success of his invention. The persecution of the Jews, perhaps the vilest and worst that the world has ever seen, runs through the whole gamut, from public baiting to imprisonment, from boycott to the private tortures of the concentration camp and even to murder. Jewish middlemen, shopkeepers, workers, lawyers and doctors, none of them are spared. They are accused of the most varied offences—failing to give the Hitler salute or alternatively, giving it; loving an Aryan girl; being successful in their business.

There are many other victims, taken from all classes and ranks of society, "carpers and cavillers," often women who have complained of the rising prices and the steadily falling income; poor and middle peasants who have omitted to provide the requisitions of the S.A. or who have commented more temperately than the *Völkischer Beobachter* upon the 'People's' gift of a landed estate to Darré; small traders and shopkeepers who have told their employees not to join the Hitler Youth, or who have openly expressed doubts of the official version of the Reichstag fire; S.A. men who believed that the 25 points of the National-Socialist programme were really unalterable, as Hitler had said and the party had decided, or who believed that their leaders would strive, as they had promised, with their lives for the achievement of the policy laid down therein; Storm Troopers who have dreamed aloud of the "second revolution"; little craftsmen and artisans who have withheld membership dues, who have, in the words of the organ of the National-Socialist 'Hago' (Artisans and Craftsmen's Guild) "even dared to poach on the National-Socialist programme" (*Aufbau*, January 13th, 1934); Catholic priests and Protestant clergy who have defended their faiths and testaments against the "Aryan clause," who have said Mass for the souls of executed workers, or who have comforted condemned men as they would martyrs. Beyond all these, the bulk of the prisoners of the Hitler terror are members of the industrial working class; workmen who have printed or distributed illegal literature, who have organised opposition in the factories and workshops, who continued to contribute to the funds of their parties and organisations. Thus are the numbers in the concentration camps and prisons made up to their terrifying totals. Most of the victims have committed no offence; many of them indeed are the victims of the unbridled bloodlust, the officiousness and the personal spite of the Storm Troopers and their leaders. The old Germany no longer exists for them and for thousands of others as yet outside the prison walls and camp fences. Germany has become a land of silence, one vast concentration camp where the spirit of Potempa reigns unassuaged, and where the innocent are given over to the wiles of bloody and unscrupulous despots.

In this part of the work only a part of the vast terror will be dealt with, but that perhaps the most frightful of all its aspects, the murder of unarmed, defenceless people. A list of some seven hundred and fifty individual cases of murders has been gathered together and each single instance has been carefully examined into, the bulk of them by the members of the International Commission, and checked from several different sources. The victim in every case was defenceless. Many of the murders have taken place in concentration camps, these, almost entirely officially attributed to "attempts to escape" present some picture of the horror which reigns in the camps.

The list with which this work concludes, although it names some seven hundred and fifty authenticated cases, not fifty, not twenty-seven, as Hitler and his lieutenants would like to pretend, is by no means complete. The stream of murders has swept through April into June 1934 unabated. Even during the months which the list purports to cover, many other murders occurred. For example the Berlin section of the German Communist Party announced that fifty of the officials were murdered during the first half of November 1933. None of these murders has been included as far as is known in the appended list. Of many murders nothing is learnt by the world. The press within Germany is kept silent; the internal censorship of letters, telephone and telegrams prevents the news from leaking into the outside world; the families of the murdered are terrorised into silence. Even in the days of the Weimar Republic no exact observation could be kept on the murders committed in East Prussia, Silesia and Mecklenburg; to-day it is well-nigh impossible to discover them. The estimates of the dead made by the anti-fascist organisations run into some three thousand. There is little doubt but that this figure is on the low rather than on the high side. Many hundreds of cases of 'suicide' or of persons who have vanished without a trace are probably to be given a more sinister explanation.

Let it be well understood that no reference is made to men killed in open fighting. In the early days of the Republic, in Bavaria, in the Ruhr and in May 1929 in Berlin, there were barricades in the streets, there were guns and rifles on both sides. Life was cheap and the number of fallen was high.

But there were no barricades in Germany in 1933, there was no open warfare between contending parties. Those who were shot in the street had no more potent weapons than pamphlets in their hands; the others were shot behind the walls of the S.A. barracks, the prisons and the concentration camps. The toll of the victims of the National-Socialists' counter-revolution has been amongst the defenceless, amongst women, even children, amongst young and old alike, amongst Social-Democrats, Communists and non-party workers without difference, amongst Jews and Christians. These murders are indeed a daily occurrence. Reference to the appended list will show that hardly a day passed in the first half of 1933 without a murder. The very day when the German people were dragged to the ballot box to vote for their own political extinction, November 12th, 1933, when Hitler pronounced that the bulk of the German people stood behind him, two known murders took place. Down to this very day the murders continue without slacking. There are indications that the summer of 1934 will see the terror against the Jews and Marxists break out with renewed vigour. As the opposition of the German people to their present dictators grows so will the wave of terror against the scapegoats of the National-Socialists increase in height. All the murders, all the brutalities of the present Fascist regime are merely indications of their own internal instability, of the consciousness of their leaders that the noose is ever tightening around their necks.

Murder as a Profession

He who wishes to read the terrible omens aright must look back some way into the recent history of Germany. As early as the winter of 1918-19 the expression "shot while trying to escape" emerges, the Swastika raises itself snake-like in the political desert. In 1919 the German Government under Ebert, Scheidemann and Noske called to arms against the revolutionary workers the very persons whom the workers had disarmed and sought to render for ever powerless. Rossbach and Hammerstein, Ehrhart and Pabst, Lützow and Epp, the militarist bandits, the freebooters of the wartime days were armed and employed to suppress the workers' risings by the governments of the Weimar Republic. To-day these experts in terrorism, in the shooting of unarmed men and women, in the murdering of 'escaping' prisoners, are foremost in the ranks of the National-Socialist Party and prominent in the German Government. Such for example are Epp, now Reichsstatthalter in Bavaria, sent by Noske into Bavaria to suppress the old Bavarian Soviet Republic; and von Killinger, sent with Epp to Bavaria in 1919 and in 1920 employed by Severing against the revolting workers of the Ruhr district, who is now Prime Minister of Saxony.

Not only are the atrocities committed by the freebooting condottieri of 1919 and 1920, the mass shootings, the hostages, the murders and the tortures, repeated in their activities to-day but the personnel of the old secret military terrorist gangs are to be found in the front ranks of the National-Socialist Party. From within the Ehrhart Brigade there was formed the Organisation Consul which planned and executed the murders of Rathenau and Erzberger. The Black Reichswehr, the anti-Communist, anti-Socialist gang of terrorists, closely allied to the Organisation Consul, formed the core of the Storm Troopers and furnished the leaders of the National-Socialist Party. Two of the most prominent members of the Black Reichswehr, Heines and Schulz, to-day fill important posts in Germany. The traditions of these associations have been carried right into the Storm Troops. Their leaders are the self-same men, self-confessed murderers, unbridled militarists and terrorists, they now occupy places from which they are able to indulge themselves with killings and lootings unrestrained. The path from Noske to Epp, from Severing to Hitler is thus a clear one. The brutality of the terror finds thus its earlier parallel in the shootings, and tortures of 1918-19.

One of the Three Thousand Murders

In East Prussia, still a land of legalised serfdom, encircled by foreign territory, Junker-ridden, the working-class movement is young and thus the more bitterly hated by the National-Socialists and their supporters. Attacks upon workers, their leaders and the houses and buildings of their organisations began in East Prussia earlier than in the rest of Germany.

On August 1st, 1932, National-Socialists murdered the Chairman of the Communist Group in the local Diet in his house. From then onwards the slaughter of working-class politicians became systematic. The Nazis marked down the local Communist member of the Reichstag, Walter Schütz of Königsberg, as their prey. Schütz had volunteered for war service when seventeen years old, had been three times seriously wounded, and after the war became prominent in the revolutionary working-class movement in Königsberg and East Prussia. He had frequently been threatened by the National-Socialists. One of them named Koch, now S.A. Leader and President of the Administration of East Prussia, during a session of the Königsberg members of the Reichstag, had shouted to him:

"Wait till we catch you! Then we'll beat you to death!"

And so it happened. One night at the end of March 1933, Koch himself led a gang of Storm Troopers into Schütz's house. The subsequent events have been secretly reported by one of the persons who took part and who subsequently relented of his deed:

"Schütz was taken to a room in the old station so that his screams should not be heard. He was stripped naked. Then my companions beat him with iron rods so that after some time he collapsed unconscious. He was then douched with water. When he came to his hair was pulled out in handfuls. S.A. man Ihle exclaimed: 'We'll make a fine job of you!' A little later Schütz almost collapsed through loss of blood. Koch then began to ply him with questions: "'Where is Mattern (the Communist leader in Königsberg)?' No reply. 'Where are your weapons hidden, you swine?' No reply. 'Who are your liaison officers with Berlin?' No reply. Each question was preceded and followed by blows with whips and iron rods.

"After two and a half hours of this treatment Schütz lay prone on the floor. He was hardly a human creature, but an unrecognisable mass of still breathing flesh. My companions took him and dragged him along the whole length of the Schleusenstrasse, raining blows upon him all the time. When they arrived at the Police Headquarters they took him on their backs and sat him on a chair in the office of Landhöfer, an official in the Criminal Investigation department. Schütz immediately fell from the chair. Landhöfer later said: 'I have never seen a more dreadful sight in my life.'"

On March 28th the following announcement appeared in the National-Socialist Party organ of the Königsberg District, the *Preussische Zeitung*:

"Numerous officials of the Communist Party were subjected with *tiring and exhaustivg* methods to intensive interrogation. Walter Schütz, the leader of the

Königsberg Communist Party, was arrested by an S.S. detachment at 3 a.m. He offered no resistance to his arrest and was later handed over to the police in a *state of complete collapse*."

The italics in the above extract coming as they do from the National-Socialist official organ are pregnant with meaning. As to what was meant by the *"tiring and exhausting methods"* one may perhaps speculate. The *"state of complete collapse"* in which Walter Schütz was handed over to the police is confirmed by the report of the doctors in Königsberg Hospital that every bone in his body was broken. Schütz's son, who was taken to see his dead father, found the corpse quite black, the face disfigured and the right eye torn out. Schütz's wife, who was arrested at the same time as her husband, was informed that he had died from a heart attack. As she was led through the streets of Königsberg to prison she shouted ceaselessly:

"I am Frau Schütz. My husband was beaten to death by the Nazis."

"SHOT WHILE TRYING TO ESCAPE"

"I declared then, before thousands of my fellow-countrymen, that every bullet fired from the barrel of a police pistol was my bullet. If you call that murder, then I am the murderer. Everything has been ordered by me; I stand for it and I shall not be afraid to take the responsibility upon myself." (Göring. *Germany Reborn.* Page 25.)

A LMOST every reactionary despotism has evolved its own methods for the disposal of its adversaries. Feudal lords threw them into deep dungeons and forgot their existence. The Venetian Doges had their enemies put under the leads. The Cæsars of Rome threw them to the lions or burned them alive. With more modern refinement the Hitler dictatorship has evolved the method of shooting his opponents "while trying to escape."

A reference to the appended list will show how often this is advanced in explanation of political murders. The phrase has indeed, even in the jargon of the murderers themselves, become the synonym for deliberate cold-blooded shooting. One number of the *Volkskampf*, the organ of the Austrian National-Socialists produced a cartoon of an armed Nazi confronting the leaders of the other Austrian political parties with the phrase: "Decide amongst yourselves who is to be the first man to be shot trying to escape!"

The Murder of Four Communists

On February 3rd, 1934, an announcement appeared in the whole German press. The *Völkischer Beobachter* reproduced it under a headline which ran:

"New Communist Capital Crime. Leading Witness of Thälmann High Treason Silenced by Feme-murder."

The headline was highly cynical for there followed it the announcement of the deaths of four leading Communists alleged to have been shot while trying to escape. These four men were John Scheer, Secretary of the Central Committee of the German Communist Party and member of the Executive

Committee of the Communist International; Eugen Schönhaar, one of the organisers of the illegal Communist press; Erich Steinfurth, formerly in charge of the 'Red Aid' organisation in Berlin, and Rudolf Schwarz, an official of the Communist Youth League.

The explanation of the headline was to be found in the mysterious murder of an ex-Communist Kattner, who had been released from prison after making statements, under pressure, incriminating Thälmann of high treason. Shortly after being set free, Kattner qualified some of his statements. He was shot dead in mysterious circumstances which the police, having failed to elucidate, sought to explain with the expression 'Communist Feme-murder.' At the same time the murder apparently served as an excuse to get rid of the four Communists named above. The police reported that it had been intended to interrogate them:

"to furnish information as to the method and plans with which this 'Feme-murder' was executed."

In fact, since mid-November 1933, John Scheer had been imprisoned in the Berlin headquarters of the Gestapo, the so-called 'Columbia House.' Schönhaar had been arrested at the same time as Scheer. Steinfurth was arrested as early as March 1933 and Schwartz had been in custody since October 1933. Thus all four had been many months in custody at the time when Kattner was murdered. The murdered man had only made his incriminating statements shortly before his death. It is difficult to understand how the police could imagine that these four men, long in their hands, had anything to do with Kattner's murder or what information they could give about the matter. Stranger than the police report is the statement in the *Frankfurter Zeitung:*

". . . They were being taken to an interrogation and a confrontation in Potsdam in an open police car. . . ."

It is indeed curious that the police who have at their disposal many closed vans for the transport of prisoners should choose to send these four important Communists in an open car, more so that the night should appear a fit time to transport them to an alleged confrontation and interrogation at Potsdam at no great distance from Berlin.

The report in the *Frankfurter Zeitung* runs further:

"When the car had to slacken speed on a hilly part of the road, the four prisoners leapt out and fled into the woods. As they did not halt in response to the calls of the guards but commenced to try to attack them, the police had thus to make use of their firearms and killed them."

Four men, without weapons, after months of solitary confinement seated in an open car surrounded by police guards armed to the teeth. Night time. The prisoners do not know why nor whence they are being transported. They must know that any attempt to escape from their guards, even a suspicious movement, spells instantaneous death. The car slows down. The official version then has it that they succeeded in eluding their guards and in jumping from the car. They ran into the woods. They appear then to have returned to attack the police, who were thus forced to fire in self-defence!

In fact it is doubtful whether the four men left the Columbia House alive. There can be little doubt that the official account of the shooting is absolutely unreliable, its very improbability is eloquent. An examination of Erich Schönhaar's corpse revealed that his brain had been penetrated by a bullet which entered at his right temple and came out behind his left ear. His temple showed marks of burning, which indicated that the fatal bullet had been fired from close quarters. His throat bore definite marks of strangulation. It is also known that Schönhaar had been so maltreated during his imprisonment that he could neither lie nor sit. His fellow prisoners had to aid him in the most simple of all movements. Yet he is alleged to have jumped from a moving car, evaded his guards and fled into the woods, to say nothing of returning to attack them!

John Scheer had also been subjected to the most brutal torture at the hands of the Storm Troopers and the secret police. It is reported from a reliable source that he was several times placed in a heated oven and that the flesh on his chest and back hung in rags. It is known that the Gestapo endeavoured to extort a confession from him. Despite the tortures and brutalities which he underwent Scheer remained silent.

Erich Steinfurth's corpse was hidden. No one was permitted to examine it to establish the cause of his death.

Finally the death certificate furnished to Schönhaar's family contradicts the official report of his death, according to which

he with his three comrades was shot on Friday, February 2nd.
The certificate in respect of Schönhaar issued by the Wannsee,
Berlin Registration Office runs:

". . . died at Wansee, Berlin, near the kilometer Hill in the Potsdam woods,
at about 10.45 *p.m. on February 1st*, 1934."

In the face of all the facts it is difficult to arrive at any
conclusion other than this, that if indeed the four Communists
ever left the Columbia House alive, they were driven into the
woods by the police and there murdered in cold blood.

The Death of Felix Fechenbach

One more case will suffice to present a picture of the many
prisoners who have been shot "while trying to escape."
Felix Fechenbach had been in 1919 the secretary of the
murdered Prime Minister of the Bavarian Republic, Kurt
Eisner. After the Republic was overthrown by von Epp's
freebooters, Fechenbach wrote to a friend:

"Our friends Landauer and Leviné have been done to death with horrible
brutality. It is falsely announced that they were shot while trying to escape. If
I were ever placed in the same position I should never escape. You will understand what it means if ever it is announced that I have been shot while trying
to escape."

Fifteen years later Fechenbach was the editor of a Social-
Democratic newspaper in Detmold. The subject of bitter
hatred on the part of the Nazis he was one of the first to be
arrested in February 1933. He was kept in Detmold prison
until the beginning of August. He wrote to his wife for the
last time on August 6th and added a postscript to his letter
on August 7th:

"I have just been informed that I shall be removed from here to-day. Write
for the time being c/o the police in Munich."

At 2 p.m. on August 7th, 1933, Fechenbach mounted the
lorry which was to take him from Detmold prison to an
unknown destination. Six hours later, at 8 p.m., he was
admitted to hospital mortally wounded at Scherfede, some
fifty kilometers distant. The lorry must thus have covered
only thirty odd miles in six hours. The official Wolff Telegraph
Bureau announced on August 8th:

". . . Fechenbach was yesterday being taken to a Bavarian Concentration Camp by lorry. During the journey he tried to escape. As he failed to halt in response to repeated commands of the guards accompanying him, they fired at him. He was struck by a bullet and fell dead."

In contradiction to the official report it appears from a letter received by Frau Fechenbach from the hospital officials at Scherfede that her husband was living, although hardly conscious, when he was admitted to hospital, and not killed outright as appears from the official report. This was also confirmed by the telegram sent to Frau Fechenbach from the Detmold police. Further, the police returned Fechenbach's watch, amongst other belongings, to his widow. It was completely smashed and the wrist band torn off. How this could have occurred during his alleged attempt to escape was not stated.

The fate of the four shot Communists and of Fechenbach are merely two terrible instances of a whole series of cases. A reference to the appended list will reveal that six Jews, Benario, Goldmann, Waur, Levy, Arthur Kahn and Erwin Kahn were shot in Dachau Concentration Camp on the same day "while trying to escape." The same fate has met many other prisoners, Communists like Hausmann, Stenzer and Hartung, Social-Democrats like Eggerstedt, a former police President, and Bienemann. The two cases examined in this part of the work are examples of a method the employment of which has now been brought to refinement.

"HEADS WILL ROLL"

"My measures will not be hampered by the superstitions of jurists or bureaucrats, my task is not to do justice, but to destroy and extirpate." (Göring. To a Public Meeting at Frankfurt on March 3rd, 1933.)

"THE heads of the betrayers of the German people will roll!" So Hitler declared in 1930 whilst giving evidence in the Supreme Court in the case against the three army officers, Scheringer, Ludin and Wendt, charged with conducting National-Socialist propaganda in the Reichswehr. Now they have attained power the National-Socialist leaders have kept their word. The scaffold has been erected in the courtyard of every prison in Germany. The hand-axe has taken the place of the guillotine. The heads of many victims have rolled from their shoulders. But the heads of the tax evaders, the war and inflation profiteers, the financial extortioners, whose blood was promised to their misguided supporters by the National-Socialist leaders have remained firmly fixed. The victims of the scaffold have been all working-class men, the sons of working-class mothers. Most of them were amongst those workers who came on to the streets in 1931, 1932, and the winter of 1932-33 to resist the armed incursions of the Fascist hordes into the working-class quarters, who were involved in street fights waged in the protection of their own homes, lives and families. Some of them may have killed, but the killing in these commotions was necessarily in self-defence. The Storm Troopers, ordered out on raids into the industrial quarters, into workers' settlements and anti-fascist centres, were the aggressors. From 1930 onwards provocation of this character, regardless of human life and limb, even of their supporters became the determined policy of the National-Socialist leaders. In face of such peril every worker with a thought for the interests of his own class and the very life of its organisations as well as in defence of himself and all that was nearest to him, was bound to offer resistance. Since the National-Socialist counter-revolution it has been those very workers who have paid for their resistance with their lives, either murdered in cold blood or executed amidst all the pomp of the law with mediæval brutality.

The National-Socialist leaders themselves set about the measuring of revenge. In February 1933, Helldorf called for the murder of four Marxists for every National-Socialist killed. Later Rudolf Hess, Hitler's lieutenant, raised the number. As shown in Roehm's letter,* the Storm Troopers were given the right to execute twelve Marxists for every National-Socialist who had fallen. The Courts of the Hitler dictatorship, were not backward in setting the machinery of revenge in motion. The Dessau Criminal Court sentenced thirteen workmen to death for the murder of one Storm Trooper; the Düsseldorf Special Court condemned nine to death, but this verdict did not satisfy the Supreme Court, which accordingly raised the number of death sentences to ten. Göring's command—"to destroy and extirpate"—was faithfully followed by the minions of Hitler justice. In the decision of the Dessau Court mentioned above it was expressly found as a fact that the fatal shots were fired by two only of the accused. The remaining eleven were nevertheless sentenced to death on the following grounds:

"Although they did not shoot, they nevertheless desired the execution of the crime. They must therefore be adjudged accomplices and sentenced to death."

This is merely one instance of death sentences which have been pronounced all over Germany.

Adolf Hitler has declared that nothing happens within the National-Socialist movement without his knowledge. He has placed his representatives, the Reichsstatthalters, at the head of the Government of every State in the Reich. To them has been given the power of life and death, the right to reprieve the condemned or to send them to their slaughter. For the acts of each Reichsstatthalter Hitler is responsible. In Prussia the carrying out of executions is placed under the personal orders of Göring, who with his own hand has signed many of the decrees under which convicted anti-fascists have paid the extreme penalty. Men like Löper in Anhalt, Wagner in Hesse, and Kaufmann in Hamburg, sign the death warrants of the victims of Hitler justice. Kaufmann may be taken as typical of the political careerists who have blossomed forth

*See page 321.

under National-Socialism. Kaufmann's activities were the subject of an investigation and decision by a private National-Socialist Party Court in July 1929. The case against him was proved beyond doubt entirely by documentary evidence; he was found guilty of grave financial frauds and irregularities and of having committed serious breaches of faith and circulated slanders for his own purposes. Kaufmann escaped prison. To-day he is one of Hitler's Reichsstatthalters and in such capacity causes "heads to roll!"

On the Scaffold!

However brutal the hangmen, however bloody their methods, nothing could stay the unflinching courage and the steadfastness of executed anti-fascist workers who have mounted the scaffold fearless and sustained to the end by their firm, undying conviction in the justice of the cause for which they died. Three instances will amply illustrate the spirit which filled the beheaded men as they were about to die.

On August 31st, 1933, the execution of the four Altona workers August Luetgens, Werner Möller, Kurt Tesch and Albert Wolff took place. They had been condemned to death for the alleged murder of four Storm Troopers who were amongst the slain when the Altona Police Chief, Eggerstedt (himself later murdered in a concentration camp by Nazis) permitted an armed procession of Storm Troopers to march through the working-class quarters of Altona, where they had never previously dared to go. The four condemned men had been particularly marked down by the National-Socialists on account of their Communist activities and their heads were amongst the first to fall to Hitler's hangmen.

The families of the condemned men were not notified of the day of the execution. The first news of it came to the mother of one of them as she was listening to the news on the wireless. But the police had brought seventy-five prisoners, colleagues of the four, to witness the execution. August Luetgens was the first to mount the scaffold. At the end of the trial, in reply to the Public Prosecutor's demand for the death sentence, Luetgens had thanked him for bestowing upon him the highest honour to which he as a proletarian revolutionary could lay claim. He had requested that he should be allowed to take the penalties of his fellow prisoners upon his own shoulders. As he mounted the scaffold he raised his clenched hand in the Communist salute and cried: "Red Front! I die for the proletarian revolution." The fourth of the condemned men, Wolff, asked immediately before his decapitation whether he had any last request to make, requested to be allowed to stretch himself once again. When his bonds were removed he struck a nearby Storm Trooper to the ground with a mighty blow of his fist. Then he died.

Three weeks later towards the end of August 1933, Ludwig Büchler was executed with the hand-axe in Magdeburg. He was a member of the Reichsbanner, a courageous anti-fascist workman, and had been condemned to death for the alleged murder of a Storm Trooper. He too died like a true revolutionary. The official National-Socialist organ in Darmstadt gave the following account of his execution:

"During the journey from his cell to a garage, where the scaffold had been erected, during the reading and the execution of the judgment Büchler displayed a deliberate composure seldom shown by condemned men. Even as he mounted the scaffold and as the preparations for his beheading were made he did not manifest the least sign of regret or excitement."

At the beginning of the first chapter of Part I of this work there is reproduced the eye-witness account of the execution by the hand-axe of the six anti-fascists in the Klingelpütz prison in Cologne. The execution of these men, and the bestial manner in which it was carried through raised a storm of abhorrence both within and without Germany. A Catholic priest was moved to say Mass for the repose of the souls of the beheaded men. He was taken to a concentration camp. In order to counter the effect of the widely-spread report of the eye-witness of the execution a special official statement was issued. This statement is remarkable for the fact that it largely confirms the eye-witness's statement. The actual beheadings lasted, according to it, twenty seconds with the exception of one which took fourteen; it alleges that only in one case did the executioner fail to accomplish his work with one stroke of the axe. Like the four Altona Communists and like Ludwig Büchler, the six Cologne workmen died with courage and resignation. As these eleven men died, so died another sixty-six victims of Hitler's justice, for their activities in the interests of the working class and for the real German revolution.

A List of Seven Hundred and Forty-seven Proved Cases of Murder of Defenceless Persons in Hitler-Germany

From Hitler's Accession to Power to the Reichstag Fire

JANUARY 31ST, 1933:
WASSNER, stonemason, shot by police officers in Breslau (*Wolff Telegraph Bureau*). KUHNERT, a workman shot by police while taking part in a demonstration against Hitler (*W.T.B.*).

FEBRUARY 1ST, 1933:
PAUL SCHULZ, aged 20, young Communist workman stabbed by National-Socialists in Berlin-Charlottenburg (*Arbeiter-Zeitung, Saarbrücken*). A GENDARME, shot by National-Socialists in Hornburg, Lower-Rhineland (*W.T.B.*). HELMUTH SCHÄFER, worker, shot by S.A. men in Velberth, SASSE, Socialist worker murdered by National-Socialists in Wilhemsburg (*Witness statement*).

FEBRUARY 2ND, 1933:
PETER VERMING, Communist workman, shot by S.A. band in Gondelsheim (Rhineland) (*Witness statement*). HÖFE, Altona, worker, shot by National-Socialist (*Witness statement*). WILHELMINE STRUTH, working woman, shot by S.A. men in Hamborn (*Witness statement*).

FEBRUARY 3RD, 1933:
ERWIN BERNER, age 21, Communist workman shot by National-Socialists in Berlin (*Telegrafen-Union*). KATHE SENNHOF, Communist, working woman, and an UNKNOWN WOMAN both shot in Duisburg by S.A. men (*Witnesses statement*). WETTMANN, Berlin workman, shot by S.A. men (*Vossische Zeitung*). ILLING, Reichsbanner member, murdered by National-Socialists in Annaberg (*Vossische Zeitung*).

FEBRUARY 4TH, 1933:
ALFRED KOLLATSCH, aged about 18, a young worker murdered by National-Socialists (*Völkischer Beobachter*).

FEBRUARY 5TH, 1933:
ANNA RÖDER, aged 61, a small trader, murdered by National-Socialists in Berlin (*W.T.B.*). WALTER STEINFELDT, student and member of the Reichsbanner, shot by National-Socialists in Breslau (*Witness statement*). BADER, young Communist workman, shot by National-Socialists in Göttingen (*Witness statement*). PAUL FISCHER, member of the Reichsbanner, shot by S.A. man in Chemnitz (*Chemnitzer Tageblatt*). HERMANN KASTEN (Social-Democrat), Mayor of Stassfurt, murdered by S.A. men (*Vossische Zeitung*).

FEBRUARY 6TH, 1933:
MARTIN LEUSCHEL, a workman, shot by the National-Socialist Bornemann in Harburg-Wilhemsburg (*Police Report*).

FEBRUARY 7TH, 1933:
ROBERT RATHKE, aged 34, Communist workman, stabbed by National-Socialists in Cologne (*Witness statement*). HEINRICH LIPPS, aged 27, packer in Cologne murdered by National-Socialists (*Kölnische Zeitung*).

FEBRUARY 8TH, 1933:
WILHELM ESSER, aged 18, Communist, formerly member of the S.A., killed by several shots in Gladbach-Rheydt *Arbeiter-Zeitung, Saarbrücken*).

FEBRUARY 9TH, 1933:
A MEMBER OF THE REICHSBANNER shot by National-Socialists in Höchst am Main (*Witness statement*).

APPENDIX

FEBRUARY 10TH, 1933:
RICHARD PÖTING, 46-year old Berlin workman, murdered for "unknown reasons." The culprit escaped (*Berliner Tageblatt*).

FEBRUARY 11TH, 1933:
SZIEFLIK, a Communist, shot by National-Socialists in Hecklingen (*Witness statement*).

FEBRUARY 12TH, 1933:
JOSEF MAY, workman, killed by several shots fired by S.A. man in Bensheim (*Witness statement*). UNKNOWN AGRICULTURAL LABOURER, murdered by S.A. in Gross-Justin (*Witness statement*). BARNIKAU, Communist official shot by S.A. men in Asseln-Dortmund (*Dortmunder Anziger*). ERWIN GLOCKE, worker, shot in an attack on the Communist Party headquarters in Eisleben (*Vossische Zeitung*).

FEBRUARY 13TH, 1933:
AGRICULTURAL WORKER shot by National-Socialists in Glogau (*Witness statement*).

FEBRUARY 14TH, 1933:
KURT LOHR, Communist, murdered by National-Socialists in Duisburg (*Witness statement*). OTTO HELM and WALTER SCHNEIDER shot during an attack by National-Socialists on a working-class meeting in Eisleben (*Vossische Zeitung*). STOCK, worker of Köln-Kalk shot by S.A. men (*Kölnische Zeitung*).

FEBRUARY 19TH, 1933:
KESTLER, Communist, shot by S.A. men in Frankfurt-Bockenheim (*Saarbrückner Arbeiter Zeitung*).

After the Burning of the Reichstag

It is stated in a confidential report made by the Berlin police headquarters to the Prussian Ministry of the Interior that in the police district of Berlin no less than 247 persons were killed in "political collisions" between the burning of the Reichstag and March 25th, 1933.

MARCH 2ND, 1933:
UNKNOWN MAN (aged 70), killed in Hamburg while standing at his window by being struck through the head by a volley of shots fired by the police without warning (*T.U.*). TWO SOCIAL DEMOCRATS employed in the Trade Union office at Ohlau, by bullets (*Witness statement*). WEISS, Social-Democrat, caretaker of the People's House at Worms, shot dead (*Witness statement*). UNKNOWN GIRL AND COMMUNIST YOUTH killed during the attack on the People's House at Worms (*Witness statement*). FIVE COMMUNIST WORKMEN shot during an attack by S.A. men on the Labour Office at Gleiwitz (*Witness statement*).

MARCH 3RD, 1933:
GERDES, Communist member of the Oldenburg Diet. Shot in the street *W.T.B.*). In this connection the *Frankfurter Zeitung* reported that the proceedings against the arrested persons had been quashed by orders of the Government. UNKNOWN COMMUNIST in Homberg killed by a revolver shot (*W.T.B.*). UNKNOWN REICHSBANNER MAN, Bremen, shot in the street ; UNKNOWN WORKMAN, Bernburg, shot by National-Socialists (*W.T.B.*). GUSTAV SEGEBRECHT, Berlin, shot in the Stephan Inn, Leibenwalderstrasse 41. (*Witness statement*). BERNHARD WIRSCHING Berlin, Petristrasse 8/9, shot by S.A. men in his flat (*Witness statement*). EBELING, Magdeburg workman, killed in the Breckenstrasse by a shot in the stomach (*Witness statement*). FABIAN, Communist worker in Kellinghausen shot at and died in hospital (*W.T.B.*).

339

MARCH 4TH, 1933:
TWO UNNAMED WORKERS, Cologne, severely wounded by shots and subsequently died (*W.T.B.*). UNNAMED MEMBER OF THE IRON FRONT, Thaleschweiler, shot in the street (about 20 shots), (*W.T.B.*). FRIEDRICH MARQUARDT, Düsseldorf, Behrenstrasse 14, no party, killed by blows (*Witness statement*).

MARCH 5TH, 1933:
KLASSEN & DE LONGUEVILLE, Oberhausen (Rhine), shot dead in a school courtyard, "while attempting to escape." Both of them had bullet wounds in front of their bodies (*W.T.B. and Witness*). WARNICKE, Quickborn, shot (*W.T.B.*). UNNAMED REICHSBANNER MAN, Central Germany, stabbed to death (*W.T.B.*). TWO BROTHERS BASSY, Bankau, Upper Silesia, murdered by Storm Troopers (*Witness*). KARL TARNOW, Berlin, beaten to death in Knesebeckstrasse, Neukolln (*Witness*). UNKNOWN WOMAN, age 75, killed in a fight between Communists and Police (*Berliner Lokalanzeiger*). UNKNOWN COMMUNIST shot by unknown persons in Kellingshusen (Hollstein) (*T.U.*). UNKNOWN YOUNG MAN shot in Treves while listening to the elections results on a loud-speaker (*Berliner Lokalanzeiger*). BLESS, Reichsbanner man, killed by S.A. men in an attack on the polling station in Offenbach (*Berliner Lokalanzeiger*). BERNHARD KRAUSE, Communist workman, shot by National-Socialists in Wiesenau near Frankfurt *a-d.* Oder (*W.T.B.*).

MARCH 6TH, 1933.
GRETE MESSING, working woman, Selb, shot down in the street (*W.T.B.*). HANS BAUER, worker, never returned from the Nazi Barracks in the Hedemannstrasse, Berlin (*Witness statement*). FRIEDLÄNDER, age 19, baker's apprentice, murdered in the Nazi barracks in the Hedemannstrasse, Berlin (*Berliner Tageblatt*). THREE UNNAMED WORKERS shot in a collision between S.A. and Police and Communists in Altona (*Berliner Lokalanzeiger*).

MARCH 7TH, 1933.
TWO UNNAMED WORKMEN, Hamburg, killed in Nazi raid (*W.T.B.*). UNNAMED WORKER, Düsseldorf, killed in the Levetezowstrasse (*T.U.*). UNNAMED WORKMAN found dead, shot through the head in Wuppertal-Elbefeld (*Police Report*). HERMANN NEUMANN, Social-Democrat, President of the State Insurance Office in Hesse, Honorary member of the Senate of Giessen University, found dead; alleged suicide on account of his retirement having been requested (*Deutsche Allgemeine Zeitung*). MATHIAS WESKE, Catholic, shoemaker, shot behind the closed windows of his house, by National-Socialists in Düsseldorf-Bilk (*Witness statement*). THEODOR WOLBER, Catholic, roofing contractor, shot by National-Socialists in Düsseldorf-Bilk, in front of his yard (*Witness statement*).

MARCH 8TH, 1933:
UNNAMED REICHSBANNER MAN assaulted by Nazis and mortally wounded in Wuppertal (*T.U.*). UNNAMED COMMUNIST WORKMAN, Billstedt, near Hamburg, shot "while trying to escape" (*W.T.B.*). PHILLIPP, caretaker at the Trade Union House Breslau, shot when Nazis occupied the building (*W.T.B.*). HEINRICH SPARLICH, building worker, Breslau, killed by a bullet and a knife stab in the back (*D.A.Z.*). BALSHUKAT, NITSCHMANN and PREUSS, young workers, Schöneberg-Berlin, bodies found in Machnower Forest (*T.U.*). UNNAMED COMMUNIST WORKER, Bochum, found shot in the street (*T.U.*). UNNAMED WORKER, Bochum, shot in his flat by six "unknown men" (*T.U.*).

MARCH 9TH, 1933:
UNKNOWN WORKER, Berlin, killed in his house by six Nazis (*Witness statement*). UNKNOWN MEMBER OF THE REICHSBANNER, Munich, the body was found in the Munich Trade Union headquarters which was

occupied by the Nazis on March 1st (*Witness statement*). LANDGRAF, director of publishing house, Chemnitz, shot when the *Volksstimme* building was occupied by Nazis (*T.U.*). HELLPUCH, Communist workman, Duisburg, found shot (*W.T.B.*). MEMBER OF THE NATIONAL FLIERS' LEAGUE, shot by an S.A. Patrol in a police raid in Brunswick.

MARCH 9TH, 1933.
UNKNOWN WORKER, shot by Nazis in Zschopau (*Berliner Lokalanzeiger*).

MARCH 10TH, 1933:
ARNO FÖRSTER and MAX TENNLER, Communist workmen, shot "while trying to escape" (*Berliner Lokalanzeiger*). FRAU BICKS, aged 70, Berlin, mortally wounded by Storm Troopers who fired through her door. HANS SAILE, circulation manager, shot when the *Volksfreund* (*Social-Democrat*) offices in Brunswick were occupied (*Witness statement*). TWO UNNAMED WORKERS, Zschopau, shot by Storm Troopers (*Berliner Lokalanzeiger*). ALFRED PETZLAFF, Communist worker, Berlin-Schöneberg, taken by Nazis from his home. His body was found mutilated at Priesterweg station (*Witness statement*). SCHONFLÜGEL, a worker, Gornau, Chemnitz, "killed by a chance bullet" (*Berliner Lokalanzeiger*).

MARCH 11TH, 1933:
ERICH MEYER, young worker, Spandau, beaten to death (*Frankfurter Zeitung*). ROBERT DITTMAR, worker, Karlshorst, near Berlin, found shot (*Berliner Lokalanzeiger*). UNNAMED WORKER, Breslau, stabbed to death (*T.U.*). FORSTER and TANDLER, Communist workers, Limbach near Chemnitz, "shot while trying to escape" (*Witness statement*). PAUL KRANTZ, young worker Limbach near Chemnitz "shot when trying to escape" (*W.T.B.*). UNKNOWN MAN, no Party, Oppeln, shot on the steps of the Town Hall (*Berliner Lokalanzeiger*).

MARCH 12TH, 1933:
Councillor KRESSE, Social-Democrat, Magdeburg, shot at polling booth in Felgeleben (*T.U.*). EICHHOLZ and KATHER, workmen, Toklemith, East Prussia, "shot while trying to escape" (*T.U.*). SPEIGEL, Social-Democratic lawyer, Keil, attacked and killed in his house (*W.T.B.*). PAUL KLUTH, Elbing workman, shot on a bridge by S.A. men (*Witness statement*).

MARCH 13TH, 1933:
WORKING WOMAN, unknown, mortally wounded by a bayonet thrust on the arrest of her husband in Grottendorf, Saxony (*Witness statement*). UNKNOWN WORKER, mutilated and murdered by Nazis in Stettin (*Witness statement*). POHL, Elbing worker, found shot through the head (*T.U.*).

MARCH 14TH, 1933:
KRUG, Schweinfurth, shot "in self defence" by a Nazi (*T.U.*). UNNAMED WORKER, Hamburg, shot by detectives (*W.T.B.*).

MARCH 15TH, 1933:
JEWISH MERCHANT, found dead in a wood near Landshut with his skull smashed in and with two bullet holes, after arrest by S.A. men (*Witness statement*). WILHELM REUPKE, Social-Democratic manager of a Co-operative in Bündheim (Brunswick), died after bestial treatment by Nazis; alleged 'suicide' (*Witness statement*). THREE UNNAMED WORKERS, shot by S.A. men in Leipzig (*Witness*).

MARCH 16TH, 1933:
SEVEN ARRESTED MEN murdered in the S.A. barracks in the Friedrichstrasse, Berlin. Their bodies were carried away (*Witness statement*). BREMER, Jewish merchant, almost beaten to death by S.A. men, found 'hanged' in his cell in Seesen the next morning (*Witness statement*). LEO KRELL, Editor, Berlin, beaten to death (*Witness statement*).

MARCH 17TH, 1933:
TWO UNKNOWN PERSONS, Elbing, "shot while trying to escape" (*Nachtausgabe*).

APPENDIX

MARCH 18TH, 1933:
WALTER SCHULZ, Communist worker, Wittstock, murdered in prison (*Witness statement*). HANS SACHS, manufacturer, Chemnitz, shot (*W.T.B.*). SIEGBERT KINDERMANN, Berlin-Charlottenburg, taken to the Nazi headquarters in the Hedemannstrasse, beaten to death and thrown from the window (*Berliner Tageblatt*). UNNAMED WORKER, Berlin-Wedding, beaten to death at Nazi headquarters (*Witness statement*).

MARCH 19TH, 1933:
KREBS, Communist worker, Moabit-Berlin, shot by Storm Troopers in the street (*Witness*).

MARCH 20TH, 1933:
GÜNTHER JOACHIM, lawyer, Berlin, tortured by Nazis, died in Moabit hospital (*Vossische Zeitung*). KURT POSSANER, Berlin, shot. Possaner was for a long time the liaison officer between the German and the Austrian National-Socialists. He had been recently thrown over by the leaders and was shot whilst being taken by car to the Austrian frontier for deportation (*Neues Wiener Journal*). FRITZ SCHMITZBERG, found shot in the Grunewald Berlin (*V.Z.*).

MARCH 21ST, 1933:
OTTO SELZ, Straubing, shot (*Witness statement*).

MARCH 22ND, 1933.
WALTER BOEGE, Ebersbach, Social-Democrat, "shot while trying to escape" (*V.Z.*). WILHELM WENZEL, Communist workman, Essen, shot in the street (*W.T.B.*). He was shot by an auxiliary policeman and died in hospital shortly afterwards (*V.Z.*). DRESCHE, workman, found murdered (*Witness statement*). PAUL REUTER, Selchowerstrasse, Berlin, beaten to death by Storm Troopers (*Witness*). UNKNOWN WORKER, shot by Nazis in Berlin-Wilmersdorf (*Witness statement*).

MARCH 23RD, 1933:
ERICH LANGE, ex-S.S. man, Gelsenkirchen, shot by S.A. men (*Witness statement*). FRANCK, member of the Reichsbanner, Worms, alleged suicide. Dragged from bed, ill-treated (his hands had Swastikas cut in them) and hanged in an outhouse (*Witness statement*). HERBERT PANGERITZ, worker, Bergestrase 78, Berlin, brutally treated and died in hospital (*Witness statement*). The death was caused by serious internal lesions, crushing of the bladder and fractures of the skull, according to the medical certificate.

MARCH 24TH, 1933:
FRAU ARBETS, working woman, Gladbach, "shot while trying to escape." Heading in the *Völkischer Beobachter*. "A Communist Woman Shot." (*T.U.*). ERICH PERL, age 17, Leipzig, shot in the street after leaving the Nazi barracks (*Witness statement*).

MARCH 25TH 1933:
DRESCHER, Communist workman, found murdered in his house in Dyrotz (*Witness statement*). SOCIALIST COUNCILLOR, Wedding-Berlin, maltreated and died in hospital. He was thrown from the third storey of a building on to the street (*Witness statement*). FRAU MÜLLER, Aue, Saxony, maltreated, said to have committed suicide (*Witness statenent*).

MARCH 26TH, 1933:
GROTHENNE, Telegraph worker, member of the Reichsbanner, beaten to death in S.A. headquarters in Brunswick (*Witness statement*). NEUMANN, shopkeeper, Königsberg, beaten and used as a target (*T.U.*). His wounds were sprinkled with pepper and salt. He was taken to a Berlin hospital where he later died (*Witness*). DR. MAX PLAUT, lawyer, beaten to death in a Nazi barracks in Kassel, on account of a personal quarrel with his Nazi colleague, present Under Secretary of State Friesler, who gave the command for his beating (*Witness statement*). MAX BILECKI, Schöneberg, tortured in Nazi barracks in Berlin and died in hospital (*Witness statement*).

MARCH 29TH, 1933:
WALTER SCHÜTZ, Communist member of the Reichstag, beaten to death in Königsberg by S.A. men (*Witness statement*). (See text).

MARCH 30TH, 1933.
FRITZ ROLLE, a Siemenstadt workman, found stabbed to death (*W.T.B.*). LEIBL VOLLSCHLÄGER of Skalitzerstraase, Berlin, kidnapped and murdered. He was taken away by S.A. men and disappeared for three days. On the fourth day his body was found in the Spree (*Witness statement*). UNKNOWN JEW, Upper Hesse, hung by his feet and died (*Manchester Guardian*).

MARCH 31ST, 1933:
TWO UNNAMED COMMUNISTS, from Ebersbach, one found shot, the other tortured by S.A. men and died from injuries in the Schweidnitz asylum (*Neugerdorfer Zeitung* and *Witness statement*).

END OF MARCH, 1933:
LAUFER, member of the Reichsbanner, killed at 6 p.m. while standing in front of his parent's shop in Elberfeld, by three revolver shots fired by an S.A. squad (*Witness statement*).

BEGINNING OF APRIL, 1933:
SIX MONTHS OLD INFANT child of the Klettenburg Communist W. thrown from its cradle and killed with a blow from a steel rod by S.A. men who had broken into the house and were looking for W. (*Witness statement*). KINDERMANN, age 16, young Communist workman killed in the street in front of a provision shop in the presence of his mother, in Berlin-Weissensee.

APRIL 1ST, 1933:
WILHELM PÖTTER, baker, and KARL GÖRMANN, Communist workman, Woldenburg "shot while attempting to escape" (*Vossische Zeitung*). WILHELM DENGEMANN, steel worker, Duisburg, shot from behind in the street (*Vossische Zeitung*). FRITZ SCHUMM, lawyer, Keil, beaten to death in his cell in prison (*T.U.*). UNNAMED WORKER, aged 23, Munich, "shot while attempting to escape" (*Munich Neueste Nachrichten*). PRESSBURGER, cattle dealer, Munich, described as suicide (*Munich Neueste Nachrichten*).

APRIL 2ND, 1933:
WERTHEIMER, Kehl, alleged death from a stroke at the time of his arrest (*W.T.B.*).

APRIL 3RD, 1933:
PAUL JAROS, smith, Limbach, near Chemnitz, "shot while trying to escape" (*T.U.*). UNNAMED WORKMAN, Augsburg, alleged death from a stroke at the time of his arrest (*T.U.*). GEORG BELL, engineer, former collaborator of the Munich Brown House, and of the S.A. Chief Roehm who had fled to Austria from the Nazis and who was murdered at Kufstein, in Austria, by armed Nazis, in motor-cars who had crossed the frontier for the purpose of killing him (*Conti-W.T.B.*).

APRIL 4TH, 1933:
HEINZ BÄSSLER, a workman, formerly a member of the S.A. shot in Dusseldorf, whilst attempting to escape (The photograph of his body shows bullet wounds in his face) (*W.T.B.*). DR. PHILIPPSTAL, dental surgeon, Biesdorf, Berlin, beaten to death (*Berliner Tageblatt*).

APRIL 5TH, 1933:
WILHELM DREWS, Communist workman, Hamburg, shot in the street. Drews was followed by Nazis and then attacked from behind, late at night (*T.U.* and *Völkischer Beobachter*.) RENOIS, Communist Councillor, Bonn,— "shot while trying to escape" (*T.U.*) SAUER, member of the Social-Democratic Party, Zubachwitz, beaten to death in the concentration camp at Hohenstein (*Witness statement*). ALFRED ROTTER and WIFE, Berlin theatrical

343

manager, ambushed by German Nazis in Vaduz, Lichtenstein, taken to the Triesenberger heights and thrown over a precipice (*Vossische Zeitung*).

APRIL 6TH, 1933:
KURT FRIEDRICH, Communist workman, shot in Johangeorgenstadt, Saxony (*Witness statement*). MAX NEIDERMAYER, Communist councillor, same town, beaten to death in Zwickau prison (*Witness statement*).

APRIL 7TH, 1933:
HERSCHMANN STEINSCHNEIDER (alias ERIK JAN HANUSSEN) the Jewish National-Socialist Clairvoyant, murdered by National-Socialists probably because of his knowledge of the Reichstag fire.

APRIL 8TH, 1933:
UNKNOWN WORKMAN, Neukölln, Berlin, beaten to death by Storm Troopers (*Witness statement*). WALTER STRAUSS, locksmith, National-Socialist, age 21, shot by National-Socialists in a riot in Breslau (*Prager Tageblatt; Witness statement*). LUDWIG ZIEGLER, National-Socialist, age 23, shot by Nazis in a riot in Breslau (*Prager Tageblatt*).

APRIL 9TH, 1933:
WALTER KASCH, Hamburg, ambushed and shot by Storm Troopers (*Witness statement*).

APRIL 10TH, 1933:
FRITZ ENGLER, barber, no Party, Chemnitz, tortured and killed in the Zeisig forest (*Witness statement*).

APRIL 11TH, 1933:
MAX RUPF, Member of Reichsbanner, Chemnitz, found shot (*T.U.*). DR. ARTHUR WEINER, lawyer, Chemnitz, found shot (*Frankfurter Zeitung*), ALBERT HANSPACH, Communist worker, Friedensdorf, Zittau, shot in prison (*T.U.*).

APRIL 12TH, 1933:
DR. ODENKIRCHEN, Councillor in Düsseldorf, alleged to have hanged himself in prison (*Nachtausgabe*). DR. BEYER, Councillor in Krefeld, alleged to have hanged himself in prison (*Frankfurter Zeitung*). BENARIO, engineer; ARTHUR KAHN, Nürnberg, merchant; ERWIN KAHN, Munich, merchant; GOLDMANN, Fürth, merchant; DR. LEVY, Gmünden, lawyer and WILHELM WAUR, Munich, lawyer, all shot in Dachau Concentration Camp "whilst attempting to escape" (*W.T.B.; D.A.Z.*, etc.) According to the statement of a witness all had been shot from the front. No persons were admitted to their funerals. FRITZ KOLLOSCHE, Charlottenburg, tortured in Nazi barracks, died after admission to hospital (*Witness statement*). SALOMON KOPF, merchant, Dresden, severely maltreated whilst being taken under Storm Troopers escort to the frontier. Admitted to hospital in Warnsdorf on April 1st, 1933, together with three other Jews found lying severely wounded near the German frontier. Died of his injuries (*Czechoslovak Press Bureau*).

APRIL 13TH, 1933:
EBEL, Social-Democrat Manager of the Association of German Sick Benefit Societies, arrested and subsequently alleged to have hanged himself (*Nachtausgabe*). GUSTAV SCHÖNHERR, workman, Hamburg, tortured to death (*Witness statement*), ALBERT JANKA, Communist member of the Reichstag, alleged 'suicide' at Zwickau (*W.T.B.*).

APRIL 15TH, 1933:
SPIRO, age 17, Jewish, Berlin, tortured in Nazi rooms in the Schönhelzerstrasse, Berlin, and murdered in the Nazi barracks in the Hedemannstrasse, Berlin (*Witness statement*).

APRIL 16TH, 1933:
BREITSCHNEIDER, found shot in a wood near Siegmar, Saxony (*W.T.B.*).

APPENDIX

APRIL 17TH, 1933:
JORDAN, Communist official, shot dead in Königsberg (*Witness statement*).

APRIL 18TH, 1933:
RICHARD POLLEIT, Communist workman, Königsberg, "shot whilst attempting to escape" (*Frankfurter Zeitung*). UNKNOWN WORKMAN, Königsberg, "shot whilst attempting to escape" (*T.U.*).

APRIL 19TH, 1933:
UNNAMED RAILWAYMAN, Munich, stabbed from behind, alleged suicide. (*Münchner Neueste Nachrichten*). ALFRED ELGER, a Christian workman, beaten to death by Storm Troopers on account of his Jewish appearance (*Witness statement*).

APRIL 20TH, 1933:
UNKNOWN MEMBER OF RED SPORT ORGANISATION, stabbed to death by S.A. men on the way from the Summary Court to the prison in Königsberg (*Witness statement*). KAMINSKI, Dortmund, member of the Anti-fascist League, beaten to death in prison (*Witness statement*).

APRIL 21ST, 1933:
FRITZ DRESSEL, Chairman of the Communist Group in the Bavarian Diet alleged to have committed suicide (*Münchner Neueste Nachrichten*), but reported by several witnesses to have been murdered in Dachau Concentration Camp.

APRIL 22ND, 1933:
MAX KASSEL, dairyman, Wiesbaden, shot in his flat (*D.A.Z.*). SALOMON ROSENTRAUCH, merchant, Wiesbaden, murdered in his flat (*D.A.Z.*). PAUL PABST, workman, alleged suicide in S.A. barracks (*Germania*).

APRIL 23RD, 1933:
PAUL HERDE, workman, Lübben, shot dead (*Vossische Zeitung*). FRANZ SCHNEIDER, anti-fascist workman, Hoch, Rhineland, alleged suicide in prison (*Vossische Zeitung*). KONIETZNY, Communist workman, Oelsnitz, Erzegebirge, alleged suicide in prison (*Vossische Zeitung*). KURT BENKE, police sergeant, S.A. man, Berlin (*Angriff*).

APRIL 24TH, 1933:
UNKNOWN SQUATTER, Horner Moor, tarred and burnt, alleged suicide (*Völkischer Beobachter*). CORDES & SON, merchants, Wittmund, near Bremen, shot in a pogrom (*W.T.B.*).

APRIL 25TH, 1933:
MENDEL HABER, merchant, Dortmund, arrested by S.A. men and taken to their barracks. He was there shot and his corpse was thrown into a nearby canal. When it was retrieved and identified it was found to have bullet and knife wounds (*Dortmunder Generalanzeiger*). TWO UNKNOWN WORKERS, Heil, Lippe, found dead (*Völkischer Beobachter*). GRANITZA, workman, Königsberg, "shot whilst attempting to escape" (*Nachtausgabe*).

APRIL 26TH, 1933:
WILLY PLONSKE, workman, Berlin, found dead (*Angriff*). MAX GOLDSCHMIDT, tailor, Königsberg, aged 30, beaten to death in the rooms of the Eastern S.A. Division (*Witness statement*).

APRIL 27TH, 1933:
ERWIN VOLKMAR, boxer, Neukölln, Berlin, found shot in the street, alleged non-political murder (*Angriff*).

APRIL 28TH, 1933:
UNNAMED MAN, Wollenberg, Oberbernhim, shot and burnt to death (*Frankfurter Zeitung and police report*). FUNK, Communist member of the Reichstag, Dortmund, murdered in prison, alleged suicide (*Angriff*). FRITZ GUMBERT, Communist workman, Heidenau, beaten to death after weeks of torture (*Witness statement*).

APRIL 29TH, 1933:
UNNAMED MAN, found murdered near Werneuchen (*W.T.B.*).

APRIL 30TH, 1933:
HACKSTEIN, Communist workman, Grevenbroich, "shot whilst attempting to escape (*Kölnische Zeitung*). ANDREAS VON FLOTOV, German Nationalist landowner, arrested by Storm Troopers and shot at Neubuckow near Schwerin, "whilst attempting to escape" (*Conti*).

END OF APRIL, 1933:
UNNAMED WORKER Ebersdorf, Saxony, and HEINZ GOLDBERG, member of a Red Sport Association shot in the cellar of the Hermann Göring House in Löbau (*Witness statement*). CAPTAIN WENDT, Member of the Strasser Group, and formerly a National-Socialist, shot near the Landsberg fortress, "whilst attempting to escape" (*Official Report*). UNNAMED POLISH JEW, beaten to death in Creglingen (*Witness statement*). The official announcement to the relatives attributed the death to a heart attack. The body was handed over in a sealed coffin and only on condition that the relatives gave a written undertaking not to have it opened. S.A. men attended the funeral.

MAY 2ND, 1933:
RODENSTOCK, Social-Democrat, secretary of the Municipal Workers' Union, and TWO UNNAMED TRADE UNION OFFICIALS tortured and beaten to death in the S.A. headquarters at Duisburg (*Witness statement*). DANZIGER, Jewish merchant, Duisburg, attacked by Storm Troopers and so severely ill-treated that he died shortly afterwards (*Witness statement*).

MAY 4TH, 1933:
UNNAMED MEMBER OF THE STAHLHELM, shot in Storm Troopers quarters in Berlin (*Saarbrücken: Arbeiter Zeitung*).

MAY 5TH, 1933:
SIMON KATZ, workman, Polish, beaten to death in Berlin (*Witness statement*). UNNAMED MAN, Potsdam, trussed up and thrown into the river (*Vossische Zeitung*). SPANGENBURG, Communist worker, Bredereiche Templin, alleged suicide in prison (*Vossische Zeitung*). UNNAMED DYE WORKER, Sagan, alleged suicide, murdered in prison (*W.T.B.*).

MAY 7TH, 1933:
DR. ERNST OBERFOHREN, Chairman of the German-Nationalist Group in the Reichstag. Found dead in his house at Kiel. Alleged suicide. See text, Part I.

MAY 8TH, 1933:
DR. ECKSTEIN, leader of the Socialist Labour Party, Breslau, tortured to death (*W.T.B.*).

MAY 9TH, 1933:
DR. MEYER, Jewish, dentist, Wuppertal, arrested and mutilated by Storm Troopers then drowned (*Witness statement*). GALINOWSKI, workman Allstein, "shot whilst attempting to escape" (*W.T.B.*).

MAY 10TH, 1933:
UNNAMED YOUNG WORKMAN, member of Red Sport organisation, Wedding-Berlin, murdered in Nazi barracks in the Hedemannstrasse, his body was then thrown into the Spree canal (*Witness statement*).

MAY 11TH, 1933:
ADOLF BIEDERMANN, Social-Democrat Member of the Reichstag, Hamburg, alleged suicide (*Frankfurter Zeitung*). GLÜCKOW, Communist workman, East Berlin, tortured by Nazis and died in hospital (*Witness statement*).

MAY 12TH, 1933:
SEPP GOETZ, Communist member of the Diet, murdered in Dachau Concentration Camp after weeks of terrible torture (*Witness statement*).

MAY 13th, 1933:
HENSELER, Communist workman, Düsseldorf, shot (*Germania*).
MAY 15TH, 1933:
DR. ALFRED STRAUSS, lawyer, Munich, age 30, German Jew, arrested on the orders of his professional colleague, Frank, now Minister of Justice, severely ill-treated and beaten to death (*Witness statement*). UNNAMED MEMBER OF THE STAHLHELM, Berlin, attacked by Nazis and stabbed to death (*Witness statement*). PALETTI, worker, Berlin, tortured to death (*Witness statement*).
MID-MAY, 1933:
GERHARD ROSENBAUM, Polish Jew, age 24, severely beaten by Nazis in an S.A. barracks; died in hospital in Moabit (*Witness statement*). PETER MEINERZ, workman, Bilk, Düsseldorf, agent for workers' papers, recovered from the Rhine with his throat cut (*Witness statement*). HILARIUS and GILGES, Mulatto actors, arrested in Düsseldorf, their bodies were recovered from the Rhine on the following day (*Witness statement*). JOHANN LOPAU, Social-Democratic member of the Senate, manager for many years of the *Volksblatt* in Lüneburg. Alleged to have committed suicide (*Hamburger Nachrichten*).
MAY 17TH, 1933:
HERMANN RIEDEL, Gladbeck, alleged suicide (*Der Tag*). JOHANNES and WILHELM BURDT, Dusiburg, beaten to death (*Der Tag*).
MAY 18TH, 1933:
HONKSTEIN, Grevenbroich, "shot whilst attempting to escape" (*W.T.B.*).
MAY 19TH, 1933:
LEONHARD HAUSMANN, Communist official shot in Dachau Concentration Camp, "whilst attempting to escape" (*W.T.B.*).
MAY 20TH, 1933:
ARTHUR MÜLLER, workman, member of Reichsbanner, taken away by Nazis in a motor-car, tortured and beaten to death in the Nazi barracks in General Papestrasse, Berlin (*Witness statement*). . . . "His skull was smashed in. His right eye was torn out. The flesh was torn away all over his face. . . . . One arm was broken in two places. . . ."
MAY 22ND, 1933:
MATTIAS THEISSEN, Organiser of the Social-Democratic Building Workers' Union in Brunswick, died in the Catholic Hospital after brutal treatment at the hands of Storm Troopers (*Witness statement*). FOUR COMMUNIST PRISONERS, shot in the Concentration Camp near Chemnitz, "whilst attempting to escape" (*T.U.*).
MAY 25TH, 1933:
SCHLOSS, merchant, Nürnburg, shot in Dachau Concentration Camp (*Witness statement*).
MAY 26TH, 1933:
GROMANN, an artist, Duisburg, shot by S.S. men in the Kalkumer Forest. The murderers pinned a message to the corpse "In memory of Schlageter" (*Witness statement*).
MAY 27TH, 1933:
FRANZ LEHRBURGER, merchant, Nürnburg, aged 29, shot in Dachau Concentration Camp "whilst trying to escape" (*Fränkischer Kurier*).
MAY 29TH, 1933:
WILHELM ARON, law student, member of Reichsbanner, Bamberg, shot in Dachau Camp "whilst attempting to escape" (*Bamberger Zeitung*).
MAY 30TH, 1933:
GRALISCH, war invalid, trampled to death in Leipzig, by members of the 48th S.A. Battalion (*Witness statement*).

END OF MAY, 1933:

H. BOON, age 22, member of the Anti-fascist League, Elberfeld, taken away by Storm Troopers in a motor-car. His corpse was found next day near the town with a cut throat and many bullet wounds (*Witness statement*). FRITZ STRUNK, Klausenhof, Barmen, father of six children, taken from his house during the night, severely maltreated and killed by ten shots through the head (*Witness statement*). TWO COMMUNISTS shot in the Siegburg Concentration Camp, near Köln (*Riechspost, Vienna*).

JUNE 8TH, 1933:

OPPOSITION STORM TROOPER, Düsseldorf, shot while distributing leaflets (*Dortmunher Generalanzeiger*).

JUNE 10TH, 1933:

KARL LOTTES, Essen, Communist workman, shot "whilst attempting to escape" (*W.T.B.*). WALTER ERNST, workman, found half buried in Henningsdorf Cemetery, Berlin (*W.T.B.*). According to a witness statement he was taken there from an S.A. barracks. FRITZ KONKORENZ, opposition Storm Trooper, found shot in his house, Berlin (*Witness statement*).

JUNE 12TH, 1933:

UNNAMED WORKER, Essen, "shot whilst attempting to escape" (*T.U.*).

JUNE 15TH, 1933:

FRITZ MERSEBURG, Member of the Anti-fascist League, Elberfeld, severely ill-treated and shot dead by Storm Troopers of the Puppe Troop in Elberfeld (*Witness statement*).

MID-JUNE, 1933:

EMIL PICCARD, Social-Democratic District Secretary, for Upper Rhineland, killed by National-Socialists. Alleged Suicide (*Deutsche Freiheit*). UNNAMED WORKMAN, Meseritz, killed in the Sonnenburg Concentration Camp. WILHELM JAENECKE, Communist official, shot in "Horst Wessel" House, Berlin (*Witness statement*).

JUNE 16TH, 1933:

KIEPENHEUER, workman, Oberbilk, Düsseldorf, arrested by Storm Troopers and driven away in a car. He was shot in the head. His body was thrown from the car on the Rhine bridge and driven over (*Witness statement*).

JUNE 20TH, 1933:

WALTER KERSING, workman, member of the German-Nationalist Association in Frankfurt-on-Oder, shot by Nazis during a dispute (*W.T.B.*). ERWIN KRAYKAMP, Communist workman, Elberfeld, hit in the face before the "People's House" by S.A. leader Puppe, and shot because he retaliated. Died a few days later in hospital (*Witness statement*).

JUNE 21ST, 1933:

PAUL URBAN, workman, Brandenburg, alleged suicide in prison (*Nachtausgabe*). MARTIN HOOB, sub-District Leader of the German Communist Party in Zwickau, and TWO UNKNOWN MEN found dead in a pool, with their arms and legs bound at Neustadel near Zwickau (*12 Uhr-Mittagsblatt*).

JUNE 22ND, 1933:

BUKERT, Communist, Friedrichshagen, beaten to death by Storm Troopers in Köpenick. WILTZOG, Communist, beaten to death in Köpenick, Berlin. WILHELM SCHMAUS, murdered by Storm Troopers in Köpenick, Berlin. His son was seriously wounded by a shot through the stomach and his life despaired of. KARL POKERT, Communist, beaten to death in Köpenick, Berlin. PAUL POHL, Social-Democrat, beaten to death in Köpenick, Berlin, his body being afterwards hanged in the woods. RICHARD KRAHL, Social-Democrat, died through ill-treatment at the hands of Nazis in Köpenick, Berlin. ERICH JANITSKI, Communist, shot by Storm

Troopers in Köpenick, Berlin, after being tortured. RICHARD ASSMANN, leader of the Reichsbanner in Friedrichshagen, Berlin, tortured to death in Köpenick by Nazis. PAUL VON ESSEN, Reichsbanner Leader, Köpenick, died through ill-treatment at the hands of Storm Troopers. JOHANNES STELLING, Social-Democrat, former Prime Minister of Mecklenburg, kidnapped and murdered by Nazis in Köpenick. FLEMMING, Social-Democrat, murdered by Storm Troopers in Köpenick. KARL RAKOWSKI, workman, murdered in Köpenick by Storm Troopers. PAUL and JOSEF SPITZER, Communists, beaten to death in Köpenick. SEVEN UN-NAMED MEN arrested and beaten to death by Storm Troopers in Köpenick. UNNAMED JEW, aged 60, factory owner in Köpenick, beaten to death by Storm Troopers (*All Witnesses statements*). ALTENBURG, Communist workman, shot in Arnswalde, "whilst attempting to escape" (*D.A.Z.*).

JUNE 23RD, 1933:
EDUARD KABUS, watchmaker, Düsseldorf, found shot in the cellar of his house (*Police announcement*).

JUNE 24TH, 1933:
ARTHUR MAY, Communist official, Aachen, "shot whilst attempting to escape" (*Police announcement*).

JUNE 27TH, 1933:
FIVE NAMELESS WORKERS murdered in Elberfeld by the S.A. troop under the directions of their leader August Puppe (*Witness statement*).

JUNE 28TH, 1933:
HANS KRÄMER, WILHEM MUNCK, LEOPOLD MOSES, EMIL GRAUPNER, workmen, Bernburg, shot in Oranienburg Concentration Camp "whilst attempting to escape." They were driven out of doors late at night and shot down with machine-guns (*Witness statement*).

JUNE 30TH, 1933:
ANTON MACIOSZYK, Social-Democrat, draughtsman, Hanover, died from the results of torture undergone during an interrogation (*Witness statement*).

END OF JUNE, 1933:
GLASPER, District Leader of the Red Aid, Elberfeld. Murdered (*Witness statement*). HUNGLINGER, Police Officer, Munich, JOHANN WEIS-MANN, Munich, SEBASTIAN NEFZGER, Munich, and MICHAEL SIGMANN, Social-Democrat, Pasing, all murdered in Dachau Concentration Camp (*Witness statement*). TWO UNKNOWN WORKERS, found shot dead with bullet wounds in their stomachs, backs and chests, Elberfeld (*Witness statements*). HANS GOSMEIER, young workman, taken away in a motor-car by Storm Troopers in Elberfeld, shot and found dead in the street next day. JOSEPH RIESS, bookseller and editor, shot by Storm Troopers. GRELL, Berlin, university assistant in the Faculty of Dental Surgery arrested by Nazis, found shot next day (*Witnesses statements*).

EARLY JULY 1933:
BRUNO EHLERS, Polish Jew, shop assistant, beaten to death by Storm Troopers in Brunswick (*Witness statement*). The police report stated that he died from a heart attack while in custody. FRITZ DÄHLER, young workman, Elberfeld, found murdered. JULIUS MENNING, workman, Elberfeld, shot dead on the Platz der Republik (*Witnesses statements*).

JULY 1ST, 1933:
MAX MARGOLINER, merchant, aged 24, Breslau. Brutally tortured in the Brown House in Karlstrasse in April. Died from his injuries in South Breslau Hospital (*Witness statement*). HERMANN DASSE, Social-Demo-cratic Trade Union Secretary, thrown from the window of the "People's House" in Brunswick, after frightful ill-treatment (*Witness statement*).

APPENDIX

JULY 3RD, 1933:
  TWELVE WORKERS, killed in an attack by Storm Troopers on a workers'
  settlement in Leipzig (*Witness statement*). LANDMANN, National-Socialist,
  shot by S.A. men in Brunswick for political unreliability (*Witness statement*).
  OTTO ROSS, Reichsbanner leader, ERICH SCHELPMANN, Communist,
  and FIFTEEN UNNAMED WORKMEN maltreated in a raid by S.A.
  men and beaten to death in the Nazi Barracks in Brunswick. KARL WOLFF,
  Communist official, tortured and beaten to death in the Brunswick Nazi
  Barracks (*Witnesses statements*).

JULY 4TH, 1933:
  HERMANN BOEHME, WILLI STEINFASS, HANS GRIMMIGER,
  WALTER RÖMLING, RHEINHOLD LIESEGANG, JULIUS BLEY,
  LUDEWIG, GUSTAVO SCHMIDT, STAATH and SCHÜNEMANN.
  The above men were taken to the Brunswick S.A. barracks where they were
  severely ill-treated. They were then taken some twenty minutes' journey
  outside the town and were killed by an S.S. troop (*Witness statement*). Not
  until August 1st were the official announcements of their deaths made to
  their families. UNNAMED WORKMAN, thrown from a second floor
  window of the Breslau Brown House (*Witness statement*). THREE WORK-
  MEN, Barmen, trampled out of recognition and murdered (*Witness statement*).
  W. ZIMMERMANN, anti-fascist workman, Barmen, attacked by S.S. men
  in the street and found dead shortly afterwards (*Witness statement*).

JULY 6TH, 1933:
  UNNAMED JEWISH SHOPKEEPER, Dortmund, seized and murdered
  by Storm Troopers (*Witness statement*).

JULY 7TH, 1933:
  UNNAMED MAN, aged 25, corpse recovered from the Neukölln Canal
  (*D.A.Z.*).

JULY 8TH, 1933:
  TWO UNNAMED BODIES, found murdered in Elberfeld (*Witness statement*).

JULY 10TH, 1933:
  TEN S.A. MEN, opposition National-Socialists shot in Köslin, when a
  Storm Troop was disarmed. THIRTEEN S.A. MEN shot by S.A. guards
  in Wilsede Concentration Camp, "whilst attempting to escape" (*Witness
  statement*).

JULY 11TH, 1933:
  KARL SCHULZ, former member of the Prussian Diet, died in Spandau
  Prison from the effects of ill-treatment (*Witness statement*).

JULY 12TH, 1933:
  YEAR OLD CHILD, daughter of Communist workman, Bohle, in Schwedt,
  shot dead by Storm Troopers who were aiming at her mother (*Witness
  statement and Vossische Zeitung*). HANS OTTENBACH, workman, murdered with THREE UNKNOWN MEN by Storm Troopers in Wuppertal
  (*Witness statement*). WILFRED ANDREAS, workman, Wuppertal, tortured and then killed by nine shots (*Witness statement*).

JULY 13TH, 1933:
  HERMANN VAN T'ENDE, Communist, shot during the journey under
  escort from Münster to the Police Prison in Essen, "whilst attempting to
  escape" (*W.T.B.*). UNNAMED NATIONAL-SOCIALIST, sub-leader,
  Magdeburg district, alleged to have shot himself on being arrested in the
  presence of the District Leader of the N.S.D.A.P. and several police officials
  (*Vossische Zeitung*). POLISH SUBJECT, died in Dresden from the effects
  of torture administered by Storm Troopers (*Witness statement*). FRITZ
  LANGE, Communist, Powayen, brought from prison and lynched by a
  mob (*Völkischer Beobachter*). MESSINGER, Communist, alleged to have
  committed suicide in Bonn Court Prison (*Völkischer Beobachter*).

APPENDIX

JULY 14TH, 1933:
THREE UNNAMED COMMUNISTS from Schwerin, shot during transport under escort to Sonnenburg Concentration Camp, "whilst attempting to escape" (*W.T.B.*). COMMUNIST OFFICIAL, Warthe, Bochum, shot whilst being taken to an interrogation "while attempting to escape" (*Vossische Zeitung*). AUSTRIAN WORKMAN, murdered in the S.A. Headquarters in Frankfurt am Main on the orders of Reichstatthalter Sprenger and the Police President of Düsseldorf, S.A. Group Leader Weitzel. His body was handed over to the police in a box (*Witness statement*).

JULY 15TH, 1933:
OTTO NEU, Communist, Stettin, shot while being arrested by Storm Troopers alleged "in self-defence" (*Berliner Borsen Zeitung*). UNNAMED POLISH JEW, aged 56, dairyman in Dragonerstrasse, arrested by S.A. men for alleged distribution of communist leaflets in fact brought to his premises by S.A. men. Disappeared. Police and consular inquiries have brought no trace to light (*Witness statement*).

JULY 17TH, 1933:
ERNST WALTER, Communist workman, Rohrbeck. Beaten to death by Storm Troopers in Meinersdorf Concentration Camp (*Witness statement*). POLISH SUBJECT, beaten to death in Börnecke Concentration Camp (*Witness statement*). FRANZ BRAUN, editor of the Communist newspaper *Volkswacht*, Stettin, found 'hanged' in prison after his arrest (*Conti*).

JULY 18TH, 1933:
DR. SCHAFFER, former National-Socialist member of the Hesse Diet; thrown over a railway bridge, mortally wounded, on to the lines twenty feet below. In 1931 Schaffer had revealed the notorious Boxheim Documents (the National-Socialist terrorist plans). His murder took place within a few days of the appointment of one Dr. Best, the author of the plans, to the position of Chief of Police in Hesse (*Frankfurter Zeitung*).

JULY 20TH, 1933:
KARL STIEBEL, employee of the Soviet Oil Company, Nürnburg, beaten to death in Dachau Concentration Camp (*Witness statement*). DORNEMANN, Secretary of the Freethinkers' Organisation, murdered by Storm Troopers in Krefeld a few days after his release from preventive custody (*Police announcement*). OPPOSITION S.A. MAN, Obermenzig, near Munich, found shot (*W.T.B.*, *Conti*). WALTER HEINRICH, Trienbrietzen, found shot on his parents' estate (*Vossische Zeitung*). UNNAMED YOUNG WOMAN, Catholic, Barmen, killed at 9 p.m. in the street, shot through the head by Storm Troopers (*Witness statement*).

JULY 22ND, 1933:
HUGO FEDDERSEN, Member of the Red Front League, Hamburg, hanged in his cell by S.S. men. Alleged suicide (*Conti*).

JULY 23RD, 1933:
JASKOWIAK, unemployed National-Socialist, Leverkusen, shot on account of suspected Communist activity (*Conti*).

JULY 24TH, 1933:
THREE OPPOSITION S.A. MEN shot in Grunewald near Berlin (*Witness statement*). THREE S.S. MEN shot dead during a struggle with S.A. detachments which were being dissolved (*Witness statement*).

JULY 25TH, 1933:
UNKNOWN MAN found lying on the pavement by passers-by late in the evening in Schmargendorf, 'apparently' fallen from the window. Died on the way to hospital (*Vössische Zeitung*). UNNAMED COMMUNIST trampled to death by Storm Troopers in Werden, Ruhr (*Witness statement*).

351

APPENDIX

JULY 26TH, 1933:
ERICH AND GUSTAV RUDOLF, brothers, Dühringshof, shot "whilst attempting to escape" (*Conti*).

JULY 27TH, 1933:
UNNAMED COMMUNIST, Offenbach, shot "whilst attempting to escape" from arrest (*Berliner Borsen Zeitung*). LUDWIG ARMBRUSTER, Military wireless operator, found dead in a building in Berlin. Alleged suicide "Motives not yet elucidated" (*Vossische Zeitung*).

JULY 28TH, 1933:
KLARA WAGNER, aged 27, Secretary, found shot in Berlin Treptow (*V.Z.*). SPEER, tailor, aged 55, Berlin, found murdered during a search for small arms (*V.Z.*). TWO PRISONERS shot in Dachau concentration camp for alleged disobedience to an official (*Witness statement*).

JULY 31ST, 1933:
HEINRICH FOERDING, Coesfeld, thrown from the second storey of the police headquarters in Recklingshausen to the ground. Alleged suicide through fear of punishment (*V.Z. and Völkischer Beobachter*). TWO S.A. MEN, executed in Berlin for distributing Communist leaflets. KURT MIESKA, cigarette merchant, Berlin, arrested for alleged Communist activity. His store was plundered and his goods stolen by Storm Troopers and sold again at half price. He was taken to the S.A. Barracks in General Papestrasse and there beaten to death (*Witness statement*). ALFRED MUTTER, workman, Augsburg, found dead from several bullet wounds in Neuberg (*Münchmer N.N.*). SOLECKI, Communist and TWO UNNAMED COMMUNISTS shot "in self defence" by two auxiliary policemen in Iserlohn (*T.U.*).

END OF JULY, 1933:
TWENTY-TWO S.A. MEN died of poisoning in the Charlottenburg S.A. Barracks. It was openly stated in Charlottenburg amongst the Storm Troopers that these men had been murdered by S.A. men because they had complained that the Hitler Government was betraying Socialism (*Witness statement*). BÄSTLEIN, Communist member of the Diet, taken from prison in Frankfurt am Main by S.S. men and vanished without a trace (*Witness statement*).

AUGUST 1ST, 1933:
KARL WOLFF, AUGUST LÜTGENS, WALTER MÖLLER AND WERNER TESCH, four Communist workmen, executed in Altona (*T.U.*). ZAUBEREL, young Polish student murdered by S.A. men in Brunswick (*Witness statement*). UNKNOWN COMMUNIST, Plauen, "shot while attempting to escape" (*V.Z.*)., TWO YOUNG COMMUNISTS shot in their houses by S.A. men in Leipzigerstrasse, Ehrfurt (*Witness statement*).

AUGUST 3RD, 1933:
POCK, a Communist, who was thrown from the third storey of the prison at Dehrendorf near Düsseldorf and so killed. The press alleged 'suicide' (*Völkischer Beobachter*).

AUGUST 4TH, 1933:
WALTER KLAUSCH, a Potsdam workman, died in Oranienburg Concentration Camp, alleged suicide, through being hanged in his cell (*Witness statement*).

AUGUST 5TH, 1933:
ERICH KOH, died through severing his arteries in Oranienburg Concentration Camp. He had been driven to suicide by ill-treatment and threats of castration (*Witness statement*). JOSEPH DILLER, locksmith, Communist official in Oldenburg, "shot while attempting to escape" (*Völkischer Beobachter*). COMMUNIST OFFICIAL shot in the street by an S.A. man in Chemnitz (*V.Z.*). UNNAMED COMMUNIST died through falling from a window in an S.A. local in Berlin (*Frankfurter Zeitung*).

APPENDIX

AUGUST 7TH, 1933:
FELIX FECHENBACH, Editor of the Social-Democratic *Volksfreund* in Detmold, formerly secretary to Kurt Eisner, "shot while attempting to escape" (*see text*) (*Frankfurter Zeitung*). AUSTRIAN HEIMWEHRMAN shot dead by German Nazis on the Austrian frontier near Kiefersfelden (*Official announcement of the Bavarian Police. Frankfurter Zeitung*).

AUGUST 9TH, 1933:
THREE OPPOSITION STORM TROOPERS "shot while attempting to escape" from Dürrheim Concentration Camp (Baden) (*W.T.B.*). WILHELM VOLK, workman executed in Hamburg (*Conti*). BAUERNFEIND, arrested in Essen as a distributor of Communist leaflets and tortured to death in the Essen S.A. barracks (*Witness statement*). The press alleged that he had committed suicide by throttling himself (*Frankfurter Zeitung*).

AUGUST 10TH, 1933:
PROFESSOR DR. NEUBECK formerly Superintendent of the Central German Wireless Service, alleged 'suicide' in the Leipzig prison (*Official Report of the Leipzig Police*). MAX HOLLE, secretary of the "Red Aid" of Munich, beaten to death whilst being taken to Dachau (*Witness statement*).

AUGUST 11TH, 1933:
GLASER, Social-Democrat, from Ottendorf, Saxony, beaten to death in Hohenstein Concentration Camp (*Witness statement*). HEINRICH HERMSEN, S.A. candidate, mistaken for a Communist by an S.A. patrol in Essen and shot dead (*Völkischer Beobachter*). OTTO FATH, found hanged in his cell, alleged 'suicide' (*Frankfurter Zeitung*). UNNAMED COMMUNIST, alleged 'adjudant' of the well-known Communist leader Hesse, shot "while attempting to escape" in the Kleinenberger Forest, near Kassel (*Frankfurter Zeitung*). BARTELS, RIES, SCHAPIRO, MARSCHALL, SENTHOF, Communist officials, murdered in Erfurt Concentration Camp after severe maltreatment on the orders of von Fichte, Police Chief (*Witness statement*).

AUGUST 12TH, 1933:
ALFRED STRÄTER, Chemist, 29-year-old Social-Democratic official, alleged to have died from a heart attack whilst in preventive arrest (*Witness statement*).

AUGUST 13TH, 1933:
GERARD, a workman, murdered by a German S.A. troop in Kerkrade, Holland (*Witness statement*).

AUGUST 14TH, 1933:
CHAIM GROSS, Polish-Jew, egg-dealer, disappeared after being sentenced to 19 months' imprisonment for "atrocity propaganda." He was attacked and kidnapped by S.A. men in the neighbourhood of the Lotheringerstrasse, and since that time no trace of him can be found, despite both German and Polish official investigation (*Witness statement*).

AUGUST 15TH, 1933:
BRUNO SCHILTER, young worker, from Tilsiterstrasse, 16, Berlin, shot by S.A. men and found dead with five bullet wounds in the head on the Landsberger Chausee (*Witness statement*). THREE S.A. MEN shot by S.S. men in Hamburg (*Witness statement*). KURT STORCH, Storm Trooper, bled to death in the S.A. Barracks in General Papestrasse, Berlin (*Kurier Codcienny*).

MID-AUGUST, 1933:
MAX CRAMER, member of the League against Fascism, Gruiten near Wuppertal, taken from his house during the night and murdered by six shots in the stomach and one through the head. His body was thrown into the river (*Witness statement*). EIGNER, a workman, member of the Socialist-Workers' Party, tortured to death in the Dresden Police Headquarters (*Witness statement*). KARL SCHWESIGK, painter, tortured to death in Düsseldorf

prison. His head was shaven with a blunt knife and parts of his scalp were torn away (*Witness statement*). ANUSCHEL and HANDSCHUCH, two Opposition National-Socialists, beaten to death in Dachau Concentration Camp (*Manchester Guardian*).

AUGUST 17TH, 1933:
FRANZ BUDNIACZINS, Communist, Meseritz, "shot while attempting to escape" (*Nachtausgabe*).

AUGUST 18TH, 1933:
WILHELM TALARECK, Communist, "shot while attempting to escape" in Wanne-Eickel (*W.T.B.*).

AUGUST 20TH, 1933:
RENZ, Trade Union Official, Communist, from Coswig, beaten to death in Oranienburg Concentration Camp (*Witness statement*).

AUGUST 22ND, 1933:
FRANZ STENZER, Pasing, Member of the Central Committee of the German Communist Party, "shot while attempting to escape" from Dachau Concentration Camp (*Official Report of the Bavarian Political Police*) (*Vossische Zeitung*).

AUGUST 23RD, 1933:
OSKAR BEHREND, Official of the "Red Aid" in Gelsenkirchen, alleged found dead in his cell from "heart failure" (*Dortmunder Generalanzeiger*). Behrend is stated by reliable witnesses not to have suffered from a weak heart previous to his arrest.

AUGUST 24TH, 1933:
TWENTY-ONE WORKMEN, Communists, amongst them six officials, a work's councillor and six workmen from a large factory, were reported to have been murdered in Hanover by the National-Socialists to this date (*Witness statement*).

AUGUST 28TH, 1933:
KARL MÜLLER, former leader of the Red Front League in Wiesbaden taken from his house by eight S.A. men to the Government Offices in Lessing-strasse where he was tortured, his body trampled upon, thrown from the second floor to the street and then killed by three bullets. Amongst his murderers were the two S.A. men Krauss and Kühne, both previously convicted for acts of violence (*Witness statement*). Official report alleges "shot while attempting to escape from a concentration camp."

AUGUST 29TH, 1933:
LUDWIG BÜCHLER, Communist, beheaded in Butzbach prison (*Frankfurter Zeitung*).

AUGUST 31ST, 1933:
PROFESSOR THEODOR LESSING, murdered in his bedroom in Marien-bad, Czecho-Slovakia, by an 'unknown' assailant (*Prager Presse*). DR. ADOLF BAUER, physician from Kehl, member of a party visiting Hungary, admitted to hospital in Budapest, where he died, suffering from twenty to twenty-five large wounds (*Frankfurter Zeitung*).

END OF AUGUST, 1933:
RAILWAY OFFICIAL, from Altona, killed by Nazis in Elmshorn prison (*Witness statement*).

SEPTEMBER 2ND, 1933:
EWALD VOGT, a young workman, formerly living in Anklamerstrasse, Berlin, formerly a work's councillor in the Hennigsdorf works of the General Electric (A.E.G.), arrested and brutally maltreated by S.A. men. Some days later his mutilated body was recovered from the military canal (*Witness statement*). HANS ALEXANDER, Social-Democratic official, shot in Papenburg Concentration Camp (*Witness statement*). UNKNOWN POLITICAL PRISONER "shot while attempting to escape at Esterwege" (*Witness statement*).

APPENDIX

SEPTEMBER 3RD, 1933:
MORITZ ANFANG, Jewish egg merchant, choked to death in Berlin-Charlottenburg (*Vössische Zeitung*).

SEPTEMBER 7TH, 1933:
FRANZ WOCHNIK, aged 24, a mason, shot by "unknown persons" in Wellendorf, Silesia. (*Breslau Neueste Nachrichten*).

SEPTEMBER 8TH, 1933:
UNNAMED COMMUNIST WORKMAN shot in Esterwege "whilst attempting to escape" (*Bremer Nachrichten*).

SEPTEMBER 9TH, 1933:
HANS LACHMANN-MOSSE, nephew of the proprietor of the *Berliner Tageblatt*, murdered (*Agence Fourier*). He had been arrested and taken to a concentration camp on about September 1st, 1933. His corpse was returned to his family on September 10th, 1933, in a sealed coffin.

SEPTEMBER 10TH, 1933:
BERGMANN, Berlin Police Official, beaten to death in Papenburg Concentration Camp (*Witness statement*).

SEPTEMBER 12TH, 1933:
PROFESSOR FÖRSTER, assistant to Professor Bonnhöfer, well-known psychiatrist at Greifswald University, committed "suicide" (*Frankfurter Zeitung*). He was associated with prominent Nazis. He had superintended a "cure" undergone by Göring for his drug mania; he had also given evidence at the trial of the present Minister of Culture, Rust, for a sexual offence, that he was not responsible for his actions. He had been given leave of absence for the purpose of undergoing a thorough examination. PUTZ, Communist member of the Reichstag, found dead in the prison at Moabit. It was officially announced that he had committed suicide (*Official report*). LORENZ SCHRIEFER, Catholic worker, Laiganz, beheaded. According to official reports he behaved with perfect composure to the last moment (*Völkischer Beobachter*). REISSNER, workman, maltreated by S.A. men in his house in Berlin (Graunstrasse 33) and thrown from the window (*Witness statement*).

MID-SEPTEMBER, 1933:
OTTO KIEFER, workman, Mainz, stabbed by S.A. man Weiss (*Witness statement*). KÖTZLE, Social-Democrat, teacher from Münster (Stuttgart) two months imprisoned in Heuberg Concentration Camp, died in hospital form a "heart attack" and "blood poisoning" (*Witness statement*). WINKELMEIER, student, opposition National-Socialist, shot in Dachau Concentration Camp (*Manchester Guardian*). COMMUNIST OFFICIAL, in charge of propaganda in Baden, alleged to bear the pseudonym Rolf, tortured to death after his arrest in Karlsruhe. The Nazi press alleged that he hanged himself (*Führer, Karlsruhe*). BARUCH, Jew, no Party, shot dead by S.S. man Nolte in Neusustrum (Papanburg) Concentration Camp (*Witness statement*). POLICE CHIEF GUHSE, from Bochum-Gerthe, murdered in Neusustrum Concentration Camp (*Witness statement*). UNNAMED BARBER shot dead in Papenburg Concentration Camp (*Witness statement*). UNNAMED WORKMAN, beaten to death in Sonnenburg Concentration Camp (*Witness statement*).

SEPTEMBER 16TH, 1933:
ALBIN FRITSCH, Director and Chairman of the Plauen Social-Democratic Party, severely maltreated in Hohenstein Concentration Camp and killed through falling from the wall of the camp (*Witness statement and Obererzgebirgische Zeitung*).

SEPTEMBER 17TH, 1933:
EMIL S., murdered and thrown into the Wansee near Berlin. The press wrote of "suicide for unknown reasons" (*Vössische Zeitung*). HARTUNG, Communist official and two unknown workmen shot in Hamburg-Fühlsbüttel

APPENDIX

Concentration Camp "whilst attempting to escape" (*Witness statement*). UNNAMED WORKMAN, age 20, shot by S.A. men in Neusustrum Concentration Camp (*Witness statement*).

SEPTEMBER 18TH, 1933:
KARL KAHDING, workman, member of the Reichsbanner, condemned to death by the Special Courts, alleged committed "suicide" in Lübeck prison (*W.T.B.*).

SEPTEMBER 10TH, 1933:
DR. SOLMITZ, editor of the Social-Democrat *Volksboten* in Lübeck, found "hanged" in his cell in the Concentration Camp at Hamburg Fülhsbüttel (*W.T.B.*). In fact, Dr. Solmitz, was severely maltreated and then beaten to death. NEID, Communist workman, Hamburg, beaten to death in Fühlsbüttel Concentration Camp (*Witness statement*).

SEPTEMBER 22ND, 1933:
HERMANN SCHEFFLER, Trade Union and Communist Party Official, tortured to death in the S.A. barracks in the Chausseestrasse, Berlin (*Bulletin of the Mortuary*). WERNER ABEL, formerly National-Socialist, alleged to have committed "suicide" in prison (*Witness statement*).

SEPTEMBER 23RD, 1933:
HANS BLENDOWSKY, Jewish workman, N. Berlin, beaten to death in the S.A. auxiliary police barracks in Prinz Albrechtstrasse (*Witness statement*)

SEPTEMBER 25TH, 1933:
E. BERGMANN, Communist, Wattenburg, Ruhr, "shot while attempting to escape" (*Witness statement*). UNNAMED WORKMAN, father of four children, shot by a bailiff "in self defence" on Rohrau estate (*Vossische Zeitung*). KURT GÜLLE and BRUNO LÜPKE, foreman and cook respectively of the Labour Service Camp in Lebbin, found shot in the vicinity of the Camp. "It is established as a result of the official inquiries that the cook was mortally wounded by a shot fired in drunkenness and that Gülle had apparently committed suicide" (*Conti*). DR. LANDSBERG, head of the Brandenburg Medical Association arrested for alleged fraudulent practices. Found hanged in his cell, stated to be 'suicide' (*V.Z.*).

SEPTEMBER 26TH, 1933:
UNNAMED JEW, aged about 30, probably from Nürnburg, murdered by Nazis and thrown into the Danube (*Official report of the Provincial Government of Linz*). According to a witness the corpse bore marks of having been burnt and crucified. Both hands were bored through by a sharp knife. Blood was still flowing from the wounds.

SEPTEMBER 27TH, 1933:
HANS MARTIN, young workman from Köln-Kalk (Nöfestrasse 8) leader in the German Communist League of Youth, thrown by S.A. men from a third floor window of the Köln police headquarters and crushed to death (*Westdeutscher Beobachter*).

SEPTEMBER 28TH, 1933:
JAN TEMPLIN, director of the "Unity" Stevedores Friendly Society in Hamburg, alleged to have committed "suicide" in Fühlsbüttel prison (*Witness statement*). DANIELY, workman, Upper Silesia, shot dead in Papenburg Concentration Camp (*Witness statement*).

EARLY OCTOBER, 1933:
KARL STETTER, workman, Rheinau, died of acute inflammation of the lungs in Heuberg Concentration Camp through lack of medical attention and exposure (*Witness statement*).

OCTOBER 2ND, 1933:
SCHFRANSKI, S.A. and auxiliary policeman in Brunswick, executed for killing an S.A. man (*Braunschweiger Landeszeitung*). UNKNOWN WORKMAN shot between Aachen and Gelsenkirchen in the course of a Nazi raid

356

(*Witness statement*). KARL WEITHÖNER, crane driver, Essen-Dellwig, cell leader in Nazi Workers' Organisation, stabbed to death by unknown assailants during the night at the door of a café (*Angriff*).

OCTOBER 3RD, 1933:
JOSEF SCHMITZ and TONI ENGELMANN, Members of the Anti-Fascist Fighter League, tortured and murdered by S.A. men in Frechen, Köln (*Witness statement*).

OCTOBER 5TH, 1933:
DR. ARTHUR LANDSBERGER, well-known author of sensational novels arrested after he had been refused leave to go abroad. Tortured and hanged in the Gestapo Prison in Prinz Albrechtstrasse, Berlin (*Witness statement*).

OCTOBER 7TH, 1933:
WALTER EHRICHT, Head Cashier of the Bruckdorf-Neitlebener Mining Company. Found dead at the steering wheel of a motor-car in a garage in Halle. Alleged suicide (*Leipziger Neueste Nachrichten*). UNKNOWN YOUNG MAN found murdered in the bushes in the Rabeninsel near Halle (Saale) *Leipziger Neueste Nachrichten*). His head and a part of the trunk were missing. Nevertheless according to the announcement he had placed a piece of dynamite in his mouth and had left a note near his body: "Tired of life."

OCTOBER 15TH, 1933:
SCHMIDT, member of the Nazi Party, stabbed by an official of the Labour Service (*Saarfront*). SIX S.A. MEN shot dead in an encounter with Reichs-wehr soldiers in Breslau (*Witness statement*).

OCTOBER 17TH, 1933:
ROLF, Dresden District Secretary of the German Communist Party, beaten to death in the Dresden Police Headquarters (*Witness statement*). EGGER-STEDT, former Social-Democratic Police Chief of Altona, shot by an S.S. leader of the Aachen Troop, and an S.S. man of the 19th Koblenz Troop at Börgermoor Concentration Camp just after dark (*Witness statement*). At about the same time S.S. Leader Faust, the Superintendent of the Börgemoor Concentration Camp announced that five anti-fasicsts had been killed. This statement has not so far been confirmed. EMIL SCHILTER, workman, Petersmühle, executed in Meseritz (*Kölnische Zeitung*).

OCTOBER 20TH, 1933:
TWO S.A. MEN members of Heines bodyguard, shot by Heines (Police President of Breslau) (*Witness statement*).

OCTOBER 22ND, 1933:
ALEXANDER, lawyer, Leader of the Reichsbanner, killed in Breslau prison after severe maltreatment (*Witness statement*).

OCTOBER 24TH, 1933:
YOUNG UNNAMED COMMUNIST, found dead in his cell in the Nürnburg prison (*Witness statement*).

OCTOBER 25TH, 1933:
AUGUST DOSENBACH, Communist official, shot at Karlsruhe "whilst attempting to escape" (*Witness statement*).

OCTOBER 28TH, 1933:
HERMANN RENKEN, Official of the United Union of Sea and Harbour Workers, murdered in prison in Hamburg through having live coals placed in his mouth (*Witness statement*).

END OF OCTOBER, 1933:
SCHOCH, Communist official, Mannheim, murdered in prison. Alleged to have hanged himself (*T.U.*). KARL LESCH, sailor, beaten to death in Fühlsbüttel Concentration Camp (Witness statement). ALI VON DER REITH, sailor, murdered in Fühlsbüttel Concentration Camp (*Witness statement*).

APPENDIX

EARLY NOVEMBER, 1933:
THREE OPPOSITION S.A. MEN tortured to death in Dachau Concentration Camp (*Witness statement*).

NOVEMBER 1ST, 1933:
WILHELM LAXA, young worker, Gleiwitz-Petersdorf, beaten to death in the Nazi barracks by Troop 33 of the Gleiwitz S.A. under the orders of S.A. man Schoja (*Witness statement*). According to the witness his body bore several stabs, wounds from life preservers and a bullet wound in the stomach.

NOVEMBER 3RD, 1933:
VESPER, workman aged 50, Mahlsdorf, Berlin, arrested and murdered by S.A. men. His skull was broken and his body trampled upon (*Witness statement*). UNKNOWN COMMUNIST shot by the Police at Gelsenkirchen "whilst attempting to escape."

NOVEMBER 6TH, 1933:
MARTIN BECKER, workman, Saarbrücken, shot by National-Socialists (*Saarbrücken Arbeiterzeitung*).

NOVEMBER 7TH, 1933:
FRITZ LUX, Hamburg docker, formerly member of the Hamburg Corporation and Member of the Central Committee of the German Communist Party, one of the most popular working-class leaders in Hamburg, murdered in Fühlsbüttel Concentration Camp (*Witness statement*).

NOVEMBER 9TH, 1933:
UNKNOWN COMMUNIST WORKMAN, shot from behind in the Lindenplatz, Berlin-Weissensee (*Witness statement*).

NOVEMBER 10TH, 1933:
DR. KATZ, Jewish physician, murdered in Dachau Concentration Camp on the day of his release, because he had seen and treated too many maltreated prisoners (*Witness statement*).

NOVEMBER 11TH, 1933:
NEUSTÄDTER, Jewish merchant and owner of a large china store in Hamborn, killed by kicks in the stomach from S.A. men (*Witness statement*).

NOVEMBER 12TH, 1933:
KRONAD DWORATZEK, workman, shot by police officials, whilst distributing Communist pamphlets in Dortmund (*Dortmunder Generalanzeiger*). The Official Prussian Press Service hailed this killing with the statement that the order to shoot at sight given by the Prussian Prime Minister on October 4th, 1933, had been successfully carried out. OTTO WYRGATSCH, formerly Editor-in-Chief of the Königsberg Social-Democratic *Volkszeitung*, died in Kopenhagen from the effects of bullet wounds received at the hands of the Nazis (*Witness statement*). FRITZ BÜRK, Communist official, Memmingen, killed by several shots in the Dachau Concentration Camp, alleged to have been received when he attacked a guard (*Leipziger Neueste Nachrichten*).

NOVEMBER 14TH, 1933:
HEINRICH ESSER, age 22, S.A. man killed by a shot in the stomach in Hochneukirch (*W.T.B.*). From the announcement of the W.T.B. it is plain that the murder was committed by another S.A. man. JOHN TRETTIN, Communist official, Hamburg, beaten to death in Fühlsbüttel Concentration Camp (*Witness statement*).

MID-NOVEMBER, 1933:
WILLI NABEL, Berlin-Mariendorf, Rathaustrasse 91, formerly head of the Red Front League of Mariendorf. He was arrested in March 1933 and so severely maltreated by S.A. men in General Papestrasse that his back took more than four months to heal. After a lengthy treatment in hospital he was discharged. In the middle of November he was suddenly summoned for interrogation. He attended in answer to the summons and was then warned by an official not to show his face in Sonnenburg again. The following

morning Nabel went out of his house as usual but never returned. He was officially reported to be missing (*Witness statement*).

NOVEMBER 18TH, 1933:
KONRAD LANG, Chairman of the Communist Representatives Group of Frankfurt, and Member of the Provincial State Council, died following maltreatment in a Concentration Camp (*Witness statement*).

NOVEMBER 20TH, 1933:
JANEK, Communist workman, Benrath, tortured to death by police officials in the Police Headquarters in Düsseldorf. His family were informed that he had "committed suicide." His body was, however, covered from head to foot with blue and black bruises and weals (*Witness statement*).

NOVEMBER 24TH, 1933:
HANS OTTO, actor in the Berlin Staatstheater, of revolutionary views, tortured in a Berlin S.A. barracks. Died of compound fracture of the skull. (*Witness statement*).

NOVEMBER 28TH, 1933:
BENKE, aged 42, workman and father of five children, following his release, after terrible maltreatment, from Sonnenburg Concentration Camp, found shot in the forest near Furstenwalde (*Witness statement*). KURT GERBER, worker, member of the Reichsbanner, Maliers, condemned to death by the Breslau Special Tribunal, executed in Breslau prison by the hand-axe (*W.T.B.*). KIRZNIEWZIK, Communist workman, Leipzig, tortured to death by the Gestapo in Prinz Albrechtstrasse, Berlin, and then hanged to give the appearance of suicide (*Witness statement*).

NOVEMBER 30TH, 1933:
KONRAD, Communist workman, shot "whilst attempting to escape" giving out pamphlets in Flensburg (*W.T.B.*). FABER, aged 19, son of a Jewish merchant, Berlin, "shot whilst attempting to escape" (*Angriff*) HAMACHER WAESER, WILLMS, HORSCH, MORITZ and ENGELS, anti-fascist workmen, Köln, condemned to death by the Köln Special Tribunal and executed by the hand-axe in the courtyard of Köln prison (*W.T.B.*).

EARLY DECEMBER, 1933:
TWO S.A. MEN, shot "whilst attempting to escape" from Brandenburg Concentration Camp (*Witness statement*).

DECEMBER 2ND, 1933:
MAX LUKAS, anti-fascist workman, found shot in Neukölln, Berlin, killed by an unkown person (*Vossische Zeitung*).

DECEMBER 3RD, 1933:
PETER WEINHERR, Austrian electrician, Salzburg, shot by police officials in front of the Hotel Kaiserhof in Munich (*Münchner Neueste Nachrichten*). THEODOR EBERS, Communist leader in Essen, Commander of the Red Army in the Ruhr in 1920, "shot whilst attempting to escape" between Düsseldorf and Essen (*Frankfurter Zeitung*).

DECEMBER 4TH, 1933:
KARL ACKERT, Communist workman, tried and acquitted in 1932 for the murder of the Nazi artist Ernst Schwatrz. Re-arrested by S.A. men and tortured by the Gestapo in order to extort a confession from him. Died in hospital from his injuries (*Angriff*).

DECEMBER 6TH, 1933:
UNKNOWN STONEMASON, arrested for slandering the S.S., wounded by the police by two shots and beaten to death by S.A. men (*Official announcement of the Bavarian Political Police*).

DECEMBER 9TH, 1933:
HANS MALTER, waiter, disabled in the war, shot in Dortmund by police officials (*Vossische Zeitung*).

APPENDIX

DECEMBER 12TH, 1933:
WERNER KÜMMEL, clergyman, kidnapped and murdered in Berlin by S.S. men (*Witness statement*).

MID-DECEMBER, 1933:
ERICH THORNSEIFER, young Communist, arrested by S.A. men in Moabit, Berlin and beaten to death (*Witness statement*). WILLI FRANZ, Communist official, shot by S.S. guards in the Dachau Concentration Camp (*Witness statement*).

DECEMBER 18TH, 1933:
GERTRUD PIEPER, working woman, tortured to death in Brandenburg Concentration Camp (*Witness statement*). The Vossische Zeitung stated that she had hanged herself in her cell. PAUL SCHULTZ, Communist official in Lichtenberg, Berlin, "fell" from the fourth floor of the police headquarters into the street (*Witness statement*).

DECEMBER 20TH, 1933:
FRITZ RAU, formerly editor of the Halle Communist newspaper *Klassenkampf*, beaten to death in the Moabit prison (*Witness statement.*)

DECEMBER 21ST, 1933:
AUGUST THIELE, Communist official, Duisburg, kidnapped and murdered by Storm Troopers under the orders of the Nazi Hardt (*Witness statement*).

DECEMBER 23RD, 1933:
UNKNOWN WORKMAN, murdered in the Augsburg prison (*Witness statement*).

DECEMBER 31ST, 1933:
UNKNOWN MAN, shot by National-Socialists in an inn at Kohlscheid. Died in hospital of his wounds. (*Witness statement*). SULLEY, merchant, Zoppot, formerly a National-Socialist, murdered by Nazis in the Danzig Judicial Prison (*Witness statement*).

EARLY JANUARY, 1934:
SPRINGMANN, Opposition S.A. man, Kehl, shot dead by S.A. men on the Rhine bridge at Kehl (*Witness statement*). The Kehl press announced that the death was due to suicide.

JANUARY 6TH, 1934:
STEPHAN, P., age 27, stonemason, no party, shot in the Wittmoor Concentration Camp near Hamburg, "whilst attempting to escape" (*Witness statement*).

JANUARY 9TH, 1934:
LUDWIG PAPPENHEIM, formerly leader writer in the Social-Democratic *Volksstimme*, shot in Börgermoor Concentration Camp, "whilst trying to escape" (*Frankfurter Zeitung*). AUGUST HENNIG, Communist, took part in the 1918 Revolution as a member of the Marine Brigade in Kiel, shot in a Concentration Camp, "whilst attempting to escape" (*Frankfurter Zeitung*) PAUL WYSTUB, S.A. leader in Oppeln, found beaten to death after a dance (*Deutsche Allgemeine Zeitung*).

JANUARY 10TH, 1934:
MARINUS VAN DER LUBBE, the Reichstag incendiary, executed.

JANUARY 12TH, 1934:
ERNST LINDAU, condemned to death on December 30th, 1933, executed by the hand-axe in Hamburg (*Frankfurter Zeitung*). KURT WILLKOMM, Communist official, murdered by the State Police in Hanover (*Witness statement*). ERICH SCHALOW, Police sergeant, Pyritz, shot whilst on patrol duty. SUTZ, shoemaker, no Party, found shot in Pyritz (*Frankfurter Zeitung*).

JANUARY 15TH, 1934:
STEPHAN KAPTUR, Communist workman, condemned to death on December 6th, 1933, found 'hanged' in his cell (*Official announcement*).

JANUARY 19TH, 1933:
MOSES, age 49, cattle dealer, Wesseling, near Bonn, died from the effects of injuries received the previous September when he was beaten and trampled on by Storm Troopers acting under orders (*Witness statement*).

JANUARY 21ST, 1934:
UNKNOWN MAN, aged about 30, found shot in Oberhausen (*Dortmunder General Anzeiger*). GEORG STOLT, Communist official, arrested in Moabit Berlin, handed over to the Mortuary with a bullet wound in the head (*Witness statement*).

JANUARY 22ND, 1934:
FRANZ WENSKI, agent, Herne, shot in Duisburg (*Kölnische Zeitung*).

JANUARY 24TH, 1934:
WILLY DOLGNER, Communist official, tortured for 24 hours in the Hamburg Prison, beaten to death and then hanged. The Nazi officials announced it as a 'suicide' (*Witness statement*).

JANUARY 25TH, 1934:
TIMM, Communist official, found hanged in Neumünster prison, alleged suicide (*Völkischer Beobachter*). WALTER, farmer, found dead in Kontopp Prison, alleged suicide. DETTMEIER, blacksmith, Quetzen, alleged to have committed suicide in Petershagen Court Prison.

END OF JANUARY, 1934:
TWENTY-NINE MURDERS in Fühlsbüttel Concentration Camp. From the statement of a prisoner released from Fühlsbüttel it appears that at least 29 persons were either shot or beaten to death during the period between September 1st, 1933, and January 31st, 1934; no less than 600 of the prisoners were seriously injured.

FEBRUARY 3RD, 1934:
JOHN SCHEER, Member of the Central Committee of the German Communist Party and of the Executive Committee of the Communist International, Deputy of Thälmann; EUGENE SCHÖNHAAR, Organiser of the Illegal Press; ERICH STEINFURTH, Leader of the Berlin Red Aid, and RUDOLF SCHWARZ, Communist official, shot, near Potsdam, at night, "whilst attempting to escape" (*see text*).

FEBRUARY 4TH, 1934:
TWO S.A. MEN, shot in Brandenburg Concentration Camp, "whilst attempting to escape" (*Witness statement*).

FEBRUARY 9TH, 1934:
RETSLAG, anti-fascist workman, executed in Hamburg Prison.

FEBRUARY 10TH, 1934:
UNKNOWN S.A. MAN, from Oberschöneweide, Berlin, shot in Berlin as an act of vengeance by several S.A. men (*Witness statement*).

FEBRUARY 15TH, 1934:
ZIEGER, former Leader of the Eisenach District of the German Communist Party, found dead in Erfurt Prison (*Witness statement*).

FEBRUARY 24TH, 1934:
GEORG ARBEITER, Member of the Reichsbanner, murdered by S.A. man Edgar Müller, in Neisse, Breslau (*Witness statement*).

EARLY MARCH, 1934:
CHRISTIAN HEUCK, former Communist member of the Reichstag, beaten to death by National-Socialists in Kiel Prison (*Witness statement*). WALTER HARNACKER and WILLI WALZ, young anti-fascist workmen, beaten to death in the cellars of the "Maikowski House" in Charlottenburg, Berlin, by Kühn, Naterüller, Sudermann and Kramm, all officers in the Storm Troops (*Witness statement*).

APPENDIX

MARCH 1ST, 1934:

ZETSCHE, former Director of the State Savings Bank in Eisenberg, arrested by the police, "killed himself whilst he was being taken under escort by shooting himself through the head" (*Berliner Tageblatt*). ALBERT JUNG, Communist factory worker in Pirmaesens, murdered in prison, alleged suicide (*Official announcement*).

MARCH 2ND, 1934:

HANACK, sentenced to death on February 28th, 1934, for shooting at police officials who were following him in October 1933, executed in Hamburg.

MARCH 5TH, 1934:

UNKNOWN YOUNG MAN, shot by police officials, "whilst attempting to escape" (*Frankfurter Zeitung*).

MARCH 7TH, 1934:

YEAR-OLD INFANT, child of the Communist Boehm, killed by a bullet aimed at Boehm's wife by an S.A. man (*Vossische Zeitung*).

MARCH 9TH, 1934:

FICK, member of the Reichsbanner, condemned to death by the Lübeck Criminal Court on September 16th, 1933, executed (*Frankfurter Zeitung*).

MID-MARCH, 1934:

WILLI SIEBE, District Secretary of the Social-Democratic Party, Cologne, so severely ill-treated in a concentration camp, that he died from the effects after his release (*Freiheit*).

MARCH 20TH, 1934:

FRITZ LANGE and WALTER SIEDELMANN, condemned to death by the Königsberg Criminal Court for the joint murder of an S.A. man. Executed.

MARCH 27TH, 1934:

PETER HUPPERTZ, EMIL SCHMIDT, OTTO LUKATZ, three anti-fascist workmen executed by the hand-axe in Düsseldorf.

MARCH 30TH, 1934:

HOHLFELD, Bank Clerk, alleged to have escaped from Hohenstein Concentration Camp, shot by an S.A. man whilst attempting to cross the frontier (*Witness statement*).

MARCH 31ST, 1934:

MARUM, former Social-Democratic member of the Reichstag, Karlsruhe, alleged, according to a Gestapo Report to have committed suicide by hanging in Kieslau Concentration Camp (*The Leader*).

END OF MARCH, 1934:

TWO JEWISH SHOPKEEPERS, taken and beaten severely by S.A. men in Gunzenhausen. One of them was found dead with four knife thrusts in his body, the other is alleged to have hanged himself from despair (*Manchester Guardian*).

(List Concluded at the end of March 1934).